NO BAD SOLDIERS

119 Infantry Brigade and Brigadier-General Frank Percy Crozier in the Great War

Michael Anthony Taylor

Helion & Company

Helion & Company Limited
Unit 8 Amherst Business Centre
Budbrooke Road
Warwick
CV34 5WE
England
Tel. 01926 499 619
Email: info@helion.co.uk
Website: www.helion.co.uk
Twitter: @helionbooks
Visit our blog at blog.helion.co.uk

Published by Helion & Company 2022
Designed and typeset by Mach 3 Solutions (www.mach3solutions.co.uk)
Cover designed by Paul Hewitt, Battlefield Design (www.battlefield-design.co.uk)

Text © Michael Anthony Taylor 2022
Images © as individually credited
Maps drawn by George Anderson © Helion and Company Ltd 2022

Every reasonable effort has been made to trace copyright holders and to obtain their permission for the use of copyright material. The author and publisher apologize for any errors or omissions in this work and would be grateful if notified of any corrections that should be incorporated in future reprints or editions of this book.

ISBN 978-1-915070-84-5

British Library Cataloguing-in-Publication Data.
A catalogue record for this book is available from the British Library.

All rights reserved. No part of this publication may be reproduced, stored in a retrieval system, or transmitted, in any form, or by any means, electronic, mechanical, photocopying, recording or otherwise, without the express written consent of Helion & Company Limited.

For details of other military history titles published by Helion & Company Limited contact the above address or visit our website: http://www.helion.co.uk.

We always welcome receipt of book proposals from prospective authors.

Contents

List of Illustrations	iv
List of Maps	vi
List of Tables	vii
Abbreviations	viii
Acknowledgements	x
Foreword	xi
Introduction	xiii
1 The Welsh Bantam Brigade	23
2 The Brigade Goes to War	71
3 Crozier: A Reputation Won and Lost	104
4 Crozier's Brigade	131
5 Reorganisation, Destruction and Reconstruction	164
Conclusion	214
Postscript	221

Appendices

I	Bourlon and Mametz: A brief comparison	223
II	40th Division Cambrai – Original Plan for Advance to the Sensée River	226
III	Attack Orders – Bourlon Wood	231
IV	Preparations for Defence March 1918	234
V	40th Division Lessons of the Recent Fighting, April 1918	236
VI	Biographies	238

Bibliography	252
Index	263

List of Illustrations

Recruits for the 17th Welsh. (Undated press cutting, author)	30
Lt-Col C. J. Wilkie. (Williams Collection)	31
'C' Company, 12th SWB, Newport, July 1915. Lt-Col Pope seated front row centre. (Author)	37
Five, possibly under-age, bantams, 19th RWF, Llandudno Junction, 1915. (Imperial War Museum, Fraser Papers)	47
Band of the 17th Welsh, August 1915. Major E.H. St George Gilbert seated centre left. (Author)	63
17th Welsh, route march, Prees Heath, summer 1915. (Author)	65
11 Platoon, 19th RWF. Prees Heath, summer 1915. Sergeant with bantam mascot seated centre front. (Author)	65
Signal Section, 17th Welsh, 1916. (Author)	68
'All British Boys' by Cpl (later Sergeant) Jack Franklin, 17th Welsh. (Author)	69
Brig-Gen C. S. Prichard on the crossing to France, June 1916. Pencil sketch by 2/Lt Morris Meredith Williams. (Williams Collection)	74
Ration party, Maroc, 1916. Pencil sketch by 2/Lt Morris Meredith Williams. (Williams Collection)	84
The Double Crassier, Loos, seen from Maroc, October 1916. Pencil sketch by 2/Lt Morris Meredith Williams. (Williams Collection)	84
2/Lts William Hopkins Beaumont and James Donald Ellis,19th RWF, 'Billets 18 August 1916'. (Author)	89
119 Bde Staff, 18 September 1916. Front row L to R: Capt Granville Soames, Brigade Major; Brig-Gen Charles Cunliffe Owen; Capt. Percy Hone, Staff Captain. (Royal Welsh Regimental Museum, Brecon)	92
The Gamecocks, 1917. Sergeant J.F. Franklin, 17th Welsh, standing front left. (*Twenty Years After*)	102
Crozier, centre, a great fan of theatre, in lighter mood. (Royal Welsh Regimental Museum, Brecon)	102
Brig-Gen Frank Percy Crozier. The late Charles Messenger noticed that, despite the date, the photo must date from 1917, after Crozier's DSO had been awarded. (*A Brass Hat In No Man's Land*)	132
Trenches at Rancourt, December 1916. Pencil sketch by 2/Lt Morris Meredith Williams. (Williams Collection)	137
Lt-Col C. B. Hore, 17th Welsh, at work. Pencil sketch by 2/Lt Morris Meredith Williams. (Williams Collection)	139
Lt-Col Robert Benzie. (*Aberdeen Press and Journal*)	139
119 Bde Staff, 1917. Front row L to R: Major Guy Vernon Goodliffe, Brigade Major; Brig-Gen F.P. Crozier; Capt Percy Hone, Staff Captain. (Royal Welsh Regimental Museum, Brecon)	142
Lt-Col Richard John Andrews. (Jill Blackmore)	148
Lt-Col William Kennedy. (*Glasgow High School Roll of Honour*)	151

119 Brigade Christmas card, 1917. The galvanising effect of the appearance of an officer. (Author) 166

Lt-Col H.C. Metcalfe. (*History of the Northamptonshire and Rutland Militia*) 180

119 Bde Staff late 1918. Front row L to R: Lt-Col James Frederick Plunkett; Brig-Gen Frank Percy Crozier; Capt Anthony John Muirhead, Brigade Major; Lt Reggie May, Staff Captain. (*A Brass Hat In No Man's Land*) 191

Men of the 12th North Staffordshire Regiment, 1918, wearing 40th Division patches. On right 44820 Pte August William Cooper, age 20, who had previously served with the DLI, W. Yorks and Labour Corps. (Ian Cooper) 194

List of Maps

1	Locations associated with 119 Brigade, 1916-18.	80
2	Fifteen Ravine, 21 April 1917.	143
3	Villers Plouich, 24 April 1917.	147
4	Bourlon Wood, 23 November 1917.	158
5	Area of 119 Brigade actions, 22-24 March 1918.	174
6	119 Brigade positions, 9-12 April 1918.	182

List of Tables

1	Discharges due to ill health or poor fitness	44
2	Discharges due to under-age enlistment	45
3	Soldiers of Welsh Birth (Williams, 2007)	49
4	Soldiers of Welsh Origin	50
5	17th Welsh – Origins	50
6	18th Welsh – Origins	51
7	19th RWF – Origins	52
8	12th SWB – Origins	53
9	Civilian Occupations 119 Brigade	54
10	Trials by District Courts Martial, 119 Brigade	58
11	Offences tried by District Courts Martial during training period	59
12	Geographical origin of officers by residence	75
13	Comparative age profiles	77
14	Participants in the 12th SWB 'mutiny' of 21 November 1916	97
15	Field General Courts Martial, 119 Brigade June 1916 to July 1918	99
16	Offences tried by Field General Courts Martial June 1916 – July 1918	100
17	Sentences of Field General Courts Martial June 1916 – July 1918	100
18	119 Brigade casualties Battle of the Lys	187
19	Background of 119 Brigade troops 1918	193
20	Training carried out by the 13th East Lancs June-August 1918	195
21	Field General Courts Martial, 119 Brigade, July 1918 – June 1919	198
22	Offences tried by Field General Courts Martial, 119 Brigade, July 1918 – June 1919	199
23	Sentences of Field General Courts Martial, 119 Brigade, July 1918 – June 1919	199

Abbreviations

2iC	Second in Command
A&Q	Adjutant and Quartermaster
A&SH	Argyll and Sutherland Highlanders
ADC	Aide-de-Camp
AG	Adjutant General
AOD	Army Ordnance Depot
APM	Assistant Provost Marshall
BEF	British Expeditionary Force
BGGS	Brigadier-General General Staff
BGRA	Brigadier-General Royal Artillery
BM	Brigade Major
CinC	Commander in Chief (in this case, of the BEF)
CO	Commanding Officer
CWGC	Commonwealth War Graves Commission
DAAG	Deputy Assistant Adjutant General
DIM	Deputy Inspector of Musketry
DSO	Distinguished Service Order
DT	Director of Transport
FGCM	Field General Court Martial
FP	Field Punishment
FSR	Field Service Regulations
GHQ	General Headquarters
GOC	General Officer Commanding
GQG	Grand Quartier Générale (French equivalent of GHQ)
GSO1	General Staff Officer Grade One
GSO2	General Staff Officer Grade Two
GSO3	General Staff Officer Grade Three
HQ	Headquarters
HLI	Highland Light Infantry
IBD	Infantry Base Depot
IGC	Inspector General of Communications
KORL	King's Own (Royal Lancaster Regiment)
KOSB	King's Own Scottish Borderers
KOYLI	King's Own Yorkshire Light Infantry
MGC	Machine Gun Company
MC	Military Cross
MS	Military Secretary
MT	Motor Transport
NAM	National Army Museum
NCO	Non-Commissioned Officer
NEC	National Executive Committee (of the Welsh Army Corps)
NLW	National Library of Wales

OC	Officer Commanding
ORs	Other Ranks
POW(s)	Prisoner(s) of War
psc	Passed Staff College
Q	Quartermaster General's Branch of the General Staff
RA	Royal Artillery
RAP	Regimental Aid Post
RC	Railhead Commandant
RD	Recruiting District
RE	Royal Engineers
RIF	Royal Inniskilling Fusiliers
RIRifles	Royal Irish Rifles
RO	Recruiting Officer
RWF	Royal Welsh Fusiliers
SDR	Special Despatch Rider
SWB	South Wales Borderers
TF	Territorial Force
TMB	Trench Mortar Battery
TNA	The National Archives
WAC	Welsh Army Corps
WO	War Office

Acknowledgements

This book is dedicated to the memory of all who served with 119 Infantry Brigade during the Great War. The brigade's achievement in capturing and holding the important Bourlon Wood position in 1917 has been largely overshadowed by the deeds of fellow Welshmen at Mametz in 1916 and I hope that this study will redress the balance a little as well as showing how a brigade can survive upheaval and reorganisation. Brigade-level studies are not exactly thick on the ground, most historians preferring the broad-brush divisional level of investigation or the detailed study of particular battalions. This book is neither, but I have greatly enjoyed getting to know the men of the brigade.

In retrospect it was perhaps a tactical error in choosing a subject that comprised largely Welsh battalions whilst I was living in Scotland. Key sources are at Kew and Aberystwyth and digitisation was a little way off even ten years ago but archive, museum and library staff were consistently helpful and my task progressed. My acknowledgements are therefore many and heartfelt. I would particularly like to thank The National Archives, Kew; the National Library of Wales, Aberystwyth; the Imperial War Museum, London; the National Army Museum, Chelsea; the Public Record Office of Northern Ireland, Belfast; the Liddell Hart Military Archive at King's College, London; the Royal Welsh Regimental Museum, Brecon; Blair Castle Archive, Perthshire; the Random House Group Archive, Rushden; the archives of the London School of Economics and Reading University's Jonathan Cape Archive for access and, where appropriate, for permission to quote key sources or use images. The British Newspaper Archive was an invaluable source that is still growing. Clive Hughes was generous with his knowledge of recruiting in North Wales in the Great War and his Welsh language skills. Simon Justice kindly took the time to elaborate on his work on the BEF reorganization of 1918. Mrs Carol Germa, Ontario, (Crozier's granddaughter) made available much family history compiled by the late Ryan Taylor, and Charles Roberts, Hampshire (Grace Crozier's nephew), kindly copied the family archive of news cuttings and the typescript of his aunt's biography of her husband *Guns and God* – my thanks to Mr Des Rees, another family member, for permission to use these. These family resources were also used by the late Charles Messenger in his biography of Crozier, *Broken Sword*. Any help I was able to give to Charles was more than reciprocated. He is missed. Since my thesis was submitted one major new source has emerged. The archive of Morris Meredith Williams (late 17th Welsh) and his talented wife Alice have been made available by their custodian Phyllida Shaw via her two books *An Artist's War* and *Undaunted Spirit*. I thank Phyllida for her transcripts of correspondence, the use of sketches and photos to illustrate this book, and her encouragement. Thanks also to George Anderson for working his magic in producing the maps.

I owe a debt of gratitude to Professor Peter Simkins whose queries about the 'bantam Welsh coal miners' formed the basis of my investigations, and whose encyclopaedic knowledge is always available; and to Professor John Bourne for his supervision of my doctoral thesis, for contributing the Foreword to this book and for his chats about our common birthplace, the city of Stoke-on-Trent.

To all of my family and friends who encouraged and tolerated my endeavours, the biggest thank you.

Finally, none of this would have happened without the *post mortem* influence of my grandfather 313445 Gunner Wilfred Taylor, 2/1st North Midland (Staffordshire) Heavy Battery (TF), 1896-1957, whom I barely remember but whose war service sparked my interest and kept me searching. He would never have dreamt of seeing his (or my) name in print. Thanks Grandad.

Foreword

There were more than 1,200 general officers who served in the British Expeditionary Force (BEF) on the Western Front during the Great War. Unsurprisingly, the largest group were those at the bottom of the general officer pyramid, brigadier-generals. These could be found across the BEF – at GHQ, corps and divisional levels – as heads of department, staff officers, gunners, sappers and logisticians, but by far the largest group (635 men) were the commanders of infantry brigades. There is truth in Liddell Hart's depiction of the BEF as 'an army of brigadiers'. Infantry brigade command experienced the war's challenges at the 'sharp end' as these changed over time, from the early days of 'open warfare', involving retreat, counter-attack and epic encounter battles, through the resource-starved beginnings of 'attrition' in 1915 and the impact of the unprecedented 'mass citizen army', first of volunteers and then of conscripts, to the renewed 'semi open warfare' of the 'Great Advance' of 1918 in which the trenches were finally abandoned and a resource-rich BEF fought its way deep into the Hindenburg Line, facing – daily – new tactical problems presented by natural and artificial watercourses, woods and shattered villages and towns. Infantry brigade command tested to the utmost the physical, moral and professional resources of the men who held the post. Not all proved up to the job and the turnover was considerable, but others – including some unusual men from unusual backgrounds – prospered, displaying leadership, courage, initiative and military judgement of a high order.

Richard Holmes famously declared that in order to be an infantry brigade commander at the end of the war you had to have been a Regular army subaltern at the start of war and still be alive. There is substance to this, though the most commonly held rank of the infantry brigade commanders in place at the start of the attack on the Hindenburg Line in September 1918 was actually captain. They were certainly young men. On 29 September 1918 125 brigade commanders were aged under 45, 49 were aged under 40, the youngest being the 28 year-old Bernard Freyberg VC. Twenty-eight brigade commanders under the age of 35 were appointed during the war, the youngest of whom was the twenty-five year old Roland Bradford VC. Although infantry brigade command was dominated by British Regular officers, it was not a Regular army monopoly. A number of 'exotics' forged distinguished careers despite limited or non-existent pre-war military experience, including George Gater (an educational administrator when the war began) and the architect Arthur Hubback. Perhaps no one was more 'exotic' than the subject of this fascinating new book, Frank Crozier.

Crozier is, arguably, the most famous British brigade commander of the Great War, though his fame, some would say infamy, rests on what he wrote about the war in the 1920s and 1930s rather than what he achieved during it. That he rose to general officer rank at all was extraordinary, given that he had been compelled to resign his Regular commission in 1908, under the threat of being dismissed for failing to honour cheques, a lifelong weakness. He was described in April 1909 as 'totally unfit to hold H.M.'s commission'. Crozier's military rehabilitation began in Ulster during his pre-war involvement with the Protestant paramilitaries, the Ulster Volunteer Force, an important contributor of troops to the 36th (Ulster) Division. He soon found himself second in command of the 9th Battalion Royal Irish Rifles and became its CO in November 1915. A year later, he was given command of the 119 (Welsh Bantam) Brigade, 40th Division, at the age of 37. He retained the post until the end of the war, one of only 27 commanders of New Army infantry brigades to remain in command for more than two years. As Mike Taylor points out, Crozier was told when he assumed command of 119 Brigade, that it was '*very bad* – quite the worst in the division'. One of the strengths of this book is that it is as much a history of 119 Brigade as it is of Crozier. This is to be welcomed, as its achievements, particularly its role in the capture of Bourlon Wood (November 1917), described by Liddell Hart as 'an epic feat of arms', have not received the recognition that was due. Crozier's role in the transformation of the brigade is subjected to careful scrutiny and a balanced account emerges. 'Balance' is not something that is easy to achieve when considering the life and career of Frank Crozier.

Crozier was one of those men, familiar to military history, who were good at war and bad at peace. He was described during an exchange of letters in 1919 between Sir William Peyton, one of Crozier's former divisional commanders, and the Adjutant-General's department, as 'that well known type, a regular swashbuckler'. This depiction was not intended as a compliment. Despite recommendations from Peyton and another of Crozier's divisional commanders, Sir Harold Ruggles-Brise, later Military Secretary of the BEF, Crozier's application to be retained in the Regular army was refused. The adjustment to civilian life proved painful. Confronted by the unyielding enmity of the 'military establishment', he found it impossible to secure official employment following his resignation from command of an auxiliary division of the Royal Irish Constabulary and took up his pen to make a living. Crozier's enduring fame/notoriety rests on what he wrote about the war and his part in the Anglo-Irish war, when he seemed to court controversy, not least to bolster the stridently pacifist position this most warlike of men adopted during the 1920s.

One of the major problems with Crozier, as Mike Taylor argues, is that the main source for Crozier's life and career is Crozier himself and Crozier's relationship to the truth was – to put it mildly – somewhat loose. Taylor charts a masterly and scholarly course through Crozier's turbulent post-war public and private life, demonstrating that his post-war writings distort as much as they reveal about his command of 119 Brigade, largely to the detriment of what he actually achieved as a brigade commander and how he achieved it. This is a very welcome addition to Helion's First World War titles.

John Bourne
University of Wolverhampton

Introduction

On 20 November 1916 the newly promoted Brigadier-General Frank Percy Crozier (1879-1937) took command of 119 Infantry Brigade, one of three brigades that made up the 40th Division (119, 120 and 121 Brigades). The purpose of this book is to bring the history and achievements of the brigade to a wider audience and add to the story of the controversial Frank Crozier. The study examines the four infantry battalions of the brigade. It does not detail the other components, the 119th Trench Mortar Battery, the 119th Machine-Gun Company or the Field Ambulances that supported the brigade.

Raised in 1915 and originally intended as a formation of the Welsh Army Corps, 119 Brigade, consisting of four battalions of Welsh bantams, had crossed to France in June 1916 – more than a year after it was formed – as a part of the last of the New Army divisions to join the BEF. It had then spent an undistinguished few months in the Loos sector.[1] According to Crozier, on his arrival at divisional headquarters, the GSO1 made it clear to him that the brigade was "*very bad* – quite the worst in the Division". Crozier, firmly believing, he says, that there were no such things as bad soldiers, only bad colonels, claims to have transformed the brigade in six months and in the process removed "a brigade-major, a brigade signalling officer, nearly a dozen commanding officers in turn, a few seconds in command, three adjutants, several doctors, quartermasters and transport officers and one or two sergeant majors".[2] Certainly the brigade seems to have performed well in April 1917 around Villers Plouich and later, most famously, at Bourlon Wood in November 1917. After the major army reorganisation of February 1918, the brigade was reconstituted with a majority of new battalions in time to be severely mauled in the German Spring Offensives but, reconstituted once again (largely with men considered unfit for front line service), it nevertheless seems to have performed creditably in the final months of the war.

Despite these upheavals Crozier remained as GOC until after the end of hostilities and was one of just twenty-seven New Army brigadier-generals to remain in command for more than two years.[3] Was he simply lucky or was he doing a good job? Of the divisions of the Fifth New Army the 40th Division has received almost no attention and the spotlight has, for example, been

---

1 'Bantams' were recruits who were between 5ft and 5ft 3 inches in height. Given Crozier's own lack of height (he was 5ft 3½ inches tall) it is tempting to speculate that someone in high command was indulging their sense of humour by posting him to command a bantam brigade. 40th Division merits just one line in the Official History volumes for 1916 and 119 Brigade is not mentioned at all.
2 F.P. Crozier, *Impressions and Recollections* (London: T. Werner Laurie Ltd, 1930), p.184. The GSO1 at this time was Lieutenant-Colonel Henry Alexander Walker (1874-1953), later Brigadier-General H.A. Walker CB CMG DSO HP. Crozier had previously used the 'no bad soldiers, only bad colonels' maxim in *Brasshat in No Man's Land* (London: Jonathan Cape, 1930), p.131 where he ascribed it to Napoleon Bonaparte. There does not seem to be any evidence for this attribution. It is not referred to in L.E. Henry, *Napoleon's War Maxims* (London: Gale and Polden Ltd., 1899) yet the attribution persists. H.R.H. The Prince of Wales used it in a eulogy in 2006. See *Prince of Wales and Duchess of Cornwall* <http://www.princeofwales.gov.uk/media/speeches/eulogy-hrh-the-prince-of-wales-memorial-service-zaki-badawi> (accessed 1 January 2015).
3 Figure derived from A.F. Becke, *Order of Battle of Divisions, Part 3a – New Army Divisions (9-26)* (London: HMSO, 1938) and *Part 3b – New Army Divisions (30-41) and 63rd (R.N.) Division* (London: HMSO, 1945)

directed on the 35th Division as the prime example of a bantam formation, or on the origins and development of the 36th (Ulster) and 38th (Welsh) Divisions as examples of formations with distinct national identities and a strong political dimension to their creation.[4] The story of 119 Brigade is unique. As a 'left-over' brigade of the Welsh Army Corps the story of its development sheds light on the creation of the last of the volunteer army formations. The examination of its 'national' identity shows how this may have affected its morale and performance while the identification of the social and geographic origins of its officers and other ranks gives new insight to changes taking place within the 'sharp end' of the BEF during the final two years of the war.

What were the origins of 119 brigade? What were the backgrounds of the officers and other ranks in its three incarnations? How good was the brigade and how did it evolve? How crucial was Crozier's leadership and what was his command style? Did Crozier do what he said he did by dismissing ineffective officers and assembling an effective group of subordinates? This book describes the history of the brigade, examines how it developed and attempts to form an objective view of its GOC. When writing his own books and articles in the 1930s Crozier had an agenda. He had failed to gain post-war employment in the regular army and had a bitter dispute with the establishment in the aftermath of his resignation from the Auxiliary Division of the Royal Irish Constabulary in 1921. By the time that his last and most controversial book, *The Men I Killed*, was published in 1937 he was an active and passionate advocate for the Peace Pledge Union. As an author he courted controversy and he can still generate emotional, intemperate and sometimes irrational criticism, much of which is sparked by his own descriptions of his part in the trial and execution of Rifleman James Crozier in February 1916, his 'confession' to at least one summary execution during the German Spring offensive on the Lys in April 1918 and his involvement in Ireland in 1920-21. The late Richard Holmes noted how his copy of Crozier's *A Brass Hat in No Man's Land* (1930) had been re-titled by a previous owner as *'A Fat Arse in No Man's Land'*.[5] A one-time subordinate in the Royal Irish Rifles also reported how the then Lieutenant-Colonel Crozier was regarded as a "callous and overbearing martinet".[6] Yet when Lieutenant H.A.J. Lamb took over as brigade signalling officer in April 1918, he noted that he had "taken over a good section. Brig. Gen. Crozier most awfully nice".[7] After Crozier's death Basil Liddell Hart wrote in *The Times*, "I have had the opportunity of questioning many who served with or under him, both war-time and professional soldiers, and have heard on all sides the most fervent admiration expressed for his qualities as a fighting leader. Some who had wide experience considered that he was the best brigade commander they saw in action".[8] Whatever his own character, Crozier gathered around him a group of senior officers in whom he had confidence. An examination of the war diaries of the brigade and its constituent battalions shows that the brigade major at the time of Crozier's promotion to the brigade was replaced within a month. The CO of the 17th Welsh was relieved of

---

4　For the most recent detailed examination of bantam units see Peter Simkins, *"Each One a Pocket Hercules": The Bantam Experiment and the Case of the Thirty-fifth Division* in Sanders Marble (ed.), *Scraping the Barrel: The Military Use of Sub-Standard Manpower* (New York: Fordham University Press, 2012), pp.79-104. For 36th (Ulster) Division see Phillip Orr, *The Road to the Somme* (Belfast: Blackstaff Press, 1987). For 38th (Welsh) Division see Colin Hughes, *Mametz: Lloyd George's 'Welsh Army' at the Battle of the Somme* (Norwich: Gliddon Books, 2nd Edition, 1990).

5　Richard Holmes, *Tommy: The British Soldier on the Western Front 1914-1918* (London: Harper Collins, 2004), p.642.

6　J.L. Stewart-Moore, quoted in Timothy Bowman, *Irish Regiments in the Great War: Discipline and Morale* (Manchester: MUP, 2003), p.30. This description has now been quoted (out of context) more than once and will be discussed later.

7　Imperial War Museum (IWM), Department of Manuscripts: 01/9/01. H.A.J. Lamb, Lieutenant RE, Diary 1915-18, 27 April, 1918.

8　*The Times*, 4 September 1937.

his command in January 1917 following 113 cases of trench foot in his battalion during a single tour of duty in the front line. The 19th Royal Welsh Fusiliers had three COs between January and May 1917 and when Lieutenant-Colonel B.J. Jones returned in June having recovered from wounds sustained in the previous year he was replaced within two months. The replacement for the wounded CO of 12th South Wales Borderers also lasted two months before being replaced himself. There is enough substance in Crozier's claims of wholesale officer replacement to warrant investigation.

Previous Research

The infantry division is the most common commonly studied higher formation and histories of just a handful of New Army infantry brigades were published in the immediate post-war period: one of these is effectively a collation of four battalion histories; two are of brigades of 30th Division and two of brigades of 34th Division.[9] The same two brigades of 34th Division are the subject of one of a clutch of more recently written accounts as are 89 Brigade (30th Division) and 92 Brigade (31st Division). 90 Brigade (again) and 91 Brigades (both 30th Division) are covered in a one volume study of the Manchester Pals. A study of a territorial brigade has also been added to the list recently.[10]

In 2004 Peter Simkins put infantry brigades firmly into the academic spotlight when he identified them as the 'building blocks' of the BEF's offensive operations. Military administration and the role of the brigade staff was the focus of Aimée Fox's 2010 dissertation and subsequent book.[11] Recently, the role and function of brigadier-generals during the Battle of Arras in 1917 has been examined by Trevor Harvey who concluded that "their most significant contribution was to ensure, despite the unglamorous treadmill of building and rebuilding their brigades, that they retained the capacity of their brigades for battle".[12] This has gone some way to addressing the point made by Simkins that "[Brigadier-Generals] have remained individually and collectively unknown to the general public" with just a few, including Crozier, leaving published memoirs or biographies.

While Crozier has attracted the attention of several authors, 119 Brigade has attracted almost none. F.E. Whitton's *History of the 40th Division* (1926) was for many years the only study of the

---

9   J. Keating and F. Lavery, *Irish Heroes in the War: The Story of the Tyneside Irish Brigade* (London: Everett, 1917); Anon, *History of the 50th Infantry Brigade, 1914-1919* (London: 1919); F.C. Stanley, *The History of the 89th Brigade* (Liverpool: Daily Post, 1919); H.L. James (ed.), *Sixteenth, Seventeenth, Eighteenth, Nineteenth Battalions, the Manchester Regiment: A Record 1914-1918* (Manchester: Sherratt and Hughes, 1923); T. Ternan, *The Story of the Tyneside Scottish* (Newcastle: Northumberland Press, 1919); E.W.J. Rowan, *The 54th Infantry Brigade, 1914-1918: Some Records of Battle and Laughter in France* (Aldershot: Gale and Polden, 1919).

10 J. Sheen, *Tyneside Irish: A History of the Tyneside Irish Brigade Raised in the North East in World War One* (Barnley: Pen and Sword, 1998); G. Stewart and J. Sheen, *Tyneside Scottish: A History of the Tyneside Scottish Brigade Raised in the North East in World War One* (Barnsley: Pen and Sword, 1999); D. Bilton, *Hull Pals: A History of 92 Infantry Brigade, 31st Division* (Barnsley: Pen and Sword, 1999); M Stedman, *Manchester Pals, 16th, 17th, 18th, 19th, 20th, 21st, 22nd and 23rd Battalions of the Manchester Regiment: A History of the Two Manchester Brigades* (London: Leo Cooper, 1994); Alan Isaac Grint, *A Sturdy Race of Men: 149th Brigade [50th Division] – A History of the Northumberland Fusiliers Territorial Battalions in The Great War* (Barnsley: Pen and Sword, 2018).

11 Peter Simkins, 'Building Blocks: Aspects of Command and Control at Brigade Level in the BEF's Offensive Operations, 1916-1918' in Gary Sheffield and Dan Todman (eds.), *Command and Control on the Western Front: The British Army's Experience 1914-18* (Staplehurst: Spellmount, 2004), pp.141-171.

12 Trevor Gordon Harvey, "An Army of Brigadiers': British Brigade Commanders at the Battle of Arras 1917', University of Birmingham, PhD Thesis, 2015, abstract.

formation.¹³ Whitton evidently had access to the war diaries of the division and its formations and units along with accounts from a few individuals but it seems simply assembled them into a narrative history which ignores the origins of all of the division's constituent brigades. The 119 Brigade is not singled out for any particular attention within the story although it is possible to detect contributions that probably came from James Frederick (Freddy) Plunkett (see Chapter Four).¹⁴ Crozier certainly submitted his own comments to Sir James Edmonds on the content of the volume of the Official History that dealt with the German Offensive on the Somme in March 1918 and the Battle of the Lys in April 1918 but the volume that dealt with Cambrai was not published until after Crozier's death and so the description of Bourlon Wood contains no obvious contribution from him.

Troop morale and discipline are two military factors which are intimately related. Timothy Bowman has defined morale as an internal factor that can be influenced by external factors and discipline as a largely external one.¹⁵ J. G. Fuller, quoting S.L.A. Marshall on his experience of Second World War combat, says that "one of the oldest myths in the military book [is] that morale comes from discipline ... The process is exactly the reverse ... true discipline is the product of morale".¹⁶ Good discipline and good morale are key to combat success and have been the focus of several studies that have attempted to use quantitative data to gauge the level of both in particular units and formations. This book extends that methodology to 119 Brigade. In 2003 Timothy Bowman presented data from the courts-martial records for the units and formations of the 16th (Irish) Division and the 36th (Ulster) Division during their periods of training and on the Western Front. Similar data sets were published by Stephen Sandford for the 10th (Irish) Division and compared with Bowman's data.¹⁷ However, the 10th (Irish) Division did not serve on the Western Front and can only be used as a comparator in this book for its period of home service. Sandford also uses data on the 13th (Western) Division which fought at Gallipoli alongside the 10th (Irish) Division. Figures from all these studies are compared in this book with data relating to the units of 119 Brigade to form a view of the relative level of discipline within the brigade.

40th Division's part in the battle of Cambrai during which it distinguished itself in the attempt to take and hold the wooded ridge at Bourlon and the adjacent village has been described in several works, including William Moore's *A Wood Called Bourlon* (1988), Jack Horsfall and Nigel Cave's battlefield guide *Bourlon Wood* (2002), Alexander Turner's *Cambrai* (2007), Bryn Hammond's *Cambrai 1917* (2008) and Andrew Rawson's *The Cambrai Campaign* (2017).¹⁸

The actions of the brigade prior to Cambrai have largely escaped attention but Bill Mitchinson's battlefield guide *Villers-Plouich* (1999) is an exception. The period immediately after Cambrai features in Colin Taylor's *'I Wish They'd Killed You in A Decent Show'* (2014) and Chris Baker's *The*

---

13   F.E. Whitton, *History of the 40th Division* (London: Gale &, 1926).
14   See for example Whitton, *History of the 40th Division*, p.143.
15   Timothy Bowman, *Irish Regiments in the Great War: Discipline and Morale* (Manchester: Manchester University Press, 2003), p.10.
16   J.G. Fuller, *Troop Morale and Popular Culture in the British and Dominion Armies 1914-1918* (Oxford: Clarendon Press, 1990), p.52. Marshall (1900-1977) was a US Army combat historian in the Second World War and Korea and author of *Men Against Fire: The Problem of Battle Command* (New York: William Morrow, 1947). The validity of his work on 'ratio of fire' values in this work has since been challenged.
17   Stephen Sandford, *Neither Unionist Nor Nationalist: The 10th (Irish) Division in the Great War* (Sallins: Irish Academic Press, 2015).
18   William Moore, *A Wood Called Bourlon: the cover-up after Cambrai* (London: Leo Cooper, 1981); Jack Horsfall & Nigel Cave, *Bourlon Wood* (Barnsley: Leo Cooper, 2002); Alexander Turner, *Cambrai* (Oxford: Osprey, 2007; Bryn Hammond, *Cambrai 1917: The Myth of the First Great Tank Battle* (London: Wiedenfeld & Nicolson, 2008); Andrew Rawson, *The Cambrai Campaign* (Barnsley: Pen & Sword, 2017).

Battle for Flanders (2011) covers the Lys battles of April 1918.[19] The reconstituted division's part in the final stages of the war has not been described in detail before.

The units which made up the 40th Division feature, along with other bantam units, in Sidney Allinson's *The Bantams* (1981)[20]. Stephen McGreal's *Cheshire Bantams* (2006) is a detailed history of the 15th and 16th Battalions Cheshire Regiment (105 Brigade, 35th Division) and 17th (Reserve) Battalion of the Cheshire Regiment that also includes some basic information on the raising of the 40th Division as the only other bantam formation in the New Armies.[21] Caroline Scott's *The Manchester Bantams* (23rd Manchester Regiment, 104 Brigade, 35th Division) is a detailed account of another bantam unit of 35th Division which, although reprising the origin of bantam formations generally, makes no mention of the bantam and part-bantam formations of 40th Division.[22]

Much has been written on the history of the 38th (Welsh) Division, its origins in the movement to create a Welsh Army Corps and its most famous action at Mametz Wood but useful general context for Wales in the Great War is now available through the works of Chris Williams and Robin Barlow.[23] These will be used as a baseline for the Welsh aspects of this study and Williams' work in particular is used to provide comparative data.

Crozier (rather than his later command) is referred to in several works on the Great War, most of which cite his actions as an officer of the 36th (Ulster) Division and in particular his roles in the court martial mentioned above and on the first day of the Somme.[24] The repercussions of his description of the collapse of the Portuguese 2nd Division on the Lys have been examined in A.D. Harvey's *Muse of Fire* (1998).[25] His later actions as commander of the Auxiliary Division in Ireland in 1920-21 are noted in several studies of that episode.[26] Professor Brian Bond included a chapter on Crozier in his study of memoirs of the Western Front *Survivors of a Kind* (2008). This has a

---

19 K.W. Mitchinson, *Villers Plouich and the Five Ridges* (Barnsley: Leo Cooper, 1999); Chris Baker, *The Battle for Flanders: German defeat on the Lys 1918* (Barnsley: Pen & Sword, 2011); Colin Taylor, *'I Wish They'd Killed You in A Decent Show': The Struggle for the Hindenburg Line between Croisilles and Fontaine-les-Croisilles, March 1917 to August 1918* (Brighton: Reveille Press, 2014).

20 Sadly, Mr Allinson's notes and correspondence with surviving bantams are not available for further study. Sidney Allinson, 'Re: Bantams etc'. Email correspondence (15 April and 21 November 2010). Sidney Allinson, *The Bantams: the untold story of World War 1* (London: Howard Baker, 1981). The book has been reprinted with minor revisions and no subtitle (Barnsley: Pen & Sword, 2009).

21 Stephen McGreal, *Cheshire Bantams: the 15th, 16th and 17th Battalions of the Cheshire Regiment* (Barnsley: Pen & Sword, 2006).

22 Caroline Scott, *The Manchester Bantams: The Story of a Pals Battalion and a City at War; 23rd (Service) Battalion The Manchester Regiment (8th City)* (Barnsley: Pen & Sword, 2016).

23 Robin Barlow, *Wales and World War One* (Llandysul: Gomer Press, 2014) contains useful social background that will be used for comparison, as does Chris Williams 'Taffs in the Trenches: identity and military service 1914-1915' in Matthew Cragoe and Chris Williams (eds), *Wales and War: Society, Politics and Religion in the Nineteenth and Twentieth Centuries* (Cardiff: University of Wales, 2007), 126-164. For a very measured reassessment of 38th Division and Mametz Wood see Chris Williams, 'A Question of 'Legitimate Pride'? The 38th (Welsh) Division at the Battle of Mametz Wood, July 1916', *Welsh History Review / Cylchgrawn Hanes Cymru*, 28:4 (2017), pp.723-752.

24 See for example Phillip Orr, *The Road to the Somme* (Belfast: Blackstaff Press, 1987); Myles Dungan, *Irish Voices from the Great War* (Dublin: Irish Academic Press, 1995); Stephen Walker, *Forgotten Soldiers: the Irishmen shot at dawn* (Dublin: Gill and Macmillan, 2007); Richard Grayson, *Belfast Boys* (London: Continuum, 2009).

25 A.D Harvey, *A Muse of Fire: Literature, Art and War* (London: Hambeldon Press, 1998).

26 See for example Richard Bennett, *The Black and Tans* (Stroud: Spellmount 2006 – first published 1959); Ernest McCall, *Tudor's Toughs* (Newtonards: Red Coat Publishing, 2010); David M Leeson, *The Black & Tans: British Police and Auxiliaries in the Irish War of Independence, 1920-1921* (Oxford: Oxford University Press, 2011).

strong biographical thread at its core but is based largely on Crozier's own publications. As we shall see, Crozier was economical with the truth about his own life in his books and great care must be taken when using them as sources of fact. Bond's analysis of Crozier as "not an easy man to like" leaves room to exercise one's own judgement.[27]

Until recently the main source of information on Frank Crozier was Crozier himself – which is probably exactly what he intended. As the present author has confirmed, the discovery of any new information beyond these sources involves the investment of large amounts of time with no guarantee of a favourable outcome. This situation has now been improved by publication of a biography by Charles Messenger. *Broken Sword* (2013) at last gives an account of Crozier's life and travails including much hitherto unpublished personal detail which allows a more rounded picture of the man to emerge.[28] Despite seeking out new information, Crozier's books remain key sources and this reinforces the need for more information about their context and Crozier's motives for writing them.[29]

The brigade does not feature in any detail in academic work or research papers and the sources for this book are largely unpublished. Absolutely key to the study of the brigade and its battalions are the war diaries (WO 95 series) in The National Archives (TNA), Kew. As is always the case, these vary in detail and in legibility but examination shows the brigade headquarters diary to be reasonably detailed and with a considerable number of appendices containing operational orders. The battalion diaries are much more variable in the quality of their content and many of their appendices are lost. TNA also contains the correspondence generated during the compilation of the official histories, including letters from Crozier, his subordinates, and representatives of divisional and corps command. At least one of Crozier's letters to Edmonds has found its way into Crozier's personal file although this potentially key source has also suffered from substantial 'weeding'. The files of several of the brigade's senior officers have also been located within TNA although again they have been 'weeded'. Unfortunately, several key figures concerned with the 119 Brigade continued to serve with the army after 1920 and their files have not been released to the public.[30] James Frederick Plunkett stands out as the only one of the senior officers of the brigade to leave a written account of his service albeit written up in the 1920s from his wartime notes. Rather strangely, Crozier rarely features in this account.[31] In order to build a picture of the origins and character of the brigade a considerable number of junior officers' personal files have been examined and as many soldiers records as can be traced have also been studied. These will be described in detail in Chapter One (men) and Chapter Two (officers). TNA Series WO 86 and WO 213 contain valuable data on courts martial during the Great War, including information relating to 119 Brigade's units, which are included later.[32]

Outside TNA the records of the Welsh Army Corps (WAC) at the National Library of Wales (NLW), Aberystwyth, provide a detailed and, to date, under-utilised resource containing important information on the formation of the Corps and on the origins of the units that would comprise

---

27 Brian Bond. *Survivors of a Kind* (London: Continuum, 2008), p.129.
28 Charles Messenger, *Broken Sword: The Tumultuous Life of General Frank Crozier 1879-1937* (Barnsley: Praetorian Press, 2013).
29 Timothy Bowman, 'Review of Broken Sword by Charles Messenger', *History Ireland*, 22 (July/August 2014), p.63 also identifies this issue.
30 For example, Anthony Muirhead (Brigade Major), Reggie May (Staff Captain), James Plunkett (Battalion CO).
31 NAM: 1994-05-398. Crozier often expresses his approval of Plunkett in his books but it is possible that, as a regular soldier, Plunkett deferred to his GOC and avoided openly commenting.
32 TNA WO 86. Judge Advocate General's Office: District Courts Martial Registers; WO 213. Judge Advocate General's Office: Field General Courts Martial and Military Courts Registers.

119 Brigade.[33] The Public Record Office of Northern Ireland (PRONI), Belfast, contains key sources relating to the 36th (Ulster) Division and Crozier's time with the 9th Royal Irish Rifles.

Several other repositories contain documents generated by individuals who served with 40th Division. Sir John Ponsonby, one of the three commanders of 40th Division during the Great War, left a very patchy diary which is at the National Army Museum (NAM). His predecessor in divisional command, Harold Ruggles-Brise, is also represented in the NAM collections, while his letters to his wife are in the Blair Castle Archive, Perthshire. The regimental museums of the various units that made up the brigade also contain items created by officers and men of those units, although these are not numerous.

The 119 Brigade did not apparently harbour notable literary talents.[34] The post-war output of Frank Crozier is well known but only two other war-inspired publications by members of the brigade have been identified. *Ar Orwel Pell* (1965) is a short account in Welsh of his wartime service by Evan Beynon Davies.[35] *Never Again: A Diary of the Great War* (1934) is an anti-war memoir that may have been inspired by Crozier's *Brass Hat*, by H. Gregory, an ex-member of 119th Machine Gun Company[36] The letters of John Saunders Lewis (second-lieutenant, 12th SWB) were published in 1993 and a selection appeared in *Wales on the Western Front* (1994).[37]

Some sources are still in private hands. An unpublished (and incomplete) biography of Crozier by his second wife has been traced and further ephemera are with descendants in Canada. The letters and sketchbooks of Second-Lieutenant Morris Meredith Williams, 17th Welsh, have recently provided material for the beautifully illustrated *An Artist's War* by Phyllida Shaw.[38] A copy of the diary of Lieutenant H.A.J. Lamb, RE, Brigade Signals Officer from April 1918, is in the Imperial War Museum (IWM). The IWM also contains Private David Starrett's account of his time as Crozier's servant throughout the war. Starrett's typescript is a particularly useful source giving a view of events that to some extent balances the extremes of Crozier's own descriptions. The IWM also holds the papers of Captain B.D. Gibbs, 18th Welsh, and Lieutenant C.L. Morgan, 21st Middlesex, as well as a few short memoirs by ORs.

---

33 The WAC records at NLW, Aberystwyth have been little used being for many years both geographically inaccessible and poorly arranged. The latter problem was dealt with by the production of a catalogue in 1993. Attention was drawn to the existence of the records by Clive Hughes in 'The Welsh Army Corps, 1914-15: shortages of khaki and basic equipment promote a 'national' uniform', *Imperial War Museum Review*, No.1, 1986, pp.91-100. Since the completion of the current author's researches the WAC records have been digitised and are now available online at http://cymru1914.org/en/view/archive/3992732.

34 The poet Isaac Rosenberg (1890-1918) enlisted in the 12th Suffolk (121 Brigade, 40th Division) in October 1915, was transferred to the 12th South Lancs (120 Brigade, 40th Division) and then the 11th King's Own (120 Brigade) until that battalion was disbanded in February1918. He was killed while serving with the 1st King's Own (12 Brigade, 4th Division).

35 Evan Beynon Davies, *Ar Orwel Pell* (Llandysul: Gomer Press, 1965). I am indebted to Clive Hughes for all the translations from this work which appear in this book. The title translates as '*On a Distant Horizon*' – part of a line from poet Hedd Wyn's poem '*Rhyfel*'[*War*]. Davies was commissioned from the 15th Royal Welsh Fusiliers (London Welsh) to be a second-lieutenant in the 19th RWF in March 1915.

36 H. Gregory, *Never Again: A Diary of the Great War* (London: Arthur H. Stockwell, 1934). 85744 Pte Herbert Gregory MM (1889-1966) of Nelson, Lancashire, was also the author of *Prisoners of War: Krieg Gefangeners: A Play* (London: Stockwell, 1934). His MM was awarded for his actions at Bourlon Wood.

37 Mair Saunders Jones, Ned Thomas and Harri Pritchard Jones (eds), *Letters to Margaret Gilcreist* (Cardiff: University of Wales Press, 1993). John Saunders Lewis (1893-1985) went on to be a significant author and prominent Welsh Nationalist. He was propelled into the spotlight by the court case that followed his attempt to burn down the newly established RAF camp at Penyberth, North Wales in 1936; John Richards (ed), *Wales on the Western Front* (Cardiff: University of Wales Press, 1994).

38 Phyllida Shaw, *An Artist's War: The Art and Letters of Morris and Alice Meredith Williams* (Stroud: The History Press, 2017).

The relative paucity of original sources about Crozier and his command have led in the past to an over-reliance on his own books as reference material. This has led to a repetitive 'churn' of facts about him, a situation that has only recently been improved by Charles Messenger's biography. The lack of obvious additional sources has also resulted in a dearth of published references to or assessments of 119 Brigade and the 40th Division. It is hoped that this book will to some extent address this gap and augment the limited historiography of infantry brigades and brigadier-generals.

The Chapters

While it would be possible to adopt a subject by subject approach to the study of a brigade that examined, for example, recruiting, training, equipment, discipline and other key areas in relative isolation, there is no existing history of the brigade to give such a study context. To address this the detailed examination of particular areas of interest in this book is set within a broadly chronological framework; starting with the brigade's origins and composition, moving through its activities in Flanders and its later restructurings in the last year of the war. It will examine the arrival of Crozier as GOC Brigade, his military background, his writing – on which so much history has previously been based – and his methods.

Chapter one will describe the origin of the brigade within the twin contexts of the drive to realise Lloyd George's vision of a Welsh Army Corps of at least two divisions and the extension of New Army recruiting across Britain to include men who would previously have been rejected on the grounds of their modest stature. The chapter develops the picture of the brigade as originally formed by examining the social background of the other ranks in the light of previous work on recruiting Welsh units, the progress of recruiting and the effects of the weeding of unsuitable individuals from the constituent battalions.[39] It also includes such information as is available on the training of the battalions.

Chapter two moves on to examine both the senior and junior officers of the brigade and how they may have influenced its internal culture as it prepared for service overseas. Data on the social background of officers will be compared with previous work on other formations.[40] The chapter includes the actions and operations of the brigade once on active service in France and show how it adapted to conditions there up to the arrival of Frank Crozier as GOC. Comment on and analysis of the effectiveness of the unit at this time will be made to compare with the later period of Crozier's command and a view presented of the success or otherwise of this element of the bantam 'experiment' by comparison with the experiences of the wholly bantam 35th Division.

Chapter three briefly examines Crozier's career up to the date when he joined 119 Brigade. To do this effectively it includes a summary of his active service with the 36th (Ulster) Division with observations on his character, reputation and *modus operandi* as a CO. Given its continuing impact and the effect it had on his reputation, his post-war literary output is examined in detail.

Chapter four examines the impact that Crozier made on the brigade, its operations in the area around Villers-Plouich/La Vacquerie in the spring of 1917 and how it met the challenge of its first offensive actions. The larger part of this chapter describes the action at Bourlon Wood during

---

39 Robin Barlow, *Wales and World War One* (Llandysul: Gomer Press, 2014) contains useful social background that will be used for comparison, as does Chris Williams 'Taffs in the Trenches: identity and military service 1914-1915' in Matthew Cragoe and Chris Williams (eds), *Wales and War: Society, Politics and Religion in the Nineteenth and Twentieth Centuries* (Cardiff: University of Wales, 2007), pp.126-164.

40 Comparisons of the social and military background of officers in the New Armies are facilitated by the work of Timothy Bowman, 'Officering Kitchener's Armies: A case study of the 36th (Ulster) Division', *War in History*, 2009 (2), pp.189-212.

the Battle of Cambrai in November 1917 which saw the virtual destruction of the brigade. A comparison of this attack with the 38th (Welsh) Division's well-documented attack on Mametz Wood during the previous year is presented as an Appendix.

The period of rebuilding the brigade after Bourlon Wood was curtailed by the major reorganisation of BEF divisions in February 1918. Chapter five describes the effects of this on 40th Division and the 119 Brigade in particular. The performance of the 'new' brigade during the German offensives on the Somme in March and the Lys in April which involved holding actions and fighting retreats in the face of sometimes overwhelming odds is outlined along with the actions of the GOC and other senior officers of the brigade and division. The chapter describes how the later losses on the Lys necessitated the temporary replacement of the traditional brigade structure with *ad hoc* arrangements in an attempt to hold back the German offensive and then moves on to look at the period of near-dissolution of a much diminished brigade and its reconstitution with men of supposedly poor quality. A view of the effectiveness of the brigade in its final incarnation as part of the British Second Army in the Advance to Victory is presented along with an assessment of the effectiveness of Crozier at a crucial moment. Finally, these threads are drawn together in a conclusion which presents a view of the brigade, its development and effectiveness and the role of Brigadier-General Frank Percy Crozier as its GOC.

This introduction has set the scope and structure of this book and examined the relevant historiography and the sources used. A context has been established demonstrating the absence of previous detailed studies of 119 Brigade, 40th Division and of Frank Percy Crozier. Despite the recent publication of Crozier's biography, there is still a need to explore his career during the Great War in more detail. With few published studies of brigadier-generals or of infantry brigades there is a clear need to assemble and consider information that might illuminate Peter Simkins' view of brigades (and their commanders) as the 'building blocks' of the BEF's offensive operations.

Recent work on Wales in the Great War and the geographical and social affiliations of its soldiers will be enhanced by the story of 119 Brigade as will existing work on 36th (Ulster) Division and 38th (Welsh) Division. While these previous studies contain quantitative data on the social and geographical make up of infantry battalions and their discipline and morale they are few in number. In answering key questions about 119 Brigade, that number will be augmented and new data presented to inform potential future studies. The presentation here of information derived from the service records of officers and men develops a picture of this brigade at different stages of the war and highlights the contrast between the volunteers of 1915 and the 'B1' men used to keep the formation in the front line in 1918. A detailed examination of the brigade's record in action presents information absent from the general works on battles and campaigns noted above and demonstrates the utility of the brigade on the battlefields of the Great War.

1

The Welsh Bantam Brigade

The infantry brigade that Frank Crozier would eventually command had an interesting and complicated birth. F.E. Whitton described in his divisional history how the 40th Division was formed in September 1915 as its constituent units and staff assembled at Aldershot but the 119 Infantry Brigade had a longer history than the division to which it was ultimately allocated. This gestation period is not described at all by Whitton and is here described in detail for the first time.

The genesis of the brigade was driven by two initiatives within the context of New Army recruitment. The first was the ambition to form a Welsh Army Corps of at least two divisions given momentum by the energy of David Lloyd George in September 1914. The second was the extension of recruiting from November 1914 to men who would previously have been considered too short for army service to form new 'Bantam' battalions. The brigade's origins were apparently quickly forgotten. The 1920 account of the formation of the 38th (Welsh) Division stated with startling inaccuracy:

> The Division [*sic*] originally comprised four battalions of Bantams … they were the 18th and 19th Royal Welsh Fusiliers, the 12th South Wales Borderers and the 17th Welsh. These Battalions were left behind in North Wales when the [38th] Division moved to Winchester and formed part of another Division.[1]

The Welsh Army

The background to the creation of the Welsh Army Corps has been described by several authors but is elaborated here because it gives essential background to the development of 119 Brigade.[2]

At the end of August 1914 the War Office, struggling to administer the growth of the New Armies and the flood of recruits into existing units, was content to sanction the formation of locally-raised battalions that drew on men's sense of community – whether community of geography or of workplace. Against the burgeoning of these 'Pals' battalions it was inevitable that there would be pressure to recruit regionally or nationally-badged formations that embodied a higher level sense of identity. After the 36th (Ulster) Division was given War Office approval on 3 September it was not long before the idea of a national army from Wales found a champion:

---

1   J.E. Munby (ed.), *A History of the 38th (Welsh) Division* (London: Hugh Rees Ltd, 1920), p.12. The correct makeup of the brigade and its location(s) are provided elsewhere in this volume.
2   See for example Colin Hughes, *Mametz: Lloyd George's 'Welsh Army' at the Battle of the Somme* (Norwich: Gliddon Books, 2nd Edition, 1990); Peter Simkins, *Kitchener's Army* (Manchester: Manchester University Press, 1988); Robin Barlow, *Wales and World War One* (Llandysul: Gomer Press, 2014); Jonathon Riley, *Ghosts of Old Companions: Lloyd George's Welsh Army, The Kaiser's Reichsheer and the Battle for Mametz Wood, 1914-1916* (Warwick: Helion and Company, 2019).

> I should like to see a Welsh Army in the field. I should like to see the race who faced the Normans for hundreds of years in their struggle for freedom, the race that helped to win the battle of Crecy, the race that fought for a generation under Glyndwr against the greatest captain in Europe – I should like to see that race give a good taste of its quality in this struggle and they are going to do it.[3]

Lloyd George's inspiring speech at the Queen's Hall, London, on 19 September 1914 fostered a positive image of the Welsh people's martial past and reprised their historical role as 'freedom-fighters' now moved to defend a fellow small nation (Belgium) from the ravages of an oppressive invader.[4] A follow-up public meeting in Cardiff on 29 September set the target of a two-division corps and established a National Executive Committee (NEC) to administer the project.

The NEC received official approval for the raising of the WAC in a letter from the War Office dated 10 October 1914. It was not without caveats. The most potentially restricting of these stated that 'every effort must be made to complete existing Welsh units to establishment before recruits are encouraged to enlist in the new units of the Welsh Army Corps' and resulted from Kitchener's 'cautious attitude towards semi-nationalist formations'.[5] Keith Grieves has pointed out that the appointment of officers via sponsors was 'a social cost Kitchener had to pay for the benefits which were derived from the local affiliation of the recruit' and one factor in the great man's opposition to the establishing of the WAC.[6]

Even before the War Office letter had been received, the Secretary of the NEC was writing to Lloyd George in response to a telegram from the War Office that spoke in a similar vein:

> Mr Owen has discussed the wire with Ld Plymouth who thinks that the proposal of the War Office to include Welsh recruits in any Army Battalion is fatal to the scheme for raising a Welsh Army Corps. Lord Plymouth asked Mr Owen to wire all the Lords Lieutenant to cancel all recruiting meetings for the time being but Mr Owen on reflection thought this ought not to be done until he had brought the matter to your notice.[7]

By 30 October Lloyd George had confronted Kitchener on more than one occasion and had removed any hindrance to recruiting for the WAC.[8] The one thing that Kitchener would not concede was the allocation of already existing battalions to the WAC and huge numbers of recent recruits were therefore denied to it. The Secretary of the NEC noted that between 2 August and 30 September 1914 47,697 Welsh volunteers had joined up and that a further 20,000-30,000 had joined the Territorial Force and the Special Reserve. He also highlighted one problem in recruiting Welshmen from outside the principality: 'Lord Derby strongly objects to any recruiting being done in Liverpool for the Welsh Army Corps … [he] is raising a new Territorial Battalion, and apparently he thinks we are encroaching.'[9]

---

3 David Lloyd George quoted in *Welsh Army Corps 1914-1919, Report of the Executive Committee* (Cardiff: Western Mail Ltd, 1921), p.3.
4 See report of meeting in the *Western Mail*, 21 September 1914.
5 See Simkins, *Kitchener's Army*, pp.94-100.
6 Keith Grieves, *The Politics of Manpower, 1914-18* (Manchester: Manchester University Press, 1988), p.10.
7 NLW WAC: C12/14: Memo to Chancellor of the Exchequer, 7 October 1914. Owen William Owen (1863-1930), Divisional Officer of Labour Exchanges of Wales, was Secretary of the WAC National Executive Committee. Robert George Windsor Clive (1857-1923), Earl of Plymouth and Lord Lieutenant of Glamorganshire, was Chairman of the NEC.
8 Simkins, *Kitchener's Army* p.99.
9 NLW WAC: C12/14: Letter outlining current status of recruiting, 22 October 1914.

Kitchener did however grant the allocation of four 'Pals' battalions that were currently recruiting to form the nucleus of the WAC. They were the 13th Royal Welsh Fusiliers (1st North Wales), 10th Welsh Regiment (1st Rhondda), 13th Welsh Regiment (2nd Rhondda) and 14th Welsh Regiment (Swansea). By the end of October 1914 the WAC had responsibility for 3,000 men; by the end of November approximately 7,000 and by the end of the year 10,000. In November a start had been made on raising a further five infantry battalions and another two would be formed in December. The first and (as it turned out) only division of the WAC was completed with the addition of a further infantry battalion plus a pioneer battalion in January 1915. The process had not been easy. 'In the first couple of months by reason of difficulties not connected with the movement [to form a WAC], the recruiting seemed slow, but by December these had disappeared and the recruits were presenting themselves in large numbers.'[10] Some of these recruits would form the first battalion of what became 119 Brigade when the Army Council gave permission for the formation of a bantam battalion of the Welsh Regiment on 15 December 1915.

The Bantams

The story of the creation of bantam battalions has, like the story of the Welsh Army Corps, been described in several works.[11] It is often surrounded with a degree of patronising sentimentality not found in the descriptions of the history of other less vertically challenged units and is debatably inherited from contemporary press accounts, which often contrast the height of recruits with their cheeky nature and fighting spirit.[12]

Presented at the time to the public as an opportunity for men under the normal regulation height to 'do their bit' for King and Country the creation of bantam units was in reality a practical response to the falling levels of voluntary enlistment during the autumn of 1914. Grieves describes how the highest figure of 30,000 recruits per day in early September 1914 had fallen to 15,000 per week by mid-October.[13] He also notes how the fluctuating height requirement acted as a disincentive to recruiting. The original minimum height for recruits of 5'4" was raised to 5'6" in September to slow down the intake of recruits. As recruiting slowed it was lowered to 5'3" in November and yet again to 5'2" in July 1915.[14] His work ignores the creation of the 'bantam' standard in November 1914. *The History of the Cheshire Regiment in the Great War* identified the catalyst for the creation of the bantams as the rejection on grounds of height of four miners who had travelled from Durham to Birkenhead to enlist.[15] This supposedly led Alfred Bigland MP, the member for Birkenhead East, who was already engaged as vice-chairman of the local recruiting committee, 'to raise a battalion of short men'[16]. However, according to Bigland himself, his initia-

---

10   *Report* WAC p.2.
11   See Sidney Allinson, *The Bantams: the untold story of World War 1* (London: Howard Baker, 1981); Stephen McGreal, *Cheshire Bantams: the 15th, 16th and 17th Battalions of the Cheshire Regiment* (Barnsley: Pen & Sword, 2006); Peter Simkins, 'Each One a Pocket Hercules': The Bantam Experiment and the Case of the Thirty-fifth Division in Sanders Marble (ed.), *Scraping the Barrel: The Military Use of Sub-Standard Manpower* (New York: Fordham University Press, 2012), pp.79-104.
12   'Little Men With Big Hearts' was a headline, for example, in the *Yorkshire Post and Leeds Intelligencer*, 30 June 1915.
13   Grieves, *The Politics of Manpower*, p.11.
14   Ibid., p.12.
15   A. Crookenden, *History of the Cheshire Regiment in the Great War* (Chester: W.H. Evans & Sons, 1939) cited in McGreal, *Cheshire Bantams*, p.21.
16   McGreal, *Cheshire Bantams*, p.21; Allinson, *Bantams*, p.36 seems to conflate the two accounts and makes the troublesome recruit a Durham miner.

tive was prompted by the case of a single, keen, rather ferocious, recruit who had been ejected from more than one recruiting office because he was one inch below the regulation height of 5'3". The recruit had been encountered by Alfred Mansfield, the Honorary Secretary of Bigland's recruiting committee, who reported the incident to Bigland with the words 'this is a serious business, when we only wanted a small army a regulation height of five feet three inches might be good, but now every available man is wanted and the subject should be reconsidered'.[17] Bigland approached Lord Kitchener who confirmed his interest in the idea via Sir Henry McKinnon, CinC Western Command, who met with Bigland in early November 1914.

> He informed me [Bigland] that the War Office was interested in the idea of bantam battalions but were too much pressed to undertake the formation of a new type of regiment. However, he had authority to say that if the Birkenhead Recruiting Committee would undertake the whole service we should have every assistance from the War Office. For specially raised battalions, regulations had already been drafted fixing a definite amount of so much for housing, a ration allowance, and payment for uniforms and equipment. The War Office would provide rifles, baggage wagons etc., but all other matters must be undertaken by the parties raising the battalion.[18]

It appears then that the bantams were benefiting from the regulations that had been developed by the War Office for the 'Pals' battalions.

Unfortunately, the Birkenhead Recruiting Committee bridled at the financial liability involved in administering the new unit and, after the Town Clerk had pointed out that the Town Council must not put itself in a position where deficit funding was a possibility, Bigland took on the financial risk himself. By 18 November 1914 he could confidently announce the creation of his unit in the local press and over the next two weeks potential recruits indicated their willingness to serve by submitting a postcard to the recruiting committee. Information about the opening of recruiting for the battalion was circulated to recruiting offices across the country on 24 November:

> 24 Nov 1915 Circular from Major P Allan, Chester to OC 24th RD Brecon
> Recruiting
> Men applying to join the Birkenhead Battalion can be medically examined and attested at all Recruiting Stations. Standard: height minimum 5'0"maximum must be under 5'3".
> 5'0" to 5'1"   Chest: 33 inches
> 5'1" to 5'2"   33½ inches
> 5'2" to 5'3"   34 inches
> These to be normal measurements without expansion. With expansion 2 inches more.
> Enlistment for the Battalion is not to commence until Monday next, November 30th, and will continue until further notice. All men passing the test, and after attestation will be given a warrant to Birkenhead and told to report themselves at the Town Hall … Inform all sub areas.[19]

Attestation officially commenced on 30 November and the unique status of the battalion ensured that it was almost up to strength in less than two days. The formation of a second bantam battalion

---

17   Quoted in McGreal, *Bantams*, p.22.
18   Bigland quoted in Allinson, *Bantams*, p.38.
19   NLW WAC 12/39: Circular from Major P. Allan, Chester to OC 24th Recruiting Depot, Brecon, 24 November 1915.

was quickly sanctioned by the War Office.[20] Recruits who had previously stood no chance of acceptance at recruiting offices flocked to Birkenhead from across the industrial north but also included men from Scotland, Lincoln and one group of fifty from London.[21] Some came from Wales.

The Welsh Bantams

The developments in Birkenhead did not go unnoticed by the WAC, which was striving to advance its own recruiting. On 25 November 1914 the NEC's secretary wrote to the Treasury:

> Recruiting – I enclose a recruiting circular issued by Major Lucas, Cardiff, from which you will see that recruiting in Wales is about to be started for the Birkenhead 'Bantam' Battalion. If recruiting for such a battalion is to be allowed in Wales, I fail to see why we should not have a Battalion of 'Bantams' here, and I wired to General Mackinnon this morning for his authority.
>
> Lord Derby, you will remember, strongly objected to our recruiting in Liverpool, which was 'his area', for the Liverpool Welsh: now we have Birkenhead, which is also in 'his area' recruiting in Wales for a Birkenhead Battalion.[22]

On the same day and certainly at the instigation of Owen, Sir Ivor Herbert, Chairman of the WAC's Recruiting Committee, wrote to Western Command:

> Please authorise reduction of standard for Welsh Army Corps to five feet as for Birkenhead Battalion in order that Welsh Army Corps may retain first call over Welshmen as indicated by War Office instructions … Recruits have been daily rejected, failing to attain the standard of 5 feet 3 inches, and there is no doubt that the units of the Welsh Army Corps would rapidly be completed if the lower limit of five feet were allowed.
>
> Pending authority for the alteration of the standard, I request that recruiting for the Birkenhead Battalion in Wales be discontinued.[23]

While the predicted swift completion of the WAC through bantam recruiting was undoubtedly an exaggeration, any move which would boost recruiting to the WAC was eagerly pursued. Western Command responded quickly to the complaint about the Earl of Derby's recruiting activities by confirming on 26 November that 'men in Welsh areas are not to be enlisted in the Birkenhead Bantam Battalion'.[24] This move was reinforced on 30 November by a reminder from Cardiff to local recruiters 'that the Birkenhead Bantam Battalion is CLOSED in this area'.[25]

The request from the WAC to Western Command to approve the formation of a Welsh bantam battalion inevitably met with a bureaucratic response. On 28 November Western Command

---

20 Originally titled the 1st and 2nd Birkenhead Bantam Battalions they were officially designated as the 15th and 16th (Service) Battalions Cheshire Regiment.
21 McGreal, pp.31-32.
22 NLW WAC: C12/14: Owen to J.T. Davies 25 November 1914. Davies was Private Secretary to David Lloyd George.
23 NLW WAC 12/39: Letter from Sir Ivor Herbert to Staff Officer Recruiting, Western Command, Chester, 25 November 1914.
24 NLW WAC C12/46: Telegram from Western Command to WAC Secretary, 26 November 1914.
25 Ibid. Glamorgan Routine Order No.137, 30 November 1914.

responded: 'Bantam Battalions treated on same lines as local battalions and each application from responsible individual or community received here is considered separately. Please send your application in writing through this office.'[26] Owen responded formally:

> Sir – I have the honour to bring to your notice the probability of our being able to raise a 'Bantam' Battalion for Glamorganshire, provided that the height is reduced from 5'3" to 5'.
>
> Major Lucas [Recruiting Officer, Cardiff] states that he has turned away many hundreds of men between these measurements, and he has not the slightest doubt but that a 'Bantam' Battalion could be raised in Glamorganshire, if the necessary authority were given, and I beg to apply that this should be done.[27]

Western Command probably forwarded Owen's request to the War Office which responded asking: '[Regarding] application for Bantam Battalion in Wales. Is it proposed to be included in Welsh Division now being formed or an extra battalion? If the latter who is responsible for raising it'.[28] Owen's reply followed a meeting of the NEC on 9 December when the committee was informed by Brigadier-General Ivor Philipps DSO that the GOC was not favourably disposed towards the inclusion of a 'Bantam' battalion in the 3rd Brigade of the division.[29] Western Command was told that the 'Bantam Battalion would be additional to First Division and raised by Welsh Army Corps Committee'.[30] Not knowing that this reply had been sent, the officer in command of troops at Porthcawl on the South Wales coast contacted the WAC Secretary about another matter but mentioned '[Western] Command wants your decision as to whether Bantam Battalions are to be included in first division. Command considers application to include would be favourably considered moreover General Philipps is anxious for inclusion.'[31] Owen retracted the previous response with indecent haste: 'Cancel my previous wire and include Bantam Battalion in first division in accordance with General Philipps wishes'.[32]

Still the questions came from the War Office via Western Command: 'Can you please say which Battalion is selected as a Bantam Battalion. Please furnish the information to this office early.'[33] This question must have produced some head-scratching within the WAC. Brigadier-General Sir Ivor Philipps telegraphed Lord Plymouth the Chairman of the NEC: '[I] Believe if Welsh Army Corps Committee approves General Mackinnon would sanction Colonel Wilkie raising Bantam Battalion of 17th Welsh Regiment [sic]. I strongly recommend to concur'.[34] Plymouth did concur with Philipps' suggestion and passed his approval on to the Secretary of the NEC who in turn contacted Western Command: 'Bantam Battalion will be 17th (Glamorganshire) Service Battalion Welsh Regiment of 3rd Brigade, Welsh Army Corps subject to your approval'. Finally the long-awaited approval came via Western Command on 15 December: 'Army Council approve

---

26 NLW WAC C12/ 39: Western Command to Secretary WAC, 28 November 1914.
27 Ibid. Secretary WAC to GOC in C Western Command, 28 November 1914.
28 Ibid. Western Command to Secretary WAC quoting War Office, 6 December 1914.
29 Ibid. Secretary WAC to Sir Ivor Philipps 15 December 1914.
30 NLW WAC C12/39: Secretary WAC to Western Command, 10 December 1914.
31 Ibid. Wilkie to Secretary WAC, 11 December 1914.
32 Ibid. Secretary WAC to Western Command, 11 December 1914.
33 Ibid. Western Command to Sec WAC quoting War Office telegram, 12 December 1914.
34 Ibid. Telegram Sir Ivor Philipps to Lord Plymouth quoted in correspondence of 15 December 1914. Philipps was promoted to command the then 43rd Division in January 1915 but, as this incident appears to show, was behaving as the head of the formation before this. The 43rd Division was renumbered as 38th (Welsh) Division on 29 April 1915.

of Bantam Battalion for Glamorganshire. Chest measurement 34 and a half inches same as regular infantry.'[35] The first element of what became 119 Brigade was about to come into being.

The 17th (Service) Battalion Welsh Regiment (1st Glamorgan)

Following War Office approval for the creation of a bantam battalion of the regiment, recruiting was officially declared open on 18 December.[36] By that time however, there had been a 'Glamorgan Service Battalion, Welsh Regiment' recruiting since 26 November as a battalion in the 3rd Brigade of the 1st Division of the WAC.[37] The county identification was transferred to the new bantam unit but evidently caused some confusion. A note to recruiting officers reminded them that: 'the Glamorgan Service Battalion is now the 'Bantam' Battalion. Cease recruiting therefore any men over 'Bantam' height for this Battalion'.[38] When recruiting opened, the Cardiff Recruiting Office 'hoped that every R.O. [Recruiting Officer] and Recruiter in the County of Glamorgan will spare no efforts to get recruits for the Bantam Battalion now in course of formation. If this is done there should be no difficulty in getting the 1,100 men required in a month'.[39]

Although there were other bantam battalions recruiting elsewhere in Britain by this time there was undoubtedly a backlog of short men who were keen to enlist. The day after recruiting opened the *Western Mail* noted that:

> Brisk recruiting has already commenced for the Glamorgan Bantam Service Battalion [*sic*] which is to form part of the Welsh Army Corps. Sir William Mackinnon happened to be present when the first recruit was sworn in at Cardiff on Friday [18 December 1914] and heartily shook the Cardiff patriot by the hand, remarking that the army had room for many more men of his stamp. Not only at Cardiff but at the various sub-recruiting stations in the county, good reports were being made throughout the day of the opportunity being seized.[40]

The proximity of Christmas seems to have influenced some men to hold back from enlisting, at least for the moment:

> Recruiting for the Bantam Battalion in the Rhondda is very satisfactory. Colour-Sergeant Jones at Tonypandy has enrolled a large number and the outlying stations Tonyrefail and Llantrisant are also doing well … many men have made arrangements to join but do not desire to leave their homes until after Christmas.[41]

---

35 NLW WAC C12/39: Telegram Western Command to Secretary WAC, 15 December 1914. The emphasis on the chest measurement was to try to ensure that the man was physically well-developed.
36 NLW WAC: C12/46: Telegram to WAC from Recruiting Officer Cardiff, 18 December 1914.
37 Ibid. Telegram from Cardiff Recruiting Office to Owen, WAC, 26 November 1914. It is probably no coincidence that the 17th Welsh was created just when it had been reported that 'both Rhondda bttns are over strength, send no more recruits' (NLW WAC: C12/46. Telegram from Cardiff Recruiting Office, 25 November 1914). No enlistments for the period prior to 15 December 1914 have been confirmed in surviving records of the 17th Welsh. It is presumed that any existing recruits over 5'3" in height were transferred to other battalions; WAC: C7/3. Letter from WO to General Officer, Western Command, 3 December 1914 places the battalion in 3 Brigade.
38 Ibid. Glamorgan Recruiting Office to Recruiting Officers, 30 December 1914.
39 Ibid. Glamorgan Recruiting Office to Recruiting Officers, 18 December 1914.
40 *Western Mail*, 19 December 1914.
41 Ibid., 22 December 1914.

Recruits for the 17th Welsh. (Undated press cutting, author)

By 1 January 1915 the WAC officially reported that the battalion had attracted 250 recruits.[42] This figure seems to have been quickly exceeded as a newspaper account stated that on the 31 December 1914 the 17th Welsh consisted of six subalterns, four trumpeters and 530 men[43]. This rush to the colours is confirmed by another enthusiastic report from the same newspaper:

> On Thursday [7 January 1915] the Bantams paraded at Porthcawl 769 strong and with the staff and the number of recruits pouring in by each train the strength at nightfall was well over 800. These figures are the more remarkable when it is borne in mind that the first batch of 50 men was received as recently as Dec 29th. Captain D. Watts Morgan, who is in temporary command of this and other units, has been kept busily occupied, with his colleagues, in dealing with the rush of recruits. The battalion has already been formed into four companies each of which is being added to daily, and everything is in complete order to close the moment full strength is reached … Colonel Wilkie will take over command directly the battalion is at full strength.[44]

Lieutenant-Colonel Charles Joseph Wilkie (1869-1916) had seen active service on the North-West Frontier of India but had been invalided home and did not serve in South Africa. He was an experienced trainer of men, had been adjutant with the volunteers before he retired from the army in

---

42 NLW WAC C7/3: Memo from Secretary WAC to DAAG, Western Command, Chester, 1 January 1915.
43 *Western Mail*, 1 January 1915.
44 Ibid., 8 January 1915. David Watts Morgan DSO CBE (1867-1933) was a miners' leader and politician. In March 1915 he was gazetted to the 17th Welsh (from the 10th Welsh) but remained active recruiting to other battalions. See Appendix VI.

1907 and became secretary of the Glamorgan Territorial Force Association in 1909. He assisted with mobilization at the start of the Great War, was promoted major in the 9th (Service) Battalion, Welsh Regiment, on 8 Oct 1914 and was given command of the 17th Welsh on 26 November when it only existed on paper and before it was designated as a bantam unit.[45]

On 19 December 1914 the *Western Mail* reported that Wilkie '(Commander of the Glamorgan Bantam Battalion) is at present acting as officer commanding the Welsh Army Corps units at Porthcawl'.[46] Porthcawl had been a pre-war camp site for the Territorial Force but had developed as a training area for various WAC units. The 16th (Cardiff City) Welsh had been formed there in November 1914 and it was a temporary home for part of the 13th Welsh. Both of these units moved to North Wales in December making room for the 17th Welsh. The crowded camp and organizational confusion were probably the cause of a telegram from the WAC to Western Command when the formation of the 17th Welsh was being contemplated: '[the] situation at Porthcawl may have bearing on Bantam Battalion proposals'.[47] Wilkie confirmed his move to Porthcawl in a telegram to the WAC that hints at some of the issues at the camp:

Lt-Col C. J. Wilkie. (Williams Collection)

> Shall take over command Porthcawl troops Monday [14 December]. Command Headquarters consider it is of utmost importance that arrangements shall be made by you under which the troops and others shall have no cause to complain of non-receipt of pay and billet money this week. I strong[ly] endorse this view and advise issue of necessary funds to existing authority.[48]

Wilkie would seem to have been an excellent choice to raise and organise a new battalion and to control the busy camp at Porthcawl but the appointment would bring him not a little anger and frustration.[49] He later wrote to the Secretary of the WAC:

---

45 *De Ruvigny's Roll of Honour, 1914-1919.* C.J. Wilkie (1869-1916) see Appendix VI. In April 1915 he published the booklet *A System of Platoon Scouts for the 17th (Glamorgan) Batt. The Welch Regiment.* What is likely to be the only surviving copy is in the Williams Papers.
46 *Western Mail*, 19 December 1914. The *Western Mail*, 2 December 1914 mentions Lieutenant-Colonel Andrew Pearson (13th Welsh) as OC Porthcawl. Pearson had moved from Cardiff to Porthcawl with half of the 13th Welsh (2nd Rhondda) on 23 November 1914, see *The Glamorgan Gazette*, 27 November 1914.
47 NLW WAC C12/39: Telegram from Secretary WAC to Western Command, 7 December 1914.
48 Ibid. Telegram from Wilkie to Secretary WAC, 11 December 1914.
49 The *Western Mail*, 23 January 1915, reported that on 22 January Porthcawl was home to 1068 men of the RFA, 707 RE, 732 Glamorgan Bantams, 587 ASC, 544 RAMC and 300 other infantry.

My seven weeks at Porthcawl very nearly laid me out – no one knows what I had to take on there or the fearsome strain it was. It was a nightmare and everyone's hand was against me but what can be said. I have the satisfaction of knowing that I saved the Welsh Army Corps Scheme from a most serious calamity although I know others will never recognise the fact.[50]

The main assembly area for the WAC was in North Wales and most new infantry units moved there to begin their serious training. Accordingly, on 15 January 1915, 551 men and four officers of A and B Companies, 17th Welsh, left Porthcawl. The arrival of the 'Welsh Gurkhas', as the press dubbed the battalion, at Colwyn Bay the next day was widely reported.[51] C and D Companies followed on 30 January.[52] For the next six months billets in the resort of Rhos on Sea would be home to the battalion and battalion HQ would be the Rhos Hydro. By 1 February 1915 the establishment of the battalion was noted as ninety-one officers [either a mistake or the battalion was massively over establishment] and 1,298 NCOs and men.[53] The goal of forming a complete battalion in less than a month had not been realized – but it was close.[54]

The 18th (Service) Battalion Welsh Regiment (2nd Glamorgan)

When the idea of the WAC was conceived, the corps was planned to consist of at least two divisions. Although this two-division concept had been approved in principle by the War Office, the GOC Western Command, Sir W.H. Mackinnon, expressed his reservations at an early stage, 'For the present I have confined the question to the formation of one division only, as I am of the opinion that it is probable that difficulty may be expected in raising a second division.'[55] With the successful raising of the 17th Welsh well under way, the Secretary of the NEC was obviously keen to press on: 'the 1st Division is now practically full … I have already written to the General Officer Commanding-in-Chief, Chester – without the authority of the [National Executive] Committee I may say – asking that official sanction for the formation of the 2nd Division be given, but no reply has yet been received'.[56]

Sanction to form a second division was never given but the development of the corps with additional units proceeded following a meeting of the NEC on 22 January. On the 29 January 1915 recruiting officers were told that:

> A second Battalion of the 'Bantams' has been authorised and it is hoped you will do everything in your power to encourage enlistment into this unit. In all probability the Battalion will be known as the '18th (Service) Battalion, Glamorgan, Welsh Regiment' and in the meantime this designation had better be entered on the attestation documents.[57]

---

50 NLW WAC: C111/25. Letter from Wilkie to Secretary WAC, 17 April 1915.
51 *The Cambria Daily Leader*, 18 January 1915.
52 *Colwyn Bay News*, 4 February 1915.
53 NLW WAC C109: Correspondence with the War Office. List of establishments dated 1 February 1915.
54 Service/Pension records for 127 men of the 17th Welsh have been traced. Of these men 91% enlisted before 31 January 1915. The 'Platoon Roll Book' for Number 16 Platoon, D Company (scanned copy in the author's possession) gives the enlistment dates of 51 men. Of these all but 5 enlisted in December 1914 (14) and January 1915 (32).
55 NLW WAC C7/1: Letter from GOC Western Command to War Office forwarding proposal for formation of a Welsh Army, 27 October 1914. Sir W.H. Mackinnon KCB KCVO (1852-1929) was GOC Western Command 1910-1916. He was previously the first Director-General of the Territorial Force.
56 NLW WAC C12/14: Secretary WAC NEC to J.T. Davies, H.M. Treasury, 20 January 1915.
57 NLW WAC C12/46: Glamorgan Recruiting Office circular to recruiting offices, 29 January 1915.

The press reported on the formation of the new battalion just two days later, 'General W.H. Mackinnon ... has authorized the raising of a second 'Bantam' Battalion to be known as the 18th Welsh (Service) Battalion, and it is hoped that the full strength will be reached by the end of February'.[58] The battalion was founded with men surplus to the needs of the 17th Welsh. It was listed in the *Weekly Return of the British Army at Home* as consisting of one officer, one sergeant and 140 other ranks on 23 January 1915 before it even officially existed.[59] There seems to have been no serious issue (yet) with the numbers of bantam-sized men offering themselves up at recruiting offices despite a newspaper referring to the previous week's recruiting at Cardiff being 'disappointing'. It reported that on 3 February there had been seventy bantams on parade but there was 'nearly a full company of about 240 men' just two days later.[60] By 16 February the *Western Mail* could report: 'Good progress is being made with the formation of a second Bantam Battalion in Glamorgan, between 400 and 500 recruits are in training at Porthcawl'. The same title had previously reported on the appointment of the CO of the battalion.[61]

Herbert Richard Homfray JP VD (1864-1940), who was given command of the 18th Welsh on 4 February 1915, was a member of a prominent Glamorgan county family with substantial financial interest in the South Wales coalfield. The third son of the family, he had been educated at Eton and then followed the same route as his elder brother into the militia (3rd Berkshire Regiment) and from there into the 1st Life Guards via a commission in the 1st Royal Irish Rifles. He resigned his subaltern's commission in 1889 and operated as a land agent in Cowbridge, Glamorgan, near the family seat at Penllyn Castle. In 1891 he became major in the 2nd Volunteer Battalion, Welsh Regiment and was the Lieutenant-Colonel Commandant of the unit between 1895-1905 when he resigned. He was a member of the Glamorgan Territorial Force Association and would have known C.J. Wilkie from his post as secretary. In 1910 he was elected a county councillor and between 1906 and 1914 he was master of the Glamorgan Foxhounds.[62] At the start of the war he was active in promoting recruiting, speaking at meetings and opening recruiting offices.[63] As a well-known county figure who had strong links with the coalfield he was a logical choice to raise a new unit in the area. The history of the WAC credits him with recruiting and training the 18th Welsh.[64]

There seems to have been some confusion about the role of the new unit. The NEC had approved the formation of a pioneer battalion for the WAC at its meeting on 6 January but had put the matter into abeyance at the next meeting.[65] The 18th Welsh though remained designated as 'Pioneers' in the *Weekly Return of the British Army* until mid-March 1915.[66] This may indicate a simple clerical error or an insight into the War Office view of the capabilities of bantams.

After the promising start, recruiting for the battalion did not proceed as quickly as it had for the 17th Welsh. The five returns for the month of March 1915 were 518, 567, 576, 652 and 733 all

---

58 NLW WAC C113/16: Press Cutting, *South Wales Daily News*, 1 February 1915.
59 TNA WO 114/26: Weekly Return of the British Army (exclusive of Territorial Force) and Dominion contingents at home [January-April 1915], 23 January 1915.
60 *Western Mail*, 6 February 1915.
61 Ibid.
62 Summary compiled from the *London Gazette* entries and local newspapers. He became Deputy Lord-Lieutenant of Glamorgan on 31 July 1915. His youngest son was killed in a motor-cycle accident in 1913 age 16 while another died at First Ypres as a lieutenant in the 1st South Wales Borderers. The eldest son was commissioned second-lieutenant Glamorgan Yeomanry in 1914.
63 See for example *Western Mail*, 6 August 1914; 28 October 1914; 6 November 1914.
64 *Welsh Army Corps 1914-1919: Report of the Executive Committee* (Cardiff: Western Mail, 1921), p.36.
65 NLW WAC C11/27 C11/28: Minutes of NEC meetings of 6 January and 22 January 1915.
66 TNA WO 114/26: Weekly Return of the British Army. 'Pioneers' last appears in connection with the 18th Welsh on 22 March 1915. It was the 19th Welsh, raised in February 1915 that was designated a pioneer battalion.

ranks and it was not until 26 April that the total reached four figures (1088). Some of the issues around recruiting will be explored later.

The initial success of bantam recruiting that led to the formation of the 18th Welsh spurred the NEC to approve the formation of two further bantam units at its meeting on 22 January 'as soon as it is considered desirable by General Mackinnon'. The first of these to be brought to the attention of the public was the 19th Royal Welsh Fusiliers (RWF).

The 19th (Service) Battalion Royal Welsh Fusiliers

Bantam recruiting in Wales had thus far been targeted at the coal mining communities of the south of the country while the WAC was concentrating in the seaside towns of the north. On 1 February 1915 it was reported that:

> It is now proposed to raise a battalion for the Welsh Division of men ranging in height from 5 ft to 5ft 3in on the lines which have proved so popular in Lancashire and South Wales. The recruiting for the 'North Wales Bantams' will probably be started immediately and the headquarters will be at Deganwy, at which charming resort … the men will be billeted for training.[67]

The RWF, the local regiment, had eighteen numbered battalions of all types by February 1915. The 'North Wales Bantams' were number nineteen. Although no doubt inspired by the success of bantam recruiting to date, the creation of this battalion was marked by a degree of caution not seen before in the growth of the WAC. It was observed that, 'So far however, authority has been given to form one company only and it depends on the success with which that is got up whether North Wales is to have its own 'Bantam' battalion'.[68] The caution was certainly justified. North Wales had not been a particularly fruitful recruiting ground for the WAC. The RWF was the 'local' regiment but samples show that during the Great War just 49 per cent of its ranks were born in Wales. Of these, the majority came from Anglesey, Caernarvonshire, Denbighshire and Flintshire with the single largest contingent (18.1%) coming from Denbighshire. South Wales provided a further 22 per cent of Welsh born recruits.[69] The Welsh-speaking, nonconformist and largely un-industrialized (the exception being slate quarrying) lands of the north were a particularly difficult nut for recruiters to crack. Clive Hughes has noted how the people of what is now the (modern) county of Gwynedd had 'small town and rural values and [a] strong nonconformist bias, had little sympathy for the military and [the county] was no great peacetime source of recruits'[70] One strategy developed by the WAC to try and improve the situation was to employ men known to their local communities in raising the new battalions. Perhaps the best known of these was Colonel Owen Thomas of Brynddu, Anglesey, a member of the NEC and a keen recruiter, who in October 1914 had recommended a scheme to improve recruiting:

---

67 *Liverpool Evening Express*, 1 February 1915.
68 *North Wales Chronicle*, 12 February 1915.
69 Chris Williams, 'Taffs in the Trenches: Welsh national identity and military service 1914-1918', in Matthew Cragoe and Chris Williams (eds), *Wales at War: Society, Politics and Religion in the Nineteenth and Twentieth Centuries* (Cardiff: University of Wales Press, 2007), pp.126-164.
70 Clive Hughes, 'Army Recruitment in Gwynedd, 1914-1916' (MA thesis, University of Wales, Bangor, 1983), p.ii. This research has been recently published as Clive Hughes, '*Arm to save your Native Land': Army Recruiting in North-West Wales, 1914-1916* (Llanwrst: Gwasg Carreg Gwalch, 2015).

Thomas believed that farmers and farm labourers, two classes largely hitherto untouched, would provide strong, healthy recruits of the best type. Upon enlistment they should not be drafted into distant depots but trained locally, and every effort made to secure staff officers fluent in the Welsh language or else with Welsh connections. Emphasis was placed on local route marches as another incentive to recruitment. To boost the ranks, they could also appeal to the strong Welsh element exiled in London, Liverpool, Manchester and other English cities.[71]

Unsurprisingly, Thomas shortly afterwards found himself propelled by the influence of David Lloyd George to the rank of Brigadier-General in command of 1 Brigade, WAC.

Further detail about recruiting and the geographical make up of battalions will follow below but the principle set out by Owen Thomas surely affected the choice of CO for the 19th RWF? The press made the announcement six weeks before the appointment appeared in the *London Gazette*: 'Colonel Lloyd Evans, JP, DL, of Broom Hall, Chwilog, has accepted a commission with the rank of Colonel in the Welsh Army Corps ... Colonel Evans will probably be gazetted to the 18th or 19th Battalions of the Royal Welsh Fusiliers, stationed at Llandudno'.[72] The press confirmed his command two weeks later by reporting that he would 'shortly' assume command of the 19th RWF.[73] The *London Gazette* finally reported on 25 May that 'Lieutenant-Colonel and Honorary Colonel Owen L.J. Evans, retired, late 4th Militia Battalion to command the battalion (19th RWF) and to be temporary Lieutenant–Colonel'.[74]

Owen Lloyd Jones Evans (1856-1928) was later described as 'a large property owner in London and North Wales'.[75] A Welsh speaker, he had graduated MA from Magdalen College, Cambridge in 1883 but had already started his service with the Royal Carnarvon Militia as a 'sub-lieutenant' in February 1877. He progressed steadily through the ranks becoming lieutenant in November 1878, captain in May 1881 and major before 1886. In 1899 he took command of the battalion. His only active service seems to have been when the 4th (Militia) Battalion RWF (the successor to the Royal Carnarvon Militia) was embodied in 1900 and briefly garrisoned the defences of Plymouth. He was an active contributor to county life, a magistrate, Deputy Lord Lieutenant and High Sherriff in 1901.[76] In May 1915 his name was used to boost recruiting in newspaper advertisements: 'Colonel Lloyd Evans of Broom Hall calls for strong men between 5ft and 5ft 3in to join the 19th R.W.F. now training at Deganwy'.[77]

Recruitment for the battalion was steady but did not demonstrate the enthusiasm evident in the growth of the 17th and 18th Welsh. The first official return of the battalion's strength was on 15 February when it was composed of one officer and thirty men. One week later it had one officer and ninety-eight men and by the end of March 442 all ranks. By 26 April, just before Owen Lloyd Jones Evans officially took command, the battalion had a total strength of 783 but this had taken eleven weeks.[78] The battalion reached full strength at some time over the summer months. On 6

---

71 David A. Pretty, *Farmer, Soldier and Politician: The life of Brigadier-General Sir Owen Thomas, MP, Father of the 'Welsh Army Corps'* (Wrexham: Bridge Books, 2011), p.89.
72 *The Chronicle*, 9 April 1915.
73 *North Wales Chronicle*, 23 April 1915.
74 *London Gazette*, 25 May 1915.
75 *Gloucester Journal*, 18 August 1928.
76 Compiled from contemporary newspaper reports and the *London Gazette*.
77 *The Cambrian News, Merioneth and Welsh Farmers Gazette*, 28 May 1915.
78 TNA WO 114/26: Weekly Return of the British Army (exclusive of Territorial Force) and Dominion contingents at home.

September 1915 it could muster 1145 all ranks.⁷⁹ At that date the final battalion of the four that made up 119 Brigade was still struggling to reach its target establishment.

12th (Service) Battalion South Wales Borderers (3rd Gwent)

The creation of the 12th South Wales Borderers (SWB) was approved by the NEC at its meeting on 22 January 1915 and received War Office sanction in time for the next meeting on 3 February, again with the proviso that just 'one company only for the present' would be formed. The press, obviously following the proceedings of the NEC closely, broadcast the news: 'New Gwent Battalion – The War Office has sanctioned the addition to the Welsh Army Corps of the 12th Battalion (3rd Gwent) South Wales Borderers which is to be raised in Monmouthshire and is to be confined to men of height 5ft to 5ft 3ins'. The same report described how men would be billeted at their own homes wherever possible and the raising of the first company would be undertaken by 'Mr C Phillip [sic], the Honorary Secretary of the Newport Defence Committee'; both moves indicating the thoughts of the NEC on the likely source of the first recruits. The first men were reported as enlisted on 8 February 1915 and the town of Newport, Monmouthshire would be the base for the unit.⁸⁰ The first official return gave the strength of the battalion as two officers, one sergeant and sixty other ranks on 15 March 1915 and on 8 April the *Liverpool Daily Post* reported that the battalion had 'made a good start'. By 20 April the adjutant could report that, 'our first company is nearing completion, being now up to a strength of 209'.⁸¹ With the completion of the first company and a start about to be made on a second, it was time for a CO to be appointed.

Once again the local press was the first to break the news of the appointment. The new CO was to be Edward Alexander Pope (1876-1919) who was promoted from major and 2iC 3rd (Reserve) Battalion Welsh Regiment. While it was noted that he was 'not a Welshman by birth', the fact that he had 'held a commission in the Welsh Regiment for fifteen years' seemed to make up for his English roots.⁸² Pope was born in Dorchester into a family of brewers. He was educated at Dorchester Grammar School and Winchester College before receiving a commission in the Dorset Militia in 1894 and becoming a Director of Eldridge Pope and Company in 1898. He became a captain in the 3rd (Militia) Battalion Welsh Regiment and, after the battalion was mobilized in 1899, sailed to South Africa where he acted as Provost-Marshal at Vryburg, Cape Colony, and commanded the armoured train *Spitfire* for seven months. Sciatica caused his return to Britain where he arrived in October 1901. He took his army career seriously, passing his 'C' and 'D' examinations in 1909 and 'Tactical Fitness to Command in' 1914. He was promoted major in 1913 and at the outbreak of war re-joined the 3rd Welsh. In common with the other three battalion COs described above, he was active in his county, becoming a County Councillor in 1904 and a JP in 1915. His promotion to command the 12th SWB was dated 21 April 1915 and was apparently due to the recommendation of Brigadier-General H.J.

---

79 TNA WO 114/27: Weekly Return of the British Army [September– December 1915]. TNA does not possess the returns for May-August 1915.
80 *South Wales Echo*, 8 February 1915. 'Mr C Phillip' was Charles David Phillips, a mechanical engineer and businessman from Newport who was gazetted as second-lieutenant, 12th SWB, dated 30 January 1915. He must have been a well-known figure in the town which presented him with a sword and pistol in July 1915. By this time he was Acting Adjutant of the battalion.
81 TNA WO 114/26: Weekly Return of the British Army; *Liverpool Daily Post and Mercury*, 8 April 1915; NLW WAC: C31/2: Letter from Second-Lieutenant C.D. Phillips to Secretary WAC, 20 April 1915.
82 *South Wales Daily News*, 22 April 1915; *South Wales Echo*, 22 April 1915.

'C' Company, 12th SWB, Newport, July 1915. Lt-Col Pope seated front row centre. (Author)

Evans.[83] Evans (1861-1932) had been OC No.4 District, Western Command, which included the Welsh Regiment Depot, and would have known Pope. In February 1915 Evans had taken over command of 43rd (Welsh) Division's 115 Brigade (then known as the '3rd Brigade') from Ivor Philipps on the latter's promotion to command the division and acted as divisional commander during Philipps' absence while attached to the Ministry of Munitions. The 12th SWB were nominally attached to this brigade. A word from Evans to Philipps in connection with Pope's advancement would surely have been likely.

Pope lost no time in publicizing recruitment to his battalion, writing to the local press urging on recruits and stating that 'we now have about 220 men and require at least 1250'.[84] This battalion though would not benefit from any rush to the colours. Recruitment figures for the summer of 1915 are missing from both the TNA records and the NLW. However, by 15 May 471 greatcoats and 475 pairs of puttees had been issued to the men of the battalion, so a mid-May strength of approximately 470 can be inferred.[85] By the end of September, when the other three battalions were up to establishment, the 12th SWB was struggling with strengths in the mid-900s. The battalion would not reach full strength until the end of the year.[86] By then the position of both the battalion and the brigade in the British Army's Order of Battle had been settled.

---

83 Anon., *A Book of Remembrance: being a short summary of the Service and Sacrifice rendered to the Empire during the Great War by one of the many Patriotic Families of Wessex, the Popes of Wrackleford, Co. Dorset* (London: Chiswick Press, 1919).
84 *Monmouthshire Evening Post*, 23 April 1915.
85 NLW WAC C31/2: Clothing return, 12th SWB, to 15 May 1915.
86 TNA WO 114/27: Weekly Return of the British Army.

The Brigade emerges

In January 1915 the WAC still aspired to recruit a second division as had been envisaged at the formation of the corps. The War Office position was more practical:

> On the assumption that all the units of the 1st Welsh Division [43rd Division] are, or shortly will be, completed. One reserve company of 250 all ranks will first be added to each battalion … if other recruits are forthcoming after all units and their reserves are completed, two battalions may be formed per Brigade … and the army Council will then decide whether the additional battalions thus formed are considered reserves or whether they will form part of a second Welsh Division.[87]

This move put a damper on the ambition of the NEC, which had resolved at its 22 January meeting: 'To transfer 17th Bat WR (Glam) to a new 4th Brigade (from 3rd Brigade). To raise a 4th Brigade consisting of the 17th WR, 18th WR, 19th RWF, 12th SWB. The 4th Brigade to be recruited at the 'Bantam' standard.'[88] The resolution at the NEC meeting of 3 February that 'The three new battalions to form the nucleus of 4th Brigade, if agreed, to otherwise to go to 18th Batt. (Bantam) WR' seems to show that the high level of enlistment was not expected to continue.

As the four battalions expanded and completing them to establishment looked more likely, they needed to be slotted into the structure of the WAC. For some reason, perhaps because the WAC or the War Office did not wish to be seen to embark on the creation of the WAC's 2nd Division, the 'bantam brigade' seems not to have been officially created despite the NEC decisions noted above. The oldest of the four battalions, the 17th Welsh, was already one of the four battalions of the 43rd Division's '3rd Brigade' (officially 130 Brigade, later renumbered 115 Brigade) but, in absence of the hoped-for WAC 2nd Division, what was to be done with the three other bantam battalions? The solution was simply to 'attach' them to the existing structure. A list dated 15 February 1915 has the 19th RWF attached to 128 Brigade (which consisted entirely of RWF battalions) and the 12th SWB and 18th Welsh attached to 130 Brigade (which contained a mix of battalions from the Welsh, RWF and SWB).[89] This arrangement was repeated in a War Office letter of 24 March. With one bantam battalion as a part of the division's structure and three 'attached' how did the WAC view their future? In February Major-General Ivor Philipps had started a letter to the WAC secretary by writing, 'Now that the whole of the 43rd Welsh Division of the Welsh Army Corps is concentrated in North Wales'.[90] With two battalions still recruiting in South Wales this was obviously incorrect but may indicate a view of the status of the bantams as within the WAC but additional to its first division.

The fulfilment of the concept of a WAC demanded the creation of a second division. As late as June 1915 Ivor Philipps was keen to press on:

> It seems to me most necessary that the Second Division should be commenced now in order to furnish, in the first instance, reinforcement for the First Division, the organization then being on the same lines as that adopted with T.F. Divisions. When the Second Division is

---

87 NLW WAC C106: Memo from War Office to Western Command, 26 January 1915.
88 NLW WAC C11/22: Minutes of NEC meeting, 22 January 1915.
89 NLW WAC C109: Correspondence with War Office. List dated 15 February 1915. 129 Brigade was made up of Welsh Regiment battalions.
90 NLW WAC C8/6: Letter from Ivor Philipps to WAC Secretary, 8 February 1915.

complete, it would then become a first line Division and a 3rd Division to supply reinforcements for the 1st and 2nd Divisions would be initiated.[91]

Taking up this argument, the NEC tried one final push:

> Some members of the Committee urged that steps be taken to lay before the Army Council their conviction that it was only by keeping together the unity of the Welsh Army Corps, and forming a Second Division ... that recruiting could be successfully continued ... On the other hand it was admitted that General Sir Henry Mackinnon had, on more than one occasion, since January 1st, informed the Committee that providing Drafts for Battalions at the Front, and Reserve Companies for the new army, were of greater importance than the forming of new battalions.[92]

The WAC's second division was never raised. Its development progressed only as far as the creation of the four bantam battalions but the official designation of a bantam brigade had been finally approved by the War Office on 27 May 1915:

> I am commanded by the Army Council to inform you that the extra battalions and reserve companies of the 38th (Welsh) Division will be organised as follows:
> The 17th (S) Battalion, Welsh Regiment (1st Glamorgan) will be replaced in the 115th Brigade by the 17th (S) Battalion Royal Welsh Fusiliers (2nd North Wales).
> A 'Bantam' Brigade will be formed consisting of:
> 17th (S) Battalion Welsh Regiment (1st Glamorgan)
> 18th (S) Battalion Welsh Regiment (2nd Glamorgan)
> 19th (S) Battalion Royal Welsh Fusiliers
> 12th (S) Battalion South Wales Borderers
> Any of these battalions which has not yet raised its extra company may do so.[93]

Conspicuous by its absence from this instruction is any suggestion of what would happen to the bantam brigade.

The creation of a brigade required the appointment of a brigadier-general to command it. From the start of recruiting for the Welsh bantams the continued expansion of the WAC had opened up more opportunities for those wishing promotion. Colonel Mainwaring 'late of the 1st RWF and OC 23rd RWF Recruiting District' speculated, 'Perhaps if they also add a 12th Battalion [of the SWB] they will form and add an additional Welsh Brigade in which case I should very much like to get the Brigade command'.[94] Mainwaring was too far ahead of the game and it was not until July that the press suggested that Lieutenant-Colonel Homfray (CO 17th Welsh) was appointed to command a brigade. Two days later the same newspaper 'was officially informed that pending the appointment of a brigadier-general to command the Welsh Bantam Brigade of the 38th Welsh Division, Brigadier-General P. E. Buston is appointed to the temporary command of

---

91 NLW WAC C11/37: Brigadier-General [sic] Commanding 38th (Welsh) Division to HQ Western Command, 27 June 1915.
92 NLW WAC C11/36: Minutes of the NEC Meeting of 14 July 1915.
93 NLW WAC C110/26: War Office letter to GOC Western Command, 27 May 1915. The 43rd (Welsh) Division had been renumbered as 38th (Welsh) Division on 29 April 1915 following the breaking up of the original six divisions of the Fourth New Army to provide reinforcements for existing New Army formations.
94 NLW WAC BM87: Letter from Mainwaring to Secretary WAC, 9 January 1915. Rowland Broughton Mainwaring, CMG (1850-1926) see Appendix VI.

this brigade'.[95] The author has been unable to trace any other evidence of this appointment and Buston was in any case supplanted just one week later by Rodney Charles Style.

Style commanded the bantam brigade from 22 July 1915 to 7 May 1916 and was appointed just after the four battalions concentrated in one place for the first time. During the week beginning 12 July 1915 the battalions moved from Colwyn Bay (17th Welsh), Porthcawl (18th Welsh), Deganwy (19th RWF) and Newport (12th SWB) to the new hutted camp at Prees Heath near Whitchurch, Shropshire. The 38th (Welsh) Division had meantime started its own concentration at Winchester and the bantam brigade was, for the moment at least, effectively unattached to a division. At this time the administrators of the WAC did not, it seems, regard the bantam battalions as anything but their own. A printed list of the 38th (Welsh) Division establishment dated 28 July recognises the move of the bantams to Prees Heath but lists the four battalions under 'Supernumerary Welsh Infantry Brigade'.[96] However, the future of the bantams was decided on 27 August 1915 when the military authorities took over the administration of the 38th Division and of the bantam brigade which for the first time was listed as 119 Brigade in 40th Division.[97] This may have annoyed the WAC administration who continued to address correspondence to the GOC 'Supernumerary Welsh Brigade' or ' GOC, 119th Infantry Brigade, 38th Welsh Division' well into November 1915.[98]

At Prees Heath the unit started to train under its new GOC. Rodney Charles Style (1863-1957) was the fourth son of the 9th Baronet Style of Wateringbury, Kent. He started his army career as a lieutenant in the 3rd (Militia) Battalion of the Queen's Own (Royal West Kent Regiment) in October 1882, transferring to a regular battalion of the regiment in February 1883. In January 1893 he was promoted to captain, became major in January 1903 and lieutenant-colonel of the 1st Battalion in March 1908. He retired in March 1912. He had seen action in the Sudan, and in India where he was wounded in September 1897. His Welsh connection was through his mother Rosamond (née Morgan) who was a daughter of Lord Tredegar. We do not know what he thought of his new command when he saw it at Prees Heath.

Whilst having the four battalions of the brigade in one place was a great improvement, conditions at Prees Heath were not good. Captain B.D. Gibbs of the 18th Welsh wrote to his sweetheart to tell her, 'It's been raining here every day since the 15th of July and the place is just one big bog and I think very unhealthy'.[99] The brigade remained at Prees Heath for two months before moving to Aldershot where the other two brigades of the 40th Division were also assembling. Becke describes how 'in early September 1915 the first divisional staff officer reached Stanhope Lines, Aldershot, and within a short time the remainder of the divisional staff assembled. Units also began to arrive …'[100] As the battalions arrived, not all went smoothly. Captain Gibbs arrived ahead of his battalion and reported, 'we are sharing these barracks [Salamanca Barracks] with the 17th [Welsh] and I found on 'taking over' that there is insufficient [accommodation] for all the chaps in our battalion so I have had to arrange tents for one company and it was some job I can tell you to fix this up'.[101]

---

95   *Western Mail*, 13 and 15 July 1915. Philip Thomas Buston CB CMG DSO (1853-1938). See Appendix VI.
96   NLW WAC C48/6: Correspondence of GOC regarding accounts etc. Printed list 38th Division establishment, 28 July 1915.
97   NLW WAC: Western Command Orders, 19 August 1915.
98   For example: NLW WAC C49/1: Letter dated 28 October 1915; NLW WAC C10/25: Letter dated 6 November 1915.
99   IWM, Documents: 72/11/1. Papers of Captain B.D. Gibbs. Letter, 17 August 1915.
100   A.F. Becke, *Order of Battle of Divisions, Part 3b – New Army Divisions (30-41) and 63rd (R.N.) Division* (London: HMSO, 1945), p.106. A source quoted by Whitton in the divisional history (p.10) gives 7 September as the precise date.
101   IWM: Gibbs Papers. Letter, 9 September 1915.

Now, with the division assembled, it was necessary to appoint a commanding officer for the new formation. In September 1915 Brigadier-General Harold Goodeve Ruggles-Brise was in Britain recovering from a severe shoulder wound received at Ypres on 2 November 1914 while GOC 20 Brigade, 7th Division. On 14 September Sir Archibald Murray, the Deputy Chief of the Imperial General Staff, wrote to him, 'My Dear Ruggles – I want to get you a division of the New Army. Are you medically fit now or is it 'light duty only'? I have sounded Robb and he is very good about it'.[102] This enquiry must have met with a positive reply as just a week later Ruggles-Brise wrote to his wife, 'I went before my medical board and I think they passed me fit for general service but that does mean that I shall go abroad. They thought that I had made a wonderful recovery. Murray is not coming down now so I shan't hear about a division. I am afraid it is too good to be true'.[103] Ruggles-Brise was being too pessimistic. He was appointed to command 40th Division just four days later.

So far we have established a previously absent chronology in order to define just how 119 Brigade came into being as part of the WAC and how, in the eyes of the WAC at least, it was regarded as a 'Welsh' unit. In moving on to discuss various aspects of the brigade, including the geographical origins of its officers and men, we will discover how 'Welsh' it actually was.

The Men

An assessment of the character and state of the Welsh bantams appeared in an article by a Mr T. Andrew Richards in March 1915 under the headline 'The Bantam Collier-Soldier':

> I have tried to sketch the collier soldier as he is. He has been billeted in our homes and I want people to see him as we have found him, not without faults, but at heart a gentleman and a hero. The European War has produced many unique things, nothing perhaps of greater uniqueness than the 'Bantam' soldier of the Rhondda Valley. Distinctly collier in type, he is a sort of hybrid creature in a chrysalis state, putting off the collier and putting on the soldier, and his destination in common with that of all other Tommies, is Hell. His patriotism, for such it truly is, has made him leave the hell of the mine for the greater hell of the battlefield. In the ranks of the first Bantam Battalion (sometimes called the Welsh Gurkhas [*sic*] but officially known as the 17th Welsh) are men who, at first sight, are the roughest specimens of humanity, yet no-one would say rough as they admittedly are, that they are not in their proper setting; for in roughness – or call it what you will – no class of Britisher can out-collier a certain class of collier – especially a Welsh one. In a word the Bantam Battalion, which was brought up to strength in the incredibly short period of 16 days is composed of exceedingly raw material. Ask them what they are going to do and nine out of ten will readily answer that they are going to kill Germans ... His business is purely that of fighting, and when he arrives at that magical place called the front, he may be relied upon to deliver a good account of himself.
>
> [When asked] 'Why on earth did you join the army?', 'Because we want to fight the Germans' came the somewhat amazed answer, 'and because our butties (a distinctly collier

---

102 Blair Castle, Perthshire, Blair Papers: Bundle 880 (Ruggles-Brise correspondence). Letter from Sir Archibald Murray, 14 September 1915. Major General (Later General) Archibald James Murray (1860-1945) had been a controversial choice of Chief of Staff, BEF, in August 1914 and was replaced, becoming DCIGS from 10 February 1915 to 25 September 1915. 'Robb' is Major-General Sir Frederick Spencer Robb (1858-1948), Military Secretary to the Secretary of State for War 1914-1916.
103 Ibid. Letter from H.G. Ruggles-Brise to his wife Dorothea, 21 September 1915.

word) were joining. In appearance he strongly resembles our brave Allies the Japanese. Of an average and almost uniform height of five feet and with a chest measurement of 37 to 40 inches, coupled with strength, and accustomed to face daily the horrors of the mine, he will not feel out of place in his new sphere. His striking disregard for his personal safety when others are in danger was admirably shown at the time of the Senghenydd explosion, when the men formed themselves into search parties, took leave of their wives, and in cold blood made their wills before descending the fiery shaft to rescue their stricken comrades. We must excuse their innate roughness, and overlook the fact that the men who are billeted in our houses do not shave every day, for they are in process of transit; they are growing every day into soldiers … The collier-soldier, from his childhood, has learned the supreme business of soldiering, he knows how to die, and he knows nothing of euphemism. To him a spade is a spade, though he likes you better if you call it a nice shovel. Indeed, the whole business of soldiering comes so naturally to him, that he has a sort of feeling, in retrospect, of having been in the line before, and in a sense, he has. Perhaps his attitude to the war cannot be better set down than the word 'keen'. His one aim is to serve his country on the battlefield and to do so by becoming efficient in the quickest possible time. He does not quite understand why he should spend so many months in preparation; he could do long marches before; to and from the pit was equal to any route marches he has since accomplished, and he could do a bit of useful shooting on the mountainside. He considers that a man who can bag a hare on the wild slopes of the Welsh hills can bag a modern Hun, and in this he is probably correct. Yet he allows that his officers know more about these things than he does, and is content to wait. So far as his spirit is concerned, he is quite ready for the trenches and no amount of military training can improve it. He is a hard worker, and on results to date his officers are more than proud of him.

But of the several Rhondda battalions which have been formed at Porthcawl, the Bantams have been the most misunderstood. Because they occasionally go on parade with black eyes, they have been called uncomplimentary things, quite regardless of the fact that a man must, to a certain degree, return to the primitive state before he can successfully meet the Hun in a bayonet charge. Still, there is a lot of difference between having that indefinable fighting something in one's make up and being a primitive pure and simple, and I will show that the term, as applied to the Bantam Soldier, is quite undeserved. Little men are said to be more pugnacious than their bigger brothers, and the Bantam Soldier certainly does not prove the exception. It is quite common to see him 'squaring up' to men of other battalions who are bigger and heavier than himself. He does so because he cannot help it. Presently he is going to 'square up' to the big, stocky Germans … [104]

The article above has been quoted at length because it gives a detailed contemporary view of several aspects of the bantam recruits to 119 Brigade: recruiting, background, health, motivation, courage, officers, discipline and training are all touched on. Some of these will be examined in detail in the remainder of this chapter while others will be dealt with in subsequent chapters in relation to specific events.

Peter Simkins has described how volunteering peaked in September 1914 and then slumped with a continued decline through 1915. There were variations within the overall picture relating to the age, employment type or even geographical location of potential volunteers but the overall trend in 1915 was downwards. Simkins relates this to several factors, not all of which necessarily apply

---

104 *Cambria Daily Leader*, 12 March 1915. Although the article singles out the 17th Welsh, by the time the piece appeared they had departed Porthcawl for North Wales and the 18th Welsh were resident. 'Butty' (pl. Butties) is Welsh dialect for 'pal' or 'close friend' and was commonly applied to a workmate in the mines.

to each individual. They are: confusion over the level and administration of separation allowance for married men resulting in a reluctance by these men to join up; increasing demand for labour due to rising levels of war-related orders and loss of manpower to the army resulting in employment opportunities increasing; rising wages in sectors where labour was needed making the army less attractive; 'political factors' such as nationalism in Ireland (or indeed Wales); international worker solidarity or an adherence to a pacifist or anti-militarist doctrine and personal factors such an increasing reluctance to abandon a family business or dependants.[105] Sometimes the employers would try and stem the flow of men who were volunteering. Simkins mentions that 'as early as 4 September 1914 the Railway Executive Committee ... decreed, with War Office backing, that railwaymen who wished to volunteer had first to obtain the written consent of the company employing them'. In the coalfields of South Wales a telegram was issued on 20 March 1915 referencing an earlier restriction on the recruitment of miners from specific collieries, 'Reference Glamorgan Recruiting Orders No 112 dated 13th Nov 1914. As collieries mentioned are supplying coal for Admiralty purposes their men should not be enlisted without written approval of firm'.[106] Against this backdrop of declining recruiting how did the units of 119 Brigade fare?

The descriptions of the formation of the four original battalions of the brigade given earlier show how the formation of the 17th and 18th Welsh was relatively fast with the 18th benefitting from the initial 'backlog' of men who stature had previously stopped them from being accepted for service. Just slightly later in the year the 19th RWF and, particularly, the 12th SWB had difficulty filling their ranks. On 10 Oct 1915 Western Command wrote to the Secretary of the NEC:

> I am directed to forward the attached copy of War Office letter AG.2.B/083 of 8th October, 1915, for the information of the Welsh Army Corps Committee.
> The General Officer Commanding-in-Chief would be glad of their opinion as to the points made as early as possible please.
> [The WO letter reads:] I am directed to request that you will be good enough to report as to whether there is any prospect of the 12th Battalion, South Wales Borderers, being brought up to full establishment at an early date, and also whether any special efforts could not be made in counties other than Cardigan, Brecknock and Monmouth to assist this battalion in raising the necessary number of recruits.
> [Signed] R.A. Montgomery, Maj.Gen., Director of Recruiting.[107]

There was obviously a problem but what was it and was it anything more than the factors noted by Simkins? Certainly the general fall off in the numbers of men enlisting would have had an effect, particularly in the late spring and summer of 1915. However, in the case of bantam units further factors came into play. The first of these was highlighted in April 1915: 'By order of No4 District I have to call your attention to the large number of men who have been sent back from the Bantam Battalion as medically unfit, and to instruct you to ask Medical Officers to take every care that men are properly examined before being passed as fit.'[108] The issue did not go way and a further order was issued in September:

---

105 Peter Simkins, *Kitchener's Army: the raising of the New Armies 1914-1916* (Manchester: University of Manchester Press, 1988), pp.49-78.
106 NLW WAC C12/46: Correspondence Recruiting Headquarters, Cardiff. Telegram, 20 March 1915.
107 NLW WAC C12/64: Letter from Western Command to Secretary WAC, 10 October 1915.
108 NLW WAC C12/47: Glamorgan Recruiting Order No. 265, 21 April 1915.

It has been brought to my notice by the Officer Commanding 18th Glamorgan Battalion (Bantams) that many recruits for this unit are being passed though medically unfit. No less than 45 have been discharged during the past month for this reason.

Recruiting Officers must insist on a most careful medical examination of the recruits and should personally see them before they are dispatched so that this may not occur again as it is a useless waste of public money and unnecessary trouble to all concerned.[109]

The level of unfit recruits is confirmed by an analysis of surviving service records. The digitized versions of these were searched and 260 records of men of the four original battalions of the brigade were found.[110] 106 of these men were discharged before the brigade left for foreign service.

Table 1: Discharges due to ill health or poor fitness

Battalion	Surviving records	Discharged Unfit/Illness
17th Welsh	126	62 (49%)
18th Welsh	67	35 (52%)
19th RWF	49	6 (12%)
12th SWB	18	3 (17%)
Total	**260**	**106 (41%)**

Source: Analysis of records at <http://www.ancestry.co.uk>

Although this is a very small sample it does indicate that a problem existed with men who had what were sometimes obvious disabilities such as flat feet, deafness, hammer toes or poor eyesight that should have been spotted at enlistment. Some problems such as old injuries, tuberculosis, syphilis, arthritis or mental deficiency may have taken longer to identify but most were spotted well before the battalions went to war. In the 17th Welsh, the battalion with the largest number of surviving records, 45 out of 62 discharges took place in two batches in March and June 1915 with a further small peak (7) in February/March 1916. In the 18th Welsh a similar pattern emerges with 15 out of 35 discharges taking place in March/April 1915 with a further small peak (7) in March/April 1916. Such peaks of activity may correspond with visits from a higher authority such as that reported in the press in April 1915 when the Medical Inspector of Recruits, Western Command, visited the 18th Welsh and inspected 900 men 'individually'. Some men 'referred to the Medical Inspector were slightly under the minimum height for bantams but they all seemed good material for the army and Col. H.R. Homfray … was most anxious to retain them in his battalion. As a result of a close examination the inspecting officer was able to form the opinion that they would, with increased time and physical training reach the required standard …'[111]

While bearing in mind that the number of surviving records is very small, they seem to show that in units of 119 Brigade unfit/ill men were, with a few exceptions, weeded out within a month

---

109 NLW WAC C12/46: Glamorgan Recruiting Order No. 132, 18 September 1915.
110 Digitised service records from TNA WO 363 (British Army First World War Service Records, sometimes called the 'Burnt Documents') and WO 364 (British Army First World War Pension Records) are available at <http://www.ancestry.com>, last accessed 8 February 2016. These are very incomplete; records from certain units having been almost totally destroyed. Given a battalion strength of approximately 1,000 plus replacements, the figures for the four battalions clearly illustrate the loss of records to enemy action in the Second World War. The difficulty of finding records is increased by poor transcription and indexing in the digital records.
111 *Western Mail*, 24 April 1915. Analysis of 235 surviving service records for the 17th Welsh, 18th Welsh and 19th RWF shows the average height of the men was 61.5 inches.

or two of enlistment. Moreover the problems that caused their discharge were, in the majority of cases not linked to their stature but to their working conditions and environment – as they would have been for any labouring man at that time.[112]

There was one other problem though that may have plagued the bantams because it was less easy to detect amongst a large group of small men. Welsh Recruiting Offices were alerted to it in early September 1915: 'It has been brought to my attention that in the case of enlistment for Bantam Battalions, instances have occurred in which 'Boys' have been enlisted as 'Bantams' … This practice is not permissible and shall not be continued'.[113] Evidence of under-age enlistment is contained in the service records described above and outlined in Table 2 below.

Table 2: Discharges due to under-age enlistment

Battalion	Surviving records	Discharged under-age
17th Welsh	126	14 (11%)
18th Welsh	67	8 (12%)
19th RWF	49	0
12th SWB	18	5 (28%)
Total	**260**	**27 (10%)**

Source: Analysis of service records at <http://www.ancestry.co.uk>

Again, the small sample size makes generalisation impossible and the sample consists only of those soldiers whose real ages were detected but some inferences can be drawn. The first is that the under-age soldiers in the 17th Welsh managed to last longer in the ranks before discharge than those in the other three battalions with 50% of them serving for more than ten months before discharge. 25613 Private James Clifford enlisted in December 1914 and chalked up twenty months service and eleven disciplinary charges before his discharge in August 1916. Another December 1914 recruit, 25346 Private John Glyn Samuel, enlisted aged 16 and was discharged eighteen months later not because he was under-age but because he was 'a potential criminal'. In contrast only two of the 18th Welsh's under-age soldiers managed to serve more than eleven months and only one man of the 12th SWB had eleven months service at discharge. Under-age enlistments peaked in January 1915 (9), March (6) and May (5) with only three thereafter. By contrast the discharges are less clustered but with slight increases in May 1915 (3) and June (3) with a major grouping in October/December (9), and January 1916 (5). The small sample will self-evidently not include a record of those under-age youths who successfully evaded detection and it is impossible to determine an accurate figure. 23553 Private William Edward Taylor, 12th SWB, died at home on 11 December 1915 aged 17.[114] Some lads did get as far as the front line.[115] 28469 Lance Corporal Harold Chadwick, 19th RWF, was 18 years old when he was killed at

---

112 The importance of health issues is shown by the rejection of 20% of 1,739 men from Anglesey who volunteered for the WAC under the Derby Scheme. See Clive Hughes 'The New Armies' in Ian F.W. Beckett and Keith Simpson (eds), *A Nation in Arms: the British Army in the First World War* (Manchester: Manchester University Press, 1985), p.118.
113 NLW WAC C12/48: Glamorgan and Monmouthshire Recruiting Order No. 403 [quoting War Office letter of 30 August 1915], 3 September 1915.
114 Private Taylor was born in July 1898 and is buried at West Norwood Cemetery.
115 TNA WO 95/2607: War Diary 18th Welsh 9 September 1916 records two men transferred to Base Depot, Rouen underage, followed on 1 November by 28187 Private J. Llewellyn 'being under 18½ years of age' and two further soldiers on 14 and 15 November. Two final underage soldiers were sent to the Base Depot on 7 and 18 February 1917.

Bourlon Wood.[116] 25447 Private Ernest Rogers, 17th Welsh, enlisted in January 1914 aged 16. He was killed serving with the 18th Welsh in August 1918 aged 21.[117] Some were more fortunate. In the 12th SWB, Captain Eric Whitworth recalled how 'he had come across a tearful seventeen-year-old who could no longer stand the trials that overseas service presented. Whitworth managed to find the boy a 'cushy job' with the military police. He also observed:

> But we ought not to have these boys with us … the genuine bantam is a fully developed man of small height and most are very fine men; the Bantam was never meant to be growing boys, as 40% or 50% of ours are, in the eagerness to join up at the beginning of the war. One can only blame the authorities.[118]

Whitworth may have been exaggerating the number of youths in the battalion to make his point because he also wrote:

> The men were all volunteers, many from the mines in South Wales, and they were men who, but for this concession as to height, would not have been accepted for service. Subsequent events amply justified the decision of the War Office, and the Bantams proved themselves in France equal to all that was demanded of them in trench warfare and later in offensive operations.[119]

In making this assertion he is, in effect, contradicting his statement about the preponderance of youths who would surely not have acquitted themselves so well under fire if present in large numbers? Some support for his view of enthusiastic youths joining up does come from an analysis of surviving service records. While the average age of recruits to three battalions of the brigade varies from 23 years to 25 years the most common stated age at enlistment is 19 years.[120] This same over-representation of nineteen year-olds was noted by Clive Hughes in the 16th RWF, a standard-height battalion, so the phenomenon may not have been restricted to bantam units.[121] The loss of so many of 119 Brigade's service records during the Blitz on London means that no conclusive answer can be forthcoming.

---

116 Chadwick was born in the last quarter of 1899. He enlisted on 8 March 1915 giving his age as 19 years and 97 days when he was only 15 years old. Despite a May 1915 recommendation for discharge which noted his 'apparent age' as 17 years and which was accepted by his CO, the Medical Inspector of Recruits, Western Command stated on 1 June 1915 'Give him a chance to develop. Fit for Home Service. This is in accordance with W.O. Instructions'. From Service Record for Harold Chadwick in TNA WO 363 available at <http://www.ancestry.com>. L/Corporal Chadwick is buried in Anneux British Cemetery.
117 Rogers was born in the April quarter of 1897. *South Wales Gazette,* 8 December 1916 reports him at the front and having enlisted two years previously. His regimental number indicates an early recruit to the battalion. He is buried at Senlis French National Cemetery where his parents visited his grave in 1922. *South Wales Gazette,* 9 June 1922.
118 Richard van Emden, *Boy Soldiers of the Great War* (London: Bloomsbury, 2012), pp.144-145. van Emden outlines the campaign against under-age recruitment which gained momentum in the second half of 1915. This may account for the spike in discharges from October 1915 to January 1916. There were also other factors at work which are described in the following pages.
119 Royal Regiment of Wales Museum, Brecon: 1992: 22 Captain E.E.A. Whitworth Memoir, p.94. This memoir was started in the 1950s and added to after 1966. The three manuscript volumes were typed up by Allen Whitworth, of Guernsey in 1990/91 but possibly not everything was included as the typescript starts on p.94.
120 Analysis of service records as follows: 17th Welsh (127) average age 24.6 years; 18th Welsh (67) 25.1 years; 19th RWF (50) 23.4 years. The mode in each case was 19 years. This is also shown in the No 16 Platoon Roll Book, 17th Welsh (authors collection), where 15 out of the 35 men whose ages were recorded were 19 years old.
121 Hughes, *Arm to Serve Your Native Land*, p.68.

Five, possibly under-age, bantams, 19th RWF, Llandudno Junction, 1915. (Imperial War Museum, Fraser Papers)

The problems that 119 Brigade had with its manpower were as nothing compared with the other two brigades in 40th Division that were also composed of bantam battalions. The 120 Brigade was originally made up of 11th King's Own (formed August 1915), 13th Cameronians (formed July 1915), 14th Highland Light Infantry (formed July 1915) and 12th South Lancashire (formed June 1915). The 121 Brigade was originally made up of 12th Suffolk (formed July 1915), 13th Yorkshire (formed July 1915), 18th Sherwood Foresters (formed July 1915) and 22nd Middlesex (formed June 1915).[122] All of these units were formed well after the initial rush of bantam men to enlist and it obviously led to difficulties. Whitton described the result in the divisional history:

> Several of the units were under strength, but more contained a large proportion of unfit men; and the divisional and brigade commanders too realized that a drastic weeding-out would be necessary before the Division could proceed overseas. This weeding-out began almost at once and was continued through the winter of 1915/1916 and into the early spring of the latter year, as it became more and more evident that many of the men were unfit to undergo even the training to which they were submitted at home. How drastic this weeding-out process ultimately became may be shown by quoting the case of one battalion, which joined the Division at Aldershot over 1,000 strong, and later was reduced by medical rejections to little over two hundred.[123]

---

122 E.A. James, *British Regiments 1914-1918* (Dallington: Naval and Military Press, 1998 reprint of 1929 edition) provided the dates of formation for these battalions.
123 Whitton, *History of the 40th Division*, p.8.

There was obviously a major problem with the quality of bantam recruits in the battalions formed in mid-1915. Whitton notes that the 'wastage was not being made good from ordinary sources of supply' and that a staff officer was dispatched to Lancashire, Glasgow and Edinburgh to trawl for recruits. In December 1915 the War Office raised the maximum height for bantam recruits to five feet four inches.[124]

> In the case of the Welsh Bde (the 119th) this difficulty was not felt to the same extent as in the other brigades, and notably in the two Scottish battalions; Scotland could not produce 'Bantams'. The drafts of recruits which joined the battalions consisted in the most part of underfed badly grown men of poor stamina, or boys of 14 to 16 who in their zeal to serve had stated false ages. The officers of the RAMC were kept very busy during these days, medical boards were being continually held and the battalions suffered a constant weeding out process. The men rejected were for the most part classed medically under the term 'Immature'. Batches of hundreds of 'Immatures' were sent away from the Division every week; the wags called them 'Immatures, Prematures and Caricatures'. The battalions necessarily suffered under this system of posting recruits who were immediately rejected as it was not possible to proceed with their training. The battalion staffs were occupied with making out nominal rolls of men who were joining and of men who were leaving rather than the more important work of welding a battalion and training for the fight.[125]

The divisional commander wrote to his wife: 'I am also much bothered about my Divn. I was told to get the infantry ready for service and I have not been given the men to get ready. I am going over first thing tomorrow to see Sir A. Hunter and shall ask him if I can go to see Lord French's staff and try to get the matter put right'.[126] Three weeks later he wrote, 'I have been so worried over my miniature bantams that I have not had a minute to write'. In February 1916 Sir John French inspected the division:

> Our inspection went off very well. Ld French said that the bantams were much better than he expected and that he was very much pleased with the whole turn-out, that it was bad luck having such immature men, and that he would do all he could to help us get more seasoned men and get rid of the wasters. He also said it was very creditable having trained them up to their present standard.[127]

The solution was eventually found: 'We got a message yesterday that the 118th Bde is to come to our Divn, but we have not yet got it in writing. This will fill us up in men and we shall probably go abroad in May ... However, don't say too much about it until it is accomplished fact'[128].

The 118 Brigade (a brigade of normal height battalions) was indeed taken from 39th Division and broken up. In 120 Brigade the 12th South Lancashire was absorbed by the 11th Kings Own and the 13th Cameronians were absorbed by the 14th HLI. They were joined by the 13th East Surrey and the 14th Argyll and Sutherland Highlanders from 118 Brigade. In 121 Brigade the 18th Sherwood Foresters were absorbed by the 13th Yorkshire and the 22nd Middlesex was absorbed by

---

124 NLW WAC C12/48: Glamorgan and Monmouthshire Recruiting Order No 532, 9 Dec 1915.
125 NAM 8002-40-34 [Ms] 'Some Records of the 40th Divn prior to arriving in France'.
126 Blair Castle, Blair Paper, Bundle 878. Letter from Major-General Ruggles-Brise, 30 January 1916. Archibald Hunter (1856-1936) was at this time GOC-in-C, Aldershot, responsible for training the New Armies and John French (1852-1925) was C-in-C Home Forces.
127 Ibid. Letter from Ruggles-Brise, 21 February 1916.
128 Ibid. Letter from Ruggles-Brise, 2 March 1916.

the 12th Suffolk. They were joined by the 20th and 21st Middlesex from 118 Brigade. The 40th Division was now complete but the loss of four of its bantam battalions made it a strange amalgam of eight bantam battalions and four standard height battalions. The introduction of new units also meant that the identity of two out of three of the brigades was very different, and debatably weaker, than the identity of 119 Brigade which had ridden out the storm of reorganization intact. Throughout the period beginning September 1915 to the end of May 1916 the individual establishments of each of 119 Brigade's battalions never dropped below 939 and for most of the period were well over 1,000.[129]

How 'Welsh' was 119 Brigade? In his important paper, 'Taffs in the Trenches', Chris Williams has explored the concept of national identity in Welsh regiments during the First World War employing *Soldiers Died in the Great War 1914-19* (SDGW) as a source of quantitative data on the national origins of the men who enlisted. His results will be compared below with data relating to the men of 119 Brigade and additional data will be presented.[130] The data used in this book differs slightly from that extracted by Williams as the information from *SDGW* was supplemented by data from surviving service records and from the war dead database of the Commonwealth War Graves Commission (CWGC) so that almost all identified fatalities of 119 Brigade can be given a geographical origin using their birthplace or their place of residence at the time of enlistment.[131]

Table 3: Soldiers of Welsh Birth (Williams, 2007)

Battalion	Sample size	Welsh birth
17th Welsh	223	62.0%
18th Welsh[132]	406	44.3%
19th RWF	222	36.5%
12th SWB	218	28.0%
Total	**1,069**	

Williams' data show that, based on the county of birth of recruits, some battalions of Welsh regiments were more 'Welsh' than others. Williams made a decision not to use the place of residence of recruits as an indicator of national origin because the place of residence in *SDGW* is often not given and yields a smaller sample size for analysis.[133] The level of mobility within the workforce at

---

129 TNA WO 114/27; WO 114/28; WO 114/29: Weekly return of the British Army.
130 *Soldiers Died in the Great War 1914-1919* (London: HMSO, 1921) was originally published in eighty-one volumes each of which covered (approximately) one regiment or corps. Martin G. Staunton first brought to attention the potential of the series if the data were entered into an electronic database system in '*Soldiers Died in the Great War 1914-19* as historical source material', *Stand To!*, 27 (1989) pp.6-8. This resource informed the work of Nick Perry (see bibliography) and the release of the whole data set on CD-ROM by Naval and Military Press in 1998 gave access to a much wider audience. In the absence of a complete set of service records for the period, this data provides the only large, detailed sample of the British Army in the period 1914-1919.
131 The CWGC data was extracted with 'Geoff's 1914-1921 DB Search Engine' at the *Hut Six* website: <http://www.hut-six.co.uk/cgi-bin/search1421.php> (Accessed 5 February 2016).
132 The 18th Welsh was the only original battalion of 119 Brigade to survive to the end of the war and was heavily engaged during its final stages. Its total for fatalities was therefore correspondingly higher than those of the other three battalions.
133 The data from SDGW has been enhanced by the inference of county of residence at the time of enlistment in cases where an individual's county of birth is the same as the county of enlistment or (in a small number of cases) where the CWGC data gives the residence of a widow who still has her late husband's surname. Although, even after this enhancement, samples for residence data are still smaller, they are still significant. Percentages are given to one decimal point and rounded up.

the time also confuses the picture of national affiliation with, for example, men from the Somerset, Yorkshire and Lancashire coalfields moving to take up work in South Wales and subsequently enlisting in the 'local' regiment.[134] The distinction between 'true' Welsh nationals and 'economic migrants' is felt to be of less importance for this study and data relating to the birthplace and residence of recruits will be presented for comparison. While Williams' study was designed to examine national identity the present work is more concerned with unit identity. If a man who was born in Lancashire but who moved to work in Glamorgan enlisted in a Welsh Regiment battalion along with others from his work community did his presence dilute the sense of 'belonging' within the battalion? As a member of a Welsh community (and a tight-knit one at that) would his presence make the battalion less 'Welsh'? The evidence described in the previous part of this chapter suggest strongly that to outsiders at least the brigade was regarded as 'Welsh' and I suggest that this identity was reflected back on to the brigade's four battalions, even those where the non-Welsh elements were in the majority.

Using the data gathered for this study a similar picture to that outlined by Williams emerges confirming the differences in degrees of 'Welshness' between battalions but the use of residence data introduces some subtle but important variations (see Table 4).

Table 4: Soldiers of Welsh Origin

Battalion	Welsh Birth	Welsh Residence
17th Welsh	62.7% (225)	73.0% (156)
18th Welsh	44.7% (409)	52.3% (350)
19th RWF	38.4% (232)	41.6% (219)
12th SWB	27.6% (232)	36.1% (210)

Source: SDGW and CWGC

The 17th Welsh had the greatest percentage of Welsh-born and Welsh-resident soldiers and it may have been even higher than these figures indicate. An analysis of the 125 surviving service records of men from this battalion shows that 114 of them (91.2%) gave addresses in Wales and of these ninety-three (74.5% of the sample) were living in Glamorgan.

Table 5: 17th Welsh – Origins[135]

County	Whole sample		To 30/11/1917		To 31/5/1917	
	Birth (225)	Residence (156)	Birth (190)	Residence (137)	Birth (89)	Residence (64)
Glamorgan	40.0% (90)	51.9% (81)	41.6% (79)	51.8 (71)	36.0% (32)	51.6% (33)
Lancs	6.7% (15)	4.5% (7)	4.8% (8)	2.1% (3)	5.6% (5)	3.1% (2)
Monmouth	6.2% (14)	9.0% (14)	6.8% (13)	10.2% (14)	7.9% (7)	10.9% (7)
Gloucs	4.9% (11)	1.3% (2)	4.7% (9)	0.0% (0)	2.2% 2)	0.0% (0)
Middlesex	4.9% (11)	4.5% (7)	5.3% (10)	5.1% (7)	7.9% (7)	6.2% (4)
Pembroke	4.0% (9)	3.2% (5)	3.7% (7)	3.6% (5)	2.2% (2)	3.1% (4)
Hereford	2.7% (6)	0.0% (0)	3.7% (7)	0.0% (0)	4.5% (4)	0.0% (0)
Somerset	2.6% (6)	0.6% (1)	3.2% (6)	0.0% (0)	3.4% (3)	0.0% (0)

---

134 As an example, the analysis of the dataset for the 19th RWF shows that 23% of men had a different birth county to the county of enlistment.
135 The table depicts results from the top eight counties only. Thirty-one counties plus Ireland and the USA supplied recruits for the battalion.

The counties of origin of the men have been analysed for each battalion of 119 Brigade and three samples for each battalion are given. One is based on the total fatalities of the battalion; the second is based on fatalities up to 31 May 1917 (after the brigade's first offensive action) and the third is based on total fatalities to 30 November 1917 (after the fierce fighting for Bourlon Wood) after which the influx of new drafts is likely to have obscured the original composition of the brigade.

While acknowledging the weaknesses in the dataset, such as the small sample size for the earliest date, Table 5 does show some interesting points. Firstly, it confirms Glamorgan as the major source of recruits for the 17th Welsh, dwarfing the contribution of other Welsh counties. Secondly, it highlights the role of the industrial county of Lancashire as a source of recruits and shows a marked difference in the number of soldiers born in the county and the numbers resident there at the time of enlistment (the small samples for Somerset and Gloucestershire show a similar situation) indicating an outward migration. Thirdly, it shows how the residence figures for Glamorgan and Monmouthshire show a larger residence than birthplace percentage indicating inward migration prior to the Great War. Fourthly, it shows the position of Middlesex (and by inference London) as a source of recruits. Finally, it shows how little the character of the battalion (as expressed in the origins of its men) had changed by the time of the losses at Bourlon Wood.

Table 6: 18th Welsh – Origins[136]

County	Whole sample		To 30/11/1917		To 31/5/1917	
	Birth (409)	Residence (350)	Birth (213)	Residence (173)	Birth (88)	Residence (73)
Glamorgan	29.0% (119)	39.1% (137)	30.5% (65)	42.2% (73)	29.5% (26)	45.2% (33)
Lancs	16.9% (69)	17.1% (60)	11.7% (25)	12.1% (21)	6.8% (6)	5.5% (4)
Cheshire	5.6% (23)	6.3% (22)	6.1% (13)	7.5% (13)	5.7% (5)	6.8% (5)
Middlesex	5.1% (21)	3.1% (11)	5.6% (12)	3.5% (6)	9.1% (8)	4.1% (3)
Staffs	4.2% (17)	3.7% (13)	4.7% (10)	3.5% (6)	6.8% (6)	5.5% (4)
Monmouth	3.9% (16)	3.7% (13)	3.8% (8)	2.3% (4)	2.3% (2)	2.7% (2)
Carmarthen	2.9% (12)	2.6% (9)	3.3% (7)	2.9% (5)	3.4% (3)	4.1% (3)
Surrey	2.7% (11)	3.1% (11)	1.9% (4)	2.3% (4)	0.0% (0)	0.0% (0)

The tabulated fatalities from the 18th Welsh (Table 6) show a slightly different picture from that of its sister battalion. Though designated '2nd Glamorgan' the number of recruits from that county had fallen significantly – although it was still the largest source – with Lancashire again being the next most important. Cheshire, Staffordshire and Middlesex (mainly districts of London) also provided significant numbers of recruits. This seems to confirm that the pool of small Glamorgan miners had already been reduced by the creation of the 17th Welsh (1st Glamorgan) and that the battalion had to be made up by recruits from elsewhere. However another contributory factor to this increased diversity may be that recruits from outside South Wales took a little more time to organise their affairs and travel to South Wales. This is supported by the analysis of place of enlistment which shows that 51.3% of the battalion enlisted in Glamorgan with just 10% in each of Lancashire and Cheshire.[137]

---

136 The table depicts results from the top eight counties only. Thirty-seven counties plus Ireland and New Zealand supplied recruits for the battalion.
137 Based on fatalities to 30 November 1917. Sample size 216.

Clive Hughes has stated that 'the six counties of North Wales had not been a fertile recruiting ground before 1914' and Chris Williams has shown how the Royal Welsh Fusiliers, whose recruiting area was centred on North Wales, continued to look beyond the Principality in order to fill its ranks.[138] Table 7 (below) confirms Williams' general statements in respect of the RWF although in the case of the 19th Battalion the nickname 'Birmingham Fusiliers' would more appropriately be the 'Lancashire Fusiliers' as 25% of the battalion's total dead were from that county – a significantly larger proportion than from anywhere else. This high figure did fall as the war progressed, as did the proportion of men from Staffordshire, while numbers from the important recruiting area of Glamorgan rose. The percentage of Welsh-born men in the battalion's dead over the course of the war was 38.4%, a considerable increase on the 24.4% represented in the fatalities to 31 May 1917.

The key areas for recruiting for the 19th RWF are confirmed by the account of Captain Evan Beynon Davies, 19th RWF, who noted 'the Bantams were a pretty mixed lot linguistically, and the proportion of Welsh soldiers was less than in the other units at Llandudno. Some of them came from Liverpool and Manchester, from the coal districts of Staffordshire, and from the Potteries [Stoke-on-Trent]'.[139] While it is tempting to emphasise the battalion's lack of 'Welshness' the number of Welsh-born men in its ranks was still substantial (Table 7).

Table 7: 19th RWF – Origins[140]

County	Whole sample		To 30/11/1917		To 31/5/1917	
	Birth (232)	Residence (219)	Birth (177)	Residence (165)	Birth (86)	Residence (77)
Lancs	25.4% (59)	25.6% (56)	26.0% (46)	27.3% (45)	31.4% (27)	35.1% (27)
Staffs	10.3% (24)	10.5% (23)	9.6% (17)	11.5% (19)	14.0% (12)	18.2% (14)
Glamorgan	9.0% (21)	9.6% (21)	6.8% (12)	7.3% (12)	4.7% (4)	2.6% (2)
Caernarfon	7.8% (18)	8.7% (19)	6.8% (12)	7.9% (13)	4.7% (4)	6.5% (5)
Denbigh	6.9% (16)	7.3% (16)	7.9% (14)	8.5% (14)	8.1% (7)	9.1% (7)
London	6.9% (16)	6.8% (15)	6.8% (12)	5.5% (9)	4.7% (4)	3.9% (3)
Cheshire	3.9% (9)	4.6% (10)	5.1% (9)	6.0% (10)	1.2% (1)	2.6% (2)
Yorkshire	3.0% (7)	0.9% (2)	2.8% (5)	1.2% (2)	5.8% (5)	2.6% (2)

The South Wales Borderers whose 12th Battalion made up the final unit of 119 Brigade has been identified by Chris Williams as the 'least Welsh of all the Welsh Regiments'.[141] The analysis of the 12th SWB's war dead seems to confirm Williams' conclusion (Table 8). The regiment's recruiting area centred on Monmouthshire, Breconshire and Radnorshire and while Monmouthshire supplied the largest proportion of men the very low contribution of the latter two counties (less than 1% in both cases) may be explained by the 'pull' of the Monmouthshire Regiment (the local Territorial Force unit that Williams identifies as 62.9% Welsh-born), the active recruiting that had occurred in the counties before the formation of the 12th SWB and the relatively small number of large industrial communities in the two counties.

---

138 Hughes, *New Armies*, p.114. Williams, 'Taffs in the Trenches', pp.138-140.
139 Evan Beynon Davies, *Ar Orwel Pell* (Llandysul: Gomer Press, 1965), p.26. William's work on the national make-up of Welsh battalions shows that Davies was incorrect in emphasising the lack of Welshmen in the 19th RWF compared with other units then forming at Llandudno.
140 The table shows results from the top eight counties only. Thirty counties plus Ireland and Gibraltar supplied recruits for the battalion.
141 Williams, 'Taffs in the Trenches', p.140.

Table 8: 12th SWB – Origins[142]

County	Whole sample		To 30/11/1917		To 31/5/1917	
	Birth (232)	Residence (210)	Birth (211)	Residence (191)	Birth (111)	Residence (98)
Monmouth	12.1% (28)	16.2% (34)	11.4% (24)	15.2% (29)	12.6% (14)	17.3% (17)
Yorkshire	12.1% (28)	12.9% (27)	11.8% (25)	13.6% (26)	11.7% (13)	14.3% (14)
Glamorgan	8.6% (20)	12.9% (27)	8.1% (17)	12.0% (23)	7.2% (8)	8.2% (8)
Lancs	7.6% (18)	7.1% (15)	8.1% (17)	12.0% (23)	8.1% (9)	6.1% (6)
London	6.5% (15)	6.7% (14)	5.7% (12)	6.8% (13)	8.1% (9)	10.2% (10)
Staffs	5.2% (12)	3.3% (7)	5.2% (11)	1.6% (3)	5.4% (6)	5.1% (5)
Gloucs	4.7% (11)	1.0% (2)	5.2% (11)	1.0% (2)	3.6% (4)	1.0% (1)
Durham	3.4% (8)	2.6% (6)	3.8% (8)	3.1% (6)	3.6% (4)	4.0% (4)

The number of men from Monmouthshire in the 12th SWB is matched by the number of men from Yorkshire with Glamorgan, Staffordshire and London again making substantial contributions. Twenty-nine counties (plus Ireland) were represented in the battalion by May 1917 while the number rises to forty (plus Ireland and the Channel Islands) over the course of the war. This might indicate that the battalion would have struggled to establish a coherent identity (one outbreak of collective indiscipline that will be described later may indeed have originated within a group of disgruntled Yorkshiremen) but the fact that the number of Welsh-born men in the battalion seems to have stayed steady at around 27% (over 30% for Welsh residents) plus the very strong regimental bond within the regiment (the heroes of Rorke's Drift, January 1879) would surely have mitigated this effect? Alexander Watson states that the regimental tradition is less important in unit cohesion than local connections and that these are strong when men of similar geographical origin serve together.[143] In this case both are probably important factors.

Language is an important factor in group identity. Robin Barlow has stated that the men of predominantly Welsh-speaking counties were less likely to volunteer than those from predominantly English-speaking counties.[144] If the proportion of Welsh speakers identified in the 1911 census of Wales (43.5%) is applied to the Welsh-born element of 119 Brigade an approximate figure of 18.8% Welsh-speakers within the brigade is obtained. There is a noticeable and not unexpected variation in the proportion of Welsh speakers between the battalions.[145] With a fifth of its soldiers speaking Welsh (at least off the parade-ground) the image of the brigade as 'Welsh' would have been reinforced. At the front, during trials of a field telephone prior to a trench raid by the 18th Welsh in July 1916, it was proudly recorded that the conversations were conducted entirely in Welsh.[146]

In referring to the 119 Brigade as 'entirely Welsh' the divisional historian was almost certainly referring to the national reference in the four battalion names.[147] The figures presented above show

---

142 The table depicts results from the top eight counties only. Forty counties plus Ireland and the Channel Islands supplied recruits for the battalion.
143 Alexander Watson, *Enduring the Great War: Combat, Morale and Collapse in the German and British Armies, 1914-1918* (Cambridge: Cambridge University Press), p.64.
144 Robin Barlow, *Wales and World War One* (Llandysul: Gomer Press, 2014), p.115.
145 If the percentages of Welsh speakers per county identified in the 1911 census are applied to the Welsh-born soldiers in the brigade's battalions the results were 17th Welsh 25.1%; 18th Welsh 18.6%; 19th RWF 23.3%; 12th SWB 8.7%.
146 TNA WO 95/2604: War Diary 119 Brigade HQ, July 1916, appendices.
147 Whitton, *History of the 40th Division*, p.20.

the variable but none the less strong degree of 'Welshness' within the brigade.[148] Mark Connelly has stated that the four battalions of The Buffs (East Kent Regiment) that he studied still had by 1918 a 'significant number' of men connected with Kent in their ranks (27%; 23%; 23% and 17%) enabling them to maintain 'a geographical cohesion of a sort'.[149] The Welsh identity of 119 Brigade was very strong indeed by comparison.

Having established the geographical origins of the men in the ranks what was their social background? Clive Hughes has previously presented some data based on analysis of the occupations of a single company of the 16th RWF showing that 89% of the men were 'working class'. This figure was made up of 27% miners; 24% labourers and other heavy manual workers; 20% transport, manufacturing and other workers and 18% clerks, salesmen and servants.[150] Figures based on the available data for the battalions of 119 Brigade show a similar picture while varying in certain key details (Table 9).[151] Within the category of 'heavy manual work' the largest proportion of men were miners (41.2% across the brigade) closely followed by general labourers. David Starrett's perception of the brigade as 'coal miners mostly' was a little wide of the mark but within the battalions they usually formed the single largest group.[152] The 17th Welsh had 53.2% miners; the 18th Welsh 31.3%; the 19th RWF 32% and the 12th SWB 17.6%.[153]

Table 9: Civilian Occupations 119 Brigade (sample sizes in brackets)

Category	17th Welsh (126)	18th Welsh (67)	19th RWF (50)	12th SWB (17)	119 Brigade overall (260)
Heavy Manual Work	81.7%	68.6%	64%	76.4%	74.6%
Manufacturing, Transport and other	7.9%	19.4%	22%	11.8%	13.8%
Clerks, Salesmen and Servants	8.7%	6%	8%	–	7.3%
Shopkeepers	–	6%	6%	11.8%	3.5%
Professional Classes	–	–	–	–	–
Miscellaneous	1.6%	–	–	–	0.8%

The figure for the 17th Welsh receives some additional corroboration from the entries in the 'Platoon Roll Book' for Number 16 Platoon, D Company. Of the sixty-five names in the book, forty-four (67.7%) give the civilian occupation of the soldier: twenty-three of these were colliers (52.3%); six (13.6%) were labourers; three were tin workers; two were moulders and the variety was extended with one each of a baker, barber, bricklayer, butcher, hotel servant, painter, papermaker, seaman, shunter, [blacksmith's] striker and tailor.[154] The apparent absence of the professional classes and

---

148 Hughes, *Welsh Army Corps*, p.91 refers to the 'inherent Welshness' of the WAC as an aid to recruiting.
149 Mark Connelly, *Steady the Buffs! A Regiment, a Region & the Great War* (Oxford: Oxford University Press, 2006), p.29 and p.34.
150 Hughes, *Recruiting in Gwynedd*, p.48; Hughes, *The New Armies*, p.120.
151 For another analysis of occupations, origins etc of a service battalion see J.M. Bourne, 'A New Army Battalion at Gallipoli: The 7th Battalion The Prince of Wales's (North Staffordshire) Regiment' in Rhys Crawley and Michael LoCicero (eds.), *Gallipoli: New Perspectives on the Mediterranean Expeditionary Force, 1915-16* (Warwick: Helion, 2018), pp.507-530.
152 IWM Documents: 79/39/1 David Starrett, *Batman*, unpublished typescript. David (Davie) Starrett was Frank Crozier's servant/batman throughout the Great War.
153 The sample for the 12th SWB is so small that results must be treated with caution.
154 A scanned copy of the original (location now unknown) was obtained by the author from the vendor when the original appeared on an online auction site in May 2011. Comparisons with other documents seen later

the very low representation of middle-class traders may indicate that these bantam battalions were seen by potential recruits (and recruiters?) as the preserve of short, strong men from the labouring classes.

One further element of common identity is religion. At the beginning of the twentieth century Wales was dominated by Nonconformity. Barlow describes how figures gathered in 1905 relating to communicants in Wales show that only 26% came from the Church of England while 71% belonged to Nonconformist denominations. He contrasts these figures with those from the roll book of a single company of the 16th RWF which lists only 38.5% Nonconformists and 54.9% Church of England and suggests that this evidence indicates the unwillingness of North Wales Nonconformists to join up. He is dismissive of the point made by Gervase Phillips that the army only seemed to recognise Anglicanism and Roman Catholicism but Phillips' view receives some support here from the only piece of evidence relating to the religious affiliation of troops of 119 Brigade.[155] The Platoon Roll Book of 16 Platoon, 17th Welsh gives denominations for fifty-four of sixty-five soldiers. Of these, no less than forty (74.1%) are listed as Church of England, six as Roman Catholic (13.6%) and the remainder as one of three categories of Nonconformist. If correct, this indicates a remarkably uniform religious affiliation among the platoon, the greater part of which was composed of miners from the Rhondda. It seems more probable that the over-representation of Anglicans is due either to the unwillingness of the men to be singled out as Nonconformists or to a subaltern's enthusiasm to enter something in the space in the Roll Book.[156]

Discipline

The volunteers of Kitchener's New Armies were enthusiastic; they were also, quite understandably, unused to the strict rules and regulations that governed army life. In June 1915 Saunders Lewis (12th SWB) observed:

> The discipline of the battalion is very poor at present; the men, and most of them are boys, have little idea of military discipline, and as most of the officers are men of little experience, we are not allowed to take things into our own hands and assert ourselves … they are amusingly like bantams in one thing. They have a strong tendency for fighting. It is hard not to laugh when marching in front of them. They spend the whole time they are marching at ease in threatening all dire things against each other, and the first stop they get into rings and we have to step in to stop any pugilistic exhibitions.[157]

Whilst the majority of volunteers completed their army service with a clean disciplinary record, the surviving service records of the men of 119 Brigade give an indication of how many did not. The largest sample is of men from the 17th Welsh (127) twenty-two per cent of which (28) had one or more offences on their records. Most offences took place during home service and consisted of absences or overstaying of leave although six men were punished for drunkenness (less than five per cent). There are few single offences and men tended to repeat offending. Only five men in the sample are recorded as committing offences in a theatre of war. In the 18th Welsh (67 records) only

---

show that it was completed by Second-Lieutenant Morris Meredith Williams.
155 Barlow, *Wales and World War One*, pp.107-112. Gervase Phillips' work was published as 'Dai Bach y Soldiwr', *Llafur*, 6/2 (1993), pp.93-105.
156 Platoon Roll Book, 16 Platoon, 17th Welsh, author's collection.
157 Mair Saunders Jones, Ned Thomas and Harri Pritchard Jones (eds), *Letters to Margaret Gilcreist* (Cardiff: University of Wales Press, 1993), p.112. Letters dated 2 and 5 June 1915.

twelve per cent of records contain offences while the records of men of the 19th RWF (50 records) have no less than forty-four per cent showing offences. The small surviving sample of men from the 12th SWB (18 records) has twenty-two per cent with offences.[158] In overview the predominance of absence as an offence seems to indicate a reluctance to give up the ties to home while 'home' was still within easy travelling distance. Three absentees charged at Cardiff in July 1915 were noted as being 'about seventeen years of age' and presumably preferred home to the camp at Prees Heath.[159] Occurrences of insolence to NCOs, lateness for parades, dirty buttons etc., indicate a lack of appreciation of the need for conformity and standards within the system.

The relatively small number of surviving service records provides a glimpse of the disciplinary records of individual soldiers. The state of discipline of organised units such as battalions is rarely recorded explicitly although several examples of collective indiscipline among the volunteers of the New Armies are known particularly from the autumn of 1914 when shortages of rations and suitable accommodation were common in the rapidly expanding forces.[160] These causes of complaint had been largely eliminated by 1915 but there is some evidence for acts of collective indiscipline in at least two of the battalions of 119 Brigade.

In Llandudno in May 1915 men from the 17th Welsh, along with men from the 16th Welsh (Cardiff City) battalion and the 10th SWB (1st Gwent) were involved in disturbances that resulted in Caitlin's Pierrots and Reynold's Serenaders closing their shows after rowdy troops demanded of male performers 'Why don't you join the army?'[161]

In January 1917 Mr A.L. Gardner, representing the Welsh National Council of the YMCA, was speaking on the war work of the institution and recalled that:

> He was once told by the late Brigadier-General Dunn that a Bantam company had 'struck' and he (Gardner) was asked to ascertain what was the matter. He went down to the men, found what the difficulty was, it was remedied by the Brigadier and in a short time the Bantams were soldiering again.[162]

In this case the cause of the 'strike' was not stated but other examples were clearly related to the reaction of volunteers to perceived ill-treatment. William Edwards recalled that during the training of the 18th Welsh at Porthcawl in May 1915 'at the hands of instructors drawn from the Metropolitan Police and the regiment of Guards [sic]':

> One of the young soldiers was struck on a very sore arm by one of these Sergeant-Majors with a heavy stick which they always carried. The boy sank to the ground in great pain, his comrades went to his defence and loudly expressed their anger, actually threatening the offender. After parade, meetings were held and it was decided to refuse to 'Fall In' the next morning. This was 100% successful, there was to be no further parades until the instructors were sent away. The 3rd Battalion Welsh Regt. were sent to Porthcawl from Cardiff to 'persuade' us to parade, they failed in their mission. We remained in our billets for four days, we were fed as usual by

---

158 The data comes from service records contained in TNA WO 363 (British Army WW1 Service Records, sometimes called the 'Burnt Documents') and WO 364 (British Army WW1 Pension Records) available at <http://www.ancestry.com>.
159 *Western Mail*, 30 July 1915.
160 Simkins, *Kitchener's Army*, pp.200, 239, 243.
161 *North Wales Chronicle*, 28 May 1915. There is no evidence of disciplinary action resulting from this incident.
162 Ibid., 26 January 1917. This must refer to either the 17th Welsh or 19th RWF both of which were based in North Wales prior to July 1915 but neither battalion was in Dunn's 2nd Brigade (later 129 then 114 Brigade).

our civilian landlords. We were then informed that the instructors were transferred elsewhere and accordingly we resumed our training ...[163]

This event has some similarities to an incident reported in the press early in the following month. The prosecution of a civilian under the provisions of the Defence of the Realm Act for 'having uttered words likely to be prejudicial to the discipline of His Majesty's Forces and also with having obstructed a police officer' was reported in detail under headlines that told of a 'Big Rumpus at Porthcawl' and 'Bloodshed and a Frightful Riot Averted'.[164] In summary, following the witnessing of an 'alleged act of severity by a non-commissioned officer to one of the recruits on the afternoon of 1 June 1915', a noisy crowd of around two hundred soldiers and civilians assembled outside the orderly room of the 18th Welsh in John Street, Porthcawl. The CO, Lieutenant-Colonel Homfray, sent his adjutant (Captain Pugh) to investigate along with Sergeant-Major King – who it is implied was the NCO that had been involved.[165] The accused was then allegedly heard to say that King 'ought to be ------- well murdered' and Pugh arrested him. The situation might have become worse when one officer, Second-Lieutenant J. Edward Walter Edwards, drew his revolver to discourage soldiers who were possibly moving to attempt the release of the prisoner. Pugh ordered the guard turned out and the street to be cleared. The disturbance died down but armed patrols policed the streets until 12.30 a.m. The prosecuting council emphasised that 'in these days ... discipline and training were the greatest assets of the state and that if interfered with then it would destroy the morale of the battalion'. The defendant, William John Rees, aged 25, an insurance agent from Tondu near Bridgend was found guilty and fined five pounds or, if in default, one month's imprisonment. The newspaper reports contain no reference to the refusal to parade as in the incident recalled by Edwards and so this may be additional event.

Edwards related a further incident in August 1915 when 'the battalion again refused orders to parade, until they had received an undertaking that Field Punishment No. 1 ... would be less frequently imposed'.[166] No other evidence of this particular incident or of the events leading up to it has been found. The 18th Welsh was likely to have been one of the two battalions 'where the lack of discipline was notorious' and which received the attention of Brigadier-General Style to 'remove [their] rough edges' following the move to Aldershot in September 1915.[167] This receives some support from the data presented below (Table 10). Collective indiscipline among the volunteers of the New Armies was mainly confined to the autumn of 1914 when shortages of rations and suitable accommodation were particularly acute.[168] The actions of the 18th Welsh at Porthcawl more than six months later indicate that the army had not yet assimilated all of the lessons learned from earlier troubles with volunteer recruits; particularly when, as suggested by Dallas and Gill, those recruits came from a pool of organised labour such as the miners of the South Wales coalfield and proved to be 'less malleable' than most.[169] In the instance of the disturbance at Porthcawl the relative inexperience of the officers on the spot may also have been a contributory factor.

Routine matters of discipline were dealt with by the battalion CO but more serious offences were tried at a District Court Martial. The examination of the District Courts Martial Registers

---

163 Quoted in Gloden Dallas and Douglas Gill, *The Unknown Army* (London: Verso, 1985), p.44. The original letter dated 23 September 1965 does not seem to have survived.
164 *Glamorgan Gazette*, 11 June 1915. Also *Western Mail*, 8 June 1915.
165 The *Porthcawl News*, 18 March 1915, listed Sergeant King as one of six drill instructors loaned from the Metropolitan Police and had previously described him as an 'ex-sergeant of the Scots'.
166 Dallas and Gill. *Unknown Army*, p.44.
167 RRW Museum, Whitworth memoir, pp.523-524.
168 Simkins, *Kitchener's Army*, pp.200, 239, 243.
169 Dallas and Gill. *Unknown Army*, p.44.

produces no additional information on the cases noted above. Indeed there are no courts martial involving men of the 18th Welsh until September 1915. It does however show a marked difference between the number of cases per battalion and a distinct rise in the number of cases across the brigade after the concentration at Aldershot in September 1915 (Table 10).

Table 10: Trials by District Courts Martial, 119 Brigade (Number of offences in brackets)

	17th Welsh	18th Welsh	19th RWF	12th SWB	Total
Apr 1915	2 (3)	–	–	–	2 (3)
May	–	–	–	–	0
June	1 (1)	–	–	–	1 (1)
July	1 (2)	–	–	–	1 (2)
Aug	2 (3)	–	–	–	2 (3)
Sept	–	1 (2)	–	–	1 (2)
Oct	1 (1)	3 (3)	–	–	4 (4)
Nov	–	1 (2)	–	1 (1)	2 (3)
Dec	–	–	–	–	0
Total	**7 (10)**	**5 (7)**	**0**	**1 (1)**	**13 (18)**
Jan 1916	1 (1)	1 (2)	1 (1)	2 (3)	5 (7)
Feb	3 (5)	–	1 (2)	3 (4)	7 (11)
Mar	2 (3)	2 (3)	1 (1)	5 (7)	10 (14)
Apr	4 (7)	2 (2)	1 (3)	1 (1)	8 (13)
May	2 (2)	5 (7)	1 (2)	3 (7)	11 (18)
Total	**12 (18)**	**10 (14)**	**5 (9)**	**14 (22)**	**41 (63)**
Overall	**19 (28)**	**15 (21)**	**5 (9)**	**15 (23)**	**54 (81)**

Source: TNA WO 86/64-70

The brigade's first courts martial took place in April 1915 when two privates of the 17th Welsh were tried on charges of insubordination (to a lieutenant) and desertion with theft. The 17th Welsh had the worst record of the four battalions during 1915. The 18th Welsh start to close the gap following the move to Aldershot while the 19th RWF and 12th SWB have almost no trials. The number of trials increased markedly in 1916 with 76% of the total of fifty-four occurring in the five months before the brigade left for France. In comparison, in nine months of training at home the men of the three brigades of 10th (Irish) Division (29, 30 and 31 Brigades) were tried for 274, 249 and 118 offences respectively.[170] In fourteen months just eighty-one offences were tried within 119 Brigade's units. Battalion-level figures given in Bowman's and Sandford's works vary enormously.[171] The figures for four sample battalions from the 36th (Ulster) Division during their training at home are: 10th Royal Inniskilling Fusiliers, 18; 9th RIRifles, 47; 13th RIRifles, 9; 14th RIRifles, 5. While in the 10th (Irish) Division figures range from 150 in the 6th Royal Dublin Fusiliers to just 10 in the 7th battalion of the same regiment (both 30 Brigade). There is an average of 69, 62 and 30 trials per battalion in 29, 30 and 31 Brigades respectively during their training period. The battalions of 119 Brigade seem to have remarkably well behaved in comparison. These soldiers were predominantly labouring men and, while it is tempting to think of them

---

170 Compiled from tables in Stephen Sandford, *Neither Unionist Nor Nationalist: The 10th (Irish) Division in the Great War* (Sallins: Irish Academic Press, 2015), pp.242-243.
171 Bowman, Irish *Regiments*, p.87.

as well-behaved, chapel-going Welshmen, the presence of large numbers of men from England in two battalions (one of which has the fewest trials by courts martial) would indicate that discipline was not a function of nationality. The variations in the number of trials / offences between battalions in the same formation supports Bowman's conclusion that the application of military justice was not consistent and did indeed vary from unit to unit.[172]

What type of offence was tried by court martial in 119 Brigade? The most common offences were absence which featured either alone or with other offences in fourteen cases (17% of all offences); insubordination in thirteen cases (24%); desertion in ten cases (19%) and drunkenness in just eight cases (15%): a picture that is broadly similar to that for other New Army formations (Table 11) although once again each formation seems to have its own unique profile.

Table 11: Offences tried by District Courts Martial during training period

Offence	119 Brigade (number of occurrences in brackets)	10th (Irish) Division[173]	13th (Western) Division	36th (Ulster) Division (sample of 4 battalions)[174]
Absence	17% (14)	28%	16%	14%
Drunkenness	10% (8)	9%	7%	4%
Insubordination	16% (13)	8%	12%	5%
Desertion	12% (10)	22%	10%	17%
Loss of public property	11% (9)	15%	17%	–
Violence	6% (5)	12%	8%	3%
Miscellaneous military offences	14% (11)	9%	12%	50%
Theft	4% (3)	4%	2%	4%

The accused was found not guilty in only three of the fifty-four trials of 119 Brigade soldiers. The most common sentence was a period of detention (42 instances) while loss of property resulted in the imposition of stoppages (7 instances). Drunkenness and other offences by NCOs invariably resulted in reduction in rank (9 instances). There were only three instances of sentencing to a period of hard labour and two of those were commuted to detention. In all there were seven cases where sentences were commuted or remitted. The figures presented by Sandford show that the sentencing records of battalions were as varied as the number and type of charges but that detention was consistently the most common sentence.[175] Data on Field General Courts Martial overseas is given in later chapters.

Uniform, Equipment and Training

The process of equipping and training the New Armies for war has been ably described by Peter Simkins, who has highlighted the effects of widespread shortages of uniform and equipment in

---

172 Ibid., p.88.
173 Figures for 10th and 13th Divisions from Sandford, *Neither Unionist nor Nationalist*, Figure 7.2, p.236. There are four additional offences each less than 2% of total.
174 Figures compiled from Bowman, *Irish Regiments*, p.87, Table 3.1. There are four additional cases of 'Miscellaneous Civil Offences'.
175 Sandford, *Neither Unionist Nor Nationalist*, p.246, Figure 7.4.

1914-1915.[176] These shortages also affected the troops of the nascent WAC. Clive Hughes has described how the NEC tackled the shortage of khaki uniforms in the WAC by commissioning its own distinctive uniforms in 'Brethyn Llwyd' – a Welsh grey homespun cloth – which started to be issued in December 1914. A total of 8,440 sets of Brethyn Llwyd jackets and trousers was purchased for the WAC and distributed unevenly across its units including to some troops of what became 119 Brigade. WAC records show that Kitchener Blue trousers, caps, jackets and greatcoats were purchased along with the official khaki and Brethyn Llwyd items.[177] Sometimes the same unit received different colours of clothing. Lieutenant-Colonel Homfray, OC 18th Welsh, objected to the issue of Brethyn Llwyd to his battalion:

> I beg to bring to notice that the following clothing has been received here for men of my battalion, viz: 160 suits of Khaki; 400 suits of Brethin Llwyd from Messrs Trippe & Sons and Messrs John Howell & Co respectively.
>
> In view of the fact that the former suits have already been issued, I most strongly protest against issuing two different types of clothing to the men of my regiment.
>
> Messrs Trippe & Sons of Cardiff have satisfied me they are in a position to supply the balance of the suits of Khaki as quickly as I require same which I entirely agree with.
>
> I wish my men clothed in Khaki and quite consider that I am entitled to have them clothed uniformly.[178]

Homfray reinforced his argument in a letter to the Chairman of the WAC Clothing Committee:

> I feel sure that if this be insisted on, the whole show will be spoilt, as we have already issued 256 suits, 576 greatcoats and 698 caps, all of Khaki, and to have some of the men in this material and some in something else would make us a laughing stock, and absolutely ruin our 'Esprit de Corps'. I hope you will do all you can to insist on our getting Khaki as soon as possible.[179]

His outrage and his attempt to go his own way in sourcing clothing did not get far in the face of the NEC's desire for centralised supply. On 2 March 1915 he was told that 'To complete the requirements of your Battalion 332 Brethyn Llwyd suits have been ordered from Messrs Masters & Co. Ltd, Cardiff'.[180] A note dated 28 September 1915 to the OC 18th Welsh enquiring about how a discrepancy amounting to two suits between the number of Brethyn Llwyd uniforms reported by the battalion (1453) and those issued by the WAC (1455) came about seems to indicate that this battalion was still wearing the style at the time although the supply had already dried up. As early as 12 July the WAC Secretary was telling the Corps Storekeeper, in response to a request for additional clothing from the 18th Welsh, to use up stocks of Brethyn Llwyd to the nearest size possible because WAC contracts had expired and 'there are no instructions to enter into new ones'. The Storekeeper issued 142 suits of sizes 5'3" to 5'6" to the battalion and the CO was informed that no more 'Bantam' sizes remained.[181] A photograph of B Company, 18th Welsh, at Aldershot in 1915

---

176 Simkins, *Kitchener's Army*.
177 Cited in Hughes, *Welsh Army Corps*, p.92 et seq.
178 NLW WAC C33/5: Correspondence regarding supplies of clothing and necessaries. OC 18th Welsh to Secretary WAC, 22 February 1915.
179 NLW WAC C111/9: Letter from OC 18th Welsh to Mr D.A. Thomas (1856-1918, later Lord Rhondda) 24 February 1915.
180 Ibid. Memorandum from Secretary WAC to OC 18th Welsh, 2 March 1915.
181 NLW WAC C17/1: Copy memoranda dated 12 and 16 July 1915.

shows some men wearing distinctly lighter shades of uniform. These may well be the remnants of the Brethyn Llwyd issue.[182]

An account of three hundred men of the 19th RWF marching from Llandudno to Deganwy in March 1915 describes how they were 'all clad in their new khaki suits and appeared remarkably smart and soldierlike'.[183] The battalion had achieved its soldierly appearance by breaking purchasing rules (along with the 15th and 17th RWF) prompting the WAC Secretary to complain:

> We had already provided for all their requirements at full strength and now we are unexpectedly informed that they have entered into contracts with the manufacturers direct. As a civilian, I would suggest that the officers might be better employed in training their men than in taking upon themselves duties which have been delegated to the Clothing Committee … I would suggest that, inasmuch as the Committee is directly responsible to the War Office for all goods entered into, the Committee should themselves make their own contracts without any regard to Officers Commanding.[184]

There is no direct evidence to indicate that the 17th Welsh were issued with Brethyn Llwyd clothing but a photograph of the battalion signal section shows six of twenty-five men wearing a distinctly paler shade of uniform.[185] However, in May 1915 the battalion quartermaster requested three hundred and eighty-two khaki suits for 'men who have not yet been supplied with Khaki Service Dress'.[186] The 12th SWB seems always to have been clad in khaki and a photograph of A Company dated July 1915 shows a uniform appearance of the ranks.[187] There is no evidence in the WAC records of any issue of Brethyn Llwyd to the battalion.

The presence of battalions of small men within the WAC added to the confusion of supply. In March 1915 the 15th Welsh at Rhyl received an order of bantam-sized greatcoats intended for the 18th Welsh at Porthcawl and Lieutenant-Colonel Wilkie (OC 17th Welsh) had to point out that hundreds of caps and pairs of boots 'owing to their large size are unsuitable for the men in the unit under my command'.[188] The following month an urgent request went out from the 18th Welsh for boots of sizes five, six and seven. The 19th RWF also urgently requested boots during the same month emphasising that 'the prevailing sizes for men of this battalion [are] 5-6-7'.[189] The Platoon Roll Book of 16 Platoon, 17th Welsh records the shoe size of thirty-six of its sixty-five men. Four were size five; nineteen were size six; twelve were size seven and just one was size eight.[190]

Even without the special requirements of the bantams the system struggled with the same demands as those generated by most of the New Army units in the process of formation. An early photograph of the 17th Welsh at Porthcawl shows a sight typical of the early weeks of most New Army battalions with the men parading in their civilian overcoats and flat caps.[191] A press reporter commenting on the 18th Welsh, then forming at Porthcawl, remarked on 'a rather unusual sight being a number of men from Lancashire drilling with clogs on'.[192] The WAC files record constant requests for clothing and kit of all types. Cap badges and numerals, NCO's chevrons and warrant

---

182 Museum of the Royal Welsh, Brecon. Un-numbered photograph.
183 *Liverpool Daily Post*, 15 March 1915.
184 NLW WAC C111/9: WAC Secretary to D.A. Thomas.
185 Author's Collection.
186 NLW WAC C111/9: Memorandum to WAC Secretary from Quartermaster 17th Welsh, 3 May 1915.
187 Museum of the Royal Welsh, Brecon. Un-numbered photograph.
188 NLW WAC C27/2 and C32/3: Memoranda 18 March 1915 and 20 April 1915.
189 NLW WAC C34/4: Telegram to WAC Secretary from OC 19th Welsh, 30 April 1915.
190 Platoon Roll Book, 16 Platoon, 17th Welsh, author's collection.
191 *Daily Mirror*, 19 January 1915.
192 *Western Mail*, 6 February 1915.

officer's crowns were urgently needed to help bolster the identity of the new units and their personnel. The 18th Welsh obtained badges from a local supplier near the Prees Heath camp as late as August 1915 and the photograph of A Company 12th SWB mentioned above shows many men without cap badges.[193] In April only half the men of the 19th RWF had greatcoats and there were no shirts or drawers. Even by June it was reported that 'men remain unclothed' due to shortage of uniform. Given the rapid growth of the New Armies such shortages were probably inevitable.

In addition to problems with 'official' supplies some equipment was not forthcoming from official sources. The press reported that 'a number of items which the War Office do not provide are still wanted, including field-glasses for non-commissioned officers, spades for trenching work, field cookers and a motor ambulance'.[194] In an effort to provide entertainment and boost morale during marches, at least three of the battalions established bands. In March 1915 Mr W.J. Tatem presented instruments to the 18th Welsh at Porthcawl to form a band that gave its first concert in June. In North Wales, after Lieutenant-Colonel Wilkie had expressed his wish to form a band for the 17th Welsh, Madame Riviere stepped in and raised funds for a set of bugles and drums with accessories. A photographic postcard taken at Prees Heath shows the 12th SWB in column led by a small band.[195] The battalions were also gifted, or acquired for themselves, mascots. Photographs of the 17th and 18th Welsh and the 19th RWF all show men holding examples of bantam poultry while the 17th Welsh was gifted a goat by Alderman Benjamin Jones of Swansea. Indeed, so strong was the urge to give goats that two weeks after the donation to the 17th Welsh the authorities at Porthcawl were moved to appeal that, due to a surfeit of presentation goats, donors check with the relevant CO before proceeding.[196]

Despite the shortages of kit the four battalions of 119 Brigade had befitted from the experiences of the first three New Armies in other ways. The first formations struggled to find acceptable accommodation and for many there was no alternative to the use of tents. When the weather broke in October 1914 the War Office hutting programme was seriously behind schedule and the tented camps became quagmires. The War Office solution was to approve the greatly increased use of billets and to delegate arrangements for this to local Area Quartering Committees. By the time that the 119 Brigade's battalions were formed, systems were well established at Porthcawl and in the seaside resorts of North Wales so that all of the battalions were able to use billets rather than tents or overcrowded public or industrial buildings. Brigadier-General Owen Thomas, 113 Brigade, 43rd (later 38th) (Welsh) Division, noted that 'One thing I feel certain about is the fact that these men are billeted with respectable people has a splendid effect on their behaviour'.[197] Meanwhile the creation of new camps included the hutted camp at Prees Heath, Shropshire where the brigade first came together in July 1915.[198] While the use of billets had some advantages for the men, their dispersal even across a relatively small area created problems in gathering men together promptly for parades and training.

While there was a clear syllabus for the training of new infantry recruits over a period of six months the lack of sources prevents a detailed picture of how this was applied to the four battalions of 119 Brigade. Some of the men of the brigade (particularly those of the 17th Welsh) would complete eighteen months of service before proceeding abroad and the sheer boredom must have

---

193 NLW WAC C33/5: Adjutant 18th Welsh to WAC Secretary, 3 December 1915.
194 *Western Mail*, 11 March 1915.
195 Ibid; *Liverpool Daily Post*, 30 March 1915; *Glamorgan Gazette*, 4 June 1915. W.J. Tatem was a Cardiff ship owner and philanthropist. Madame Riviere was the widow of Jules Riviere (died December 1900) a well-known and successful French musician who had settled in Colwyn Bay. 12th SWB postcard author's collection.
196 *Western Mail*, 23 January 1915.
197 *Liverpool Daily Post*, 22 January 1915.
198 See Simkins, *Kitchener's Army*, pp.237-244 concerning the new camps and the issues around them.

Band of the 17th Welsh, August 1915. Major E.H. St George Gilbert seated centre left. (Author)

been disheartening. Lieutenant E.E.A. Whitworth, 12th SWB, certainly found it 'irksome and disappointing, and … some of us wondered whether we should ever see active service at all'.[199] On the other hand the brigade had a head start in training matters over its sister brigades that were recruited later in 1915 and over the additional battalions brought in to bolster them in February 1916. Alexander Watson has stated that the average training period for a New Army battalion was 9.4 months which was 'adequate to enable strong primary group bonds and feelings of *esprit de corps* to form'.[200] These had the chance to develop further in 119 Brigade.

The basics of drill occupied the first part of the training syllabus and as this required neither arms nor equipment it could and did occupy the troops even while battalions were being recruited. The promenades and beaches of Porthcawl, Rhos-on-Sea and Llandudno provided parade grounds and in Newport the 12th SWB used the municipal park. Battalions were lucky if they had some experienced soldiers to call on. Second-Lieutenant Evan Beynon Davies, 19th RWF, noted that Sergeant J.E. Jones and Quartermaster Keating were the only experienced soldiers in the battalion. At Newport, Second-Lieutenant J. Saunders Lewis, 12th SWB, noted that 'the sergeants of another battalion are lent to us for training in early parts of work' while at Porthcawl the 18th Welsh were lent the services of lieutenants Bracher and Pugh and sergeants Davies and Prangley by the 16th Welsh.[201] Prior to Lieutenant-Colonel Homfray taking command of the battalion the two junior officers acted as OC and 2iC respectively and, although the loan was 'a temporary measure only', Pugh transferred to the battalion in the next month as captain and adjutant. In addition to these officers it was reported that 'there are no fewer than ten competent instructors on duty, some of whom have seen considerable service in South Africa and elsewhere. One of the instructors holds the DCM'.[202]

---

199 RRW Museum, Whitworth memoir, p.96.
200 Alexander Watson, *Enduring the Great War*, p.64.
201 Jones, *Letters to Margaret Gilcreist*, p.112. Sidney Walter Pugh (1883-1943). See Appendix VI.
202 *Western Mail*, 6 February 1915.

Even though the 18th Welsh was still recruiting it was reported in March that it was making:

> Rapid strides towards efficiency, thanks to the keenness of officers, non-commissioned officers and men. This week A Company carried out their first night march and outpost work and were visited at certain points by Colonel H.R. Homfray [and] Adjutant Sidney W. Pugh, who took an entirely different route, in order to see whether the work was properly carried out. So well were the duties performed that they were unable to get through the lines unchallenged.[203]

In Newport with the 12th SWB, Saunders Lewis noted how 'The Battalion is in a curious way now; there are some here who have had three months of training, and many a few days, and new men come in daily; so that our work as officers will range from the entirely elementary to the very advanced.'[204] This must have been both confusing and frustrating for the officers concerned but there were other, unforeseen, problems:

> I was put in charge of the scouts and signalling section of our battalion; in fact I was set to form and instruct them; and as there is a great deal of writing to do in these tasks I soon discovered that a big proportion of the men is quite illiterate, and that to read, write and spell fluently is quite exceptional – and it made my job next to impossible.
>
> The only thing I could think of to remedy matters was to institute a night school in the battalion, and I suggested that to the men. They seemed to take to the proposal very readily; so I said that if I could get a reasonable number of men keen on joining I should myself get a room in Newport and start classes two nights a week …[205] only a few of them cannot write at all, it is dictation and spelling [that] they are weak in.[206]

His classes seem to have progressed but after a spell away at a signalling course he found that much depended on his own dedication to the task after 'finding a man who had temporarily undertaken my work had succeeded in a few weeks in ruining all I'd tried to do at Newport and had given the Colonel an idea that I had not taught the signallers a single thing. I really felt like throwing up my old commission'.[207]

Beynon Davies, 19th RWF, contrasted the 'warm and happy atmosphere in Wales' with the realization, following the move to Prees Heath, 'that we were finally in reality going to war and that we had a day of busy bending to the task ahead of us'.[208] Quite what that task consisted of is not clear as no description of the training undertaken at Prees Heath has been traced. Two photographs taken by a local photographer show men of the 17th Welsh returning to Prees Heath in column behind their band. The men have 1914 Pattern leather equipment and approximately one in three carries a Lee-Metford rifle – the type commonly issued (often in small quantities) to New Army units for initial training. Clive Hughes has described how 'the WAC received a few condemned rifles at the start of 1915, otherwise the men had to use walking sticks or other improvised arms' and how after attending the 128 Brigade St David's Day parade at Llandudno, at which arms were conspicuous by their absence, Lloyd George interceded with Lord Kitchener.

---

203 *Western Mail*, 11 March 1915. According to the syllabus for Recruit Training in General Staff, War Office, *Infantry Training* (London: HMSO, 1914) instruction in night work is introduced in the third fortnight of training but is seriously pursued only after the seventh fortnight.
204 Jones et al, *Letters to Margaret Gilcreist*, p.111. Letter dated 4 June 1915.
205 Ibid., p.115. Letter dated 11 June 1915.
206 Ibid., p.119. Letter dated 30 June1915.
207 Ibid. p.149. Letter dated 7 October 1915.
208 Davies, *Ar Orwel Pell*, p.33.

17th Welsh, route march, Prees Heath, summer 1915. (Author)

11 Platoon, 19th RWF. Prees Heath, summer 1915. Sergeant with bantam mascot seated centre front. (Author)

'As a result each battalion [of the WAC] received a hundred Boer War firearms'.[209] Captain E.E.A. Whitworth, 12th SWB, noted that following the move to Aldershot 'the men had not been issued with their service rifles and each company had a certain number of 'D.P.s' (Drill Purpose, that is rifles not fit to fire) on its strength'.[210] It must be assumed that the training at Prees Heath focused on drill along with route marches and running while a start was made on rifle drill using the few weapons available. Beynon Davies records that the arms drill in summertime was no great problem and 'reinforced our health and strength under the smiles of the sun'.[211] Saunders Lewis noted that his writing classes might not take place because 'in camp there is night work so often, there may not be time'.[212]

Training moved up a gear once the brigade moved to Aldershot and then, in December 1915, to nearby Blackdown:

> We came to know a lot about the geography of England within about fifty miles of Aldershot, and we knew how hard it was to live in an open trench, what it was to fight with bayonets and mills bombs, how to read a map and how to withstand a gas attack. After being at it for hours training in the heat of the day it was grand to be able to return to barracks and to hear the boys singing 'Tipperary', 'When I get my civvy clothes on', and 'Waltzing Matilda'.[213]

By Christmas 1915 he thought that they 'had become seasoned soldiers, and that we had hardened sufficiently to face anything on the battlefield'.[214] Captain Whitworth, 12th SWB, observed that 'at this stage in our training we were frequently practising by companies outpost and the attack' and 'I was happy and fully occupied with the work of a company commander; the week's training ended on each Saturday morning with a route march of 10 or 12 miles in full marching order and the Bantams, despite the weight of equipment and ammunition, responded well'.[215] Saunders Lewis was also having a better time of it: 'I am at work now I think would interest you, teaching map-reading and compass work; explaining contours and scales. Tomorrow, if the snow abates, I am taking half a dozen NCOs out on bicycles with me cycling on compass bearings and doing practical map-reading in the country. It is work I really enjoy'.[216] He was having problems though in finding NCOs to take on responsibility:

> Sometimes work is very depressing. I have had my class of nearly sixty men now for nearly eight months, and constantly training, lecturing, exhorting, yet now when I want to make more NCOs, out of fifty-odd men I can scarcely find one whom I can trust to take responsibly and be strong and be able to command men. Even of the four NCOs I have, one who has been with me since the beginning is utterly weak and impotent to take command and care, the others are fairly successful. Results like these make me very doubtful and rather hopeless. You can preach, teach, command, persuade, bully, appeal, attempt to exemplify but unless they are in a man, nothing you (or I) do can give them the qualities I strive for. I wish I had some

---

209 Hughes, *Arm to Save Your Native Land*, p.82.
210 RRW Museum, Whitworth memoir, p.521. The syllabus for recruit training places the issue of rifles in the second fortnight after which there are never less than ten hours of musketry instruction per fortnight. This would be impossible to deliver in the absence of adequate numbers of rifles.
211 Davies, *Ar Orwel Pell*, p.34.
212 Jones et al, *Letters to Margaret Gilcreist*, p.124. Letter dated 15 July 1915.
213 Davies, *Ar Orwel Pell*, p.41.
214 Ibid., p.39.
215 RRW Museum, Whitworth Memoir, pp.95, 521.
216 Jones et al, *Letters to Margaret Gilcreist*, p.188. Letter dated 28 February 1916.

training in teaching or in psychology before I started this work. Often I feel at a disadvantage in dealing with men. For surely every man may be approached and won some way.[217]

On 4 January 1916 Captain Gibbs, 18th Welsh, noted that they had been firing on the ranges but a new hardness was entering his correspondence:

> Unpleasant things happen and have to be done every day in the Army and life doesn't go smoothly as in peace time. In fact to carry on properly one has to be hard and think of nothing but the one job, work night and day, read, think and live for one end – killing Germans. It's horrid I know but the sooner it's over the better and the more one gets right into it the sooner it will be over.[218]

With the final musketry courses fired and the division made up to strength the frustrations of the long wait to go overseas were almost over.[219] Gibbs reported how the difficult job of an officer was bearing fruit:

> There are things that must be studied quite apart from drill and field work and these have to be gradually planted in every man's heart unknown to himself even, so that when the time comes the men of the 18th will not be found lacking in courage. It means really that every man now serving must feel in himself that it matters little if he dies in June of this year or Dec of 1996. He must also have the feeling that he's going to come through the war quite alright and this in itself will help him through. But it's a bit of a job kid isn't it – to impart this unknown to them, but I believe it's bearing fruit already as on the march today A Coy were singing to the top of their voices about what would happen if anyone would only show them a German. It was a topping song and I didn't know where they got it from … though the language was perhaps not quite as it should have been.[220]

The bantams distinguished themselves in other ways that helped to strengthen their identity and build morale:

> There was a big cross country race here today – a team of 20 men from each battalion. There were over 700 running. Our little Bantams ran and were 6th team home. Every one finished (of ours) and all were in the first 100. Can you imagine the sight? Little wee fellows running against 6ft Australians, Canadians and goodness knows what – and beat them too. The King started the race.[221]

The King paid one more visit to the bantams. On 25 May 1916 the whole of 40th Division was paraded for a royal inspection and was told afterwards that 'The Major General is much pleased at being able to inform all ranks that General Sir Archibald Hunter, Commanding the Aldershot Command, has notified that the parade of the 40th Division on the 25th of May on the occasion

---

217 Ibid., p.187. Letter dated 18 February 1916.
218 IWM, Documents: 72/11/1, Gibbs papers. Letter dated 23 March 1916.
219 The only evidence for the efficacy of the musketry training undertaken comes from the 16 Platoon Roll Book, 17th Welsh (author's collection). Of 65 names 54 have musketry grades. There were just six first class shots, eleven second class and 37 third class.
220 IWM, Documents: 72/11/1, Gibbs papers. Letter dated 23 March 1916.
221 Ibid. Letter dated 26 April 1916.

Signal Section, 17th Welsh, 1916. (Author)

of its inspection by His Majesty the King, was quite the best witnessed on Laffin's Plain since the outbreak of the War.'[222]

The proprietorial attitude of the WAC Executive Committee towards 'its' bantam brigade has been noted earlier in this chapter. It was clearly demonstrated for a final time by the reaction of the NEC Secretary, Owen, to the arrangements for the otherwise successful royal inspection. Under the headlines 'WHAT WAS LACKING/WHY WELSH MUNICIPALITIES WERE NOT REPRESENTED' the correspondent of the Cardiff-based *Western Mail* reported:

> So remarkable was [*sic*] the circumstances that none of the Welsh municipalities were represented [at the inspection] that I afterwards made inquiries as to what had happened. Mr. O.W. Owen, the secretary of the Welsh Army Corps, told me quite frankly that he had not been consulted at all with regards to the arrangements for today, and that he had only heard casually that certain private invitations were being sent out [Lord Plymouth and Sir Ivor Philipps were present at the inspection].
>
> 'I was not asked,' he said, 'to communicate any invitations to members of the committee of the Welsh Army Corps, who have been working so hard in connection with the whole recruiting scheme, though, as you know, most of them, together with several Welsh members of Parliament, journeyed to Winchester specially to send off the [38th] Welsh Division.'
>
> The matter is certainly one which calls for inquiry, and when one recalls the extraordinarily pleasant scenes at Winchester, when distinguished visitors from the various townships went

---

[222] RRW Museum., Brecon Ref 99.88: Scrapbook of W.E. Brown 12th SWB. Note from HQ 40th Division, 29 May 1916.

"ALL BRITISH BOYS."

Dedicated to Col. Wilkie, Officers and Men of the "17th Glamorgan Service Batt. The Welsh Regiment"—"The Bantams."

Original Words and Music by
Corporal J. F. Franklin, Bantam Battalion.

Sold in Aid of the BANTAMS BAND FUND

There have been threats of an invasion
Of "Old Englands Shore"
By a foe from a foreign land
But we've used the same persuasion
As we've done in days of "yore,"
Just to make them stay their hand,
We've an Army and a Navy,
Who in history have won fame,
So there's very little cause to be afraid,
For the "World" we can defy,
And we surely can rely on our Gallant Little
               Bantam Brigade.

CHORUS.

For they are all "British Boys"
Bull-dogs one and all,
All "British Boys," and plucky though they may
               be small,
Standing by their guns, ever staunch and true.
And if there's a "Rantom"
Well? the gallant little Bantam
Will help to pull old England through.

They will pot this Potsdam Butcher and his
               murderous gang,
And his thieving Crown Prince too,
The "Gallant little Bantams" will get at him with
               a bang.
Tho' they are scarcely five feet two,
With a man like "Colonel Wilkie"
To lead them in the fight
They will prove their training was not all in vain.
They will smash this "Germ(hun) Boss"
And his cherished "Iron Cross"
The Bantams don't forget Louvain.

'All British Boys' by Cpl (later Sergeant) Jack Franklin, 17th Welsh. (Author)

among the troops distributing pipes and good wishes, one could not fail to appreciate what was lacking in today's proceedings.[223]

On 28 May 1916 an advanced party of officers left for France and the division followed three days later.

In summary, this chapter has established a previously absent history of 119 Brigade for the period before it became a part of 40th Division and added detail for the period from September 1915 up to its departure for France. The brigade's origins within the Welsh Army Corps at the commencement of recruiting bantams to the Fifth New Army and some of the issues surrounding recruiting and equipping bantams in 1915 have been explored. The individual histories of the four infantry battalions have been presented along with quantitative data on geographic and social origins of the men establishing that the brigade was indeed strongly 'Welsh' and composed almost entirely of men from the labouring classes. Data on language and religion were also used to augment the picture of a formation with a distinct national identity. Quantitative data was again used, along with examples to establish the disciplinary records of the battalions while they remained in the United Kingdom and showing that, compared with other brigades for which data has been published, discipline in the 119 Brigade was good. It is suggested that the extended period of training undergone by the brigade likely enhanced *esprit de corps* and how, at the end of that training, the Welsh identity of the formation was still to the fore.

---

223 *Western Mail*, 26 May 1916.

2

The Brigade Goes to War

Chapter 1 established a chronology for the formation of 119 Brigade, explored the geographical and social composition of its other ranks and examined how it was equipped and trained prior to despatch to a theatre of war. This chapter will focus on the leaders that took the unit to France in June 1916 and examine its development and record in the field before the arrival of Frank Crozier as GOC in November 1916. Evidence will be presented to establish whether the Welsh identity of the ORs was shared by the battalion officers and data presented to illuminate the disciplinary record of the brigade on active service. The record of the brigade's participation in the controversial tactic of trench raiding will be examined and the perception of the value of bantam formations as fighting units challenged.

Senior Officers

Changes were made to the senior command before the brigade proceeded overseas. At the battalion level two of the four battalions lost their existing commanding officers. The first to go was the OC 19th RWF, Lieutenant-Colonel Owen Lloyd Jones Evans, who as a prominent landowner and Welsh speaker had proved useful during the recruiting of the battalion but whose total lack of combat experience and age (he was 59) marked him for replacement. According to Beynon Davies, who had noticed his age, he was also 'uncommunicative'.[1] His successor was very different. Forty-one year old Lieutenant-Colonel Bryan John Jones (1874-1918) had spent his army career in the Leinster Regiment rising from second-lieutenant to major and gaining combat experience in South Africa from 1899-1902 where he was mentioned in despatches. He later acted as adjutant to the Royal Meath Militia (1905-1909) and to the 1st Leinsters (1910-1912) and was a dedicated professional soldier. He was slightly wounded on 22 January 1915 at Dickebusch and probably wounded again later in the year.[2] The citation for the later bar to his DSO gives an impression of his capabilities:

> For conspicuous gallantry and devotion to duty on the 14th of October 1918, in the Moorseele Sector. When it was impossible to get accurate information on the location of the troops during the attack, he went forward and organised his battalion while fighting in the streets of Moorseele, and personally placed his machine guns in action, causing the village to be soon cleared of the enemy. He personally shot a machine gunner who was holding up the advance.

---

1 Evan Beynon Davies, *Ar Orwel Pell* (Llandysul: Gomer Press, 1965), p.28.
2 *De Ruvigny's Roll of Honour, 1914-1919*, (5) p.97. Bryan John Jones (1874-1918) see Appendix VI.

His fine example and leadership were mainly responsible for the great success obtained by his battalion.³

He assumed command of the 19th RWF on 12 November 1915.

In the 18th Welsh, the fifty-two year old Lieutenant-Colonel Homfray was cast in the same mould as Evans. A well-known figure in the county of Glamorgan, he had proved useful in recruiting the battalion, had not seen Regular Army service since 1889 and had no experience of combat. His replacement was the newly-promoted forty-eight year old Lieutenant-Colonel Richard Stirling Grant-Thorold (1868-1953) whose military career had been long but fragmented.⁴ The son of Alexander William Thorold Grant, one time High Sherriff of Lincolnshire, after leaving Eton in 1886 he attended the Royal Military College and was commissioned lieutenant in the RWF in February 1888. He resigned his commission in January 1891 but joined the South African Light Horse as a lieutenant at the outbreak of the Boer War and was mentioned in dispatches.⁵ He left South Africa in March 1902 and in May was commissioned as captain in the Lincolnshire Imperial Yeomanry. He resigned in March 1905 and seems to have travelled.⁶ It was reported that in 1913 he was a breeder of polo ponies in British Columbia and was importing stallions from Australia.⁷ At the outbreak of the Great War he was in Australia where he applied for and was granted a commission as captain in C Company of the Australian Naval and Military Expeditionary Force that captured the German colony of Papua New Guinea; after which he was appointed district administrator for New Ireland.⁸ In March 1915 his commission was 'terminated' (the record gives no details) and he returned to Britain on 25 April 1915 to be appointed temporary major in the 8th Royal Fusiliers in May 1915 just before the battalion sailed for France.⁹ He was wounded and invalided home in August 1915.¹⁰ He took command of the 18th Welsh on 17 January 1916, saw the battalion to France and stayed with it until he was wounded on 3 January 1917. He did not hold a field command again and relinquished his commission with the rank of colonel on 27 March 1919.¹¹

Lieutenant-Colonels Wilkie (age 47) and Pope (age 40) took the 17th Welsh and the 12th SWB respectively to France. The four battalion commanders were all in their forties with varying degrees of experience of combat, three had served in South Africa where two were mentioned in despatches.

At brigade level Rodney Style had commanded since the brigade was formally constituted but he would not lead it on active service. In retrospect his appointment can be seen as a stop-gap;

---

3 *The Edinburgh Gazette*, Supplement, 8 October 1919, p.3188.
4 The account of his appointment appearing in the *Western Mail*, 17 January 1916, is a case of mistaken identity and actually refers to H.D. Thorold 'who until recently was in charge of the military records office in Lichfield'. Brevet Colonel Hayford Douglas Thorold (1861-1934), West Riding Regiment, had seen service in South Africa.
5 Queens South Africa Medal (six clasps) and the Kings South Africa Medal (one clasp).
6 'Outgoing and Incoming Passenger Lists' <http://www.ancestry.co.uk> (accessed 1 April 2015). In August 1895 he departed London for Adelaide, a trip he made several times. He also made at least two journeys to New Brunswick. *The British Museum* <http://www.britishmuseum.org/research/collection_online/search.aspx?people=34901&peoA=34901-3-9 > (accessed 1 April 2015) indicates that in 1911 he donated two items from Papua New Guinea to the British Museum.
7 *Yorkshire Post and Leeds Intelligencer*, 5 February 1913 and *Western Daily Press*, 13 February 1913.
8 <http://recordsearch.naa.gov.au/NameSearch/Interface/ItemDetail.aspx?Barcode=4663024&isAv=N> (accessed 12 April 2015).
9 'Incoming passenger lists' <http:// www.ancestry.co.uk>, accessed 1 April 2015.
10 *Western Mail*, 31 January 1916.
11 In July 1917 he was sent by Eastern Command to inspect the 2nd Cambridgeshire Volunteers. *Cambridge Daily News*, 25 July 1917.

with little combat experience, none of it in South Africa and none above the rank of captain, he could not have been expected to continue on into action. His role was to bring the discipline of the regular army to a crowd of inexperienced volunteers. Captain Whitworth (12th SWB) noted that Style was:

> The old type of regular soldier ... pre-eminently a 'pukka-sahib' himself he did not understand the material the New Army was accepting as officers ... this led to much unnecessary friction and discontent ... The GOC became intensely unpopular and young officers were disheartened instead of encouraged ... [yet] the strictness and severity of the GOC was invaluable in removing the rough edges off two battalions where the lack of discipline was notorious ... It is true that in war ... the individual must always be sacrificed to efficiency and the attainment of any necessary object, and this was one of the stern lessons of warfare taught by the GOC before he left the Brigade. Later we learned that he was suffering from an internal complaint but he did not allow this to interfere with his work, and, although harsh and unsympathetic to individuals, his dignified presence always demanded respect as well as fear.[12]

Even without a possible health issue it is clear that Style was not the man to take the brigade to war. His replacement took command on 8 May 1916 just three weeks before the brigade joined the BEF.

At fifty-four Charles Stewart Prichard (1861-1942) was a year older than Rodney Style (showing that age was not necessarily an impediment for command) but his background was a marked contrast. Educated at Marlborough he joined the Northamptonshire Regiment from Sandhurst as a subaltern in 1882 and became captain in 1889. He served with distinction in South Africa, was mentioned in despatches twice and received the DSO. He was wounded in November 1914 and again at Neuve Chapelle on 12 March 1915 while commanding the 2nd Northamptonshire Regiment, became a Companion of the Order of the Bath (Military) on 9 December that year and was mentioned in despatches.[13] Captain Whitworth's view of the new GOC was considerably more positive than the last:

> [He] was a man who's equal for charm of personality I have rarely if ever met in any sphere of life. He was older than most Brigadiers appointed to the New Army but a man of great activity ... To many he had two great characteristics as a General; his study of the men, their capabilities and necessities, was incessant, and like all great soldiers the idea of the impossible was abhorrent to him ... in all things a very high standard was demanded by the GOC and this was certainly true of his inspections.[14]

The first brigade major also impressed Captain Whitworth who described him as 'brilliant' and giving 'invaluable lectures on tactics and training'.[15] Robert Emile Shepherd Prentice (1872-1953) took up his appointment on 22 July 1915 (the day after Style became the first GOC 119 Brigade) and stayed only until 24 October 1915 when he returned to the Western Front to command his battalion (2nd HLI). He was a veteran of the BEF's 1914 campaign and had been wounded by shrapnel on 8 April 1915 a few days after taking up an appointment as Brigade Major, 2

---

12 RRW Museum, Brecon: Memoir of Captain Eric E. A. Whitworth, pp.523-524.
13 Charles Stewart Prichard (1861-1942). See Appendix VI.
14 RRW Museum, Whitworth memoir, p.525.
15 Ibid, p.524.

Brigade, 1st Division. His appointment to 119 Brigade was only a short one but his injection of recent practical experience was clearly welcome.[16]

The brigade major who succeeded Prentice and went to war with 119 Brigade was Captain Arthur Granville Soames (1886-1962), Coldstream Guards. Soames was a member of an upwardly mobile family. His father was a prosperous brewer and Arthur was educated at Eton, attended the Royal Military College, commissioned second-lieutenant, Coldstream Guards, in 1905 and lieutenant in 1907. He was appointed adjutant at the Guards Depot in September 1913 and Staff Captain, 4 Infantry Brigade, 2nd Division, on 25 August 1914. Soames was wounded, probably in the ferocious fighting on the Aisne in September, returned to England, promoted to captain in February 1915 and appointed Brigade Major, 119 Brigade on 25 October 1915. His practical experience enabled him to write the twelve-page *Standing Orders for War, 119th Infantry Brigade*.[17] He was still in post when Frank Crozier took command of the brigade on 20 November 1916.[18]

Brig-Gen C. S. Prichard on the crossing to France, June 1916. Pencil sketch by 2/Lt Morris Meredith Williams. (Williams Collection)

Battalion Officers

So far, we have examined the other ranks of 119 Brigade, the brigade staff and the commanding officers of the four infantry battalions that made up the brigade. This section will look at the less senior officers and their origins and form a view of their 'Welshness'.

Writing in 1917 Captain Eric Whitworth looked back at the system of officer recruitment in place in 1915:

> Commissions were granted on the recommendation of Colonels after the applicants had been given a personal interview. Some of these had served several months in the ranks, others came

---

16　Robert Emile Shepherd Prentice CB CMG DSO (1872-1953). See Appendix VI.
17　Copy in the Williams Papers. The booklet mentions *Divisional War Standing Orders* issued by 40th Division HQ. I have been unable to locate a copy.
18　Compiled from the *London Gazette*. Soames' wounding was reported in the *Aberdeen Journal*, 3 October 1914 and must have occurred shortly prior to that date (there is no 4 Brigade HQ War Diary for this period). See Appendix VI.

straight from a school OTC, while not a few were men who, however suitable they might be, had done no previous military training at all. In all these cases there was no system of intensive training from the point of view of making them efficient officers before they joined their battalions; nor was there any opportunity of seeing whether those who had served in the ranks were really suitable to hold commissions … the training which these officers received consisted of a general course of instruction immediately after they were granted commissions.[19]

Whitworth makes no observations on the geographical origins of these officers nor on their occupations in civil life. In order to address this an analysis of surviving officer personal files in TNA series WO 339 and WO 374 was carried out.[20] A total of 209 personal files of officers who served in units of 119 Brigade 1914-1918 were identified and examined. Of these 156 belong to officers from the four original battalions of the brigade. How many of these were Welsh? County of birth is only given in fifty per cent of cases and analysis shows a high number of Welsh-born officers (67.5%) but almost all the records give residency information (146) and this shows that sixty-one per cent of the officers found were Welsh residents (Table 12). The figures vary across the battalions with only fifty per cent of 12th SWB officers Welsh resident – going a little way to confirming Second-Lieutenant J. Saunders Lewis' observation that 'there are more English (and one or two Irish) than Welsh officers in the [12th] SWB'.[21] Surprisingly the 19th RWF, the least Welsh battalion in its other ranks, has the largest number of Welsh residents amongst its officers at more than seventy-three per cent (73.7%). The battalion also has more Welsh counties represented and although the number of officers from Glamorgan in all battalions confirms the pre-eminent role of that county in recruiting, in the 19th RWF the rural counties of North Wales predominate. The 17th Welsh have sixty-one per cent of officers Welsh residents (61.3%) and the 18th Welsh sixty-five per cent (65.9%). A surviving post-war address list for the Officers' Association of the 18th Welsh gives a lower (although still high) figure of fifty-four per cent of officers with Welsh addresses.[22] As a comparison Timothy Bowman's work on the 36th (Ulster) Division, a formation with strong political and geographical affiliations, shows that eighty-one per cent of its officers were resident in the nine counties of Ulster.

Both Gary Sheffield and Timothy Bowman have shown how the perception of the wartime officer class as being dominated by the products of the public school system is incorrect.[23] Nevertheless, the Officer Training Corps, created in 1908 and consisting in 1914 of twenty-four university-based units and 166 public school and grammar school-based units, was an important source of officers. Between August 1915 and March 1915 20,577 men with OTC backgrounds were commissioned.[24]

---

19 RRW Museum, Whitworth Memoir, p.517.
20 The files were identified by extracting names of officer fatalities for the four battalions from *Officers Died in the Great War* and then supplementing this list with names found in a range of sources including battalion war diaries, nominal rolls (where they exist) and the Army List. By no means all of the names have a corresponding file. Records of most members of the Territorial Force and officers who served beyond 1921 (still held by the Ministry of Defence) are absent. Some of the surviving files have almost no useful information, having been severely 'weeded' in the past.
21 Mair Saunders Jones, Ned Thomas and Harri Pritchard Jones (eds), *Letters to Margaret Gilcreist* (Cardiff: University of Wales Press, 1993), p.158.
22 IWM Documents, 72/11/1 Gibbs Papers.
23 Gary Sheffield, *Leadership in the Trenches: Officer-man Relations, Morale and Discipline in the British Army in the Era of the First World War* (London: Macmillan, 2000). Timothy Bowman, 'Officering Kitchener's Armies: a case study of the 36th (Ulster) Division', *War in History*, 16 (2), 2009, pp.189-212. See also Keith Simpson, 'The Officers' in Ian F. W. Beckett and Keith Simpson (eds.), *A Nation in Arms: the British Army in the First World War* (Manchester: Manchester University Press, 1985), pp.63-96.
24 Peter Simkins, *Kitchener's Army: The Raising of the New Armies 1914-1916* (Manchester: Manchester Unversity Press, 1988), p.221.

The number of OTC men available seems, not unexpectedly, to have decreased markedly in 1915. In the personal files identified at TNA of 108 commissions to units of 119 Brigade in 1915 just eighteen (17%) can be identified with men with experience at an OTC unit.[25] These are not distributed evenly across the brigade: the 17th Welsh and 19th RWF having just two each while the 18th Welsh and 12th SWB each had seven. The lack of military knowledge amongst the officers of the brigade must have been conspicuous. This is in marked contrast with the situation in 1916/17 after the introduction of Officer Cadet Battalions in February 1916 to address the training of officers. In 1916-17 thirty of forty-seven commissions to the brigade's units (64%) are known to have been given to OCB graduates while a further eight went to OTC members – a vast improvement in the number of trained officers.

Table 12: Geographical origin of officers by residence (sample sizes in brackets)

Welsh County	17th Welsh (31)	18th Welsh (41)	19th RWF (38)	12th SWB (36)
Anglesey	–	–	3	–
Brecknock	–	–	1	–
Caernarfon	1	–	9	–
Carmarthen	–	3	3	–
Cardigan	–	1	2	–
Denbigh	–	–	2	2
Glamorgan	17	19	8	6
Monmouth	–	4	–	10
Pembroke	1	–	–	–
Non-Welsh Resident	12	14	10	18
% Welsh Resident	61.3%	65.9%	73.7%	50%

Source: TNA: WO 339 and WO 374 Series.

Gary Sheffield has pointed out that analysis of the civilian occupations of army officers carried out at demobilization showed that the largest numbers belonged to the 'commercial and clerical' (27%), 'students and teachers' (18%), 'professional men' (15%) and 'engineering' (8%) classes. In 119 Brigade a similar picture emerges when the 127 records for the officers of the four original battalions that give an occupation are examined. Schoolteachers and students are thirty-one per cent of commissioned officers while clerks / bank clerks / bank cashiers make up thirty four per cent, engineers and shopkeepers each make up five per cent. If the records examined are restricted to those commissioned up to 1916 (91) the picture changes with schoolteacher/students making up thirty-three per cent and clerks/bank clerks making up twenty-four per cent (29% if civil servants are included). The officers of 119 Brigade were overwhelmingly middle class throughout the war. It is noteworthy that the single commissioned miner, labourer, painter and cotton-spinner all came through the OCB route.

Bowman's study profiles the ages of the 36th (Ulster) Division officers and here a considerable difference with the ages of 119 Brigade officers emerges. The Ulstermen had more older officers (Table 13) and this may be due in part to the deliberate selection 'of older men who had held

---

25 This would tend to support Timothy Bowman's observation that 'previous OTC membership was not as important a prerequisite for a commission as some historians have suggested'. Bowman, 'Officering Kitchener's Armies', p.211.

positions of responsibility in the business world'.[26] The men of the 119 Brigade in contrast were clearly younger even allowing for Bowman's dataset containing more of the senior officers of the 36th and 38th Divisions. Despite its small size the sample of data from 38th Division suggests that its age profile is more akin to that of 119 Brigade. Despite the first impression of the brigade's officer corps consisting of a large group of young, inexperienced officers a surprising number of them had gained some military knowledge before commissioning. Of 109 commissions given before the brigade left Britain no less than seventy-seven (69%) went to men who had already enlisted. Seventeen of these came from the Territorial Force – mainly the Welsh Horse, Glamorgan Yeomanry and field artillery units while the largest single number (20) came from the 13th RWF which had started recruiting in September 1914. The surplus men from the 13th RWF were the basis of the 16th RWF which contributed a further five men for commission in 119 Brigade. Four men came from the 14th Royal Warwickshire Regiment (raised September 1914) and three came from the 21st Royal Fusiliers (Public Schools Battalion).

Table 13: Comparative age profiles (sample sizes in brackets)

Year class	36th (Ulster) Division (228)	38th (Welsh) Division (37)	119 Brigade (144)
1855-1859	3.0% (7)	2.7% (1)	–
1860-1864	3.9% (9)	2.7% (1)	–
1865-1869	7.5% (17)	–	–
1870-1874	7.0 % (16)	2.7% (1)	–
1875-1879	13.6% (31)	2.7% (1)	2.8% (4)
1880-1884	19.7% (45)	21.6% (8)	11.1% (16)
1885-1889	17.1% (39)	16.2% (6)	23.6% (34)
1890-1894	22.8% (52)	37.8% (14)	45.8% (66)
1895-1899	5.3% (12)	13.5% (5)	16.7% (24)

Source: Bowman, 'Officering Kitchener's Armies' for 36th and 38th Division data.

Selection seems to have been in the hands of the OC battalion and most early applications seen were approved by the divisional general Sir Ivor Philipps. John Saunders Lewis, a student at Liverpool University, had enlisted in the 19th King's (Liverpool Regiment) in the early days of the war. In May 1915 he wrote that his application for a commission 'kept me very busy, so many forms I had to sign, so many letters to write, so many officers to interview; the Vice-Chancellor has given me a recommendation but it will be many weeks or months perhaps before I hear anything of it'.[27] A little later 'The preliminary part of my application for a commission is now over, and if it were not I should myself annul everything, for I am tired of the endless interviewing and correspondence. Yesterday, however, I was called to the Colonel and he seems willing to send my papers off. Thank the Lord'. At the end of the month he was called to an interview with Lieutenant-Colonel Pope, OC 12th SWB. '[I] had my interview today, a horrid one, was sent from the room, thought it was all over and almost felt thankful, called back and found myself accepted, and sent by the next train back to London to buy my outfit … They gave me £50 to do it.'[28]

26　Bowman, 'Officering Kitchener's Armies', p.212.
27　Jones et al, *Letters to Margaret Gilcreist*, pp.101-109.
28　Ibid.

Eric Whitworth was a territorial officer, one of the men who did have a public school background and had an even more difficult time than Lewis. When war broke out he was an assistant master at Rugby School, and in December 1914 found himself at Southend as a second-lieutenant with the 14th (Reserve) Battalion The Rifle Brigade. He was obviously not happy with his lot but used his connections:

> I met Lt Colonel Haig-Browne who had commanded the Lancing contingent of the OTC and I told him of the conditions at Southend. His brother-in-law, Lt Colonel A. Pope, was raising a service battalion of the South Wales Borderers and was very short of officers with any experience at all to take command of the companies, and he offered me command of a company with the rank of Captain. My colonel refused his consent to the transfer and I demanded an interview with the Brigadier. I pointed out that I had two years' service as a Territorial Officer, including attachments to the Northamptonshire and Warwickshire regiments and that the transfer offered me not only promotion but the chance to make use of my previous service. The Brigadier no doubt realised the unsatisfactory state of affairs in the 14th Rifle Brigade and authorised the transfer.[29]

These were the type of men, overwhelmingly Welsh, educated, middle class, inexperienced and in their twenties and thirties, who would lead companies and platoons in France. The challenge of rubbing along with fellow officers who might not be the type of men one would normally have as close acquaintances proved difficult for some. Francophile Second-Lieutenant Morris Meredith Williams, 17th Welsh, wrote 'the surroundings and pleasant kind French people seemed to bring out the dull, ill-conditioned vulgarity of our officers as never before. I never felt so heartily ashamed of them, and sick of the lot'.[30] Shortly afterwards he wrote, 'The greatest trial of the campaign so far is being forced to live at such close quarters with people one despises and dislikes. Like all that class, they do not improve on acquaintance!'[31] The bonds of comradeship had still to be forged on the battlefield.

Early Days in France

After crossing the English Channel 119 Brigade completed its concentration in the French villages of Bourecq and St Hilaire (just west of Lillers in the Pas de Calais) on 5 June 1916 and was attached to 1st Division, I Corps, for instruction. The system for inducting new divisions to the practicalities of trench warfare had been evolving through the previous year and usually involved attaching units from the newly-arrived division to units of one or more (often two) experienced divisions in a relatively quiet sector of the front. When the first division of the New Armies, 9th (Scottish) Division, arrived in France in May 1915 it received its induction in the line from 6th Division to which each of its brigades was attached for two days. Following additional intensive training out of the line in the skills of bombing, the division relieved 7th Division in the line near Festubert on

---

29 RRW Museum: Whitworth Memoir. Eric Edward Allen Whitworth MC (1889-1971. See Appendix VI. Whitworth had been commissioned from the Cambridge University OTC as second-lieutenant in the Territorial Force in February 1913 for service with the Rugby School OTC. He was perhaps over-emphasising his 'two years' experience'. Alan Roderick Haig-Brown (1877-1918) was indeed Pope's brother-in-law and a fellow master in a public school. See Appendix VI.
30 Williams Papers: Letter to his wife Alice, 3 June 1916.
31 Ibid. Letter, 22 June 1916.

the night of 1/2 July.³² By the time that Frank Crozier arrived in France in October 1915 as 2iC 9th Royal Irish Rifles [RIRifles], 107 Brigade, 36th (Ulster) Division, GHQ had decided to augment the usual five day attachment to an experienced division (in this case the 4th and 48th Divisions) by removing one brigade for a longer attachment to another division and replacing it temporarily with a brigade of regulars from that division. Thus Crozier found himself along with 107 Brigade in 4th Division for two months until the brigades were returned to their original divisions.³³ This highly disruptive system did not last long. When 38th (Welsh) Division arrived in December 1915 its battalions were attached in rotation over three weeks to the Guards and 19th Divisions in XI Corps, followed by attachment by complete brigades for a further two weeks before relieving 19th Division and taking over its sector of the line on 24 January 1916.³⁴

By the time that the bantams of 35th Division arrived at the front in February 1916 the induction period seems to have shortened and the division's units were attached to 19th and 38th Divisions in XI Corps, for just ten days before relieving 19th Division in the line on 7 March.³⁵ The transfer of 40th Division to France was delayed by the need to absorb and train the replacement battalions in 120 and 121 Brigades and so it was the 41st Division that arrived first. On 14 May 1916 their first parties were despatched to the front for instruction in II Corps sector. Two sections per company were given two days supervised induction in the trenches that their respective platoons would eventually occupy. By 1 June 41st Division had relieved the 9th (Scottish) Division in the line.³⁶ Trench induction followed a similar although slightly extended pattern for 40th Division. Starting on 8 June two battalions of 119 Brigade spent two days paired with men from the brigades of 1st Division at a one to one ratio. Ruggles-Brise reported to his wife, 'Tomorrow I am sending two of my little bantam Battns up to the trenches for instruction. I think they will get on all right. They go up by twos until they are all finished'.³⁷ The initial two days was followed by a further two days with the battalions attached on a platoon to platoon basis. Once all battalions had completed this they were given a further two days in the front or support line retaining their company organisation. By 5 July 1916 40th Division had relieved 1st Division in the I Corps right sector. 119 Brigade manned the Calonne section, 121 Brigade was responsible for the Maroc section and 120 Brigade formed the reserve.³⁸ With an adjustment to extend the length of front occupied, 119 Brigade would spend the next four months in this area.

Things had not started well for the brigade. When the 17th Welsh and 19th RWF left for the trenches it was noted that after ten miles their march discipline was 'very bad'. This did not escape the GOC Division who displayed some sympathy: 'our little bantams did not do a very good march and they make them march much too far at the finish ... This is rather annoying as I thought that I had taken every precaution'.³⁹ The records show that there was another, more serious, issue relating to discipline and training. During its first tour in the trenches the brigade suffered a total of nineteen killed and fifty-four wounded. The brigade war diary notes that in seven of these cases (almost 10%) the causes were 'accidental'. Some occurred in the front line, others during training. The war diary of 12th SWB notes that on 22 June 'a sniper (Kemp) coming into a dugout in a shaky

---

32 John Ewing, *The History of the 9th (Scottish) Division 1914-1919* (London: John Murray, 1921), pp.12-15.
33 Cyril Falls, *The History of the 36th (Ulster) Division* (London: Constable, 1922), pp.24-28.
34 TNA: WO 95/2539/1. War Diary 38th (Welsh) Division General Staff.
35 H.M. Davson, *The History of the 35th Division in the Great War* (London: Sifton, Praed & Co., 1926), pp.8-9.
36 TNA WO 95/2617/1: War Diary 41st Division General Staff.
37 Blair Castle Archives: Ruggles-Brise correspondence.
38 TNA WO 95/2604: War Diary 119 Brigade HQ.
39 Blair Castle Archives: Ruggles-Brise correspondence.

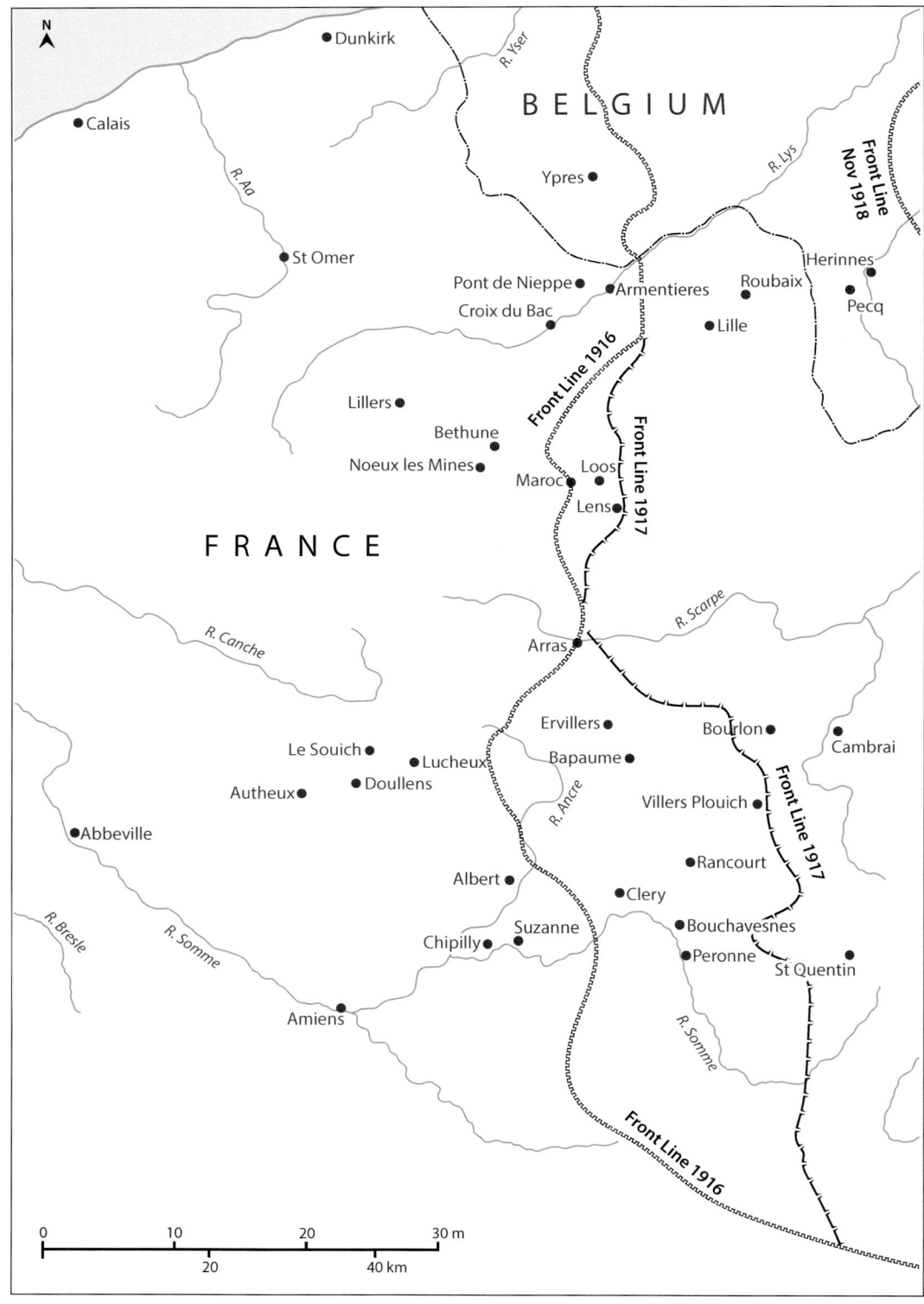

Map 1 Locations associated with 119 Brigade, 1916-18.

state accidentally shot Pte Oliver who died later'.[40] The death of Lieutenant Alfred Newman, 12th SWB, on the bombing range on 1 July 1916 provides a useful case study of the hazards encountered there. The statement provided by Captain J.W. Foreman, 12th SWB, details the incident:

> On the afternoon of July 1st I accompanied A Coy 12th S W Borderers to a field in the neighbourhood of Marles Les Mines for the purpose of carrying out live bomb practise under the supervision of the Batt Bombing Officer Lt A Newman 12 SWB. About 3pm it was Private E Wesson's turn to throw. He was given a bomb and fully instructed by Lt Newman what to do with it. How to hold the bomb. How to draw the pin and where to throw it. The man drew the pin and threw the bomb which hit the parapet in front of him and rolled back into the trench at the man's feet. I am sure that his hand did not hit the back of the parapet. The man in accordance with the instructions given stood still and upright. Lt Newman who was standing to the right rear of the man stepped forward, stooped and picked up the bomb and threw it in a half right direction. The bomb fell on the parapet and again rolled in to the trench between Lt Newman and myself. Seeing this Lt Newman immediately doubled off to the left and I doubled to the right. When I last saw Wesson he was still standing at attention as if rooted to the spot and in my opinion impeded Lt Newman from getting into the sap. Before I got to the bend in the trench the bomb exploded and I felt a burning sensation in my back. As soon as the explosion was over Capt Whitworth and I rushed along the trench and found Lt Newman lying on his back with Wesson lying on his side on top of Lt Newman.

Both men died. A statement from Captain E.E.A.Whitworth commanding A Company confirmed the general sequence of events:

> About 6 men had thrown a bomb when No 23446 Pte Wesson, E. 12th SWB whose turn it was to throw after extracting the safety pin dropped the bomb when his hand was in the backward position for throwing. I saw Lt Newman throw himself forward and pick it up and throw it. I then lowered myself in the trench and waited for the explosion not knowing that an accident had occurred. On stepping forward after the explosion, I saw Lt Newman lying in the trench wounded and apparently unconscious together with Pte Wesson in the same condition.

Platoon Sergeant R.D. Howell was clear that the man's hand had hit the back of the trench:

> After about six men had thrown it was Pte Wesson's turn to throw. Capt Foreman 12th SWB warned him to come forward a little so that he would not catch the back of the trench. He went forward. He then started to throw the bomb but his hand caught the back of the trench and he dropped the bomb. I saw Lt Newman make a dive for the bomb. He slipped on to his knees and I saw him throw the bomb as he was on his knees. I saw the bomb hit the parapet and roll back into the trench. I then took cover and heard the explosion…

The situation did not escape the attentions of the divisional commander who appended a note to the reports: 'AAG, First Army. This is the 2nd accident of the sort that has occurred lately. I am

---

40 TNA WO 95/2606: 23721 Pte Ernest Kemp of Hunslett Carr was tried by Field General Court Martial on 29 June 1916 for the manslaughter of 23497 Pte John Charles Oliver of Aberbargoed. He was sentenced to one year's imprisonment but the sentence is recorded as quashed – TNA WO 213. Kemp was killed by shellfire on 9 July 1916 and is now buried at Loos British Cemetery. Pte Oliver is buried in Bully-Grenay Communal Cemetery British Extension.

taking up the whole question as to how to prevent a recurrence. Hitherto, the orders already issued have been found of little worth'.⁴¹ The bombing range was undoubtedly a dangerous place. On 20 August Second-Lieutenant P.J. Farmer, 17th Welsh, and one man were accidentally wounded at the brigade bombing school despite the earlier attention of the GOC division.⁴²

There were other indicators of the inexperience of the brigade. The brigade war diary implies a degree of annoyance in an entry for 20 July: 'Frequent vacillation on the subject of reliefs as there was for the move from Bully Grenay and vicinity (June 22-25) to Marle-les-Mines and from the latter place to Les Brebis (July 3-4). In this instance 4 separate and distinct rosters have been issued the 4th being definitely approved. Since then neither of the Brigade reliefs due to take place (121st-120th Brigade and 120th-119th Brigade) have happened on the days scheduled.' And the next day: 'Orders, counter-orders and disorders resultant once more. 120th Bde is now to take over all Calonne Section on 22nd and half Maroc Section on 21st. Two battalions 119th Bde are to be in Brigade Reserve to 120th and 121st Bdes respectively'.⁴³ Inexperience showed in other ways. In the early hours of 8 July following heavy German shelling to the left of the brigade's sector Brigade HQ received an SOS message from the 17th Welsh that quickly resulted in a protective artillery barrage being fired but which proved to be a false alarm. Later that night the same battalion passed on a false gas alarm 'despite it not being a gas wind' which caused the adjacent 12th SWB to don gas hoods. On 10 July 'there was another gas alarm owing to Brigade Operations sending out 'Gas Alarm' rather than "Gas Alert".⁴⁴ Other matters were actioned successfully. A conference at divisional HQ attended by the GSO1, GSO2, three brigade majors, CRE and the OCs of 255 Tunnelling Company, RE and an un-named tunnelling company resolved that all requests for infantry working parties for RE purposes should be channelled via the divisional HQ for apportioning to the brigades and that the maximum demand on a brigade in reserve would be 500 men per day.⁴⁵

Administrative problems notwithstanding, how did the brigade settle down to fight the war? As far as the British Official History is concerned, after recording the arrival of 40th Division in France, it was invisible and it may have been this period that led its men naming it as the 'forgotten fortieth'.⁴⁶ From its arrival to the end of October 1916 it was located in the old Loos battlefield in an area of mining villages dominated by spoil heaps or *crassiers*. The village houses provided billets for units out of the line and even those in support could use their cellars for comfort and protection. During the summer of 1916 I Corps was responsible for the line from Loos to the La Bassée canal which it held initially with three divisions. The southernmost (right) sector was allocated to 40th Division. Once it was given responsibility for a sector the division followed standard practice and normally placed two of its brigades in the line and one in reserve.⁴⁷ Each brigade then placed two battalions in the front line, one in support and one in reserve. Each battalion spent four to six days in its allotted role before it was relieved and rotated through the cycle of line / support /

---

41   TNA WO 339/36300: Personal file, Lieutenant Alfred Newman, 12th SWB. Newman was 23 years old. 23446 Private Wesson was 38. The first incident had taken place in 121 Brigade on 21 June 1916 when the Bombing Officer of 12th Suffolks, Captain Nisbet, and one man were accidentally wounded during bombing practice. Nisbet died from his wounds.
42   TNA WO 95/2607: War Diary 17th Welsh.
43   TNA WO95/2604: War Diary 119 Brigade HQ.
44   TNA WO 95/2604: War Diary 119 Brigade HQ; WO 95/2606. War Diary 12th SWB.
45   Ibid.
46   Sir James Edmonds, *Military Operations: France and Belgium 1916 Vol.1* (London: HMSO, 1932) p.24; Whitton, *History of the 40th Division*, p.157.
47   The extension of the divisional front in August 1916 led to all three brigades occupying the front line.

reserve.[48] A similar rotation was operated at brigade level. These reliefs required a huge effort of organisation and it is not surprising that the resulting paperwork dominates the surviving records in the brigade war diary. Reports of the brigade's actions did reach home occasionally. In July 1916 under the headline 'Brave Bantams/Praise for Welsh Miners at the Front' the *Western Mail*, published an extract from a letter written by the wife of a member of Lord Rhondda's staff (Percy Hone, Staff Captain 119 Brigade):

> It is a matter of great pride to us all how well the Welsh miners forming his brigade (Bantams all) have, so far, done. They went almost at once into action and remained in the front line trenches for a fortnight, my husband being with them for six or seven hours at a stretch. He spoke of their undaunted cheerfulness, their pluck and daring, and of how they would march back singing at the top of their voices, and highly pleased with themselves. One of the first nights two of the little men went out into No-man's Land, and seeing two six-feet Bosches, lay in wait for them: each marked his man and then bayoneted him. The brigade major, a Guardsman [Soames], has great faith in the Welsh miners: my husband's pride in them, however, is beyond words.[49]

Second-Lieutenant M.M. Williams noted that 'I have never seen 'Percy' since coming out. I don't suppose he has ever been to the trenches. They laugh at him rather. Some rot about the Brigade appeared in a S. Wales paper and people say Mrs Hone put it in'.[50]

Following their loss of ground to the BEF in the battle of Loos in September and October 1915 the German army had consolidated and strengthened its new line to the south and east of the village of Loos. It was here that 119 Brigade gained experience and suffered the first losses from its ranks while thirty miles to the south the BEF was engaged in the Somme offensive. On 9 July the war diary of the 17th Welsh noted Captain H.N. Sheppard, CO D Company as 'wounded' much to the delight of Second-Lieutenant M.M. Williams who did not get on with Sheppard. He wrote 'Sheppard has gone home "collapsed!!" so life will be a good deal pleasanter … It is only what I expected and you predicted. He was putting the whisky away at a great rate lately'.[51]

Despite its use as an area where new divisions could be introduced to trench warfare the area around Loos was far from 'quiet' and the British lines were frequently subjected to artillery bombardment. The 19th RWF lost four men killed by shell fire between 10-14 June and another five between 18-20 June. Artillery, particularly trench mortars would cause the majority of the brigade's casualties while it occupied this sector. The 12th SWB lost Captain H.C. Rees on 5 August to a direct hit by an 'aerial dart' (*Granatenwerfer*). He was 'an able and popular officer, much loved by his men, and his death will be greatly felt by all of us'.[52] However much the brigade's units might wish to exact revenge on the enemy, the BEF had proved in 1915 that this was not favourable ground for a major offensive and neither side had any such plans but, by the summer of 1916, the BEF had developed trench-raiding tactics, now well-established, for harassing the enemy, gaining intelligence and causing him casualties.

---

48 This was the usual arrangements but local conditions and the lengthening and adjustment of corps, division and brigade frontages occasionally resulted in all three brigades manning the line each with three battalions up and one contributing to the division reserve.
49 *Western Mail*, 1 July 1916. There is no corroboration for this incident.
50 Williams Papers, Letter to his wife, 11 July 1916.
51 Ibid, Letter 10 July 1916. Henry Nathaniel Sheppard (1878-1952). Sheppard was dismissed the Service by sentence of General Court-martial, December 1916. See Appendix VI.
52 TNA WO 95/2606: War Diary 12th SWB. Henry Charles Rees (1883-1916). See Appendix VI.

The Double Crassier, Loos, seen from Maroc, October 1916. Pencil sketch by 2/Lt Morris Meredith Williams. (Williams Collection)

Ration party, Maroc, 1916. Pencil sketch by 2/Lt Morris Meredith Williams. (Williams Collection)

Tony Ashworth examined trench raids as one element of his survey of the 'live and let live' system that evolved at times on all fronts during the war.[53] Anthony Saunders' work looked in more detail at raiding and has described the development raiding of tactics and how raids on enemy trenches were initially promoted by GHQ in 1915 'since they relieve monotony and improve the moral[e] of our troops, while they have a corresponding detrimental effect on the moral[e] of the enemy's troops and tend in a variety of ways to their exhaustion and general disquiet'. Saunders notes that there seems to be no evidence for these positive aspects of raiding nor indeed that 'enterprises of this nature constitute the most effective form of defence, since by throwing upon the enemy anxiety for his own security, they help to relieve our own troops from the wearying and demoralising effects produced by expected attacks on the part of the enemy'.[54] The probability of casualties among the raiding party and the almost certain German retaliation do not seem to feature in the concept of trench raiding. While Ashworth concluded that in non-elite units raiding had a 'good effect' on the non-raiding members of that unit, Mark Connelly acknowledged that the controversy over raiding has not yet reached a consensus among historians and that 'the issue of raiding and its value is a complex one that makes it difficult to sustain a simple and clear conclusion as to its value and impact'.[55]

Although raids had taken place in 1915 the pressures of trench construction and other duties on the limited number of troops available when not actively engaged in the year's offensives meant that raiding was not as enthusiastically promoted as GHQ had hoped. Nevertheless, some raids did take place and were given new impetus by a directive from Second Army HQ to encourage aggressive action over the winter of 1915 – 1916. Experience of best practice from these raids was accumulated, set down and circulated by the time that 119 Brigade arrived in France.

SS107 Notes on Minor Enterprises was issued by the General Staff in March 1916 and offered practical guidance 'compiled as a result of the experience gained in certain minor operations during the past few months. No definite rules for the conduct of such operations can be laid down but the suggestions contained in these notes may be useful as a guide in future enterprises'. The notes emphasise the importance of thorough preparation, reconnaissance, secrecy, training and surprise in securing a successful outcome to a raid and displays its realistic approach by suggesting that 'it is seldom advisable to persevere in a minor enterprise if the enemy are found ready and prepared'. So did the minor enterprises planned by 119 Brigade follow best practice?

Originally conceived and executed at battalion level, the approval of raids had become the responsibility of brigade and divisional staffs by 1916. In summer the strategic context of raiding was the Somme offensive. First, Second and Third Armies carried out forty-three raids in the week preceding the start of the battle on 1 July in an attempt to distract German attention from the very obvious preparations in Fourth Army's sector on the Somme. Between July and November 1916 as the battle progressed the three armies carried out three hundred and ten raids. Analysis of the formations taking part has shown that in the period July-October 1916 (when 40th Division operated as part of I Corps and had completed its induction) I Corps carried out fifty-eight of these raids – the highest number within First Army and sixteen more than XI Corps – the second most active raiders. The XI Corps Commander, Lieutenant-General Sir Richard Haking (1862-1945)

---

53 Tony Ashworth, *Trench Warfare 1914-1918: The Live and Let Live System* (London: Macmillan, 1980).
54 CGS to Army and Corps HQs 5 February 1915 quoted in Anthony Saunders, *Raiding on the Western Front* (Barnsley: Pen and Sword, 2012), p.4 and 6. For the most recent analysis of the evolution and utility of trench raiding see Kenneth Radley, *On the Dangerous Edge: British and Canadian Trench Raiding on the Western Front* (Warwick: Helion, 2018).
55 Mark Connelly, *Steady the Buffs! A Regiment, a Region & the Great War* (Oxford: Oxford University Press, 2006), p.77.

'was committed to, and always conformed with, the policies of his superiors'.[56] He enthusiastically endorsed his Commander in Chief, Sir Douglas Haig's policy 'making raiding and aggression in no man's land a key part of his general strategy of attrition'.[57] The relevance of Haking's attitude will become apparent below.

Orders to reconnoitre the German wire 'with a view to organising a raid' were received by the 17th Welsh 16 July 1916 but no raid resulted as the original plan for two simultaneous raids by the 17th and 18th Welsh were reduced to a raid by a single battalion.[58] The first raid from 40th Division's front was therefore carried out by the 18th Welsh on the night of 18/19 July in response to 119 Brigade Operational Order No.8 issued on the previous day. Captain Gibbs wrote to his sweetheart anticipating success: 'they'll be brave boys and by gum kid they're a brave lot, fine hearts and MEN'.[59]

The objects of the raid on the German front line trench just west of *Puits 16 bis* were defined as to obtain identification; to obtain prisoners and to damage the enemy's defensive system. Following reconnaissance patrols during the night of 16 July, details were discussed at a meeting held at Brigade HQ on the 17 July attended by the GOC 40th Division, his GSO1, GOC RA, BMRA, GOC 119 Brigade, BM 119 Brigade and OC Right Group RA (which covered the area to be raided). The stated impossibility of wire cutting by the artillery resulted in amended orders being issued but on the next day reports of unsuccessful wire cutting prompted a reconvened meeting.[60] The resulting amended orders were modified yet again following suggestions from the OC 18th Welsh who attended neither of the planning meetings. The scope of the orders issued by the OC 18th Welsh seems very complicated for inexperienced troops. Each party of one officer and sixteen other ranks had a range of tasks:

> The artillery barrage will commence at 12.15am and by this time you must be up to the gap in the wire. Immediately the barrage begins you will rush to your positions, 2nd Lt Salisbury with 3 bayonet men and 4 bombers will enter the trench at point G and clear trench up to point A.
>
> Simultaneously 3 bayonet men enter at point G and work down to B also 1 NCO and 4 bombers keep on parapet and work from G to B.
>
> Remaining 3 enter at G and follow others to B. Three of the six then at B will work a little way down towards C and three towards H.
>
> 2nd Lt R.D. Grossart's party:
>
> 3 bayonet men and 3 bombers will rush across trench at E and move on to D where the three bayonet men and look out, one up and one down the trench with the other between them. The 3 bombers will remain on the parapet above the bayonet men who will themselves carry bombs.
>
> Two bayonet men will enter the trench at point E and two bombers, one each side of the trench, will remain on the parapet. Three bayonet men with bombs will enter the trench at E and work towards H meeting 2nd Lt Salisbury's party when they will both move down towards D.

---

56 Michael Senior, *Haking – a Dutiful Soldier: a Study in Corps Command* (Barnsley: Pen and Sword, 2012), p.286. To be fair to XI Corps they had between two and four divisions in the line during the summer of 1916 compared with I Corps' four.
57 Ibid, p.276.
58 TNA WO 95/2607: War Diary 17th Welsh.
59 IWM: Documents 72/11/1, Gibbs Papers, letter 18 July 1916.
60 The amended orders removed any involvement by the 17th Welsh who were adjacent to the 18th Welsh.

Yellow ribbon (distinguishing badges) will be removed and pay books and any letters or papers handed in.

Wire 'footballs' will be taken for blocking trench.

Telephone wire will be run out to gap as soon as dark.

NCO and 5 scouts will move out at dark and carefully watch the gaps and report any movement there to the telephone operator.

C Coy will furnish a covering party on the right of 1 NCO and 8 men who will move out with the scouts.[61]

The raid was unsuccessful and recorded in the brigade war diary as 'a costly failure. Total bag two rifles'. There were seven casualties among the raiders including one officer wounded and one man killed. The OC 18th Welsh reported:

I regret the failure of the operation due, I consider, to the following causes:

(a) the moon was bright and it was impossible to actually go through the wire before the attack, so strands of wire left by artillery delayed some of the parties.
(b) we encountered a strong working party of Germans who were evidently there to mend their wire and although we had taken out 144 bombs these were exhausted and 2nd Lt Grossart's party had to retire for want of ammunition when he had dead and wounded Germans in the pit in front of him.
(c) 2nd Lt Salisbury being wounded left his party without a leader. This was a great misfortune.
(d) the finding of German trench running out in front of gap left out by our artillery on left caused a certain confusion as it was not shown on our aeroplane photograph and the party that should have got to point G did not get there as quickly as they should.[62]

The raid was obviously organised with the guidance of *SS107* but the bright night and the lack of reconnaissance immediately prior to the raid to confirm that the wire was cut and the gap clear of Germans were the errors of inexperienced leaders. The wounding of Second-Lieutenant Salisbury removed command and control of the bombing fight and any direction to obtain identification from German casualties. Two 'shorts' from British artillery plus enemy machine-gun fire caused casualties and speeded the withdrawal. Although there were at least two planning meetings for the raid, there is no mention of any training over similar terrain – an essential prerequisite according to *SS107*. Given the situation on the Somme it is possible that there was a degree of pressure from above to organise raids quickly but if this was so it did not result in a flurry of raiding. The next raid from the brigade did not take place until 13 August and was carried out by the 12th SWB.

It may have been the likelihood of planning raids that prompted Colonel Wilkie, 17th Welsh, to build a model of the local terrain as described by Second-Lieutenant M.M. Williams:

---

61 TNA WO 95/2607: War Diary 18th Welsh. This is an abbreviated version – the full order is in TNA WO 95/2604, War Diary 119 Brigade Appendices for July 1916. The 'yellow ribbon' was the distinguishing shoulder patch for the battalion. A yellow cloth rectangle worn at the base of the shoulder straps distinguished the 18th Welsh. The 17th Welsh used a dark blue triangle on the arms. The 12th SWB used a horizontal green bar at the top of the arms and the 19th RWF a red over blue rectangle. See David Bilton, *The Badges of Kitchener's Army – Infantry* (Barnsley: Pen and Sword, 2018). Some sketches of the men of the 17th Welsh made by M.M. Williams (Williams Papers) show an upward pointing triangle on the rear of the tunic below the collar.

62 Ibid.

> The C.O. has an idea of making a plain model of trenches on the ground, with little houses, railways etc. built out of old brick and we have been working at it today, on a waste piece of ground which has been levelled. You should have seen the Colonel busily building with bricks and digging. As he said, "As we can't go to Margate, we come here." It was great fun. He twice pocketed my foot rule and it could not be found anywhere and after he had vehemently denied having it, it was found in his pocket! Bell [Williams' servant] was collecting brick and carrying bags of slag for us. The C.O. said it was like laying out a garden. He really enjoyed himself, I think.[63]

Originally planned for the night of 11/12 August, the 12th SWB raid was delayed for a day after a patrol discovered that the wire was insufficiently cut. The detailed orders for the raid which was undertaken solely to secure identification of the German unit opposite had been issued by the battalion on 8 August (and were approved by the GOC 40th Division) allowing time for preparation. Two and a half typed foolscap pages detail the composition, equipment and deployment of three assaulting parties each of one officer, one NCO and twelve men plus a supporting party of one NCO and six men. Each attacking party consisted of eight bombers and four riflemen and the importance of an adequate supply of Mills bombs is apparent as each bomber wore a waistcoat with ten bombs and carried a canvas bucket of bombs (these would normally hold twenty or twenty-four bombs); each rifleman also carried a bucket of bombs and each of the support party carried two buckets and were to return for more if needed. The raiders therefore carried at least 1220 bombs in total – a considerable increase on the 144 carried by the 18th Welsh on their raid three weeks earlier even allowing for the increased number of raiders. Each party had a light ladder to aid exit from the enemy trench, the men's faces were darkened and each bomber carried a trench club. Riflemen carried a loaded rifle with bayonet fixed and a bandolier of ammunition. Fifteen 'bombproof jackets' were available and were to be worn by all officers and NCOs with the remainder issued to men identified by the officer in charge of the raid, Captain Pritchard.[64] White disks were to be placed by the support party to mark the route to the two gaps in the wire cut previously by the artillery and the return route. The left and right parties would isolate a section of trench between its junctions with communication trenches and prevent enemy attacks while the centre party would deal with two saps in its sector. Seventy-five minutes were allowed for the parties to be in place before the start of a forty-five minute barrage to cover the raid. Thirty minutes after the barrage started the retire signal would be given from the British front line by two buglers sounding the cookhouse call. Routes for the evacuation of prisoners and medical arrangements were also in place.

The battalion war diary noted that the raid 'was planned with great care, every detail was thoroughly considered and everyone engaged was completely familiar with the part he had to play'. The raiders reached the enemy wire just in time for the barrage at midnight. Rushing forward the parties met the enemy response of rifle, machine-gun and shell fire. Captain Pritchard was

---

63 Williams Papers, Letter to his wife, 7 August 1916. The use of a model in the planning of the 1917 Messines attack is well known but this 1916 instance has not been previously noted.

64 These 'bombproof jackets' were likely to have been a version of the Dayfield Body Shield, the most widely used protective 'jacket' during 1916. See Anthony Saunders, *Dominating the Enemy: War in the Trenches 1914-1918* (Stroud: Sutton, 2000), pp.42-59. Captain Pritchard 'was a Welsh International Rugby football forward and one of the most delightful companions in the officers mess. He was a man of immense physique, over six feet in height, and at home he had always spoken up for the Bantams, at times in the face of some mild ridicule, for he was confident that the boys, as he called them, would fight when the time came and he was right' – RRW Museum, Whitworth Memoir. For more on Pritchard see Peter Jones, *He did his Bit: The Stories Behind the Shirt Collection of Welsh Rugby Legend Charlie Pritchard* (Llandysul: Gomer, 2020).

wounded almost at once but refused aid, leapt into the trench and shot and captured a German. The order to retire was given as soon as the prisoner was secured but Pritchard, already weak from loss of blood, was hit again. Second-Lieutenant Wood brought in the prisoner while Second-Lieutenant Enright helped the stricken Pritchard back to the British line. The whole of the party were back by 12.53 a.m. although one man was found to be missing later. Two men were killed and twenty wounded (none seriously) but Captain Pritchard died later of his wounds. 'The battalion is congratulating itself today after accomplishing a quite successful raid ... we cannot be but greatly pleased that our battalion was responsible for the first prisoner taken by the 40th Division ... [the raid] was carried out with great dash and all concerned behaved extremely well ... the officers engaged behaved with great gallantry, admirable judgement and keen enthusiasm quite in keeping with the best traditions of the Army and set a fine example to their men who eagerly and enthusiastically followed it.'[65]

2/Lts William Hopkins Beaumont and James Donald Ellis, 19th RWF, 'Billets 18 August 1916'. (Author)

On 25 September both the 12th SWB and the 17th Welsh carried out raids to obtain identification from the enemy. Both raids were unsuccessful. For the 17th Welsh it was their first minor enterprise and its methods illustrate another approach to raiding. The one page order issued by Lieutenant-Colonel Wilkie was much more succinct than that issued for the 12th SWB raid described above but there was obviously a lot of planning behind it. In his post-raid report Wilkie described how the two parties involved (of one officer, two sergeants and fifteen men, and one officer, two sergeants and twenty-one men), advanced to the gaps in the enemy wire under cover of the battalion's Lewis guns 'without a single hostile shot' and how when the artillery barrage opened 'none [of the raiders] received any injury from our own gun fire. This must inspire the greatest confidence in future operations'. Once through the wire the two parties worked along the trench each with a 'driving party' covered by a flanking support party. Both parties found the trench

---

65 TNA WO 95/2606: War Diary 12th SWB.

empty and although dugouts were bombed no identifications or prisoners were obtained. Five men were wounded. Nevertheless Wilkie could report 'the raid itself was carried out to programme without a hitch ... Captain Lyne trained the raiding parties most successfully, Lt Rees and 2nd Lt Walton (the leaders of the two parties) exhibited great coolness and handled their parties well. The rank and file performed their tasks like clockwork.' The GOC 119 Brigade endorsed the report with 'I consider the raid was well carried out according to the rehearsed programme ... It was unfortunate that no prisoners were taken'.[66]

119 Brigade carried out eight raids from July to October 1916 while 120 Brigade carried out ten and 121 Brigade sixteen. Was this comparatively low number a cause for concern? It was certainly more than were occurring in some places. For example, 41st Division (XV Corps, Fourth Army) carried out no raids until 3 December 1916 while between the start of July and the end of September 1916 only two brigades of 12th (Eastern) Division carried out one raid each and in 24th Division again just two brigades organised raids with one carrying out two raids and the other just one.[67] On 15 August the newly-appointed (but temporary) commander of First Army, the energetic and aggressive Lieutenant-General Richard Haking, addressed his corps commanders at an Army conference: 'we must at all costs do our utmost to wear down the enemy, to reduce his moral[e] and at the same time improve the moral[e] of our own troops, and prove to them, by their own action, that they can get into the German trenches whenever they are called upon to do so. This can only be done by raids'.[68] That same day Haking visited Brigadier-General Prichard at 119 Brigade HQ. Prichard left for England the next day. There is no cited reason for Prichard's departure but the brigade had carried out only two raids by this date and the low tally surely counted against him.[69] Prichard wrote to Lieutenant-Colonel Pope, 12th SWB, (who had the one successful raid under his belt), 'Time did not allow me to say goodbye and to thank you for all the good work you have done while we served together. You can be justly proud of your battalion and if it continues to improve as it undoubtedly has under the strain of the trenches, I shall look forward to great things'.[70]

Perhaps thinking of Prichard, the GOC 40th Division, Harold Ruggles-Brise wrote to his wife on 15 August 'several of the older men in my Divn have already fallen out, they cannot stand the strain and the hard work, but so far no-one of any great importance'.[71] Others were also finding life at the front challenging. The 2iC 17th Welsh, Major Edmund Harry St George Gilbert was fifty-three, two years younger than Prichard, but became ill in mid-July. Second-Lieutenant Morris Meredith Williams wrote that 'I don't know what is the matter with him but he is elderly and cannot stand the discomforts of life out here'.[72] An actor and unlikely soldier, Gilbert was given the job of Town Major in Les Brebis, the first of several 'rear-area' appointments. By the war's end he was a lieutenant-colonel supervising units of the Chinese Labour Corps.[73]

Prichard's replacement as GOC 119 Brigade arrived on 17 August. Charles Cunliffe-Owen (1863-1932) was a regular soldier and the second son of Major-General Charles Henry Owen, sometime Professor of Artillery at the Royal Military Academy, Woolwich. Educated privately

---

66 TNA WO 95/2607: War Diary 119 Brigade HQ, Appendices.
67 Kenneth Radley, *On the Dangerous Edge: British and Canadian Trench Raiding on the Western Front* (Warwick: Helion, 2018) p.315. Connelly, *Steady the Buffs!*, pp.248-249. Both 12th and 24th Divisions were engaged on the Somme and raiding was probably not a priority.
68 Quoted in Senior, *Haking*, p.279.
69 It cannot have been the only reason for his dismissal as 120 Brigade had carried out no raids by this date.
70 TNA WO 95/2606: War Diary 12th SWB.
71 Blair Castle: Archives, Ruggles-Brise correspondence. Letter dated 15 August 1916.
72 Private collection, Williams Papers. Letter to his wife Alice dated 18 July 1916.
73 Edmund Harry St George Gilbert (1863-1947) see Appendix VI.

and at the RMA, he was gazetted lieutenant in the Royal Artillery in 1883, captain (1891), major (1900), lieutenant-colonel (1909) and substantive colonel (October 1914). His surname was changed to Cunliffe-Owen by deed poll in January 1905.[74] He saw service at home and in India and action in the South African War from 1899-1901 (including the relief of Ladysmith) for which he received the Queen's South Africa Medal with six clasps and was mentioned in dispatches. At the outbreak of the Great War he took XXVI Brigade, RFA (1st Division), to France and was given temporary command of 2nd Infantry Brigade between 10 and 23 November 1914. On 19 January 1915 he was appointed to BGRA, Australian and New Zealand Army Corps and landed at Anzac Cove Gallipoli on 25 April. He was BGRA, MEF from November 1915 to February 1916 and arrived in France with the ANZACs on 2 April.

While 119 Brigade was finding its feet to the north, on the Somme the fighting had moved to the village of Pozières where a complex situation was demanding ever more complex artillery plans. On 25 July the C-in-C, Sir Douglas Haig wrote:

> After lunch I visited … HQ Australian Corps … The situation seems all very new and strange to Australian HQ. The fighting here and shell fire is much more severe than anything experienced at Gallipoli! The German too, is a different enemy to the Turk! … I spoke to Birdwood about his CRA, Brigadier General Cunliffe Owen. The latter had served with me at the beginning of war but soon left France and so had no experience of our present artillery or the methods which had developed during the war. I therefore wished to give him an up to date CRA. He thanked me and said he would take anyone I selected … I also saw Cunliffe Owen and explained how sorry I was to have to move him, but in the present situation I would be failing in my duty to my country if I ran the risk of the Australians meeting with a check through faulty artillery arrangements.[75]

Cunliffe-Owen was immediately replaced by Brigadier-General W.J. Napier and just over two weeks later assumed command of 119 Brigade. His choice as GOC seems odd; he was first and foremost an artilleryman with one two-week period in 1914 in command of infantry. Captain Whitworth, 12th SWB, was clear why Cunliffe-Owen was posted to the brigade: 'Rumour said he only came to us to gain further experience of infantry work previous to a higher command, and for once a rumour was possibly true'.[76] If this was indeed the case, he only received thirteen weeks experience before he was relieved of the command, leaving for England on 18 November. Perhaps this brief experience was enough because he went on to command 54 Brigade, 18th Division, from 6 April to 22 October 1917.[77] If he gained experience of infantry work what did the brigade learn from him? Whitworth's further comments indicate that perhaps it was not much: 'Nothing escaped his eye as regards march discipline. Officers could no longer carry a waterproof on the back of the saddle, nor an officer's servant carry the acetylene lamp of the company mess outside his pack! The transport officer had a more difficult task and was up before the Colonel [sic] at every halt'.[78] During his time with 119 Brigade the number of raids increased markedly (only two before

---

74 His younger brother Frederick (born 1868) also started his career in the Royal Artillery and also adopted the surname Cunliffe-Owen by deed poll. Both men were involved in different capacities in the Dardanelles leading some authors to confuse them. See Robert Rhodes James, *Gallipoli* (London: Pan, 1984), p.374 and John Laffin, *Damn the Dardanelles* (Stroud: Sutton, 1989), p.15.
75 Gary Sheffield and John Bourne (eds.), *Douglas Haig, War Diaries and Letters, 1914-1918* (London: Weidenfeld and Nicolson, 2005), p.209.
76 RRW Museum, Whitworth Memoir p.526.
77 In November 1917 he became GOC 206 Brigade, 69th Division – a 2nd line TF division.
78 RRW Museum, Whitworth Memoir p.526.

119 Bde Staff, 18 September 1916. Front row L to R: Capt Granville Soames, Brigade Major; Brig-Gen Charles Cunliffe Owen; Capt. Percy Hone, Staff Captain. (Royal Welsh Regimental Museum, Brecon)

his arrival, six afterwards) but only two of six were successful.[79] It may be that although Cunliffe-Owen acted on the wishes of GOC First Army it was the number of raids that counted in the eyes of the First Army commander rather than their success rate. Cunliffe-Owen's departure came not long after Lieutenant-General Sir C. A. Anderson took over I Corps and Major-General H.S. Horne became commander of First Army – both on 30 September 1916 – and he might have fallen victim to two 'new brooms'.

In what condition did he leave the brigade? There are no descriptions of its capabilities at this point in the war although Horne, writing to the CGS, Sir Launcelot Kiggell, on 5 October noted that 40th Division was 'coming on' but had 'many 'bantams' and has not been distinguished in

---

79 Overall 119 Brigade had 37% of its eight raids achieve their goals; 120 Brigade only 10% (of 10) and 121 Brigade 31% (of 16).

trench warfare'.[80] At the end of the month the division had a strength of 17,439 all ranks and had not been massively depleted by five months in the trenches.[81] An appendix to the October war diary of the 18th Welsh indicates the level of attrition:

> There have been about 279 casualties of which 110 either remained at duty or have since returned leaving a permanent loss of 169. Casualties to officers have been few, no officer being wounded in the trenches by enemy fire. Of the 9 officer casualties 3 were wounded on raids, 1 in 'No Man's Land' (very slightly), 1 accidentally in our line and 4 were sick.[82]

The sectors that 119 Brigade occupied suffered from regular bombardment, particularly by German trench mortars, and most fatalities were caused in this way. In five months the brigade lost nine officers and 163 men.[83] The most senior of these were Lieutenant-Colonel Wilkie (17th Welsh) and his acting 2iC, Captain C.V. Lyne, both killed by a high explosive shell on 18 October while on a tour of the battalion's line.[84] Replacements for casualties were few. War diaries record that the 19th RWF received a draft of eighty men on 26 September, the 17th Welsh received twenty-five men on 10 October and the 18th Welsh received thirty-eight men on 4 November. When Frank Crozier took command on 20 November 1916, the brigade had essentially the same make up as it had when it left England in June.

At about the same time that Horne was telling Kiggell that the 40th Division was 'coming on' Harold Ruggles-Brise was writing to his wife: 'I do not know why the Divn was not taken down to the Somme. I think possibly because they are bantams and the bantams that have already been there did not last very long – at least so I am told … Lately we have done rather well, and my little lads have shown great gallantry, and some of their performances have been mentioned in communiqués'.[85] Was he right? Was it the performance of the bantam 35th Division that kept the 40th Division from being deployed to the Somme?

While 119 Brigade was manning the line around Loos the Somme battle was consuming British infantry divisions at an alarming rate. The original thirteen attacking divisions on 1 July 1916 had been increased as the battle became one of attrition. Fifty-three divisions of eleven corps, including Canadian, New Zealand, Australian and South African formations, fought on the Somme between July and November during which time the average death rate per day was 893.[86] Why did 40th Division not take part? 41st Division was only a month longer in France and did well at Flers-Courcelette on 15 September as part of XV Corps. The bantams of 35th Division which had arrived in February and received initial instruction as part of Haking's XI Corps had by contrast done rather poorly as part of XIII Corps. Perhaps they were just not ready? Peter Simkins has described how the division's 'morale and resilience apparently became increasingly and unexpectedly fragile' in the second half of 1916 whilst acknowledging four extenuating factors: during its time on the Somme the division never fought as a coherent unit, being committed as single brigades or single battalions; the men were used extensively on trench digging and carrying duties,

---

80 TNA WO 158/186 quoted in Simon Robbins, *British Generalship during the Great War: The Military Career of Sir Henry Horne (1861-1929)* (Farnham: Ashgate, 2010), p.275.
81 TNA: WO 394, Statistical abstracts of information regarding the armies at home and abroad.
82 TNA WO 95/2607: War Diary 18th Welsh.
83 *SDGW*. Fatalities in the battalions June-October 1916 were: 17th Welsh – 3 officers and 31 men; 18th Welsh – 42 men; 19th RWF – 3 officers and 39 men and the 12th SWB 3 Officers and 51 men.
84 The 2iC, Major Appleby, had left just seven days previously to attend the new Senior Officers' School at Aldershot. He was also lucky enough to be posted from the battalion just before Bourlon Wood. Digby Appleby (1880-1945). See Appendix VI.
85 Blair Castle: Archives, Bundle 880. Letter 9 October 1916.
86 Gary Sheffield, *The Somme* (London: Cassell, 2003), p.152.

were exhausted and were losing men to German bombardments to which they could not retaliate; the sector in which they fought was an inherently difficult one flanked by the French Sixth Army and finally the period of July-August was one when Fourth Army repeatedly launched small-scale attacks against difficult targets with little chance of success. Senior officers of the division did not blame the original bantams but focused on the nature of new recruits to their battalions. Brigadier-General A.H. Marindin, 105 Brigade, wrote 'The class of men we are now getting … are no longer the 'Bantams' proper but are either half-grown lads or degenerates'. While acknowledging that the recruits were 'sorely needed' Simkins also doubts that the losses in the battalions before the Somme battle were enough for the numbers of later sub-standard recruits to have made a difference to the effectiveness of the division.[87] Casualties up to June 1916 were 819 – 7% of the division's infantry but by the end of July the total was 3,728 or just less than 32% of the division's infantry.[88] With this level of casualties a drop in the morale of the division might be expected and new recruits would not have the same *esprit de corps*. The division had a bad time over a protracted period. All of these factors combined in a complex mix that, along with poor handling, resulted in the below-par performance of 35th Division. That a number of the original 1915 recruits were amongst the twenty-six men of the 19th Durham Light Infantry (106 Brigade) tried for cowardice in December highlights the need for further detailed study of 35th Division in 1916.

There also seems to have been an issue with the quality of new drafts to the Cheshire Regiment beyond 35th Division. On 3 June 1916, Alexander Johnston, the Brigade Major of 7 Brigade (25th Division), noted after a visit to the 10th Cheshires (which was not a bantam battalion) that 'They have just received a perfectly useless draft of 80 'Bantams' who cannot march or carry their full equipment and seem to have had very little training. I can't think what the authorities can be thinking about …'[89] The influx of new, apparently poor-quality recruits at just the wrong time focussed attention on the physical and mental state of the bantams and led to a major weeding out exercise in 35th Division later in the year. By mid-January drafts totalling 1,350 new men had been absorbed and the division performed creditably in the second half of 1917 and in 1918. Meanwhile, the bantams' reputation as a fighting force was at rock-bottom. It is very likely then that Harold Ruggles-Brise was correct in attributing the lack of involvement of 40th Division in the Somme fighting to the perceived defects of 35th Division.[90]

On 6 December the officers of 35th Division received a circular advising them that due to the shortage of recruits all battalions of the BEF were now accepting small men, that replacements would now be of average height and that the 35th would no longer be referred to as a bantam division.[91] This was forcefully restated by the new GOC, Major-General H.J.S. Landon, on 18 December making it clear that 'in reorganising [the] Division … [the] Bantam standard must be disregarded for good and all'.[92] The consequences impacted on 40th Division:

---

87   Peter Simkins, '"Each One a Pocket Hercules": The Bantam Experiment and the Case of the Thirty-fifth Division' in Sanders Marble (ed.), *Scraping the Barrel: The Military Use of Sub-Standard Manpower* (New York: Fordham University Press, 2012), pp.79-104.
88   H.M. Davson, *The History of the 35th Division in the Great War* (London: Sifton Praed & Co, 1926), pp.308-312. Battalion casualty figures from the appendix have been used to compile the totals given above.
89   Edwin Astill, *The Great War Diaries of Brigadier General Alexander Johnston 1914-1917* (Barnsley: Pen & Sword, 2007, p.159.
90   Simkins' study notwithstanding, the relationships between morale, poor discipline and performance, and other factors such as training, leadership and command remain to be explored in the case of 35th Division.
91   Stephen McGreal, *Cheshire Bantams: The 15th, 16th and 17th Battalions of the Cheshire Regiment* (Barnsley: Pen & Sword, 2006), p.135.
92   TNA WO 95/2468: War Diary 35th Division General Staff.

Use of the term Bantam for designation of certain Inf[antry] units to be discontinued. No further bantam drafts.[93]

The order came in to inform us that the [40th] Bantam Division would cease to exist as such and would be reinforced by men of any physique (I believe this was caused by the failure of the 35th Division, the original Bantams, to carry out the work of bigger men on the Somme). Our Division of Bantams had performed exceedingly well and took great pride in the fact that they were Bantams. It was therefore a blow to us all when we ceased to be a Bantam Division.[94]

Second-Lieutenant Morris Meredith Williams, 17th Welsh, reported:

A large draft of men have joined us. They are big men & are reported to be from the Dragoon Gds, some of them … You cannot tell us from an ordinary Regt now. We have such a lot of tall men.[95]

A slightly different opinion was given by Captain Whitworth, 12th SWB:

I have had another draft of men – some fine type of men among them; it is a great thing to see some of the Bantam element going; they will never have the real spirit of soldiering, yet some of these recent [word missing] men – almost conscripts – are splendid.[96]

Given other events within his battalion at the time (described below), his negativity is understandable. Meanwhile the general weeding out of unfit and small men in 35th Division did not extend to 40th Division.[97]

Discipline in France

In addition to dealing with the enemy the officers of 119 Brigade had to come to terms with dealing with problems amongst the ranks. Mark Connelly has written that 'the final test of internal cohesion and morale is the disciplinary record of the battalions'.[98] The battalion war diaries do not usually record minor disciplinary matters but a few surviving service files give an indications of the issues dealt with in the early months of active service. On 24 June 1916 the loss of part of his kit 'by neglect' resulted in 25274 Private Robert Jones, 17th Welsh, being stopped three days' pay and, a month later, 28728 Private Richard Thomas, 19th RWF, received two days Field Punishment Number Two for appearing 'dirty on parade'. On 25th July 25613 Private Robert Jones, 17th Welsh, was sentenced to twenty-eight days Field Punishment Number Two for 'not complying with an order' while on 26

---

93 TNA WO 95/2594: War Diary 40th Division A&Q, 22 January 1917.
94 National Army Museum (NAM) 1994/05/398/1: 'Diary of the war by J.F. Plunkett. Copied from my rough notes taken in the field'. Undated entry but post-October 1916. Plunkett was at this time 2iC 12th Suffolk Regiment, 121 Brigade.
95 Private Collection, Williams Papers. Letter to his wife 14 December 1916. The draft was of 160 men (War Diary) but I have found no evidence of cavalrymen.
96 RRW Museum: Whitworth Memoir. Letter from Captain Whitworth (12th SWB) to his mother 1 December 1916.
97 It is interesting to note that the war diary of 106 Brigade, 35th Division for January 1917 notes that 'in this period the rejection of all unfits and men of the Bantam standard was undertaken' [my emphasis].
98 Mark Connelly, Steady the Buffs! A Regiment, a Region & the Great War (Oxford: Oxford University Press, 2006), p.29.

August 25262 Private George Rogers, 17th Welsh was convicted of 'being absent from parade for [the] trenches and being drunk'. He received fourteen days Field Punishment Number One and was docked twenty-eight days' pay. Although varying in degrees of misconduct and punishment these instances highlight the adjustments that needed to be made by troops on active service and the necessary realization that they were now 'in' the war. For some this was hard to do.

On 29 June 1916 after less than four weeks in France Private N. Morris, 12th SWB, was convicted of desertion by Field General Court Martial. His death sentence was 'commuted to ten years penal servitude, sentence suspended'. On 8 July Private Morris shot himself in the foot while on sentry and was placed under arrest.[99] Despite his previous offence and existing suspended sentence his FGCM on 21 July sentenced him to two years hard labour commuted to three months Field Punishment Number One.[100] It seems that the military authorities were going out of their way to be lenient at this early stage of the battalion's war. There must have been extenuating circumstances to be considered when 23355 Private John Dalton, also of the 12th SWB, 're-joined from desertion' on 10 December 1916 and was simply forfeit twenty-six days' pay.[101]

These last two examples of misconduct occurred in the ranks of the 12th SWB and something does seem to have been amiss in this battalion in the second half of 1916 despite Eric Whitworth's description of Lieutenant-Colonel Pope having 'immense drive and [being] determined to make his Battalion the best in the Brigade. He was good with personal relationships with the men who liked and respected him and responded well to his exacting demands. He was too, a disciplinarian, intolerant of inefficiency whether it concerned an officer, NCO or men in the ranks'.[102] The 12th South Wales Borderers were later regarded by Crozier as the best of his battalions 'because they had been properly grounded, when young, by Colonel Pope'.[103] Despite this reputation the battalion was the only one of the four original battalions in the brigade to record acts of collective indiscipline while on active service in France.

Alcohol was a favourite target for theft by British troops.[104] On 7 November 1916, members of A Company appropriated fifty-two bottles of wine from a cellar in the village of Autheux while out of the line. Having investigated, Lieutenant-Colonel Pope 'referred the matter to brigade'. The battalion had arrived at its billets in Autheux on 5 November. Its training programme had been curtailed by rain on the 6 November and had to be abandoned completely on the day of the offence.[105] Presumably the men were bored and 'apparently aggrieved with the owner of their billet and thought 'to get their own back … 10 Francs paid by unit and charged against the [approximately twenty] men concerned'.[106] The next day 'by order of the Brigadier General [Cunliffe-Owen] the whole of A Coy vacated their billets and moved to Mon Plaisir Farm'.[107] Presumably the removal from billets to the isolated farm was intended as a sanction on the whole of A Company.

The second incident involving the battalion occurred later in the same month but was apparently unrelated. The battalion war diary records that on 1 December 1916 there was a 'FGCM on 20 men of D Coy for disobeying an order to fall in on defaulters parade'. The entry for Sunday 3

---

99 TNA WO 95/2606: War Diary 12th SWB, 8 July 1916; Gerard Oram, *Death Sentences Passed by Military Courts of the British Army 1914-1924* (London: Francis Boutle, 1998), p.36.
100 TNA WO 213/10: Register of FGCMs.
101 TNA WO 95/2606: War Diary 12th SWB, December 1916.
102 RRW Museum: Whitworth Memoir.
103 Frank Percy Crozier. *Impressions and Recollections* (London: T. Werner Laurie, 1930), p.184.
104 Craig Gibson, *Behind the Front: British Soldiers and French Civilians, 1914-18* (Cambridge: Cambridge University Press, 2014), pp.89-90.
105 TNA WO 95/2606: War Diary 12th SWB, November 1916.
106 TNA WO 95/2594: War Diary 40th Division HQ, A&Q.
107 TNA WO 95/2606: War Diary 12th SWB. Mon Plaisir Farm is in an isolated location 2.1km north-east of Autheux village.

December records the 'promulgation of the FGCM for disobeying an order and the CO read out sections 4 to 44 of the Army Act' confirming that the accused had been charged with mutiny and disobedience. Using the information from the papers of the Judge Advocate General as published by Julian Putkowski, it is possible to name the nineteen accused (not twenty as stated in the battalion war diary).[108] Although this source does not give the men's service numbers it is possible to identify all but two of them with some confidence. The service record of one of the accused, 24203 Private Walter Sutton, has survived and allows the sequence of events to be elaborated.

Sutton, a twenty-three year old platelayer from Swinton, Yorkshire, was placed under arrest awaiting trial on 21 November 1916 (presumably along with the other eighteen accused) and tried by FGCM on 1 December for 'disobeying a lawful command given by his superior officer, A.A. Sect 9 (2)'.[109] He was found guilty and sentenced to eighteen months hard labour. Two of the accused were found not guilty and all the rest were given the same sentence as Sutton except for privates A.W. Leather and R. Milne who (presumably because they were identified as the ringleaders) were sentenced to seven years penal servitude and two years hard labour respectively. The sentences were confirmed on 2 December by the GOC 119 Brigade (who by this time was Frank Crozier), promulgated on 3 December and the guilty men passed to the APM of 40th Division. On 18 December the GOC 40th Division, Harold Ruggles-Brise, commuted the sentences to two years hard labour for Leather and to three months Field Punishment Number One in respect of Sutton and the rest.

Table 14: Participants in the 12th SWB 'mutiny' of 21 November 1916

Surname	Forename	Rank	Service No	Verdict	Enlisted
Price	Charles R.	Pte (L/Cpl)	24178	NG	
Milne	Robert	Pte	24180	G	
Kelly	Sidney V.	Pte	24196	G	
Rustage	William	Pte	24201	G	Mexborough
Sutton	Walter	Pte	24203	G	Mexborough
Wood	William A.	Pte	24204	NG	
Leather	Albert W.	Pte	24207	G	
Marsden	Enoch	Pte	24209	G	
Cooke	Reginald	Pte	24210	G	
Walton	Robert	Pte	24229	G	
French	John	Pte	24281	G	Chesterfield
Hale	Thomas	Pte	24351	G	
Gummer	Evan	Pte	24483	G	
Watkins	Frank	Pte	35130	G	
Tough	Thomas F.	Pte	35193	G	
Samuel	Vergil	Pte	35362	G	
Claybrook	Arthur H.	Pte	39897	G	
Thomas	T.	Pte (not traced)		G	
Turner	E.	Pte (not traced)		G	

---

108 Julian Putkowski, *British Army Mutineers 1914-1922* (London: Francis Boudle, 1998), p.108.
109 Service Record 24203 Private Walter Sutton, TNA: WO 363, 'British Army Service Records, 1914-1920' <http://www.ancestry.co.uk> accessed 24 April 2014. Sutton probably never completed his sentence of Field Punishment No.1 as he was hospitalised with influenza at the end of December. In February 1918 he was posted to 2nd SWB and taken prisoner on 11 April. He survived the war and was demobilized in 1919.

The table (Table 14) clearly shows that at the core of the group that refused to obey an order are a number whose service numbers are very close together, indicating that they enlisted at roughly the same date and probably in the same place. There is no indication of the cause of this offence. It may not be coincidence that Captain H.C. Lloyd, commanding D Company, left on leave on the day of the offence which was one of 'fog and cold mists'. 'General leave' had started on 19th November and it is possible that tiredness and cold had lowered morale so that leave or the lack of it was the catalyst for the trouble. After six months in France the men could not have been as 'profoundly ignorant of the basic demands of military discipline' as they probably were when first recruited.[110] The lack of *esprit de corps* highlighted by this episode reflected badly on the 12th SWB and the GOC Division, Ruggles-Brise, addressed the situation directly:

> He rarely however spoke to the troops and the only occasion when he addressed our Battalion was a serious one. There had been two cases of collective acts of insubordination and the General came and warned all ranks of the inevitable end of such conduct, namely death by being shot, with the unpleasant corollary of the men having themselves to shoot one of their own Battalion. He spoke very shortly but to great effect. Behind his words everyone felt determination to carry them out with strength and justice. For he reminded all ranks of his duty also, to see justice was done to every officer and man in his Division.[111]

This blunt warning seems to have worked. No similar incidents were recorded and for the remainder of its time with 119 Brigade the 12th SWB had the fewest instances of trial by court martial in the brigade (Table 15). The figures for 1916 show clearly the effect of the nineteen trials for mutiny in the 12th SWB on the total. However if the mutiny cases are excluded the battalion had a lower level of trial by court martial than the 19th RWF which generated eighteen trials in 1916. It is difficult, if not impossible, to attribute causes to the variations in the number of trials between battalions and from month to month. When Freddy Plunkett took command of the 19th RWF in August 1917 he regarded discipline as bad even though there had been only seven courts martial involving men of the battalion to date that year. Changes in battalion COs may be a factor in the number of courts martial records for the 17th and 18th Welsh but do not seem to affect the lower number of trials in the 19th RWF and 12th SWB. If the number of trials is a realistic indicator of the level of discipline in a battalion then discipline was notably better in 1917 after the arrival of Crozier as GOC 119 Brigade. As a comparison, over a period of ten months from December 1915 to September 1916, the three brigades of the 16th (Irish) Division put 112, 123 and 147 men to trial by FGCM. Over twelve months from October 1915 to September 1916 the three brigades of the 36th (Ulster Division) put 122, 41 and 84 men to trial. In twelve months of 1917, 119 Brigade put just 54 men to trial.[112]

In the absence of further comparators it is not possible to prove the obvious assumption that discipline in 119 Brigade was good as it cannot be disproved that a more 'relaxed' disciplinary regime that sent fewer men to trial was in operation. Plunkett's remarks about the discipline of the 19th RWF might be taken to indicate that levels of discipline and numbers of FGCMs may not be closely related.

---

110 Sheffield, *Leadership in the Trenches*, p.73.
111 RRW Museum: Whitworth memoir, p.522. The battalion's war diary confirms that Ruggles-Brise addressed the battalion on 21 December 1916.
112 Figures compiled from Timothy Bowman, *Irish Regiments in the Great War: Discipline and Morale* (Manchester: Manchester University Press, 2003), p.113, Table 4.1 and p.120, Table 4.2.

Table 15: Field General Courts Martial, 119 Brigade June 1916 to July 1918

	17th Welsh	18th Welsh	19th RWF	12th SWB	Total
June 1916	1	–	–	5	6
July	–	–	4	6	10
Aug	4	2	3	5	14
Sept	3	1	2	2	8
Oct	1	1	1	–	3
Nov	1	1	3	–	5
Dec	2	–	5	20	27
Total	12	5	18	38	73
Jan 1917	–	1	1	1	3
Feb	–	1	–	–	1
Mar	1	–	–	–	1
Apr	1	2	–	–	3
May	1	6	–	–	7
June	–	–	2	–	2
July	5	3	4	–	12
Aug	4	2	–	–	6
Sept	–	2	–	1	3
Oct	5	1	2	5	13
Nov	–	–	–	–	0
Dec	1	1	2	–	4
Total	18	19	11	7	54
Jan 1918	–	1	4	–	5
Feb	–	2	–	2	4
Mar	1	–	–	–	1
Apr	–	–	–	3	3
May	1	–	–	–	1
June	–	–	2	–	2
July	1	–	–	–	1
Total	3	3	6	5	17
Overall	33	27	35	50	145

Source: TNA WO 213/9-23

The variation in the types of charge (Table 16) brought against members of different formations may be taken as an indicator of different standards being applied or, for example, may genuinely indicate that the men of 119 Brigade were more insubordinate and disobedient than the men of the 16th (Irish) and 36th (Ulster) Divisions but less prone to drunkenness.

Only six men of the brigade were sentenced to death during the war, one for sleeping and the rest for desertion, and all of the sentences were commuted to periods of penal servitude, suspended in one case.[113] In all, thirteen sentences were suspended and fifty-nine (30%) remitted or commuted to some degree. There seems to have been a reluctance to apply the most severe punishments and although hard labour and field punishment predominate in the sentencing regime they were used just 140 times in two years (Table 17). Field Punishment Number One seems to have been used

---

113 The 40th Division was the only New Army division to have no executions during its existence.

fairly evenly across the battalions: in the 17th Welsh 15 times; 18th Welsh 14 times; the 19th RWF 18 times and the 12th SWB 35 times including the 19 sentences for mutiny described earlier.

Table 16: Offences tried by Field General Courts Martial June 1916 – July 1918 (Instances of offence in brackets)[114]

Offence	119 Brigade*	16th (Irish) Division**	36th (Ulster) Division**
Absence	8% (15)	–	–
Drunkenness	10% (18)	24% (53)	23% (38)
Escaping confinement	1% (2)	0.4% (1)	–
Miscellaneous Military Offences	30% (56)	57% (127)	54% (89)
Cowardice	1% (2)	0.4% (1)	0.6% (1)
Desertion	5% (9)	9% (20)	11% (18)
Disobedience	17% (32)	7% (16)	v4% (7)
Insubordination	9% (16)	3% (7)	1% (2)
Resisting	0.5% (1)	–	–
Losing property	0.5% (1)	–	–
Mutiny	10% (19)	0.4% (1)	0.6% (1)
Quitting post / Sleeping	6% (10)	1% (3)	2% (4)
Offence against inhabitant	1% (2)	0.4% (1)	0.6% (1)
Theft	2% (3)	3% (6)	2% (3)
Injuring/making away w. property	–	0.4% (1)	0.6% (1)
Violence	–	0.9% (2)	–
Total Offences	**186**	**224**	**165**

*All four battalions June 1916 –July 1918, TNA WO 213/9-23
** Sample of four battalions October 1916 – February 1918

Table 17: Sentences of Field General Courts Martial June 1916 – July 1918

Sentence	Instances in 119 Brigade
Field Punishment No.1	42% (82)
Field Punishment No.2	1% (2)
Imprisonment	2% (3)
Penal Servitude	4% (8)
Hard Labour	30% (58)
Death	3% (6)
Reduction in Rank	10% (19)
Stoppages/Fine	2% (4)
Guilty but insane	0.5% (1)
Not Guilty / Quashed	5% (13)
Total Sentences	**196**

Source: TNA: WO 213/9-23

---

114 Divisional figures are compiled from Stephen Sandford, *Neither Nationalist Nor Unionist: The 10th (Irish) Division in the Great War* (Sallins: Irish Academic Press, 2014), p.261, Table 7.11.

The disciplinary regime within 119 Brigade until its reorganisation seems to have been a moderate one but more comparators are needed before its status can be defined with confidence. Other than the sources used as comparators in this study there is a notable lack of quantitative data available and the important works by Gary Sheffield, Alexander Watson and Peter Hodgkinson contain none.[115] Further data on FGCMs during the final embodiment of the brigade will be presented later.

The three studies cited above all touch on the subject of troop morale and the coping mechanisms that enabled the troops of the BEF to carry on in difficult circumstances and recognise the value of popular culture (sport, cinema, theatre, social drinking) in keeping up morale 'convincingly demonstrated' by the work of J.G. Fuller.[116] His book shows the importance of organised recreational activity, particularly football, but one other facet appears to be absent in the brigade. Fuller identified over 100 'trench magazines' produced by a variety of mainly infantry units and used as the medium for sometimes black humour and veiled swipes at the military hierarchy.[117] This particular medium does not seem to have been used by the troops of 119 Brigade or of 40th Division. The production of such magazines is reliant on a number of factors most notably the availability of materials and equipment plus the presence of motivated and literate individuals who had the time and organisational skills to commission or write copy and assemble and distribute the finished magazines. The social makeup of the brigade's units was notably lacking in the commercial and professional classes and their absence may be one reason for the absence of a trench magazine.

One form of entertainment that certainly was available to 119 Brigade was the divisional concert party. Only three New Army brigades had their own concert party but twenty-four of thirty New Army divisions had one. Fuller notes that despite the popularity of Charlie Chaplin films, only nine New Army Divisions had cinemas and that concert parties were much more important as morale boosters.[118] 40th Division's concert party 'The Gamecocks' was certainly in existence by August 1916 and continued until the division was reduced to a cadre after the German Spring Offensives.[119] Before then the 'troupe and band [had] lost most of their stage properties and instruments by enemy action' in April 1918.[120] In November 1917 the troupe was performing four times weekly and in February 1918 'The Gamecocks' gave performances in each of the three brigades' areas weekly: 'Brigade Hd.Qrs. are requested to assist Lieut. Davies as regards accommodation for the troupe and band'.[121] 'The Gamecocks' cast included Sergeant J.F. 'Jack' Franklin, 17th Welsh, a well-known music hall entertainer and comedian who had assisted recruiting at the beginning of the bantams. Away from the divisional troupe, in the 12th SWB, Lieutenant Harold Jones'

---

115 Gary Sheffield, *Leadership in the Trenches*; Alexander Watson, *Enduring the Great War: Combat, Morale and collapse in the German and British Armies, 1914-1918* (Cambridge: Cambridge University Press, 2008); Peter Hodgkinson, *'Glum Heroes': Hardship, Fear and Death – Resilience and Coping in the British Army on the Western Front 1914-1918* (Wolverhampton: Helion, 2016); Gerard Oram, 'Pious Perjury: Discipline and Morale in the British Force in Italy, 1917-1918', *War in History*, 9:4 (2002), p.412-430 gives some basic data derived from FGCM records for three divisions serving in that theatre.
116 For example, Sheffield, *Leadership in the Trenches*, pp.139 – 140. J.G. Fuller, *Troop Morale and Popular Culture in the British and Dominion Armies 1914-1918* (Oxford: Oxford University Press, 1991).
117 Fuller, *Troop Morale and Popular Culture*, p.3.
118 Ibid., pp.113, 191.
119 TNA WO 95/2564: War Diary 40th Division A&Q, 21 August 1916; IWM: Documents 66/298/1, The Papers of Captain H.J.C. (Harry) Graham. Letter 1 January 1918. Graham obtained a portable piano for the troupe.
120 TNA WO 95/2564: War Diary 40th Division A&Q, 5 November 1917 and 12 April 1918.
121 Ibid., Administrative Instruction S/122/Q, 6 February 1918. Lieutenant Ernest William Parry Davies (1891-1964). See Appendix VI.

The Gamecocks, 1917. Sergeant J.F. Franklin, 17th Welsh, standing front left. (*Twenty Years After*)

Crozier, centre, a great fan of theatre, in lighter mood. (Royal Welsh Regimental Museum, Brecon)

batman 'Lester' was also a music hall comedian.[122] In the final months of the war Crozier was pleased to have the famous baritone Charles Knowles as his orderly officer.[123]

This chapter has established the backgrounds of the senior officers of the brigade and the brigade staff and shown when and why some of them were replaced as the brigade moved to active service. While the level of 'Welshness' of the battalions' officers varied, there was still a strong national identity among them. The discipline of the battalions while on active service and their level of participation in the tactic of trench raiding have been described. The 40th Division's non-participation in the Battle of the Somme was shown to have been due to the poor opinion of the record of the bantams of 35th Division held by senior staff and that poor performance in 35th Division was the result of other factors rather than any inherent problem with the bantams themselves.

---

122 RRW Museum, Brecon: 2001.98, Diary 68, Memoir of Lieutenant Harold Jones, 12th SWB. A search of contemporary newspapers reveals no less than seven comedians with the surname Lester. None appear in the SWB medal rolls.
123 Crozier, *Impressions and Recollections*, p.230. Charles Reginald Knowles (1868-1950) was a highly accomplished and popular vocalist. See Appendix VI.

3

Crozier: A Reputation Won and Lost

Chapters 1 and 2 established the history and composition of 119 Brigade, formed a view of its national identity and examined its first six months as an under-performing formation of the BEF. This chapter will outline the background and reputation of the brigade's new GOC, Frank Percy Crozier, by briefly describing his military career before the Great War, looking in more detail at his battalion command in France and by examination of his post-war publications. In *Broken Sword* Charles Messenger described Crozier's early career in South Africa, Nigeria and with the Ulster Volunteer Force in separate chapters. His time with the 9th RIRifles is also covered in a single chapter as is the whole decade prior to Crozier's death when all his books were published.[1] Statistics derived from records of courts martial compiled by Timothy Bowman are here abstracted and interpreted to form a view of the discipline in Crozier's 9th RIRifles and 107 Brigade.[2] While this book shares some of the same sources with Charles Messenger's book, additional detail and analysis (for example of the disciplinary record of the battalion and the reception of Crozier's books) is given in order to demonstrate the fall / rise / fall of Crozier's reputation before, during and after the Great War. The surviving correspondence of one of his subordinates, Captain William Montgomery, OC A Company, 9th RIRifles, will be used here to illustrate his relationship with one of his officers. The oft-repeated observation by one subaltern that Crozier was 'particularly keen on sending out patrols to no purpose' will be challenged as will remarks made by Wilfred Spender which will be placed in context and quoted in full for the first time. The chapter will then move on to explore how Crozier's hard-won reputation as a soldier was damaged by his own post-war writings and the reaction to them. Two books in particular, *A Brass Hat in No Man's Land* (1930) and *The Men I Killed* (1937), continue to be regularly used as sources for both academic and popular publications. The examination of his output defines an important context for its previous and future use as a historical source.[3] The popular perception of Crozier created by reading his publications, particularly the two mentioned above, out of context has inhibited not just the study of the man as a brigadier-general but the study of the brigade that he commanded. This chapter will provide that context.

---

1 Charles Messenger, *Broken Sword: The Tumultuous Life of General Frank Crozier 1879-1937* (Barnsley: Pen & Sword, 2013).
2 Timothy Bowman, *Irish Regiments in the Great War: Discipline and Morale* (Manchester: Manchester University Press, 2003), pp.100-139.
3 Philip Orr's potted biography of Crozier which forms the Introduction to the 1989 reissue of *Brass Hat* is typical of works that use Crozier as the main source of information – F.P. Crozier, *A Brass Hat in No Man's Land* (Norwich: Gliddon Books, 1989); F.P. Crozier, *The Men I Killed* (London: Michael Joseph, 1937).

Crozier's Military Background

When the thirty-seven years old Frank Crozier arrived at 119 Brigade HQ at Le Souich (8km north of Doullens) on 20 November 1916 the brigade was taking a break from its long march south-west from the Loos sector to a training area east of Abbeville. Crozier had arrived in France a year earlier in October 1915 as 2iC 9th Royal Irish Rifles, 107 Brigade, 36th (Ulster) Division, was placed in temporary command of the battalion on 10 December and was confirmed as CO on 1 January 1916. As an officer with experience he had previously been given a key role in recruiting and training the battalion. How had he arrived at this point?

After two years at Wellington College, Crozier had been barred by his height and slight build from joining the Regular Army but obtained a subaltern's commission in the 4th Middlesex Rifle Volunteer Corps in June 1897. In October 1898 he ventured to Ceylon to learn the practicalities of tea planting only to leave as soon as news of the outbreak of the Second Boer War arrived. He gained experience on active service in South Africa as a private then as a NCO in Thorneycroft's Mounted Infantry and was present at the battle of Spion Kop (23 January 1900).[4] While in South Africa he was commissioned as a second-lieutenant in the 2nd Manchester Regiment and left Thorneycroft's Mounted Infantry in June 1900. He departed South Africa in January 1901 having volunteered for service in the West African Field Force and spent the next four years in Nigeria. Thomas Astley Cubitt, Crozier's CO for part of this time and a witness at his marriage, later recalled that Crozier was known as 'The Bull Pup' and 'always had physical "guts"'.[5] His reputation as a soldier at this stage seems to be positive but alcoholism, ill-health, a bad marriage and a complete lack of financial awareness blighted his return to Britain and several episodes in various localities involving unpaid bills and dishonoured cheques led to bankruptcy and ended his military career. On 22 May 1909 he resigned his commission and left for Canada to farm. The failure of this venture caused his return to Britain in 1911 as a committed teetotaller and in 1913 he found a niche as a captain in the Ulster Volunteer Force where his previous transgressions were apparently unknown.[6] Wilfred Spender, the UVF's Assistant Quartermaster General and later GSO2 36th (Ulster) Division, makes no mention of Crozier's early transgressions in any of the sometimes very critical letters that he wrote.[7] When war was declared Crozier, 'late Captain, Canadian Forces', was commissioned as a captain in the 5th Royal Irish Fusiliers.[8] Using his UVF contacts

---

4   F.P. Crozier, *Angels on Horseback* (London: Jonathan Cape, 1932). The relationship between Alexander Thorneycroft and Crozier's mother may have led to her son's acceptance as a recruit. Crozier claims to have been on the summit of Spion Kop but his description in *Angels on Horseback* contains little detail that is not available elsewhere and it is possible that he was with the remainder of the unit guarding a ridge slightly to the south. Ron Lock, *Hill of Squandered Valour: The Battle for Spion Kop, 1900* (Newbury: Casemate, 2011) is a detailed account of the battle which disregards Crozier as a source. It is perhaps significant that Crozier gives no account of the action on the summit in *Impressions*.

5   University of Oxford, Bodleian Library: Lugard MS 9/7/128. Letter from Cubitt to Lord Lugard, 29 May 1936.

6   1912 is Crozier's 'missing' year, there are no accounts of his activities during this time. The Ulster Volunteer Force was a unionist paramilitary organisation formed in January 1913. Many of its officers were recruited though the League for the Defence of Ulster and like Crozier had served (or in some cases were serving) with the British Army. The UVF supplied many recruits to the 36th Ulster Division at the onset of the Great War. In 1920 the organisation reformed but was short-lived. See Timothy Bowman, *Carson's Army* (Manchester: Manchester University Press, 2007). Bowman's notes on Crozier (p.59) are inaccurate in several details – most notably placing his brigade command within 38th (Welsh) Division instead of 40th Division.

7   Margaret Baguley (ed.), *World War One and the Question of Ulster: The Correspondence of Lilian and Wilfred Spender* (Dublin: Irish Manuscripts Commission, 2009).

8   *London Gazette*, 8 September 1914. Crozier asserts that while in Canada he 'joined the local military forces and was … partly responsible for the raising of a squadron of the Saskatchewan Light Horse'. There is

and the disorder and confusion of recruiting at that time, he avoided taking up this commission and instead was commissioned into the 9th (Service) Battalion Royal Irish Rifles (West Belfast Volunteers).[9] From 4 September 1914 he was major and 2iC of the battalion.

The 9th RIRifles had at its core the West Belfast Regiment of the UVF.[10] Crozier had commanded the unit's Special Service Force and would have been familiar to many of the men and officers of the new battalion.[11] After a period under canvas at Donard Lodge the autumn weather drove the 9th RIRifles into billets before they moved to a new hutted camp at Ballykinler – much to Crozier's relief:

> It is not possible to raise a ... battalion in billets with any degree of satisfaction or hope of efficiency. The barrack rooms and the officers' and sergeants' messes are ... where discipline is forged and character moulded.

Crozier and his CO 'concentrate on two things at the outset: knocking the beer and politics out of all ranks and building up *esprit de corps* in its place ... while ...we foster, inculcate, teach and build up the blood lust for the discomfiture of the enemy'.[12] Crozier writes that the CO, Lieutenant-Colonel G.S. Ormerod, asked him to 'undertake the tactical training of the officers for war, from the theoretical point of view, by means of lectures after mess'. Each weekday evening, for (he claims) six months, Crozier lectured to the officers on subjects such as 'Field Service Regulations, Parts 1 and 2, Infantry training, combined training, a little topography, organisation and equipment, military law and certain campaigns of history'.[13] His syllabus was informed by 'a very extensive memorandum sent ... early in 1915 regarding the training required for France'. The source was Crozier's cousin, Colonel Brinsley John Hamilton Fitzgerald (1859-1931) who at that time was Sir John French's Private Secretary having previously been his ADC in South Africa.[14] While emphasising the principle of 'never retire unless you're ordered to', he also stressed the need to conquer fear: 'All soldiers ... are frightened in action at times. There comes that pain in the tummy. That you have to master. You must never let your neighbour know you are in a funk, either by word, deed or suggestion. Funk in itself is nothing. When unchained it becomes a military menace, and for that men die at the hands of their comrades'.[15] Crozier's lectures were additional to more practical exercises which he described in a letter in 1932:

---

no other evidence for military involvement while in Canada other than in the field of veteran affairs. In *Impressions* he claims that he was 'an ex-Canadian soldier' and in a note to Lord Halifax in 1935 that in 1913 he 'had come specially back from Service with the Canadian Forces' – F.P. Crozier, *Impressions and Recollections* (London: T. Werner Laurie, 1930), pp.136 and 157. Messenger, *Broken Sword*, p.43; TNA WO 374/16997.

9   *London Gazette*, 27 October 1914.
10 Richard S. Grayson, *Belfast Boys: How Unionists and Nationalists Fought and Died Together in the First World War* (London: Continuum, 2009) examines in detail the make-up of the 9th RIRifles and other West Belfast units.
11 Though the number of officers from outside the UVF varied between battalions, the senior officers of the 9th RIRifles were mainly Belfast businessmen – Timothy Bowman, 'Officering Kitchener's Armies: a case study of the 36th (Ulster) Division', *War in History*, 16:2 (2009), pp.189-212. IWM: Documents, 79/35/1, David Starrett, 'Batman' – unpublished typescript, p.13. Bowman, *Carson's Army*, p.99, notes that Crozier does not appear on a list of officers wanted for the Ulster Division.
12 Crozier, *Brass Hat*, pp.36-37.
13 Ibid, p.38. The campaigns covered included, of course, the abandonment of Spion Kop which Crozier contrasted with Smith-Dorrien's stand at Le Cateau just a few months before.
14 Crozier *Impressions*, p.175.
15 Ibid, p.40. Crozier is probably alluding here to the possibility of death by firing squad but just might be also hinting at summary killing.

When platoon drill had been mastered our routine was (1) Adjt's pde before breakfast (with the CO and myself 'observing' (2) CO's parade (steady drill 1½ hrs 10 to 10.30 am) after which we wander into the blue not knowing what was going to be done (I never knew myself till I invented the scheme, shouted out the general and special ideas, made the Adjt write the orders and the Coy cdrs give theirs and platoon cdrs explain to their men) and then got going – falling out half the officers as legitimate casualties in the first half hour to repeat the dose with the other half, putting the original half back instead and then – sounding the officers call – changing the whole scheme from A to Z – dinners in cookers and home at 4pm. After mess, discussion of the day's work – followed by a dance until 11pm, bed, sleep, up again. It made for astounding flexibility.[16]

This first instance of Crozier's promotion of practical training exercises has echoes in 1917 that will be elaborated in Chapter 4. All this training, however, was not enough. When 107 Brigade, including the 9th RIRifles, reached France there were disciplinary problems with the men, some of whom were still over-fond of drink, and capability issues among the officers.[17]

When Major-General Oliver Nugent took command of the Ulster Division in October 1915 he was not impressed. He told his assembled officers what he thought of the division, that: 'we had a good name ... but he did not know how we got it. Every rudimentary mistake that could be made had been made by officers that day [a field day]. They showed total ignorance of modern conditions and lamentable ignorance. He did not know what sort of training we had had in Ireland but it was very poor'.[18] He went on to stress the importance of discipline:

Discipline is the cement which binds every body of men into a homogeneous whole and without which any mob of solders has little to distinguish it from an ordinary mob ... It is the spirit of discipline that enables you and the men you have to lead to face losses ... [But] not all men are equally brave or equally [steady?] under fire ... those are the men who in a big fight begin to look behind them ... the bad example of one man is contagious ... A rot must always be stopped before it spreads. You would be justified in using every means even to the most decisive to prevent an individual whose nerve has one from being a cause of infection to others. You would not only be justified in any step you took to deal with such cases but I would expect it of you.' [19]

The apparent incitement to summary execution is interesting given Crozier's subsequent descriptions of his own actions – all written long after the fact – and it may be that Nugent was setting an example that Crozier sought to follow.

Just ten days after this lecture Nugent's attention focussed on 107 Brigade: 'The Belfast Brigade is awful. They have absolutely no discipline and their officers are awful. I am very much disturbed about them. I don't think they are fit for service and I should be very sorry to have to trust them ... It is all due to putting a weak man in charge of the brigade to start with and giving commissions

---

16   Kings College, London, Liddell Hart Military Archive: LH1/207, Liddell Hart Correspondence with Frank Percy Crozier. Letter 29 August 1932.
17   Timothy Bowman, *Irish Regiments*, particularly Chapter 4, pp.100-139.
18   Diary of Second-Lieutenant G.O.L. Young, 11th Royal Inniskilling Fusiliers quoted in Bowman, *Irish Regiments*, p.110.
19   Ibid. For another extract from Nugent's lecture see Nick Perry, 'Politics and Command: General Nugent, the Ulster Division and Relations with Ulster Unionism 1915-17' in Brian Bond et al, *'Look to your Front': Studies in the First World War by the British Commission for Military History* (Staplehurst: Spellmount, 1999), pp.105-120.

to men of the wrong class'.[20] The officers took the full force of Nugent's tirade which though 'not wholly deserved' was 'very good for us [and] which I shall always treasure in my mind as the most complete example of what can be said by the powerful to the powerless in the shortest space of time … in the most offensive, sarcastic and uncompromising manner possible.'[21] When 108 Brigade was selected for transfer 4th Division in exchange for 12 Brigade (at the time an experimental BEF practice) Nugent substituted 107 Brigade losing (albeit temporarily) what he thought to be his most inefficient formation.[22] His changes worried his GSO2 who wrote to his wife: 'We had officers like Crozier with plenty of experience but General N[ugent] has taken the line that they are all no good and brings over their heads men of 7 years' service'.[23] Crozier believed that it was the 9th and 10th RIRifles that 'carried the weight of the brigade on their shoulders' at this time and that the problem lay with the 8th and 15th RIRifles 'on account of the inferiority of their commanding officers'. Consequently, the 9th and 10th RIRifles 'sometimes caught the reaction caused by the other two [battalions]'.[24] Crozier may well have believed this but the evidence of the number men tried by courts martial during the division's first five months in France indicates otherwise.

From October 1915 to the end of February 1916 seventy-two men of 107 Brigade were tried while the total for 109 Brigade was thirty-eight and for 108 Brigade just nineteen. The 9th and 10th RIRifles were responsible for thirty-nine of these cases and the 8th and 15th accounted for thirty-three.[25] The number of cases from the brigade fell markedly, particularly within the 9th and 15th RIRifles, when one man from the former and two from the latter battalion were executed for desertion in February and March respectively. In commenting on the cases Brigadier-General Withycombe observed that 'the discipline of the 9th R[oyal] I[rish] Rif[le]s is good for a service battalion' while that of the 15th RIRifles was only 'fair': giving a little support perhaps to Crozier's claim that the problems lay elsewhere.[26] Crozier's role in the case and subsequent execution of 14218 Rifleman James Crozier, 9th RIRifles, on 27 February 1916 has been described in almost every work about Crozier and about the death penalty in the First World War.[27] It is interesting that, despite Crozier reporting to the court martial that:

> From a fighting point of view, this soldier is of no value. His behaviour has been that of a shirker for the past three months … I am firmly of the opinion that the crime was deliberately

---

20 Nicholas Perry (ed.), *Major-General Oliver Nugent and the Ulster Division 1915-1918* (Stroud: Sutton, 2007), p.34. On taking command of the division Nugent had replaced Brigadier-General G.H.H. Couchman (1859-1936) with the younger and more competent Brigadier-General W.M. Withycombe (1869-1951).
21 Crozier, *Brass Hat*, p.61.
22 Nicholas Perry, *Major-General Oliver Nugent: The Irishman Who Led The Ulster Division In The Great War* (Belfast: Ulster Historical Foundation, 2020), p.98.
23 PRONI D1633/1/1/81: Wilfred Spender to his wife Lilian, 29 November 1915, quoted in Margaret Baguley (ed.), *World War One and the Question of Ulster: The Correspondence of Lilian and Wilfred Spender* (Dublin: Irish Manuscripts Commission, 2009), p.21.
24 Crozier, *Impressions*, p.161.
25 Bowman, *Irish Regiments*, abstracted from Table 4.1, p.113. There is of course a possible alternative interpretation. The number of cases might be indicative of the level of discipline within a battalion as opposed to the level of indiscipline. Bowman points out that during home service the adjutant of the 14th RIRifles refused to refer 'absent without leave' cases to a court martial. This resulted in a lower number of cases for the battalion (5 compared with the 47 cases for the 9th RIRifles during the same period). Presumably, with a strict disciplinarian in charge, the number of cases would be disproportionally increased. There is as yet, however, no corroboration to confirm this alternative view.
26 Ibid., pp.116-117.
27 Anthony Babington, *For the Sake of Example: Capital Courts Martial 1914-18, the Truth* (London: Leo Cooper, 1983) is an exception. The Crozier case receives a scant mention on p.60.

committed with the intention of avoiding duty ... more particularly as he absented himself shortly after the case of another soldier had been promulgated for a similar crime. The officer commanding the man's company is of a similar opinion.

He then inserted into his statement, apparently as an afterthought: 'He has been with the Expeditionary Force since 3/10/15' – thus reminding the court that Rifleman Crozier was one of the original volunteers.[28] David Starrett, though, recalled that 'The Colonel [Crozier] was more upset than I had ever seen him. 'To have to shoot one of your own men' he kept saying ... [that evening he] buried himself in maps and plans of the line.'[29] Rifleman Crozier had been executed *pour encourager les autres*. Writing in 1937 Frank Crozier stated: 'I did not regret his death at the time ... for intuitively I felt that it would be the first and last of its kind in my regiment [*sic*]. That prediction was proved true by fact.'[30] As this was one of the episodes that coloured readers' perceptions of Crozier's character and hence his reputation we will look again at the execution of Rifleman Crozier as described by his CO later in this chapter.

Crozier was nothing if not even-handed. Just before the FGCM of Rifleman Crozier he had sent one of his junior officers for court martial. Lieutenant Arthur Annandale had previously received his CO's favour in the form of ten days leave granted (unofficially) while he received treatment for venereal disease but, when Annandale promptly bolted during a meeting with Crozier and his company commander when a German trench mortar bombardment started, he found himself in front of a FGCM. He was found guilty of conduct to the prejudice of good order and military discipline but the sentence of dismissal from His Majesty's Service was not confirmed and he was sent to England where he later relinquished his commission on health grounds.[31] Starrett observed that 'The Colonel [Crozier] was off the deep end about both [cases], and few could get anywhere near him ... if the officer did not know what he was doing, did the man?'[32] Crozier had successfully resisted having Annandale returned to duty with his battalion and wrote that as a result 'the Adjutant-General's Department at GHQ obviously tried to break me ... for reasons best known to themselves' and that he owed his survival to the support of his divisional commander, Nugent, and the GOC 107 Brigade, Withycombe.[33] Turning a blind eye to Annandale's venereal disease indicates an element of tolerance in Crozier's approach to discipline. This is also evidenced by the case of Captain George Gaffikin, OC B Company, 9th RIRifles, who Crozier discovered drunk while on front line duty during the winter of 1915/16. Perhaps because of Crozier's own battle with drink a blind eye was turned on the incident following receipt of a promise of abstinence while with the battalion.[34] Just two months after the courts martial the 9th RIRifles received a mention (along with 9th and 10th Royal Inniskilling Fusiliers, 109 Brigade) in Douglas Haig's first despatch as CinC, BEF, for 'good work in carrying out or repelling local attacks and raids'.[35]

---

28   TNA WO 71/450; The FGCM was made up of Major N.G. Burnand (8th RIRifles, President), Captain G. H. Gaffikin (9th RIRifles) and Lieutenant A.T. Blackwood (8th RIRifles). Riflemen J. Prior, 9th RIRifles, was sentenced to two years hard labour on 23 January 1916 for desertion. On 27 February – the day of James Crozier's execution – Rifleman W.J. McFarland, 9th RIRifles was sentenced to two years hard labour for quitting his post.
29   Starrett, *Batman*, p.56.
30   Crozier, *The Men I Killed*, p.52.
31   The case is described in Messenger, *Broken Sword*, p.62; TNA WO 339/14160: Personal file Arthur Annandale.
32   Starrett, *Batman*, p.56.
33   Crozier, *Brass Hat*, p.81; Crozier, *Impressions*, p.169.
34   Gaffikin, promoted major in March, was killed on 1 July 1916.
35   J.H. Boraston (ed), *Sir Douglas Haig's Despatches (December 1915-April 1919)* (London: Dent, 1979 first published 1919), pp.10-11.

Back in Ireland the mention prompted the following assessment: 'Such a distinction proves that the officers of this battalion [the 9th RIRifles], from top to bottom, have been most assiduous and successful in training their men for actual warfare'.[36] Captain George Gaffikin and Second-Lieutenant K.W. Gould of B Company, 9th RIRifles also received mentions.[37] Back in December 1915, just after he had taken command of the battalion, Crozier wrote to Captain Montgomery, OC A Company, 9th RIRifles, asking him to remain when his company had finished its time in the trenches to supervise further working parties. Montgomery remarked 'The General expects a lot, but that is the penalty we pay for a good reputation'.[38] By June 1916, the evidence indicates that the reputation of the battalion and by inference that of Crozier, was improving. How would they perform in their first major action?

Experience of the Somme

The 'local attacks and raids' mentioned above took place on a sector of the front line near the village of Auchonvillers but in March the Ulster Division gave up this northernmost part of its sector and concentrated in the area immediately north of the strategically important high ground at Thiepval. During April, May and June 1916 duty in the trenches was interspersed with provision of working parties (mainly in Thiepval Wood) creating the assembly trenches and other essential infrastructure for the planned offensive on the Fourth Army front. Between 21 – 30 April and 1 – 6 May time was found for the battalion to practice attacks over dummy trenches.[39]

The role of 107 Brigade during the battle was to support 109 Brigade, occupying 36th Division's right sector which was to attack at zero hour and capture the first three lines of German trenches known as 'A', 'B' and 'C'. 107 Brigade was to leave its position in the rear at zero, move up and attack thirty minutes after the main assault with 10th RIRifles on the right and 9th RIRifles on the left. Halting at the already captured 'C' line, their objective was to capture the fourth or 'D' line of trenches which would be consolidated by the 8th RIRifles which was in support.[40]

According to Crozier, and this is one of the many instances where there is no other source, he and his friend Lieutenant-Colonel Bernard, OC 10th RIRifles, were (rightly as it turned out) concerned about the dominating Thiepval village and chateau on their right flank.[41] In case the attack plan needed amendment they agreed to meet in no-man's-land as their battalions deployed. This ignored the orders of Major-General Nugent who had instructed that no CO should venture

---

36 *Larne Times*, 3 June 1916.
37 *London Gazette*, 15 June 1916; Boraston, *Haig's Despatches*, pp.10-11. Messenger, *Broken Sword*, p.64 mistakenly writes that the 9th RIRifles was the only battalion of the Ulster Division to receive a mention.
38 Public Record Office of Northern Ireland, Belfast: D2794/1/1/8, Note from Crozier to Captain W.A. Montgomery. William Alexander Montgomery DSO OBE (d.1932) Captain and OC A Company, 9th RIRifles, went on to be Major and 2iC, 15th RIRifles.
39 TNA WO 95/2503: War Diary, 9th RIRifles.
40 The fourth battalion of 107 Brigade, 15th RIRifles, was to support two battalions of 108 Brigade in their attack on St Pierre Divion it the right centre sector. The remainder of 108 Brigade was to attack north of the River Ancre, which split the front of the division, towards Beaucourt Station. Books about the Somme battle abound. For accounts in differing styles, from different standpoints at different times see, for example, A.H. Farrar-Hockley, *The Somme* (London: Batsford, 1964); Martin Middlebrook, *The First Day on the Somme, 1 July 1916* (London: Allan Lane, 1971); Philipp Orr, *The Road to the Somme: The Men of the Ulster Division Tell Their Story* (Belfast: Blackstaff, 1987); Gary Sheffield, *The Somme* (London: Cassell, 2003); Peter Hart, *The Somme* (London: Cassell, 2005); William Philpott, *Bloody Victory: The Sacrifice on the Somme and the Making of the Twentieth Century* (London: Little Brown, 2009).
41 Lieutenant-Colonel Herbert Clifford Bernard (1865-1916) see Appendix VI.

forward of their battalion battle HQ.[42] At zero on 1 July the 9th and 10th RIRifles advanced in parallel extended columns up the slope through Thiepval Wood to the British Front line. The 10th RIRifles to the right of the 9th RIRifles were clearly visible to the German troops at Thiepval as they passed through the now defoliated wood and were heavily shelled. Bernard was killed soon after the advance started. Crozier watched his four companies leave the British lines 'bullets cutting up the ground at his feet' but realised something was wrong to the right. He 'could not see or hear of Colonel Bernard who was to give the pre-arranged signal for the joint advance of both battalions'.[43] A sunken lane ran in front of the captured German front line about half way across no-man's-land. The men of the 9th RIRifles had formed up there where there was also a little shelter from the enfilade fire from Thiepval. 'Between the bursts Crozier doubled to the sunken road … rallied what was left of the Tenth … signalling the men on. He walked into bursts, he fell into holes, his clothing was torn by bullets, but he himself was all right. Moving about as if on the parade ground he again and again rallied his men … without him not a man would have passed the Schwaben Redoubt let alone reach[ed] the final objective'.[44] Second-Lieutenant H. Malcolm McKee, 9th RIRifles, wrote many years later 'that seeing Crozier standing in No-man's-land gave me a feeling of glee that we were in the battle together. He was a tiger – but his example inspired me lots of times not to run away!'[45] Crozier acknowledged that he 'saw red' that day.[46]

Crozier spent the rest of the day at battalion HQ on the British Front line although an adventure recounted in *Brass Hat* states that he went across to the old German front line that night.[47] Mixed-up units of the Ulster Division were clinging on in the German lines subjected to counter-attacks, bombardments and critical shortages of ammunition, bombs and water. They were also deficient in officers as the COs had been kept back and the 2iCs were part of the cadre retained for post-battle rebuilding. The wounded Captain Montgomery, OC A Company, 9th RIRifles, withdrew the few men remaining in his charge at about 10.30pm but other isolated parties remained in the German front line.[48] The night was spent collecting wounded and clearing trenches of dead and equipment. On the second day Crozier was ordered to organise a party which eventually consisted of 360 men of the 8th, 9th, 10th, and 15th RIRifles to reinforce the troops still holding on. Crozier 'had arranged to lead the force in person' but was stopped by Brigadier-General Withycombe and command given to the 2iC, 9th RIRifles, Major Woods. This enterprise was 'well conceived and gallantly executed' and succeeded in its goal.[49] Most of the exhausted men of the Ulster Division were relieved on the night of 2/3 July and, after some delay, Wood's force was relieved on the morning of 3 July having suffered 200 casualties. Crozier had been at his battle HQ at the edge of Thiepval Wood for more than forty-eight hours. Starrett, his servant, noted that even out of the line he 'could not rest, sitting or standing'.[50]

---

42 Crozier, *Brass Hat*, p.97; Crozier, *Impressions*, p.173. Starrett, *Batman*, p.64 records that 'The two Colonels confab'd [*sic*] … looking anything but happy, for they knew the strength we were up against' but does not record what was said. Confirmation of Nugent's order is given in a letter to his wife dated 11 July 1916: 'The COs were not allowed forward with their men … I absolutely forbid them to go beyond Thiepval Wood … They all protested when I told them … they are far more valuable as live men than dead heroes', Perry, op. cit., p.89.
43 TNA WO95/2503: War Diary 9th RIRifles 'Narrative of Operations 1st-3rd July 1916.
44 Starret, op.cit., p.64.
45 *Belfast Telegraph*, 30 June 1966.
46 Crozier, *Impressions*, p.174.
47 Crozier, *Brass Hat*, p.111.
48 Montgomery was suffering from a head wound, in a state of 'utter exhaustion' and had to be carried back across no-man's-land. For his gallantry on 1 July 1916, he was awarded the DSO.
49 TNA WO 95/2491: War Diary 36th Division HQ General Staff, Account of Operations of 1st July 1916.
50 Starrett, *Batman*, p.67.

Out of the line he wrote to the families of some of the dead. One letter produced an unexpected result when the parents of Lieutenant K.W. Gould who had been reported dead wrote back indignantly having received notice from the Red Cross that he was in German hands.[51] Another letter appeared in the Belfast local press, forwarded by the widow of Company Sergeant-Major Joseph Martin: 'Your husband was killed just as the battalion was about to deploy from the wood for the attack … he has persevered to remain with the battalion all this winter, despite of being ill, and when he came back from hospital it only was because he knew it was his duty to be in the firing line come what may'.[52] While not shedding any light on the action the sympathy letters do illustrate another side to Crozier, even if the latter example is a little restrained.

The 36th (Ulster) Division had suffered 5104 casualties, including 189 officers, during three days of fighting.[53] Crozier wrote that he marched out of the line with just seventy men of the 9th RIRifles. *SDGW* lists 107 men and five officers killed in the battalion and the wounded must have numbered many more.[54] Twenty officers were killed, wounded or missing – the joint highest total (the same as the 8th RIRifles) for any of the division's twelve battalions.[55] Captain Montgomery wrote that he had led 115 other ranks and four officers (including himself) into the battle and just he and thirty-four other ranks remained.[56]

On 11 July the battalion entrained and left the vicinity of the Somme for Flanders where it rested and trained. On 15 July battalion classes for Lewis gunnery, bombing and scouting commenced and 18 July was devoted to musketry training. On 28 July the battalion took up a support position in Ploegsteert Wood and its two composite companies (losses not yet having been made up) moved into the front line on 31 July. On 16 August two patrols went out to examine the enemy wire and this was repeated the next night. On 31 August 3 officers and twenty men left the trenches to raid the German trenches 'under cover of gas' but had to return when the wind refused to cooperate.[57] Further raids followed on 15 September and 12 October, both successful. Crozier wrote (fourteen years later) of three successful raids and that 'during these hectic days I receive the prisoners personally, the number of the regiments concerned being telephoned to GHQ via my report centre actually from the German lines'.[58] In fact the battalion war diary shows that he was away on leave during the second of the successful raids and it was Major Woods, the 2iC, who reported the efficacy of the telephone in this case. It was probably true though, that when Crozier wrote 'These three [sic] successful raids, on top of the Thiepval epic, stimulate the battalion to such an extent as to place it on the topmost rung of the war-ladder' – despite the losses, the morale and capability of the battalion were recovering under Crozier's command.[59]

Captain Montgomery, who had returned to the battalion, had to deal with a draft of 'undesirables' from the 3rd RIRifles. His irregular approach must surely have been known to Crozier:

> Nice and quietly I said to the Sergt Major – please arrange to have these people well beaten after parade, I don't want to be bothered writing things on their conduct sheets … If one beating isn't enough you needn't bother me about it. Just have 'em beaten every day at reveille

---

51 Crozier, *Brass Hat*, p.105.
52 Quoted in Gregson, *Belfast Boys*, p.87.
53 J.E. Edmonds, *Military Operations: France and Belgium 1916 Vol. 1* (London: Macmillan, 1932), p.421.
54 Gregson, *Belfast Boys*, p.85.
55 Anon, *The Great War 1914-1918: Ulster Greets Her Brave and Faithful Sons and Remembers Her Glorious Dead* (Belfast: Books Ulster, [1919] 2015), p.13.
56 Letter quoted in Orr, *The Road to the Somme*, p.191.
57 TNA WO 95/2305: War Diary 9th RIRifles.
58 Crozier, *Brass Hat*, p.126.
59 Ibid.

for as long as it takes to lick 'em into our shape … they don't love me much at present but are coming on quite nicely.⁶⁰

Montgomery chose this busy time to ask Crozier if he could go on a training course:

> I asked the CO the other day … and he said 'Go on a course indeed, Go to hell!' – nice polite friendly person that he is, but soldier – he did end up by telling me that any time I really needed a course I could go on any one I liked just for the asking … this CO knows men because that 'just for the asking' is a perfect masterpiece. The little ugly devil plays with the inside of us and that has made this battalion what it is. Those he cannot play on he doesn't keep.⁶¹

Crozier seems to have been generally well thought of among the officers of the 9th RIRifles. As late as January 1918 his name heads the list of the 'provisional committee' on a leaflet promoting the formation of a 9th RIRifles officers' dinner club to be known as 'The Webel's Own' [sic]. The leaflet notes that it 'was suggested by Brigadier-General Crozier DSO, when in command of the 9th Battalion Royal Irish Rifles, that steps should be taken for the maintenance of a spirit of close comradeship between all the Officers who have served with the Battalion, for as long as two such survive'.⁶²

Another, less flattering, view of Crozier has been widely repeated. In 1976 James L. Stewart-Moore, who was subaltern in the 15th RIRifles and later transferred to 107 Trench Mortar Battery in time for the Somme battle, gave his recollections of Crozier's supposed penchant for sending officers on patrol:

> Their object [officer patrols] was supposed to be the maintenance of offensive spirit but so far as I could see they never achieved anything on our part of the front. Colonel Crozier who commanded the 9th Rifles was particularly keen on sending out patrols all to no purpose except to show off. He had the reputation of being a callous and overbearing martinet.⁶³

It is not clear to which period this comment refers and Stewart-Moore was invalided home in October 1916. Post-Somme the 9th RIRifles war diary records patrols going out on four dates. Pre-Somme patrols are only listed on three dates, all in December 1915. While it is possible that the diarist did not record them, it is also possible that Stewart-Moore's recollection had been influenced by Crozier's own emphasis on patrol work in *Brass Hat* in which patrols lead to the death of one subaltern.⁶⁴ Indeed, it is quite likely that Stewart-Moore's whole image of Crozier as 'callous and overbearing' had been so influenced. If Crozier was indeed 'particularly keen' on sending out patrols it is not reflected in the available evidence and his 'unenviable reputation … due to his advocacy of trench raiding' is founded on the single quotation given above.⁶⁵

---

60 PRONI D2794/1/1/15: William Montgomery to his parents 24 July 1916.
61 PRONI D2794/1/1/14: Letter from Captain W.A. Montgomery to his father, 26 September 1916.
62 David R. Orr and David Truesdale, *'Ulster Will Fight…': Vol. 2, The 36th Ulster Division from Formation to the Armistice* (Solihull, Helion, 2016), p.64. The leaflet is reproduced as a photograph but no source is given. The other members of the 'provisional committee' were Lieutenant-Colonel G.S. Ormerod, Major William Montgomery and Major Horace Haslett. It is not known if the club was actually formed.
63 PRONI T3217/1: Random Recollections recorded by J.L. Stewart-More at Drumkillick commencing 27/1/76, Part II, The Great War, p.26. This extract was first published in Philipp Orr, *The Road to the Somme* in 1987 and has been repeated since without qualification. Stewart-Moore was not alone in his opinion of the value of patrols or trench raids, see Ashworth, *Trench Warfare*, p.192. Ashworth also uses Crozier's description of false reporting of patrol results without qualification (p.106).
64 Crozier, *Brass Hat*, pp.120-124.
65 See Bowman, *Irish Regiments*, p.30.

Some in the 9th Royal Irish Rifles anticipated that after the Somme battle promotion was in the air. Captain Montgomery, now Acting 2iC, 9th RIRifles, who had obviously developed considerable respect for Crozier, wrote to his father in September 1916: 'My CO [Crozier] is in command of the Brigade at present during the Brigadier's absence on leave. I think it is a case of 'coming events'. I hope so, if he will take me with him, otherwise not'.[66] A month later Montgomery was writing that 'I had a very straight heart to heart with the CO [Crozier] today. He has promised me that when he leaves this battalion he will fix it that I get a good job … the CO leaving the battalion depends on when he gets a Brigade. This I think must certainly occur before the Spring'. Montgomery went on: 'I couldn't leave the little devil even if I were only in command of a platoon'.[67] Montgomery was right about 'coming events'. On 19 November 1916 he wrote:

> About 4.00pm the CO [Crozier] got a wire telling him to take over command of a Brigade. He didn't know where it was, who they are, or anything, but he left here to take them over at 5.35pm … Some career in this war he has already had. Captain to Temporary Brigadier-General in two years and a month. He told me before he left that he would send for me just as soon as he finds a good job for me – preferably a staff job … From what Brigadier-General F.P. Crozier said to me before he left it [Montgomery's reversion to captain following Haslett's return] won't be for long if he can help it … no more Coy cmdg for me if I can possibly avoid it.[68]

Crozier did indeed attempt to obtain Montgomery's services in 1917 but without success as described later.

Crozier was lucky to have supportive superiors in the brigade and division – although he had tested his divisional general's patience to the limit by his actions at Thiepval on 1 July. He later wrote that 'Nugent, owing to Bernard's death kindled up such a fuss about 'disobedience' that I, for personal post battle safety, drew a very heavy veil over events. You know better than I do the <u>rules</u> laid down in old F.S.R. governing the departure from an order in the presence of the enemy. All the justifications for departure were present. I saw the original recommendation for a DSO for me, made out by Withycombe, scrawled across in red ink by Nugent … "Rank disobedience of orders, should be court-martialled"'.[69] Nugent's ire passed and Crozier was awarded a DSO in the next New Year's Honours List and was mentioned in despatches.

Nugent was obviously important to Crozier because no promotion could be forthcoming without his approval. He (Nugent) certainly had earlier reservations when considering Crozier's promotion to battalion command. Wilfred Spender, then the GSO2 in the 36th (Ulster) Division, observed later that: 'in fact General Nugent, who felt some hesitation in giving him [Crozier] promotion owing to the roughness and ruthless way in which he handled his men, spoke to me on the subject, and I recommended him thinking that his courage and leadership would counterbalance his other

---

66 Public Record Office of Northern Ireland, Belfast: D2794/1/1/14, Montgomery Family Papers, Letter from Major W.A. Montgomery to his father, 26 September 1916.
67 PRONI D2794/1/1/17: Montgomery to his father, 30 October 1916. Despite Crozier's recommendations, Montgomery was replaced as 2iC, 9th RIRifles, by the returning Major Horace Haslett, and passed over for the battalion command in favour of Major Philip Woods who returned from the Senior Officers Course at Aldershot.
68 PRONI D2794/1/1/19: Montgomery to his father, 19 November 1916.
69 TNA CAB 45/132: Letter from Crozier to Sir James Edmonds, 23 March 1930. Crozier's faith in *FSR* [General Staff, *Field Service Regulations Part 1, Operations* (London: HMSO, 1909, Reprinted with Amendments 1914)] was justified. Section 12, paragraph 13ii, stated 'A departure from either the spirit or the letter of an order is justified if the subordinate who assumes the responsibility bases his decision on some fact which could not be known to the officer who issued the order'.

disabilities.'⁷⁰ Spender implies that they did not but, nevertheless, both Withycombe, GOC 107 Brigade, and Nugent, GOC, 36th (Ulster) Division, thought well enough of Crozier's abilities to recommend him for promotion after the Somme battle. Crozier put it down to the fact that they 'were fair-minded men, as my seniority was against me. I was the junior Colonel in the brigade'.⁷¹

The quotation from Spender given in the last paragraph was first brought into the spotlight by Gary Sheffield who also highlighted Crozier's 'unbalanced views'.⁷² Spender wrote his letter just one month after the publication of *Brass Hat* and had not liked what he read. It is important to read the full extract in context:

> Brigadier-General Crozier has recently published a book which casts grave reflections on the men of the [BEF] in fact General Nugent, who felt some hesitation in giving him promotion owing to the roughness and ruthless way in which he handled his men, spoke to me on the subject, and I recommended him thinking that his courage and leadership would counterbalance his other disabilities. Perhaps the kindest view of General Crozier's mentality is to try and believe that his contact with men with very high ideals in religion and patriotism has now produced a somewhat unbalanced change of view corresponding to what sometimes takes place at a revival meeting on the minds of men whose standards had previously not been high. I refer to this matter since, if it were possible to do so, the official history of the war should show in some way the true picture which is so different to that being painted by General Crozier and other writers of similar notoriety.

The letter was obviously written in anger following his reading of *Brass Hat* and, in Spender's eyes, Crozier's unbalanced views can be seen to be a later construction and not a contemporary description of his wartime psyche.

Crozier particularly admired the working of the 107 Brigade staff which he called 'first class', singling out for praise the working relationship between Withycombe and his Brigade–Major, Maurice Fitzmaurice Day MC.⁷³ They had 'served together for years' and Day had previously been adjutant to Withycombe when he commanded the 2nd King's Own Yorkshire Light Infantry.⁷⁴ Crozier was clearly aware of the value of good brigade HQ staff. In Crozier's opinion 'General Withycombe should have got a Division at the end of 1916 but he never got one at all'.⁷⁵ 'Nugent was one of the worst treated men in the war and should have been a Corps commander, had the Gods been kind.'⁷⁶ Crozier recalled that on the day he left 36th Division, Nugent gave him 'sound advice; he always did. "Treat your four battalions like four big companies," he said, and "do not forget your oddments," advice which I always acted upon to the best of my ability'.⁷⁷

Crozier's promotion was the tangible result of his reputation as a capable commander. Subsequently that reputation has been eroded not only by the publication of the remarks made by

---

70   TNA CAB 45/137: Letter from Wilfred Spender, ex GSO2, 36th (Ulster) Division, to Sir James [Spender calls him 'Sir Thomas'] Edmonds in connection with Edmonds' Official History volume on the battle of the Somme, 3 May 1930.
71   Crozier, *Impressions*, p.174.
72   Gary Sheffield, *Leadership in the Trenches* (London: Palgrave Macmillan, 2000), p.149.
73   Maurice Day (1878-1952) see Appendix VI.
74   Withycombe started the war as CO 1st KOYLI but took command of the 2nd KOYLI from November 1914 – October 1915.
75   Crozier, *Impressions*, p.174.
76   Ibid., pp.179-180. Nugent stayed with the Ulster Division until May 1918.
77   Ibid., p.178. Presumably Nugent was referring to the Brigade HQ staff, clerks, servants, machine-gun company, trench mortar battery and brigade transport. In *Brass Hat* (p.131) Crozier gives another version of Nugent's words: 'Treat your new brigade like a big battalion'.

Stewart-Moore and Wilfred Spender cited above but particularly by public reaction to the books that he published in the 1930s. In order to understand the effect that Crozier's books have had on his reputation, the next section will examine them in some detail.

Crozier's Post-War Writing

The image of Brigadier-General Frank Percy Crozier was created largely by his books and the books that others have since written that draw on their content. Understanding how and why they were written and how they were received is crucial to the understanding of the evolution of his public image and reputation. This section examines them in detail along with some of the reviews and press notices that they generated. Although two books are very well known and often quoted he wrote seven:

Title	Publisher	Date Published
A Brass Hat in No Man's Land	Jonathan Cape	April 1930
Impressions and Recollections	T. Werner Laurie	September 1930
A Word to Gandhi	Williams & Norgate	October 1931
Five Years Hard	Jonathan Cape	February 1932
Angels on Horseback	Jonathan Cape	August 1932
Ireland for Ever	Jonathan Cape	December 1932
The Men I Killed	Michael Joseph	August 1937

These do not form a logical sequence. *Brass Hat* is a memoir of the Great War; *Impressions* is the nearest to an autobiography and covers the periods before and after the war as well as going over the same ground as *Brass Hat*; *A Word to Gandhi* is an account of British policy in Ireland and its lessons according to Crozier; *Five Years Hard* describes Crozier's service in northern Nigeria between 1901 and 1905; *Angels on Horseback* is an account of his time with Thorneycroft's Mounted Infantry in South Africa during the first half of 1900; *Ireland for Ever* returns to the subject of Ireland and British imperial policy, while *The Men I Killed* returns to the subject of the Great War.[78]

Crozier's public writing started with letters to newspapers and was initially concerned with his interest in the places where he had seen service. In 1920, for example, he wrote to *The Times* about the situation in Lithuania.[79] His resignation as commander of the Auxiliary Division of the Royal Irish Constabulary (ADRIC) in February 1921 was followed by a flurry of correspondence and articles. Ireland seems also to have been the catalyst for his first attempt at extended prose at a time when he was said to be 'burning with indignation'.[80] In rejecting a political pamphlet 'Imperial lessons from the Irish settlement' in August 1923, the managing director of The Labour

---

78   F.P. Crozier, *Five Years Hard: being an account of the fall of the Fulani Empire and a picture of the daily life of a regimental officer among the peoples of the Western Sudan* (London: Jonathan Cape, 1932); F.P. Crozier, *A Word to Gandhi: the lesson of Ireland* (London: Williams and Norgate, 1931); F.P. Crozier, *Ireland for Ever* (London: Jonathan Cape, 1932).
79   In September 1919 Crozier was appointed as Inspector General of the Lithuanian forces. The Lithuanians were fighting on three fronts against Germans, Bolsheviks and Poles. He regarded the mission as 'a ghastly failure' and was back in Britain by March 1920.
80   London School of Economics Archives, M3383, Coll Misc 1155.

Publishing Company mentions that 'I certainly remember you coming to us in regard to your book on Ireland'.[81] It would be nine years before the book on Ireland appeared.

By 1928 Crozier was a regular contributor of newspaper copy. He published articles with headlines such as 'Are we too Kind to the Modern Schoolboy?', 'Are You in Love with Your Job?' and 'Are the Professions Doomed?'.[82] He also contributed a series of 'derring-do' stories based on his experiences in the Baltic and South Africa to the boys periodical *Chums* and in 1935-1936 he was credited as 'our military expert' by *Reynold's Illustrated News* which published a series of articles on the Italian campaign in Abyssinia and the Spanish Civil War.

Why did Crozier Write?

When looking for the motivation for Crozier's writings it is impossible to disregard his financial situation. He found no employment in the Regular army after the war, his Lithuanian adventure proved abortive, the reformed UVF did not want him and he had resigned his post with the ADRIC under a massive cloud and much public recrimination in February 1921. His first wife died in April 1921 and he married for a second time later in the same month. His actress first wife had brought no fortune, contributed to the frittering away of such income that he did have and suffered from physical and mental illness that required payment of medical bills. His second wife had been employed as the nurse to his elder daughter and was also not endowed with funds. His previous bankruptcy as a junior officer in 1909 was just the first of a series of events that illustrate how he had no capacity for effective management of his own finances.

By March 1922 Crozier was Chairman and Director of the 'Ex-Officers Automobile Service', the Principal General Manager of which was Lieutenant-Colonel Richard Andrews, who served under Crozier in 119 Brigade. Tragedy struck in January 1923 when Andrews was hit in the chest and killed by a disintegrating abrasive wheel in his garage with Crozier (supposedly) at his side, effectively putting paid to that venture.[83] Crozier's subsequent attempt at a parliamentary career came to nothing when he failed to be elected as the member for Portsmouth Central in the December 1923 General Election.[84] The loss, by 3,502 votes, in what had been a marginal constituency, perhaps indicates that his reputation had suffered a knock in the aftermath of his very public resignation from the ADRIC. By the end of 1925 he was bankrupt again. At the first meeting of his creditors he declared liabilities of £600 and no assets – he also blamed his financial state on an establishment vendetta that set out to ruin him.[85] Though writing was by now not his only option – by 1929 he was also earning by speaking on behalf of the League of Nations Union – it seems that his published output was driven largely by financial necessity.[86] He needed cash.

Much has been written about the context of the explosion in war writing during the late 1920s and 1930s. Crozier published his first book at the height of the period of disenchantment with the ideals that had carried Great Britain through the Great War and the years prior to the publication

---

81 Ibid. Crozier had tried the *Daily Herald* and then contacted George Bernard Shaw in an attempt to publish his pamphlet.
82 *Daily Express*, 29 August, 13 November and 29 November 1929. The first of these was prompted by a return to his old school, Wellington College.
83 If Crozier was indeed an eyewitness it seems odd that accounts of the subsequent inquest do not record him being called to give evidence and this is probably another instance of him embellishing a narrative.
84 *The Times*, 7 December 1923. The seat had been marginal at the 1922 General Election but Crozier (standing for Labour) was 3,502 votes behind the winning Liberal candidate.
85 *Daily Mirror*, 13 February 1926.
86 *Manchester Guardian*, 4 February 1929.

of *Brass Hat* saw the appearance of Max Plowman's *A Subaltern on the Somme* (1927), Edmund Blunden's *Undertones of War* (1928), Robert Graves' *Goodbye to all That* (1929), Charles Douie's *The Weary Road* (1929) and Erich Maria Remarque's *All Quiet on the Western Front* (1929) amongst many. These books abandoned the heroic and restrained tone of earlier works; they caught the public imagination and they sold well. Cyril Falls wrote in April 1930 – the same month that *Brass Hat* was published – that 'the characteristics of this book [*All Quiet…*] and its successors, whether fiction or reminiscence are very similar; indeed it is common gossip that several writers sat down to produce one in the same vein after watching Herr Remarque's sales go soaring up into the hundred-thousands'.[87]

Crozier was not likely to admit to a financial motive to his writing. Defending his first book against the charges of sensationalism and untruth that appeared in the press, Crozier, said 'I have written my book to focus attention on the futility of war. Another war will lead to the destruction of the moral fibre of the world'.[88] His wife gave the reason for writing as 'To tell the stark truth about war, not glossing it over or idealizing it but showing its stark realities'.[89] At the time of writing *Brass Hat* Crozier was involved in the League of Nations Union and a supporter of the League's stance on peace. Just as the book was published the London Naval Conference was ending and Crozier obviously expected much good to come out of it. His 'Epilogue' at the end of *Brass Hat* describes an imagined scene in the year 2119 when a group of Boy Scouts visiting the museum which by then occupies the redundant War Office are told of the key role of the League of Nations in abolishing war and of the 'constructive advance into the realm of disarmament and cooperation' that took place at the 1930 conference.[90] Crozier would have been disillusioned with its actual outcome. In the reprinted edition of *Brass Hat* he acknowledged that he was wrong in his prediction:

> Readers may feel that owing to the failure of the World to use the League of Nations as originally intended, owing to the collapse of collective security and the breakdown of the Disarmament Conference, some of the conclusions arrived at in this book no longer hold good. They will I believe be right.[91]

Crozier's conversion to the cause of peace seems to be genuine and perhaps indicates an underlying remorse about his role as a soldier in causing the deaths of others but his enthusiastic support for the peace movement also gave him the chance to hit back at the establishment.[92]

The different titles that he penned had other motives underlying their key role as income generators. At the time of writing *Brass Hat* Crozier was developing his views on peace but aimed to push readers towards that cause by emphasising, even sensationalising, the beastliness of war by repeated reference to violence, alcohol and sex. The success of his first venture prompted T. Werner Laurie to publicise *Impressions* as 'By the author of *A Brass Hat in No Man's Land* …He lived a score of lives, each one a glamorous adventure'.[93] In fact *Impressions* is Crozier's most restrained work and

---

87 Cyril Falls, *War Books* (London: Greenhill Books, 1989 first published 1930), p.xvi.
88 *Daily Mirror*, 24 April 1930.
89 Grace Crozier, *Guns and God*, unpublished typescript, p.147. Copy in author's possession.
90 *Brass Hat*, p.263.
91 F. P. Crozier, *A Brass Hat in No Man's Land* (London: Jonathan Cape, Florin Books edition, 1937), p.7.
92 IWM: Sound Archive, AC4581. Crozier stated that he was reluctant to speak in a meeting held in church because he had so much blood on his hands. *Brass Hat* was first cited as a source in H.R.L. Sheppard, *We Say No: The Plain Man's Guide to Pacifism* (London: 1935), Chapter 6, 'The Slayer of Souls'.
93 *The Times*, 10 October 1930. It is doubtful whether Crozier would have agreed with the description of his life.

the most readable. It demonstrates the effect of tight editorial control over content and style and is the nearest thing to an autobiography that he wrote, covering his life story up to the aftermath of his resignation from the Auxiliary Division Royal Irish Constabulary (ADRIC). He does take the opportunity to air his views in departures from the narrative throughout the book and particularly in a final chapter on 'The Lessons to be Learnt', which focuses on the ills of alcohol, the need for world peace, the negative effects of bureaucracy and the need to ensure promotion within the military by merit and not favouritism. There is no reference to sex. *Impressions* also contains his first account of his resignation from the ADRIC. He returned to the subject of Ireland in the strange *A Word to Gandhi; The Lesson of Ireland* (1931). The description on the cover of that book states that the author:

> Describes with fearless frankness the disastrous policy pursued by the British Government during the Irish Rebellion. His case is that anything between martial law and concession of demands leads to reprisals, murder, and chaos. In India martial law is impossible. The choice, therefore, is between a situation infinitely worse than the Irish, or practical concession of Gandhi's terms.

Crozier sent Gandhi a copy inscribed 'Mr Gandhi will be surprised to find in a military man an admirer of his'.[94] The publishers of *A Word to Gandhi* were Williams and Norgate. This company published Henry Brinton's *The Peace Army* in the following year and their use by Crozier indicates his increasing engagement with the peace movement.[95] Money and the cause of peace were two of Crozier's motives for writing, the third (particularly in the case of the Irish-themed books) was revenge. By 1931 it was obvious to Crozier that he had lost his continuing battle with the establishment over the loss of both his reputation and his income following his resignation from the ADRIC back in 1921. To a more perceptive man it would have been obvious that the establishment was not going to budge but Crozier was nothing if not stubborn.[96]

His next three books were published by Jonathan Cape in quick succession. All three are in the mould of *Brass Hat* and written in Crozier's trademark derring-do style. Theatrical chapter titles lead into equally theatrical paragraphs of short sentences laced with florid language, extensive reported conversation and exclamation marks. The first to be published was *Five Years Hard*. Crozier uses this book to describe his experiences in northern Nigeria as a member of the West African Field Force (WAAF) and as such it forms one of the two 'prequels' to *Brass Hat*. The other is *Angels on Horseback*, which covers Crozier's service in Thorneycroft's Mounted Infantry (TMI) during the Second Boer War. Despite both these subjects appearing previously in *Impressions*, Jonathan Cape must have thought that there would be enough interest in the subjects (and their author) to warrant the investment in publication. Like *Brass Hat* both works continue Crozier's penchant for using pseudonyms for characters that were (mainly) still alive at the time of publication – although Crozier does not use the conceit consistently. As many of the characters are easily tracked down by cross-reference to the already published *Impressions* one wonders why he did this and whether it was a requirement of his publishers. Most easily recognized in *Five Years Hard* is

---

94 D.G. Tendulkar, *Mahatma: Life of Mohandas Karamchand Gandhi. Vol 3, 1930-1934* (Bombay: Jhaveri & Tendulkar, 1952), p.146.
95 Henry Brinton, *The Peace Army* (London: Williams and Norgate, 1932).
96 Crozier's last-ditch attempt to obtain a pension was a thirty-eight-page document submitted to Lord Halifax (facilitated by Dick Sheppard) outlining Crozier's version of the events in Ireland that led to his resignation. TNA WO 374/16997.

Thomas Astley Cubitt who appears in the guise of 'Tom Spindle'.[97] Anyone familiar with either Cubitt's role in the WAAF or his tall, gangly frame would have quickly identified him.

Angels on Horseback describes a period in Crozier's life before that of *Five Years Hard* and one again wonders why the books came out in the 'wrong' order. Its subject is the six months that Crozier spent in the ranks of TMI in 1899-1900. Though a short period it was an important one for the young man as he had his first taste of action and survived the battle of Spion Kop. The battle and his future step-father's role in abandoning the summit of the hill left a lasting impression on him and provided an example that he says he used time and again to his men during the Great War to illustrate the danger of retreat without orders. The book again contains the use of pseudonyms but is notable for the prominent character of Rufus 'Ginger' Ross. Ross embodies the admirable characters of the British officer: concern for duty, care for his men, obedience to orders, steadiness under fire and moral courage, but who is also someone unafraid to speak his mind when it is necessary. Ross is such an important character in the book that he deserves some study, particularly as Crozier claims to have met him again under fire in France eighteen years later.[98]

A profile of Ross can be put together from snippets in the book. The son of a general, he attended Wellington College (like Crozier), he attended the same crammer in Earl's Court as Crozier, was a 'senior subaltern' in a militia battalion before joining the Sierra Leone Frontier Police in 1896, served in Cuba against the Spanish in 1898 where he reached the rank of colonel, joined the Royal Niger Company before service with TMI and a commission in Brabant's Horse. By 1918 he was a 'colonial cavalry general'. Crozier gives the impression of hero-worship when writing of Ross so it is surprising that it has proved impossible to identify an officer with the same record. It seems likely that Ross is a composite character based on Crozier's contacts in South Africa and in Nigeria. It is noteworthy that Ross does not appear at all in *Impressions* but that Crozier describes W.C.N. Hastings (known as 'Marcus') in similar terms as Ross:

> He was at the same time not only quite a character, but perhaps the best practical soldier that the battalion possessed ... A brave man, he had considerable respect for the enemy in the field but none whatever for his superiors, should they chance to be stupid, ignorant, or lacking that sense of humour which is an essential factor in a military machine. On top of this able to superimpose his own personality, the result being that he generally got what he wanted.[99]

Combine Hastings (and a little of Crozier himself) with the like of Hugh Gilbert Gregorie, son of a Major-General, who joined TMI as a trooper on the same day as Crozier and rose to command 47 Infantry Brigade, 16th Division, in the Great War, and the character of Ross takes shape.[100] One final element may be provided by the character of Jack Seely, an unconventional soldier, whom Crozier had seen in action in South Africa and who commanded the Canadian Cavalry Brigade from 1915 to 1918.[101]

The next book, *Ireland for Ever*, was the vehicle for Crozier's vindication of his conduct as Commandant of the ADRIC. Its 301 pages outline the Irish situation in 1920 and 1921 from Crozier's perspective as he describes the organizational chaos and lack of clear policy which in his opinion led to the alienation of the population and the loss of Ireland by the 1921 treaty. Much has

---

97 Thomas Astley Cubitt (1871-1939). See Appendix VI.
98 Crozier, *Angels on Horseback*, pp.246-262.
99 Crozier, *Impressions*, p.50.
100 Hugh Gilbert Gregorie (1878-1928). See Appendix VI.
101 John Edward Bernard ('Jack') Seely (1868-1947). See Appendix VI; Crozier, *Impressions*, p.53. Crozier witnessed Seely publicly refusing an order to retire and commanding a successful rearguard – for which Seely was subsequently reprimanded following a court martial.

been made of Crozier's role there (not least by Crozier himself) but it must be remembered that he was in command of the ADRIC between 4 August 1920 and 23 November when he was involved in a serious road accident that left him hospitalised. He did not return to duty until 10 January 1921 and resigned on 19 February. His account is biased, is influenced strongly by subsequent events and therefore must be read with some scepticism.

Crozier's last and most notorious book was *The Men I Killed*. By the time it was published Crozier had formed a close friendship with Reverend H.R.L. 'Dick' Sheppard and had been instrumental with Sheppard in founding the Peace Pledge Union in 1936.[102] The book is not a good piece of writing. As one reviewer put it: 'This is a free country and General Crozier can have his convictions and have his say. His say is noisy, excited, poorly arranged, ill-argued and ill-written'.[103] The storm of criticism that greeted this particular publication is described further below.

How were these books received?

> May 15th[1930]. Have I, asks our Vicar's wife, read 'A Brass Hat in No Man's Land'? No I have not. Then, she says, don't, on any account. There are so many sad and shocking things in life as it is, that writers should confine themselves to the bright, the happy and the beautiful. This the author of 'A Brass Hat' has entirely failed to do. It subsequently turns out that our Vicar's wife has not read the book herself, but that our Vicar has skimmed it, and declared it to be very painful and unnecessary. (Mem: Put 'Brass Hat' down for 'Times' Book Club list, if not already there).[104]

The 'Provincial Lady' was one of many to seek out *Brass Hat* which ran to five impressions within a month and was eventually also produced in a cheap edition in April 1937. After the author's death extracts were also published in *The Great War, I Was There*.[105] The reviews were mixed. Robert Graves wrote in the house magazine of Jonathan Cape:

> In spite of occasional clichés of phrase and sentiment, or even not in spite of them, for they are so obvious that they save the book from being judged too strictly on its literary merits, it is the only account of fighting on the Western Front that I have been able to read with sustained interest and respect … After a book of this sort has appeared no one need bother to write more 'startling war revelations' of the Western Front. Crozier has done the job once and for all; and nobody can challenge the authenticity of Crozier as witness.[106]

The *Times Literary Supplement* reviewer (possibly Cyril Falls, who had served in the Ulster Division with Crozier) noted:

---

102 Hugh Richard Lawrie Sheppard (1880-1937) was a charismatic Anglican clergyman and pacifist. He first met Crozier in 1932 after Crozier supported Sheppard's proposal for a 'Peace Army' to place itself between combatants in war zones and they worked closely until Crozier's death.
103 *Morning Post*, 13 August 1937.
104 E.M. Delafield, *Diary of a Provincial Lady* (London: Howard Baker, 1930), p.53.
105 J. Hammerton, *The Great War: 'I Was There!'* (London: Amalgamated Press, 1938-9), pp.657, 1459.
106 R. Graves, 'Review of A Brass Hat in No Man's Land', *Then and Now* (Summer 1930), p.5. Grave's lengthy review was mainly a response to Douglas Jerrold, *The Lie about the War* (London: Faber and Faber, 1930). Jerrold rejected the torrent of new works supposedly telling 'the truth about the war' including *All Quiet on the Western Front* and Graves' *Good-bye to All That*. Crozier's *Brass Hat* was published three months later.

The author of this book had the reputation of being a man of remarkable physical bravery and a successful commander of the cut-and-thrust order; one cannot truly say that he reveals himself to be an engaging personality. It must be admitted, however, that he has a philosophy and sticks to it consistently … There are other features of the book in the highest degree reprehensible. Allusions are made to despicable conduct on the part of brother officers, not always with names mentioned, indeed, but in a fashion such that the names could be identified by hundreds who served.[107]

The *Daily Mirror* reviewer wrote:

When read carefully this egoistical book, which has aroused much discussion is not so unpleasant as some critics have supposed … If General Crozier is stern with the man who lets his fellow soldiers down, he can also be generous to the good fighter who is guilty of a temporary lapse … Much of the book is trivial or injudiciously phrased, but most of it remains an interesting eye-witness's account of war conditions and a logical explanation of the urgent military reasons underlying certain severities.[108]

The *New York Times* noted that *Brass Hat* was 'The literary sensation of the hour' and that much of 'the torrent of abuse' with which the press greeted its publication was 'simply the accusation, repeated over and over again in varying terms and at great length, that a British officer should be ashamed at himself for throwing mud at the British Army. No reputable authority has attempted to challenge the statements of fact given on General Crozier's first hand authority'.[109]

Sir Herbert Creedy at the War Office wrote to the King's Private Secretary, Colonel Sir Clive Wigram:

When we saw that Brigadier-General Crozier had published his book … we went into the question of what, if anything, could be done and finally took counsel with the Home Office. We have come to the conclusion, naturally with some regret, that there is nothing we could do which would not have the result of advertising the book and putting more money into the pockets of Crozier and his publisher.

Wigram replied 'Many thanks for your confidential note on General Crozier, which I showed to the King. He is evidently an undesirable person and, as you say, the best thing to do is to let the book slide back into the mud from which it emerged'.[110] The book sold 6,275 copies in two months and 10,000 copies of the cheap edition were printed in 1937.[111]

The furore generated by the publication of *Brass Hat* is in marked contrast to the reception of another author's work just three years before. When Max Plowman (who would later work closely with Crozier in the Peace Pledge Union) sought a publisher for *A Subaltern on the Somme,* the book was rejected by Collins for lacking 'the element of sensation' needed 'for a book on war to have any reasonable chance of success'. The book was published by Dent in September 1927, went to two

---

107 *Times Literary Supplement*, 15 May 1930. Cyril Bentham Falls CBE (1888-1971) see Appendix VI.
108 *Daily Mirror*, 2 May 1930.
109 *New York Times*, 18 May 1930.
110 TNA WO 374/16997: Personal file, F.P. Crozier.
111 University of Reading: MS 2446 Jonathan Cape Archive, Sales ledgers. Unsold copies of this edition were bound for sale as one-shilling paperbacks in 1940.

impressions in two months and received at least twenty-five favourable reviews.[112] It then faded from sight until reprinted by the Imperial War Museum in 1996. This is surprising considering that it touches on alcohol abuse by officers, sex, venereal disease, threats to shoot anyone who retires without orders, courts martial and bullying officers in the course of its 269 pages. Unlike Crozier's book, however, it lacks the strained invective and the hectoring tone. Being written by a subaltern and not a brigadier–general it certainly never attracted the attention of the establishment which suggests that the objections to Crozier's work from the higher echelons of society were related to the rank of the author as much as the content.[113]

When *Impressions* was published Cyril Falls wrote:

> The tone of the narrative is altogether less provocative and more pleasing [than in Brass Hat]. Ruthless efficiency, rather than the creation of blood lust, is here his theme; and if he sometimes seems to suggest that he was about the only ruthless Brigadier on the Western Front his enthusiasm and single-mindedness afford some excuse … the chief fault of his writing is its disjointedness. He is constantly breaking off his story to moralize, the result being that the sequence of events is often vague …It need only be said that the disjointed methods of putting before his readers his narrative … are in this case very unfortunate in view of the grave charges which he brings against both his superiors and his subordinates, and of the persistent persecution of which he declares himself to be the victim.[114]

'This comparison lacks force and meaning' was the dismissive verdict of the reviewer of *A Word to Gandhi* on Crozier's comparison of British policy in Ireland and India.[115] *Ireland for Ever* was also dismissed: 'the writer prefaces his passages on the struggle in Ireland in 1920 and 1921 with a historical summary of no great value. The rest of the book is mainly taken up with accusations against the police in Ireland in those years'.[116] At 31 December 1932, six weeks after publication, 821 of the 1,500 print run had been sold.[117]

Cyril Falls was again the *Times Literary Supplement* reviewer of *Five Years Hard*:

> Brigadier-General Crozier can write in a vivid and arresting manner as he has already proved. Apart from half a dozen phrases or paragraphs in which he insists upon saying the things that 'are not said', this is a pleasant and amusing, as well as a bright and interesting book.[118]

One of Crozier's imperial heroes, Lord Lugard, who had been the 'Chief' in Nigeria during Crozier's time there was rather less impressed.[119] When asked to review the book by the *Daily Mail*, he declined:

---

112 'Mark VII' (Max Plowman), *A Subaltern on the Somme* (London: Dent, 1927); M. Pittock, 'Max Plowman and the Literature of the First World War', *Cambridge Quarterly*, 33 (2004), pp.217-243. For Plowman's *post mortem* defence of Crozier see *Peace News*, 11 September 1937.
113 Yuval Noah Harari, 'Martial Illusions: War and Disillusionment in Twentieth-Century and Renaissance Military Memoirs', *The Journal of Military History*, 69 (2005), pp.43-72, seems to imply the Crozier was a representative of a writer from the 'junior ranks'.
114 *TLS*, 16 October 1930.
115 *TLS*, 22 October 1931.
116 *TLS*, 19 January 1933.
117 University of Reading: MS 2446 Jonathan Cape Archive, Sales ledgers.
118 *TLS*, 3 March 1932.
119 Frederick John Dealtry Lugard, 1st Baron Lugard, CMG CB DSO PC (1858–1945), soldier, explorer and colonial administrator. First High Commissioner for the Protectorate of Northern Nigeria, 1900-1906.

I am surprised that any publisher should have accepted it and hope that you will ignore it, and not give it the valuable advertisement of a review ... It represents officers of the West African Field Force ... as perpetually under the influence of liquor, to say nothing of their relationship with native women, and the account of a white woman aboard ship which is not fit for publication ... Some of the incidents Crozier relates ... would not be credible were it not that he relates the facts as having being done by himself.[120]

Lugard also brought the matter to the attention of Sir George Tomlinson at the Colonial Office: 'A man who describes with apparent gusto how he told his native soldiers to mutilate the dead (his co-religionists) in the search for gold bangles, is a disgrace to the order of the DSO ... This scandalous description of them [the officers of the WAFF] as a drunken immoral crowd is a libel on the traditions of the Corps'.[121] Tomlinson replied pragmatically: 'One can only hope that the book will be treated with the contempt it deserves and so sink into oblivion'.[122] At 30 June 1932, five months after publication, 2,027 of a print run of 5,000 had been sold.[123]

When *Angels on Horseback* was published Cyril Falls was once again the reviewer:

In previous books Brigadier-General Crozier has had something to say of the South African war. Here he describes his part in more detail. The book has the merits and demerits of its predecessors: a vivid narrative power and a gift for description on the one hand and on the other for indifferent taste and always too much reported conversation in circumstances which make it impossible for the author really to remember what was said.[124]

Crozier defended his powers of recollection – not very convincingly:

May I defend my memory on which your reviewer casts doubt? Are we not accustomed to tell our stories in detail, at our regimental dinners, thirty, yes forty, years after – then why not write them? ... I can remember conversations, in action, as vividly today as thirty-five years ago – and the settings.[125]

By the end of December 1932, five months after publication, 821 out of a print run of 2,000 had been sold.

But it was Crozier's final book that produced the greatest outrage. Publication of *The Men I Killed* triggered a blizzard of newspaper copy almost all of which was viciously condemnatory. The national and provincial press was awash with headlines such as 'Church Leaders Denounced'; 'Amazing Confession by General Crozier'; 'My Men I Shot: Killed an Officer to Prevent Panic'; 'Threats to General Who Told Truth about War'; 'War with the Lid Off: Another Sensational Book By General Crozier'; 'War Dead Slandered'; and 'General, I Wouldn't Be You', most of which led into extracts taken from the more lurid passages in the book, usually those dealing with the

---

120 Bodleian Library: Lugard MSS 9/7/123, Lord Lugard to Douglas West (Editorial Department *Daily* Mail), 5 February 1932.
121 Bodleian Library: Lugard Papers L9/7/124.
122 Ibid., L/9/7/125.
123 University of Reading: MS 2446 Jonathan Cape Archive, Sales ledgers.
124 *TLS*, 25 August 1932.
125 *TLS*, 1 September 1932. Quoted in B. Clifford, *The Men I Killed: A Selection from the Writings of General F.P. Crozier* (Belfast: Athol Books, 2002).

shooting of an unidentified subaltern during the battle of the Lys in April 1918.[126] There were a few, more considered, reviews:

> He [Crozier] tells all that is important about the men he killed in one chapter and that chapter has ensured excellent reviews, not of the book, but of that one chapter. For the rest 'The Men I Killed' is a pathetic plea for peace. It is pathetic in its tone, its reasoning, and its disregard for the facts. At times irritating. At times it is merely tiresome.[127]

> The publishers describe Gen. Crozier's book as 'sensational and important, and one of the most amazing revelations ever made by a distinguished soldier.' In this description one need only take exception to the word 'important'. Gen. Crozier's account of a few cases in which it was necessary for him to exact the extreme penalty for cowardice on active service is certainly sensational. It is no less remarkable that any former officer should have felt it necessary to write such a book. But it is not an important book … to describe in detail the execution of a private soldier is scarcely a constructive contribution to the pacifist movement Gen. Crozier has adopted. It will seem to the average Englishman a piece of crude and peculiarly ill-timed sensationalism.[128]

Those newspapers that gave Crozier the benefit of the doubt were those with some sympathy with the cause of pacifism:

> It is annoyingly and repetitively written, disfigured by wild accusations, egotism and abuse. It solves no problem and ignores the argument that a strong man well armed perhaps best guards the house of peace. But it does ask questions, and they are questions which no citizen, no statesman and, above all, no Christian priest can afford not to answer in one way or another for himself.[129]

George Orwell wrote ambivalently:

> General Crozier is a professional soldier and by his own showing spent the years between 1899 and 1921 in almost ceaseless slaughter of his fellow creatures; hence as a pacifist he makes an impressive figure, like the reformed burglar at a Salvation Army meeting … The only question is, can he advance any argument that will drive the general public an inch farther in the direction of active resistance to war?
>   Here, on the whole, the book fails. It is a rambling, incoherent book, circling vaguely round two anti-war arguments, one of them good so far as it goes, the other doubtful … if not a completely logical pacifist he is at least an engaging one. As a living contradiction that every pacifist is a Creeping Jesus, he should be of great value to his cause.[130]

Further criticism followed the publication of the book in America:

---

126 For examples see *Daily Sketch*, 16 August 1937; *Daily Express*, 12 August 1937; *Nottingham Journal and Express*, 8 August 1937; *Daily Sketch*, 9 August 1937; *Sunday Dispatch*, 8 August 1937; *Edinburgh Evening Dispatch*, 11 August 1937; *Evening Standard*, 10 August 1937.
127 *Irish Times*, 27 August 1937.
128 *Daily Telegraph*, 10 August 1937.
129 *The Spectator*, 13 August 1937. Review by Lawrence Athill.
130 *New Statesman and Nation*, 28 Aug 1937.

The Men I Killed is not a military book…[it] suffers not from lack of material but from lack of cohesion and a total absence of logic…[Crozier] repeats things that have a bearing on his arguments, and things that have no bearing on anything save his peace of mind … It is unfortunate that reading the book leaves one unhappy and thoroughly dissatisfied with General Crozier as a man and as a soldier, for occasionally flashes of characteristics come through the almost impenetrable verbiage which makes one think that General Crozier must have been a good man and an able soldier … [he] is very plainly honest. He thinks he has something to say; he is trying to say it; and it is really pitiful that he does not say it.[131]

As a result of the publicity the book went to a third reprint even before it was on the shelves.[132]

A Trustworthy Source?

Peter Buitenhuis's study *The Great War of Words* has the subtitle *Literature as Propaganda, 1914-18 and After*, and this is a particularly apt description of Crozier's literary output.[133] His work can be viewed as propaganda for the cause of peace, propaganda for the promotion of imperial policy and propaganda promoting his own position as an important historical player and honourable but ill-used patriot. In a letter to Lord Ponsonby about *The Men I Killed*, Crozier wrote confirming the propagandist agenda of the book: 'The test is will it do any good for the cause'.[134] Ponsonby replied that 'I am delighted to hear you were attacked … it gives us something to bite on … when a full-blown general comes and upsets them it makes them mad with rage … If I could go round addressing nothing but opponents who would attack me and even howl me down I should feel I were really doing something'.[135]

Can Crozier's books be used confidently as historical sources? In a review of *The Black and Tans* by Richard Bennett, Hereward Senior accused the author of accepting 'Crozier's literary pose as the conventional professional soldier outraged at the irregular proceedings of the crown forces in Ireland' and of missing 'the opportunity of entering into a long overdue discussion on the value of the much quoted Brigadier-General Crozier as a witness'.[136] Many authors have drawn and continue to draw on his texts uncritically without appreciating the context of their conception and the intent of the author. This is especially true of the two most popular works that deal with the Great War, *Brass Hat* and *The Men I Killed*.[137] The use of the latter book as a key source for the events surrounding the court martial and execution of Rifleman James Crozier by Cathryn Corns and John Hughes Wilson in their book *Blindfold and Alone* is a good example.[138] The authors

---

131 Brooke Maury, 'Review of The Men I Killed', *The Field Artillery Journal*, May-June 1938, p.252.
132 Bodleian Library, Oxford: Ponsonby Papers, C679/147, Crozier to Lord Ponsonby, 9 August 1937.
133 P. Buitenhuis, *The Great War of Words: Literature as Propaganda, 1914-18 and After* (London: Batsford, 1989).
134 Bodleian Library: Ponsonby Papers, C679/147.
135 Ponsonby to Crozier, undated, quoted in G. Crozier, *Guns and God*, p.157. Copy in author's possession.
136 H. Senior, 'Review of Richard Bennett, The Black and Tans', *Irish Historical Studies*, 47 (March 1961), pp.277-280.
137 Stephen Walker, *Forgotten Soldiers: The Irishmen Shot at Dawn* (Dublin: Gill and Macmillan, 2008) is an example of an (admittedly journalistic) work that over-relies on Crozier as a source: a chapter dealing with the execution of James Crozier in February 1916 cites Frank Crozier's *Brass Hat* and *The Men I Killed* as sources in 22 of 32 references. Craig Gibson, *Behind the Front: British Soldiers and French Civilians, 1914-18* (Cambridge: Cambridge University Press, 2008) cites *Brass Hat* as a source eight times (seven times relating to sex and once to drunkenness). Lesley A. Hall, 'Impotent ghosts from no man's land, flappers' boyfriends, or crypto-patriarchs? Men, sex and social change in 1920s Britain', *Social History*, 21 (1996), pp.54-70, again highlights the sexual references in *Brass Hat*.
138 Cathryn Corns and John Hughes-Wilson, *Blindfold and Alone: British Military Executions in the Great War* (London: Cassell, 2001), pp.304-307. The use of this episode without regard to the context in which it was

acknowledge that the only evidence of this young soldier's age is Frank Crozier's book written some twenty years after the event and that 'it may be unwise to place too much confidence' in it but then go on to use the testimony without further qualification. But Crozier quite deliberately suggested that Rifleman Crozier was an under-age soldier to heighten the impact of the story when he gave the boy's mother the words 'But you're not old enough Johnny. You're only seventeen. I'll tell on you to the officer'.[139] James Crozier was born on 6 August 1894 and was 21 when he was executed.[140]

Crozier's descriptions of the execution in *Brass Hat* and *The Men I Killed* are the most frequently quoted extracts from his works. Yet the exaggerated style of their narrative is clearly demonstrated when compared with a description published two years before *Brass Hat* and generally overlooked:

> I had had two previous experiences in other wars and I knew the difficulties. I decided to superintend personally the detailing of the firing party, the driving in of a stake into the ground to which the unfortunate man would be secured, and the allocation of warm, comfortable quarters within a few yards of the place of execution in which he could spend his last night on earth.
>
> I then gave our padre, a good fellow, half an hour in which to chat to our comrade in distress, after which I saw him myself for a few minutes before leaving him to his company commander.
>
> The fire having been stoked up, and an easy-chair, books and papers procured, and refreshments, in the shape of a cake, a bottle of whisky, and a pint of rum, placed on the table, he was left to himself.
>
> Next morning at dawn the battalion fell in on the road under my command, the condemned man having been carried out of his last billet in secret and tied to the stake – speechless, blind and quite oblivious to anything that was happening around him.
>
> I had specially selected the officer who was to command the firing party, and had warned him that at dawn, while chilled and nervous, even the best men miss their mark, he was to be ready with revolver drawn and loaded in order that, if necessary, the victim might be 'finished off' instantly.
>
> I had arranged that no words of command were to be given, save when I called the battalion to 'attention', when I saw (I was the only one who could) the officer commanding the firing party pick up a white handkerchief which was also the signal for the firing party to come to 'the present'. When he lowered his arm a volley rang out.
>
> Alas! As I had expected, although only a few yards distant from the doomed man, several bullets missed their mark, whereupon the medical officer pronouncing life not to be extinct, the officer in charge of the firing party administered the 'coup de grace' with his revolver. We buried the dead soldier in the little cemetery, with his name and the word 'Died', together with the date on his cross.[141]

Crozier refers in his books to letters, diaries and papers and the diaries do certainly seem to have existed for a photograph of two pages from a pocket diary appears in *Impressions*.[142] Yet we have

---

written continues – most recently in David Johnson, *Executed at Dawn: British Firing Squads on the Western Front 1914-1918* (Stroud: Spellmount, 2015), pp.62-64.
139 Crozier, *The Men I Killed,* pp.42-43.
140 General Register Office of Northern Ireland, Belfast: Birth Registration ref. U/1894/51/1007/41/382.
141 *Sunday Express,* 13 May 1928. Article by F.P. Crozier, 'A General's Poignant War Revelation of Man who was shot at dawn'.
142 F.P. Crozier, *Impressions,* facing p.258

already seen how Crozier admitted to relying on his memory during the creation of *Angels on Horseback*, how his recall of the number of raids made by the 9th RIRifles was faulty and how key characters had their names changed (Tom Spindle) or were composite figures (Rufus Ross). There are also deliberate omissions from the books, the most obvious being any details of the circumstances surrounding Crozier's resigning of his commission in 1909 or any details of his two marriages. Some dates are also (deliberately?) wrong. Crozier claims to have left Canada in the autumn of 1912 having worked for the government telephone construction company in the summer and autumn and having dealt with a forest fire in the Rainy River district. However, the Canadian census of 1911 places him with the telephone company in June of that year while the Rainy River fire took place in October 1910. Shipping records also indicate a return to Britain in September 1911 and not 1912 which remains a blank.[143]

The style of Crozier's writing gives the impression that the books were written hurriedly. *Brass Hat* was allegedly completed in ten days, although his wife was at pains to point out that 'He did not burn the midnight oil in accomplishing this; he wrote quickly, filled with his subject, and still found time to meet his usual social engagements'.[144] In a letter to Sir James Edmonds Crozier called the book ' a light effort at snap-shotting events in my mind, fourteen years on'.[145] His style would seem to confirm that his other works were also penned quickly and *The Men I Killed* reads like a series of harangues from a PPU platform.[146] Crozier had indeed completed a series of lectures for the PPU in the months before publication and these may well have provided material for the book.[147]

Despite misgivings, Charles Loch Mowat acknowledged that as a source (in the context of Irish history) 'General Crozier was a man with a grievance, but he was in a position to know things from the inside, and his testimony must be given weight.'[148] In respect of the Great War Crozier was also 'in a position to know' but his writings must be treated with caution. As shown above they cannot be taken at face value without investigating content and context and where possible cross referencing to confirm points.[149] In particular, *The Men I Killed* should be used as a source warily, if at all, given its clearly propagandist intent.[150]

Reputation and Character

The inescapable conclusion of a survey of Crozier's books is that, far from enhancing his reputation as a capable, honourable but poorly-treated soldier driven by duty, they ensured that it foundered:

---

143 Information from: <http//data2.collectionscanada.gc.ca/1911/pdf/e001947592.pdf>, accessed 17 March 2010 and <http://www.ancestry.co.uk> (accessed 3 March 2007). It is of course possible that Crozier returned to Canada but there is no evidence for this.
144 G. Crozier, *Guns and God*, p.144. Copy in author's possession.
145 TNA CAB 45/132: Letter from Crozier to Edmonds, 23 March 1930.
146 Crozier's obituary in the *Guardian*, 1 September 1937 says that the book was 'written in ill-health in ten days'.
147 Reports of Crozier speaking at meetings in Glasgow, Dundee and Edinburgh for example are given in *The Scotsman*, 24 November 1936, 27 January 1937 and 29 January 1937.
148 C.L. Mowat, *Britain Between the Wars, 1918-1940* (London: Methuen, 1955), p.52.
149 Crozier is still used as a source in academic (and other) works. See, for example, Bruce Cherry, *They Didn't Want to Die Virgins: Sex and Morale in the British Army on the Western Front 1914-1918* (Solihull: Helion, 2016).
150 See Brian Bond, *Survivors of a Kind* (London: Continuum, 2008), pp.125-128 for an analysis of Crozier's style in *The Men I Killed*. Bond's perceptive chapter on Crozier contains many of the points made above such as Crozier's lack of funds being a motive for writing but in some points of detail such as Crozier being a 'devoted family man' or the age of Rifleman James Crozier he is incorrect.

He scaled the heights of egotism with his ill-written and eccentric books of personal reminiscences and pontifications, and he gave English literary history one of its most tasteless book titles – The Men I Killed.[151]

His account [of the execution of James Crozier in Brass Hat] is a graphic and wretched indictment of inhumanity ... Crozier certainly lacked nothing in terms of self-belief yet paid scant attention to the sufferings of the men under his command.[152]

An intensely disagreeable and mean spirited man ... A small pudgy figure with a thin wispy moustache, he was, in many respects, the epitome of the cartoon-British officer class.[153]

Crozier was an arrogant and cynical writer whose accusations (often obvious fabrications) amount to little more than indiscriminate mudslinging; and his wartime reputation as a martinet who cared little for the lives of his men was apparently well deserved.[154]

[Crozier was] not always a reliable witness, nor did his literary approach bring him many friends.[155]

[A man] whose memoirs ... and style of command have made him a controversial figure.[156]

It is easy to see how Crozier's style, which often exaggerated the beastliness of war to drive readers toward the cause of peace, or promoted his own version of events in Ireland, overshadowed his historical narrative and to a large extent diluted its value. It is too easy to extract from his writings the more extreme descriptions of events that he may have perpetrated, witnessed or simply heard about at second hand and then present them out of context. Comments that confine themselves to Crozier's military abilities are usually more restrained:

Throughout the Great War he showed an indomitable courage and all those other qualities which made him a fine leader of men.[157]
Definitely not a man to be trifled with.[158]
The thrusting commander par excellence.[159]
Was promoted as a 'thruster' and did well in many battles...[160]
A man of rigid principle who believed in discipline, order and sobriety.[161]
A tough and uncompromising man.[162]

---

151 Orr, *Road to the Somme*, p.226.
152 Michael Stedman, *Thiepval* (Barnsley: Pen and Sword, 1995), p.116. Stedman repeats the story of Rifleman Crozier being under-age.
153 Miles Dungan, *Irish Voices from the Great War* (Dublin: Irish Academic Press, 1995).
154 Edward G. Lengel, *World War 1 Memories: An Annotated Bibliography of Personal Accounts Published in English Since 1919* (Oxford: Scarecrow Press, 2004), p.93.
155 Richard Holmes, *Tommy: The British Soldier on the Western Front 1914 – 1918* (London: Harper Collins, 2004), p.642.
156 Grayson, *Belfast Boys*, p.63. Rifleman Crozier's age is once again incorrect.
157 J. Hammerton, *The Great War: 'I Was There!'* (London: Amalgamated Press, 1938), Vol.1, p.654.
158 William Moore, *The Thin Yellow Line* (London: Leo Cooper, 1974), p.83.
159 Malcolm Brown, *Tommy Goes to War* (London: Dent, 1978), p.73.
160 Paddy Griffith, *Battle Tactics of the Western Front* (London: Yale University Press, 1994), p.28. Griffith goes on to state that Crozier's success was attributable to his 'willingness to use his revolver on his own men' thus repeating what Crozier wanted his readers to think.
161 Nick Baron, *King of Karelia: Col. P.J. Woods and the British Intervention in North Russia 1918-1919* (London: Francis Boutle), p.109.
162 Bryn Hammond, *Cambrai 1917: The Myth of the First Great Tank Battle* (London: Weidenfeld and Nicolson, 2008), p.250.

The Men I Killed was published just three weeks before Crozier's death and he was certainly aware of, and may have been pleased about, the furore that it caused.[163] He may not have been aware though of the particular resentment about one aspect of the book that was growing in Wales. Crozier's comment that at Bourlon Wood the men 'knew that it was better to die at the hands of the enemy than to be shot out of hand like rats by their officers', spurred one of his former subordinates, Lieutenant-Colonel W.E. Brown, to write to the *Western Mail* concluding:

> The widows and dependents [of the men killed] can rest assured that it was the courage and stout hearts of their husbands and sons which enabled them to fight to the end against overwhelming odds and not 'the fear of being shot out of hand like rats', a possibility which never existed except in the mind of Gen. Crozier.[164]

The case was taken up by the British Legion:

> Mr James Prince, General Secretary of the Cardiff Branch of the British Legion, which has the third largest representation in the Empire, said last night that it was their intention to circularise all Welsh MPs asking them to approach the Premier and to demand an inquiry. Mr Prince said: 'the book is a gross libel on ex-servicemen generally and on Welshmen in particular, by reason of the General's reference to Welsh troops in the Battle of Bourlon Wood … They were not only going to demand an inquiry but also, pending that, that the book should be withdrawn from circulation. He also challenged General Crozier to come before ex-Servicemen in Wales and repeat his allegations.[165]

The demand was taken up by the Opposition Whip, Sir Charles Edwards, MP for Bedwellty, who announced (ironically at Porthcawl) that he had the support of 'many Welsh MPs' for a letter that he had sent to the Secretary of State for War demanding a full inquiry, a full withdrawal and an apology to the Welsh soldiers.[166] The demand came to nothing. Six days later Crozier was dead and his reputation had been permanently damaged.

---

163 *Daily Sketch*, 9 August 1937. 'Strangers were telephoning and calling at his house … levelling criticism and abuse at him … he took it all in good part … "[I] give them a drink and a cigarette and tell them to go away and talk sense and try to prevent another war"'.
164 *Western Mail*, 19 August 1937. Brown had earlier written 'What a lie' against a newspaper article by Crozier who claimed that in Bourlon Wood 'a colonel' had shot several men of another brigade to 'save the situation' –The Royal Regiment of Wales Museum, Brown Papers, cutting from *The Sunday Express*, 13 May 1928. William Ernest Brown DSO MC* (1882-1949) See Appendix VI.
165 *The Scotsman*, 23 August 1937.
166 Ibid., 25 August 1937.

4

Crozier's Brigade

The previous chapter examined Crozier's military background and career up to his promotion to the command of 119 Brigade. It showed how his reputation as a capable soldier was earned on the Somme and, as we shall see, enhanced by his command of 119 Brigade, was damaged by his post-war publications. This chapter will move on to examine Crozier's command from his promotion up to and including the battle for Bourlon Wood in November 1917. It will show how Crozier's arrival coincided with renewed emphasis on training and how the command of the brigade's units and HQ was moulded until, in Crozier's words, the brigade was 'at the top of its form'.

Frank Crozier wrote that he heard of his promotion to GOC 119 Brigade in a telephone call from the Staff Captain of 107 Brigade on 19 November 1916, while at St. Quentin Cabaret.[1] The news was not unexpected 'because Sir William Peyton, the Military Secretary, had told my mother [that] "I had been very well reported upon"'.[2] We have already seen that the news was also anticipated within the 9th RIRifles.

When Crozier joined 40th Division on 20 November 1916 it was approximately half way through its long march from the Loos sector to billets east of Abbeville where it would train. He was driven south-west along with his servant, Starrett; his groom, McKinstry, followed.[3] On that date Divisional HQ was at Bouquemaison, just north of Doullens, while 119 Brigade HQ was at Le Souich less than three kilometres away to the north-east. Calling first at division, Crozier later described how he was 'frankly astonished' to hear from the GSO1 'to the effect that I would be very disappointed in my brigade which was *very bad* – quite the worst in the Division – the men were bantams from the coal mines of Wales and could not even carry packs, while *morale* was low'.[4] No other source suggests a problem with the men's fitness but it is not surprising to find that morale was low if indeed that was the case. The brigade had spent its first five months of trench duty sitting beneath trench mortar and artillery bombardments of varying intensity, had been passed over for duty on the Somme, had no real chance to hit back at the enemy other than by small-scale raids, had lost some popular officers and was in the middle of a long march.

Having reached the brigade, Crozier asked Starrett, for his opinion of the men. Starrett recalled:

> Sturdy lads and a bit rough … coal miners mostly, speaking of places that all seemed to commence with the letter 'Y' and using up all the letters of the alphabet in their spelling.

---

1 St Quentin Cabaret is a farm at the road junction on the southern edge of Wulverghem, 3km west of Messines, Belgium.
2 F.P. Crozier, *Impressions and Recollections* (London: T.Werner Laurie, 1930), pp.176-177. Crozier recalled the moment as 'the most pleasurable' of his working life. Peyton had served briefly in Thorneycroft's Mounted Infantry from July to October 1900 and so knew Crozier's stepfather although Crozier had left the unit in June 1900.
3 Tentatively identified as 9/15439 Rifleman Joseph McKinstry, 9th RIRifles.
4 Crozier, *Impressions*, p.182.

They were fighters and stickers and had marvellous endurance … they were second to none. The general thought so too, but not so much of the officers, who had to be put through it again and again before they were fit to lead their own men. 'Well, Starrett, what do you think of them?' and I told him what I've just said. He smiled and suggested the officers would improve. They were of good blood he said, not only of good families, as most were, but well schooled. After they got over having their cup filled to the brim with good things, they'd be all right.⁵

According to Crozier they did 'do all right': 'we gave him [the GOC 40th Division] a brigade which carried him to victory after victory, six months after the General Staff Officer had confessed to me that in the 40th Division was probably the worst brigade in the British Armies in France!'.⁶ Did the brigade improve and, if so, how did it happen?

Before Action

Change was already underway when Crozier joined his brigade as it moved from the Third Army area around Loos to that of Fourth

Brig-Gen Frank Percy Crozier. The late Charles Messenger noticed that, despite the date, the photo must date from 1917, after Crozier's DSO had been awarded. (*A Brass Hat In No Man's Land*)

Army north of the Somme. On 14 November Fourth Army HQ learned of negotiations with the French that were likely to result in the BEF extending its southern flank and inserting extra British divisions on the Somme to release three French corps.⁷ The Somme battle had been officially 'closed down' on 18 November and, with many other divisions exhausted and depleted by the summer's fighting, it seems that, bantam or not, 40th Division was now needed.⁸ The experience of the division, though, was of static warfare not the type of offensive actions that had taken place in 1916 and which were expected to continue in 1917.

---

5 Imperial War Museum Documents 79/39/1, David Starrett, *Batman,* unpublished typescript, pp.79-80. In *Brass Hat*, p132, Crozier places the conversation a week after he arrived at the brigade and Starrett's response as simply 'They'll be all right presently'.
6 Crozier, *Impressions*, p.183. Charles Messenger's view, *Broken Sword*, p.73, that Crozier being the fourth man to command the brigade was an indication of a problem brigade, is questionable.
7 Wilfred Miles, *Military Operations France and Belgium, 1916,* Vol. 2 (London: HMSO, 1938), pp.529-530.
8 In fact, 120 Brigade was diverted during its march south and spent a week from 13 November under the orders of 31st Division, XIII Corps, in the line at Hèbuterne at the northern end of the Somme battlefield. TNA WO 95/2608: War Diary 120 Brigade. XIII Corps front was held by a single division, the 31st, at this time, the other divisions having been used to reinforce other corps of Fifth Army for the Battle of the Ancre Heights. Its front had also just been extended northwards. Between 10–20 November the 40th Division was under XIII Corps command.

After five days on the march a pause allowed the introduction of a new and, for the division, novel element – training. Other than the initial induction training undertaken on arrival in France, specialised training on the bombing ranges or the focused training given to raiding parties, the brigade war diary does not mention training at all until 6 November 1916 when it records that nine days were spent around Autheux in company and battalion training with emphasis on artillery formation.[9] No other details of 119 Brigade's training are given but the two other brigades of the division were also training during this period.[10] In addition to the catch-all entry of 'training', their war diaries mention 'practice relief in the open by night' by two battalions, an all-units practice attack (both within 120 Brigade), 'units carried out a brigade outpost scheme', 'the brigade practised the attack' and 'cooperation with an aeroplane was carried out' (all by 121 Brigade).[11] There is a conspicuous lack of detail in the unit war diaries of 119 Brigade's battalions but that of the 12th SWB gives more details than the others. The programme from 2 – 21 November was as follows (missing dates indicate that the battalion was on the march):

2   Arms drill and instruction in the use of the new Small Gas Box Respirator.
3   Drill, bayonet fighting, lectures, use of Small Gas Box Respirator.
6   Company training.
7   Rain stopped training
8   Company training. CO lectured all officers on 'The Attack – Trench to Trench'.
9   Company training. 'Another useful lecture to officers.'
10   Companies practise attack trench to trench. Lecture on consolidation of captured trench.
11   Company training. CO's lectures on attack concluded.
12   Battalion training p.m.
13   Company drill.
14   Company and battalion training.
16   Battalion training and company work.
19   Company training and battalion drill.
20   Company training all day. 'Now practising trench to trench attack and artillery formation.'
21   Company training.[12]

On 20 November 40th Division was transferred to XV Corps, Fourth Army. This affected the training to be undertaken. Having finally arrived in the new area, training re-commenced on 27 November 'in accordance with XV Corps Winter Training Course'.[13] The units of 119 Brigade started intensive training in musketry, bombing, 'machine-gunnery' [sic] and Stokes mortars. Rifle ranges were constructed and 'made full use of during the hours of daylight'. Lewis gun and Vickers gun ranges were set up and a brigade training school begun to which one officer and six NCOs from each battalion were detailed to attend.[14] On 4 December, for example, the 12th SWB had 'Company training all day and range practice. Lewis gunners also fired and Capt. T.O. Jones took a party in revolver shooting. In the evening the CO gave a lecture and all Coys did rapid

---

9   TNA WO 95/2604: War Diary 119 Brigade. Autheux is 8km west of Doullens.
10   The training of 120 Brigade was cut short by its temporary move to Hèbuterne on 13 November.
11   TNA WO 95/2608: War Diary 120 Brigade; WO 95/2613, War Diary 121 Brigade.
12   TNA WO 95/2606: War Diary 12th SWB. The training may well have been guided / prompted by the issue in October 1916 of *Memorandum on Trench to Trench Attack* cited by Paddy Griffith, *Battle Tactics of the Western Front: The British Army's Art of Attack 1916-18* (London: Yale University Press, 1994), p.77.
13   TNA WO 95/2608: War Diary 120 Brigade.
14   TNA WO 95/2604: War Diary, 119 Brigade.

loading by night from 7.30 to 8.30'.[15] Training was interrupted on 9-10 December by the move east to XV Corps' 'Middle Area' in preparation for a move into the front line and was then postponed by the desperate need to improve conditions at the hutted camps 12 and 13 near Sailly Laurette which had recently been vacated by French units. Nevertheless, training was clearly now a matter of some importance and recommenced on 13 December. The brigade training school was reopened followed by the bombing and Lewis gun schools. While one company per battalion worked on camp improvements, the others trained.[16]. This extended period of training ended on 27/28 December when the brigade relieved the left brigade of 33rd Division in the Rancourt Sector of the front line.[17] All this intensive training for the brigade was not initiated by Crozier but by higher authority. What impact was his arrival having?

Having been appointed to brigade command on the basis of his performance as a battalion CO, and specifically on his performance on the first two days of the Somme battle when he demonstrated personal bravery and a willingness to grasp a difficult situation, he may legitimately be regarded as a 'thruster' who displayed energy and drive. Captain Eric Whitworth, 12th SWB, who appreciated the 'gentleman' in his superiors had another epithet for Crozier who:

> Was different in every respect from his three predecessors [Style, Prichard, Cunliffe-Owen]. He lacked the presence, charm and greatness of the three respectively, and the dignity of them all. He was essentially a hustler, who probably overestimated the results obtained by energy alone, and his authority was not strengthened by the issue of impossible orders, which could not be carried out owing to conditions he never saw. No doubt he had hustled his own battalion with great success, but his reputed boast on arrival that he had never obtained discipline in his own battalion until a man had been shot, was indicative of his own characteristics rather than of strength or greatness as a commander of men.[18]

Whitworth was obviously not impressed but the 'impossible orders' that he refers to probably relate to the terrible first tour that the brigade carried out in the Rancourt sector when 'very definite instructions' for the construction of a thirty yard communication trench were issued. These could not be fulfilled because of appallingly cold, wet and muddy conditions. Brigade 'remained dissatisfied'.[19] Yet Whitworth also says:

> Not that the efficiency of the Brigade suffered much under his [Crozier's] command; in many ways it was more efficient than it had ever been before, but this was from fear rather than as a response to any real leadership. Instead of a steady level standard of work being maintained, it was felt that a kind of game was going on in which officers were justified in doing anything so as not to be 'Caught' by the Brigadier. The word was always passed along of his approach

---

15   TNA WO 95/2606: War Diary, 12th SWB.
16   Interestingly, the brigade bombing school classes not only consisted of one officer and twenty other ranks per battalion but two men from the Trench Mortar Battery and six from the brigade's Machine-Gun Company. Crozier was taking care of his 'oddments'. TNA WO 95/2604: War Diary, 119 Brigade.
17   The picture of training fits the general developments at this date as described in Simon Robbins, *British Generalship on the Western Front 1914-18: Defeat Into Victory* (Oxford: Routledge, 2005) pp.83-97 (Chapter 6: 'Training for Victory'). Robbins references (fn. 113) 'Fourth Army Courses of Instruction During the Winter, 1 November 1916 – 1 April 1917' and it is very likely that the XV Corps syllabus followed by 40th Division was derived from this. The lessons of the Somme were being passed on. This flurry of training activities would have (mainly) missed the guidance of *SS 135: Instructions for the Training of Divisions for Offensive Action,* which was issued in December 1916 although it would have had the benefit of its antecedent *SS 119*.
18   Royal Regiment of Wales Museum, Brecon: 1992.22, Memoir of Captain Eric E.A. Whitworth, pp.526-527.
19   Ibid.

and the men soon saw the position and, until he had passed, there could be no harder working Brigade in France; when he was gone there was the inevitable relapse, tolerated often by the officers, for although they feared their general, there was no feeling at all of respect or devotion; without doubt the Battalion began to feel less the influence of the Brigade than under any previous GOC.[20]

This extract may tell us as much about Captain Whitworth as it does about Crozier. Whitworth saw Crozier in action for just four months before being invalided home after the brigade's first offensive action. January and February 1917 saw the brigade hold the line in appalling conditions. Not all of Whitworth's writing is contemporary and his opinion of Crozier may, like those of others, be coloured by Crozier's later books: 'I met him on several occasions but never near the front line in the Rancourt Sector, though he chose as a title for his reminiscences 'A Brass Hat in No Man's Land'! He was a tough and no doubt efficient staff officer but never showed any interest or sympathy with the officers of his Brigade when he met them; he was the type of 'Brass Hat' that provoked the ill feeling that was widespread against the staff'.[21] Compare that with this description from Captain B. D. Gibbs, 18th Welsh:

> At 5.46 I was asleep. Then up again at 12 noon and lucky thing too as about 12.30 the Brigadier General came to the top of the dugout steps for me. I hadn't shaved or washed for nearly a week. I had my old tommy's tunic on with the stars put up on the shoulders and I just had time to slip my jackboots on and go up. So I asked him to please excuse me being improperly dressed which he did. He wanted to know how I had got on in the line and seemed very pleased especially when I told him that I didn't have a single case of 'trench feet' in the Coy again.[22]

Whitworth does not describe the 'many ways' in which the Brigade was more efficient under Crozier. From the war diaries we know that Crozier inspected the 12th SWB which was paraded in full marching order on 7 December and, despite the lack of references, it is a safe assumption that he inspected the other three battalions at about the same date.[23] He inspected one of his 'oddments', 119 Machine Gun Company, on 9 December. He also visited both the incoming and outgoing classes at the brigade training school on 20 December.[24] On 15 December Second-Lieutenant Morris Meredith Williams, 17th Welsh, recorded his first impressions of his new GOC:

> Our new Brigadier put in an appearance for a short time. He is short and tubby, rather like a pocket edition of Soames [the Brigade Major] and covered with two rows of dazzling ribbons. I have not spoken to him so far, but they say he is a good sort.[25]

Just one day later he had noticed something more:

> We have been working at the camp and battling with the mud. Our new Brigadier seems a fussy man. He makes regulations about boots and puttees and Sam Brown belts in the midst of all this![26]

---

20 Ibid.
21 Ibid.
22 IWM: Documents 72/11/1, Papers of Captain B.D. Gibbs. Letter to his sweetheart, 17 January 1917.
23 TNA WO 95/2606: War Diary, 12th SWB.
24 TNA WO 95/2604: War Diary, 119 Brigade.
25 Private Collection, Williams Papers. Letter to his wife, 15 December 1916. See Messenger, *Broken Sword*, p.40 for Crozier's habit of sporting medals to which he was not entitled.
26 Williams Papers. Letter to his wife, 16 December 1916.

Whitworth's passing reference to Crozier's 'energy' is important. Crozier was sixteen years younger than the previous GOC, Cunliffe-Owen, and that contrast in itself would have been marked. Crozier says that he used the power of 'electricity' (in a metaphorical sense): "Electricity' had carried me from major to brigadier in nine months; it would carry this so-called bad brigade to the very height of efficiency in half that time … We 'electrified' our men into activity'.[27] For 'electricity' read 'energy'.

> The first question tackled by the Brigadier was deficiencies of equipment. The difficulty of the ordinary soldier to keep his clothing and equipment complete are almost insuperable. His pack and haversack are the only means at his disposal and it is impossible to keep his possessions separate in dark dug-outs, large barns or billets emptied of all conveniences. No doubt loss of equipment owing to slackness had reached serous dimensions and the GOC issued an order that any loss of kit was to be punished with 28 days F.P. No.1 subject to the right of trial by FGCM. The first case was punished accordingly but the sentence crushed by higher authority and the whole incident deleted. A large amount of useless work had been involved which, in addition to the injustice to the individual, was due to [the] policy of hustle. No alternative solution was offered and the serious question of loss of kit remained unsolved.[28]

Whitworth is obviously in sympathy with the other ranks and one suspects that he was the one put to 'a large amount of useless work'. The 'higher authority' would have been divisional HQ. His memoir describes the conditions in January-March 1917:

> Three months of trench warfare followed in the worst possible conditions and during a very severe winter, with temperatures constantly below freezing … There was no continuous front line or system of trenches; the line was held by the men living in isolated posts, sometimes not much better than shell hole, and by day no movement of any kind was possible. As company commander I was isolated in a small dug-out with my Company Sergeant Major and my runner from dawn to dusk; not until it was dark could I go the rounds and visit the platoons holding the front line and often it was not easy to locate them. No hot food was possible for the men beyond what they could warm in a limited supply of 'tommy-cookers'. Water and rations, wire and trench boards were brought up by pack mules to battalion HQ on the Bapaume – Péronne road, and then brought up to the front line by carrying parties at night, over ground pitted with shell holes, with 2 or 3 feet of water or slime and without any communication trench to guide them or protect them from rifle fire. On the other hand casualties were few for the sea of mud made raids or an attack unlikely and there was little artillery activity on either side. There was the risk of casualties from trench feet and this could decimate a battalion. I had given instructions to platoon commanders as to the necessity of maintaining circulation by every possible means; tight puttees were discarded and replaced by sandbags tied round the legs, and even then boots had to be removed so that the feet could be rubbed and a change of socks put on. By a lucky chance, on the evening before we left for the front line, I received from Queen Mary's needlework guild a bale of socks, hand-knitted and of much better quality than the normal issue. And I distributed a pair to

---

27 Crozier, *Impressions*, p.183.
28 RRW Museum: Whitworth Memoir, p.527; 23351 Private S.T Kerswell, 12th SWB, was tried on 8 December 1916 and found guilty of 'losing [public] property'. His sentence of 28 days FP No.1 with stoppages was quashed. TNA WO 213/1: Register of FGCMs gives the name as F.T. Kerswell. Private Kerswell later transferred to the 14th Worcs Regiment.

Trenches at Rancourt, December 1916. Pencil sketch by 2/Lt Morris Meredith Williams. (Williams Collection)

every man in the company, and our casualties from trench feet were very few. Such were the conditions in the front line during the severe winter of 1917. Each night I visited the front line posts … I found the NCOs and men, not only without complaint, but cheerful and alert with their Lewis guns kept ready for action. No company commander could have asked for greater reward.

Captain Whitworth noted another illustration of the new GOC's attention to detail:

26 December 1916 … With Brigade orders arrived a furious memorandum from the Brigadier (Crozier) that he had noticed, as the Battalion had marched past him, that many men were carrying their mess tins outside their packs instead of inside as had been ordered by the Brigade. The civilian mind had difficulty in understanding the motive of such a complaint; usually it was enough if the men arrived as fit as possible and carrying their necessary equipment. It is a paltry mind which worries how men, who that night would be holding front line trenches, carried their mess tins. Yet it is insistence on this kind of detail which largely contributes to the discipline of our troops, and slackness in this respect would indicate indifferent officers. In this actual case it was due to the mess tin being crowded out of packs by the remains of the Christmas post, though this did not satisfy the anger of the CO, who, hunted by his Brigadier, had in turn to hunt his company commanders![29]

---

29 RRW Museum: Whitworth Memoir, p.538.

On 8 February 1917 Second-Lieutenant Morris Meredith Williams noted that 'The Brigadier is coming to dinner with the Mess tomorrow night. No one likes him. We have been unfortunate in our Brigs. Pritchard was the only nice one we have had'.[30]

In addition to 'electrifying' the men, Crozier "executed' our colonels and senior officers when necessary'.[31] The first victim was the Brigade Major, A.G. Soames, who apparently made the mistake of stating that a kit inspection would be 'most inconvenient'.[32] Soames left on leave on 9 December 1916 prior to attending a Senior Officers Course and did not return to the brigade. Two other departures were not due to Crozier but to the enemy. On 3 January Lieutenant-Colonel R.S. Grant-Thorold, OC 18th Welsh, was wounded and evacuated and on the night of 22/23 January Lieutenant-Colonel B.J. Jones, OC 19th RWF, met an enemy patrol while visiting isolated posts and was severely wounded.[33] Meanwhile, another departure had been initiated by Crozier. Lieutenant-Colonel C.B. Hore, OC 17th Welsh, was relieved of his command on 8 January after 113 cases of trench feet occurred in the battalion in one six-day tour of duty.[34] Crozier placed Major B.F. Murphy, 12th SWB, in temporary command. Only Pope now remained from the four battalion commanders who had come out with their units and he would leave just before his battalion's first offensive action. On 17th April, he stumbled on some barbed wire during a visit to the line and cut his cheek open on the stake. Major Robert Benzie, who had arrived to take up the duties of 2iC just the day before, assumed the duties of CO.[35]

Three of the 'original' battalion COs had been in command for more than the six months active service that Peter Hodgkinson suggests is the mark of a 'viable' battalion commander (as indeed Crozier had been before his promotion) and had exceeded (just exceeded in the cases of Grant-Thorold and Jones) the average of eight months active service that COs attained.[36] Crozier had been deprived of, at the very least, a group of competent COs. In January 1917 he had the chance to mould his own team. The first two replacements were internal to the battalions concerned. Major Hugh Reginald Wood took command of the 18th Welsh and Major James H.R. Downes-Powell took command of the 19th RWF. Both had previously been their battalion's 2iC. Downes-Powell had been seconded to the RWF from the Glamorgan Yeomanry as 2iC in October 1916 after a spell as a staff captain (formation unknown), while Wood had been one of the original officer

---

30 Williams Papers. Letter to his wife, 8 February 1917.
31 Crozier, *Impressions*, p.183.
32 F.P. Crozier, *A Brass Hat in No Man's Land* (London: Jonathan Cape, 1930), p.132. The staff officer is not named by Crozier but, as the Staff Captain remained in post, Soames was the likely culprit. The kit inspection was possibly related to the issue about loss of kit recorded by Captain Whitworth.
33 IWM: Documents 72/11/1, Papers of Captain B.D. Gibbs. Letter to his sweetheart, 6 January 1917: 'Isn't it bad luck that the Col [Grant-Thorold] stopped it – he was just coming to look me up when he had a lovely Blighty in the leg. He'll be alright but I doubt whether he'll come out again'; TNA WO 95/2607, War Diary 19th RWF. These two COs were the only officer casualties in their battalions in January.
34 Charles Beauman Hore (1879-1965). See Appendix VI. Hore assumed command of the 17th Welsh after Lieutenant-Colonel Wilkie was killed by a shell in October 1916.
35 TNA WO 95/2606: War Diary 12th SWB. Robert Benzie DSO** (1874-1930) see Appendix VI. Captain Whitworth reported Benzie's arrival (with some inaccuracy) to his brother: 'The new 2nd in Command has arrived; a temp Captain who has been Brigade Machine Gun Officer [certainly not 119 Brigade MGO] and done similar jobs; he has never commanded a company or been permanently in the line holding it! He is a very nice fellow, and I think a pukka sahib, though he is so Scotch I can't tell' – RRW Museum: Whitworth memoir, letter 19 April 1917.
36 Peter E. Hodgkinson, *British Infantry Battalion Commanders in the First World War* (Farnham: Ashgate, 2015), pp.41-42. A 'viable' commander is one who has not succumbed to negative aspects of health, age or ability in six months active service. Hodgkinson is writing particularly in respect of 'dug-out' officers in this respect but the criteria equally well apply to all COs on active service. The fourth CO, Wilkie, had been killed after just four months on active service.

Lt-Col C. B. Hore, 17th Welsh, at work. Pencil sketch by 2/Lt Morris Meredith Williams. (Williams Collection)

Lt-Col Robert Benzie. (*Aberdeen Press and Journal*)

recruits to the 18th Welsh in 1915.[37] Both would remain in command until May 1917 and, in the absence of any evidence relating to ill-health or wounding, it is likely that they were ultimately found wanting. It seems that Crozier, presumably with the agreement of his superiors, was willing to give 2iCs a chance to prove their capability as he did three months later with Robert Benzie.[38]

Back at Crozier's old battalion Captain William Montgomery was still anticipating a move. '[Crozier] wrote me and said that if I got on the course that Horace [Haslett] went on he would apply for me as one of his COs. I didn't get on the course, so I am still here'.[39] The next month he asked his father 'to turn over in your mind the possibility of you bringing influence to bear in the event of me applying for transfer to a Welsh regiment with a view to having that transfer facilitated'.[40] Montgomery's divisional commander [Nugent] had other ideas: 'He told me that he would not let me go under any circumstances, although Gen. C[rozier] had written to him personally and asked for me.' Furthermore:

> I understand Gen. Crozier paid him [Nugent] the delicate compliment of asking for one of his Coy Cmdrs as he would be glad to have him command one of his battalions and was told politely 'to go to hell'. Gen. Nugent told me anyway quite, quite distinctly that I would not go to Gen. Crozier, in fact he had other plans for me.[41]

---

37   James Henry Richard Downes-Powell (c.1874-1958) was a solicitor and Welsh-speaker, see Appendix VI. Hugh Reginald Wood (1880-1958) was, by 1914, a Valuer and Boundary Surveyor, Irish Civil Service. See Appendix VI.
38   Crozier wrote that Ruggles-Brise (GOC 40th Division) gave him a 'free hand' in France – Crozier, *Impressions*, p.183.
39   PRONI D2794/1/1/21: Montgomery to his parents, 30 January 1917.
40   PRONI D2794/1/1/22: Montgomery to his father, 23 February 1917.
41   PRONI D2794/1/1/27: Montgomery to his father 13 May and 2 June 1917.

The first 'outsider' to find himself posted as a CO in the brigade was Lieutenant-Colonel Alan Bryant DSO who took command of the 17th Welsh on 22 January 1917 after Charles Hore was relieved of the command. Bryant was a regular soldier who had seen active service in South Africa and had been captured by the Boers. Before the outbreak of the First World War, he had served as a staff officer in several formations and in July 1914 was still GSO2 at the Canadian Military College, Ontario.[42] Crozier tells us that Bryant (whom he does not name) was:

> A delightful fellow ... [who] had friends at court and longed for advancement to command a brigade ... as a stepping stone ... he was ordered to be placed in command of a battalion, while I was ordered to report on him at the expiration of a month, as to his fitness to command a brigade.[43]

This may be true but Crozier was wrong when he wrote that Bryant arrived in April 1917 and there is no evidence for the unchallenged German lodgement in the battalion's front line trench that supposedly led Crozier to tell Bryant 'that he had better send his kit to the transport lines at once and get off on another ten days leave, during which period I would try and get him back to the staff for which he was better suited'.[44] It is unlikely that Crozier could take this initiative on his own authority and his description of the episode seems written to reinforce his own reputation as an energetic and efficient commander. By placing Bryant's arrival just before his battalion's first major offensive, and then having Bryant ask for leave to take his son to school for the first time, he diminishes Bryant's authority and capability.[45] The facts are somewhat different. Just after Bryant's arrival in January it was Bryant who as the senior CO in the brigade stood in for Crozier when he was on leave and Bryant remained as CO 17th Welsh until 15 September when he 'proceeded to [Divisional?] HQ for duty'.[46] This is well beyond both the six month period defined by Hodgkinson and just about the average length of active service for a CO. Bryant did go on leave just before the battalion's first attack in April 1917 (arriving back on 4 May) perhaps for the reason Crozier states. He also had leave from 12-26 August 1917 and had taken temporary command of 120 Brigade from 26 June to 30 July during the absence on leave of its GOC. It is likely that these regular absences would have disrupted the command chain and annoyed Crozier. On 21 July a patrol from the 17th Welsh was attacked and one officer and seven other ranks were wounded and four men reported missing. There was also a German raid on 18 June during which a Lewis gun post was bombed and five other ranks wounded plus failed raids by the 17th Welsh on the German lines on 11 July, 30 August and 31 August when the officer in command of the raid and one other man were killed and another wounded.[47] This lack of success was likely to have been a black mark for Bryant not only in Crozier's eyes but in the eyes of the new GOC 40th Division, John Ponsonby (see below), who took over from Ruggles-Brise on 24 August. Bryant's temporary command of 120 Brigade may also have alerted the high command to possible limitations to his effectiveness at that level but such speculation cannot be confirmed from the sources

---

42 Alan Bryant (1869-1917) see Appendix VI. After commanding the 17th Welsh, he took command of 9th Northumberland Fusiliers in the Ypres Salient on 2 October 1917. On 17 October 1917 his HQ dugout was hit by a shell killing him, his adjutant, medical officer and intelligence officer. Crozier, once again diminishing Bryant's role and reputation, states wrongly that 'he went; and died later – with 400 other men – the result of a mistake' – Crozier, *Brass Hat*, p.145.
43 Crozier, *Impressions*, p.190.
44 Ibid.
45 Ibid.
46 TNA WO 95/2607: War Diary, 17th Welsh.
47 Ibid.

available. Crozier's verdict was that Bryant's strengths were 'neither the command of men nor the slaughtering of the enemy'.[48]

The staff captain of 119 Brigade was Percy Frederick Hone who had been commissioned into the 17th Welsh in January 1915 and became staff captain in the new 119 brigade in October.[49] Crozier seems to have been satisfied with his performance despite Morris Meredith Williams' observation in February 1917 that 'I hear he [Hone] gets a bad time with the Brigadier'.[50] Hone's early days with the Welsh Army Corps National Executive Committee Secretary did not bode well: 'Capt. Hone I may say was Assistant Private Secretary to Mr D.A Thomas [later Viscount Rhondda], a member of the Welsh Army Corps Committee, and his services therein were lent to me by Mr Thomas last October or November. He is such a hopeless muddler in the office that I was seriously considering the advisability of dispensing with his services. I made no secret of this either in conversation with Capt. Hone himself or with my assistant, Mr Brazel, and I was very glad when he was offered a junior lieutenancy in the 17th Welsh.'[51] He remained as Staff Captain, 119 Brigade until December 1917 when he moved a step up as Acting Brigade Major.[52] His military career was a remarkable one for such a 'hopeless muddler'.

The banished Soames was temporarily replaced as brigade major in turn by Captain Seton James Montgomery (from 9 December 1916 to 5 January 1917) and Captain Harry Leslie Reed, adjutant of the 20th Middlesex (from 6 January to 17 February).[53] On 18 February Captain Guy Vernon Goodliffe arrived to be other half of Crozier's longest-lasting headquarters team. Surprisingly he receives only one passing mention in Crozier's writings and yet he was the BM throughout the remainder of 1917 which included the attacks around Villers Plouich and the brigade's greatest test at Bourlon Wood.[54] Crozier says that Goodliffe left the brigade in December 1917 when he (Crozier) nominated him for 'a six-month staff course at Cambridge University'.[55]

Disciplinary matters still needed attention. On 17 April 27603 Private William Ramscar, 18th Welsh, was reported absent as his battalion marched into the line. He was court-martialled on 4 May and his death sentence subsequently commuted to five years penal servitude.[56] Also on 17 April, Second-Lieutenant Whaley, 18th Welsh, was 'released from close arrest after interview with Brig-Gen [Crozier] and to lose leave for 12 months'.[57]

---

48 Crozier, *Brass Hat*, p.145.
49 Percy Frederick Hone (1878-1940) see Appendix VI.
50 Williams Papers. Letter to his wife, 12 February 1917.
51 National Library of Wales, Aberystwyth: Welsh Army Corps, C7/15, letter from Secretary WAC National Executive Committee to Western Command HQ, Chester, 25 August 1915.
52 TNA WO 95/2605: War Diary 119 Brigade. Hone's first signature as Acting BM is 13 December 1917 while the previous incumbent's last is 19 December indicating a period of overlap – although Hone would in effect have been 'shadowing' during his two years as staff captain.
53 Seton James Montgomery (1889-1966) is tentatively identified as a second-lieutenant who commenced his military career in the 15th Royal Scots. H. Leslie Reed (1885-1969). See Appendix VI for details of both men.
54 Crozier, *Impressions*, p.206. Guy Vernon Goodliffe (1883-1963) see Appendix VI. The lack of acknowledgement of Goodliffe's role is remarkable. Crozier wrote later that of his four BMs Hone and Muirhead were 'very good indeed' – *Impressions* p.224.
55 Crozier, *Impressions*, p.210.
56 TNA WO 95/2607: War Diary 18th Welsh; Gerard Oram, *Death Sentences Passed by Military Courts of the British Army 1914-1924* (London: Francis Boutle, 1998), p.105. Private Ramscar was 13 years old in 1911 and would have been under-age when he enlisted.
57 TNA WO 95/2607: War Diary 18th Welsh. Cecil David Whaley, commissioned second-lieutenant on 5 November 1915 and joined the 18th Welsh in France on 29 August 1916. He had re-joined the battalion from 40th Division School on 10 April 1917. There are no further details of this intriguing case. Whaley was wounded in an encounter with a hostile patrol on 22 August 1917 and evacuated to England.

119 Bde Staff, 1917. Front row L to R: Major Guy Vernon Goodliffe, Brigade Major; Brig-Gen F.P. Crozier; Capt Percy Hone, Staff Captain. (Royal Welsh Regimental Museum, Brecon)

Offensive Action

The push on training that had started in November was sustained through the winter. Despite the weather conditions, training continued when the brigade was out of the line and not providing working parties. On 29 January the brigade held a conference for COs at which 'Administration matters and the organisation of 'fighting platoons' [were] thoro'ly [sic] discussed'.[58] The next four days were spent in 'cleaning up and close order drill' after which the brigade bombing, Lewis gun and trench mortar schools were reopened. From 5 – 9 February training of fighting platoons took place in the morning and recreational training in the afternoon although it was noted that 'the fighting platoons are still in a very elementary stage'.[59] The end of February 1917 found the brigade almost completely given over to the supply of working parties under XV Corps instructions but a 'composite training company' was formed for 'training drafts and backward men of units of the Brigade'.[60]

---

58 TNA WO 95/2604: War Diary 119 Brigade.
59 Ibid. Thus was the message of *SS 143: Instructions for the Training of Platoons for Offensive Action, 1917* introduced to the brigade. The date of the first COs meeting indicates that a draft must have been available in advance of the post-14 February release of the pamphlet.
60 Ibid.

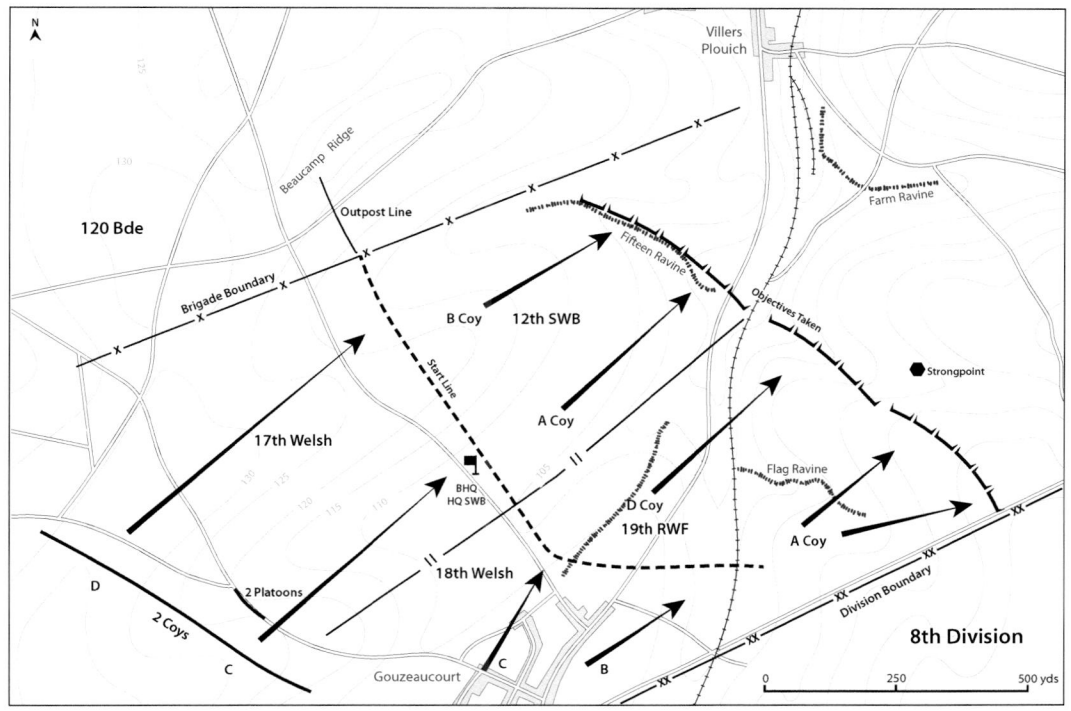

Map 2 Fifteen Ravine, 21 April 1917.

In March the brigade found itself forming the extreme right of the BEF when it took over the Clery sector abutting the right bank of the River Somme but it was out of the front line when the expected German withdrawal to the Hindenburg Line took place in the sector. Then almost a month was spent in slow forward moves or putting every available man to rebuilding the roads in the area. 'Though the hours of work were long there was still time for a game of football after the return to billets and a Brigade tournament was organised which our battalion [12th SWB] won'.[61]

One notable event during this period was the formation of a divisional mobile column for 'local protection' to be ready on twelve hours' notice. Consisting of Corps mounted troops, one section RFA, a proportion of the Divisional Ammunition Column, the 17th Welsh, one platoon of divisional pioneers (the 12th Yorkshire Regiment), one section of the 137th Field Ambulance and the 119 Brigade HQ and signals, it is not clear whose idea it was.[62] The fact that Crozier was

---

61 RRW Museum: Whitworth memoir, p.117. The final was on 14 April; 12th SWB beat the 17th Welsh 3 – 0.
62 TNA WO 95/2604: War Diary 119 Brigade; WO 95/2592: War Diary 40th Division HQ GS, Divisional Order 64 issued 7.30pm, 21 March 1917. The term 'local protection' is straight from *FSR Part 1*, p.96, which broadly defines the purpose of an advanced guard. All-arms columns had been proposed by Douglas Haig to exploit success on the Somme in 1916, see Gary Sheffield, *Douglas Haig: From the Somme to Victory* (London: Aurum Press, 2016), p.172. It is probably not coincidence that on the same day as 40th Division's mobile column was formed, 48th Division, III Corps, on the flank of 40th Division, organised a similar column known as 'Ward's Force' (commanded by Brigadier-General Ward, CRA, 48th Division) and later as 'Dobbin's Force', which was disbanded after 10 days – TNA WO 95/2746: War diary 48th Division HQ GS. Mobile all-arms columns appeared again in August 1918, see Peter Simkins, 'Building Blocks: Aspects of Command and Control at Brigade Level in the BEF's Offensive Operations, 1916-1918' in Gary Sheffield and Dan Todman (eds.), *Command and Control on the Western Front: The British Army's Experience 1914-18* (Staplehurst: Spellmount, 2004), p.164.

given command may indicate that it was his suggestion, particularly as the two other brigade commanders were senior, or it might be that as a (comparatively) young 'thruster' he was deemed suitable for the task. In the event, the force was stood down and dispersed after only three days.

The German army had moved back to the Hindenburg Line but had created an advanced outpost screen of occupied villages and high ground aligned approximately south-east/north-west. XV Corps now advanced its formations into positions from which this line could be attacked. On the right 8th Division would take the villages of Villers-Guislain and Gonnelieu. In the centre 40th Division would take Villers-Plouich and Beaucamp while on the left 20th Division would take Trescault. The central villages of Villers-Plouich and Beaucamp would have to be taken once the villages on either flank were taken. Operations on 21 April 1917 would see the flank villages secured while 40th Division undertook its first offensive by securing the German positions in front of Villers-Plouich and Beaucamp from which another forward move could take place.

On 1 April 1917 there was a conference at corps to discuss 'impending operations'.[63] On the same day it was noted that despite a draft of ninety-three men for the 17th Welsh 'the [119] Brigade is much reduced in numbers averaging about 500 per battalion' and no other drafts were recorded before the action on 21 April.[64] In planning his dispositions Crozier would have to allow for the reduced numbers. Divisional orders for the attack 'probably in a day or two' were issued on 18 April and followed up on 20 April.[65] While 8th Division attacked Gonnelieu, 40th Division would attack on its left. 119 Brigade would capture a feature known as Fifteen Ravine and the adjacent spur while, to its left, 120 Brigade would take the ground from Fifteen Ravine to the Gouzeaucourt – Trescault Road. Crozier ordered the 19th RWF to take the spur on the right and the 12th SWB to take Fifteen Ravine. Each battalion was to assault with their two forward companies in the recently-learned fighting platoon formation. The 18th Welsh would provide support and the 17th Welsh were in reserve. The disposition of an assaulting battalion is illustrated by the 12th SWB which had A Company in two platoons on the right with B Company similarly arranged to its left. Two platoons of C Company provided the 'moppers up' while the remaining two platoons plus D Company provided the supporting wave. Each man carried fifty extra rounds, two Mills bombs and two empty sandbags, while the men of C and D Companies also carried a pick and shovel.[66]

Just before zero the assaulting battalions moved out of the front line onto a taped line parallel to their objectives. At 4.20 am the artillery barrage commenced and the battalions closed up to it and advanced behind it as it moved towards the objectives which were entered at 5.15 a.m. By 5.45 all opposition had been overcome and consolidation was underway. To the left 120 Brigade had occupied its objective meeting little resistance. To the right 8th Division occupied Gonnelieu with some help from the right flank of the 19th RWF which dealt with a troublesome strongpoint. Brigade casualties were ten officers and 147 other ranks. The 12th SWB met with the greatest resistance from snipers and MGs in Fifteen Ravine. On the right the ravine was not well defined and this, plus a 'pull' to the right caused by trying to keep in touch with the 19th RWF, meant that A Company, 12th SWB (Captain E.E.A. Whitworth commanding) overshot its objective.

Captain Whitworth recalled that up to the afternoon before the attack the men were expecting to be relieved but from 3pm to 2am had to work creating advanced dumps, a battalion HQ and a dressing station. Despite their disappointment and tiredness 'they worked like heroes with pick and shovel until the work was completed. Such a response *reflects well on the discipline of a battalion* [my emphasis] where the men have learned that weariness or exhaustion are excuses no soldier will

---

63 For the context of XV Corps operations see Cyril Falls, *Military Operations France and Belgium 1917*, Vol. 1 (London: Macmillan, 1940), pp.152-162.
64 TNA WO 95/2594: War Diary 40th Division HQ A&Q.
65 TNA WO 95/2592: War Diary 40th Division HQ GS.
66 TNA WO 95/2606: War Diary 12th SWB.

plead; and it is the best reward an officer can win'.⁶⁷ Whitworth's account gives interesting detail including the fact (not mentioned in the battalion war diary or brigade report) that casualties were caused by the British artillery which was otherwise reported as 'accurate and well timed'.⁶⁸ Whitworth's own account reads:

> At 3 a.m. the companies fell in. A short explanation was given for, in an attack, every man must know sufficient to carry it out even if he has no further orders from officer or NCO. The objective was described. The advance was by the right and it would be fatal if touch was not kept. On reaching the objective the ravine was to be at once crossed and firing positions established on the top of the further bank. On no account were bombs to be thrown wildly … in the event of a counter attack we would need every bomb we had. The objective would be taken and held at all costs … The companies were at the low strength of 80 and consequently worked as two platoons, each platoon forming one wave … Owing to the length of our objective the men were extended to 15 paces …Our objective was 800 yards away and the company advanced for 300 yards before suffering a casualty … [we expected] every minute that the barrage would lift and in the dawning light we would strike the ravine.. In reality we had already missed and passed our objective … we now found ourselves, a party of two officers (one wounded), and about thirty men seeking for our objective and under heavy fire from our own artillery and, as it grew light fired at from two or three sides by German snipers. We saw an old German trench and in this took up our position … and tried to collect a few isolated parties of our own battalion … we were in an isolated position in front of the battalion on our right [the 19th RWF]. Though reluctant in any circumstances to give up ground which had cost lives to win, we decided to withdraw … Consolidation of the new line was begun at once and it was impossible to give the men any rest until early afternoon, when the defence of the line was complete. The battalion captured 40 prisoners and suffered in casualties about a third of the total number who went over.⁶⁹

Whitworth's subsequent citation for the Military Cross noted that he was:

> In charge of the assaulting line. By his careful organisation of the men under his command and his initiative and courage he was very largely responsible for the successful carrying out of the operation. Although wounded he refused to leave the line until the position had been consolidated and then only at his battalion commander's instigation.⁷⁰

Lieutenant J. Saunders Lewis, 12th SWB, was another casualty. He recalled in an undated letter (probably in July 1917) that:

> I was wounded in the left thigh and calf. Two machine-gun bullets went through the knee, and a lump of shell, I think it must have been shrapnel, blew the calf of my leg away about an hour later. The M.G. bullets have entirely healed, and the calf is rapidly healing. More than ¾ of it has already grown again. The nerves were not cut only bruised and I shall have their use again. The muscle will not be quite as pretty as that of a flapper we once saw in Bidston.⁷¹

---

67 RRW Museum: Whitworth memoir, pp.121-122.
68 TNA WO 95/2604: War Diary 119 Brigade, after action report dated 29 April 1917.
69 RRW Museum: Whitworth memoir, pp.121-122.
70 Quoted in RRW Museum: Whitworth memoir, p.125.
71 Jones, *Letters to Margaret Gilcreist*, p.257.

The 19th RWF on the right applied their newly-acquired tactical training in capturing a strongpoint: 'at the same time our Lewis gunners and snipers engaged effectively hostile machine guns … [while] at the same time D Coy was deployed to bring covering fire to bear'.[72] The battalion reached its objectives without casualties but lost two officers and forty-nine men in holding them. The first offensive action by the brigade's units had seen a pre-dawn attack pressed home successfully and an improved jumping off position secured for the next stage of the advance. Forty prisoners were taken. 'The operations were carried out with steadiness and precision and were entirely successful.'[73]

The division's next attack, on 24 April, was focussed on the capture of Villers-Plouich and Beaucamp. The task of 119 Brigade, which was once again on the right, was to take the high ground which dominated Villers-Plouich on the east. The village itself and the village of Beaucamp to the north-west were the objectives of 120 Brigade. The tactics used were different to those of three days before and would involve the two battalions that had previously provided the support and reserve for that attack. On the right the 18th Welsh advanced one company at 11.25 p.m. on 23 April and occupied without opposition the high ground to the east. Four strong points were created each to hold a garrison of one platoon with two Lewis guns to provide covering fire over the ground to the left. On the left the 17th Welsh, drawn up once again in advance of the front line, waited for the barrage at 4.15am before moving forward with two companies in line of column of platoons and two companies in support. The retaliatory barrage fell on the empty front line trench. The 119 Machine Gun Company deployed its guns to cover the high ground to the north of the village and to suppress the fire of the garrison of La Vacquerie to the east. Despite some difficulties with uncut wire all objectives were taken by 7.05a.m., surviving Germans were mopped up and the ground consolidated. On the left Villers-Plouich was taken but evacuated due to heavy shelling. The 17th Welsh had to form a defensive left flank temporarily and at the request of division plans were drawn up by the brigade to assist 120 Brigade with an attack through Villers-Plouich to take Beaucamp. The 19th RWF and 12th SWB which together made up 'the equivalent of one battalion of under-average strength', were ordered forward to the east of Villers-Plouich but the attack was cancelled and movement halted as the GOC XV Corps, Sir John Du Cane, who was visiting 119 Brigade Battle HQ, 'did not consider the situation required reinforcements at Villers-Plouich and that after the enemy intense bombardment died down [120 Brigade] would probably get their objective' – which they did.[74] However, the capture of Beaucamp was not completed by 120 Brigade until the following day after 20th Division had captured the flanking village of Trescault. Casualties in 119 Brigade were eight officers and seventy-nine other ranks. Sixty-one prisoners were taken.

The brigade had done what was asked of it and congratulations were forthcoming to 40th Division from XV Corps, Fourth Army and from the CinC himself: 'Congratulate Fifteenth Corps and 8th and 40th Divisions on the successful operations carried out this morning.'[75] Privately, though, Douglas Haig noted in his diary that 'Villers-Plouich and Beaucamp were captured by 40th Divn. The latter is a poor Div. under Ruggles Brise. Luckily they met a 'new' German Divn which did not stand!'[76] The CinC's comments seem unfair in the light of the successes. The opposing division (*256th Division*) was indeed 'new' but was later reported as being a shock division in 1917 and had

---

72 TNA WO 95/2607: War Diary 19th RWF.
73 TNA WO 95/2604: War Diary 119 Brigade, after action report dated 29 April 1917.
74 TNA WO 95/2604: War Diary 119 Brigade, after action report dated 2 May 1917.
75 TNA WO 95/2592: War Diary 40th Division HQ GS.
76 National Library of Scotland, Edinburgh: Haig Papers. Douglas Haig Manuscript Diary, 24th April 1917.

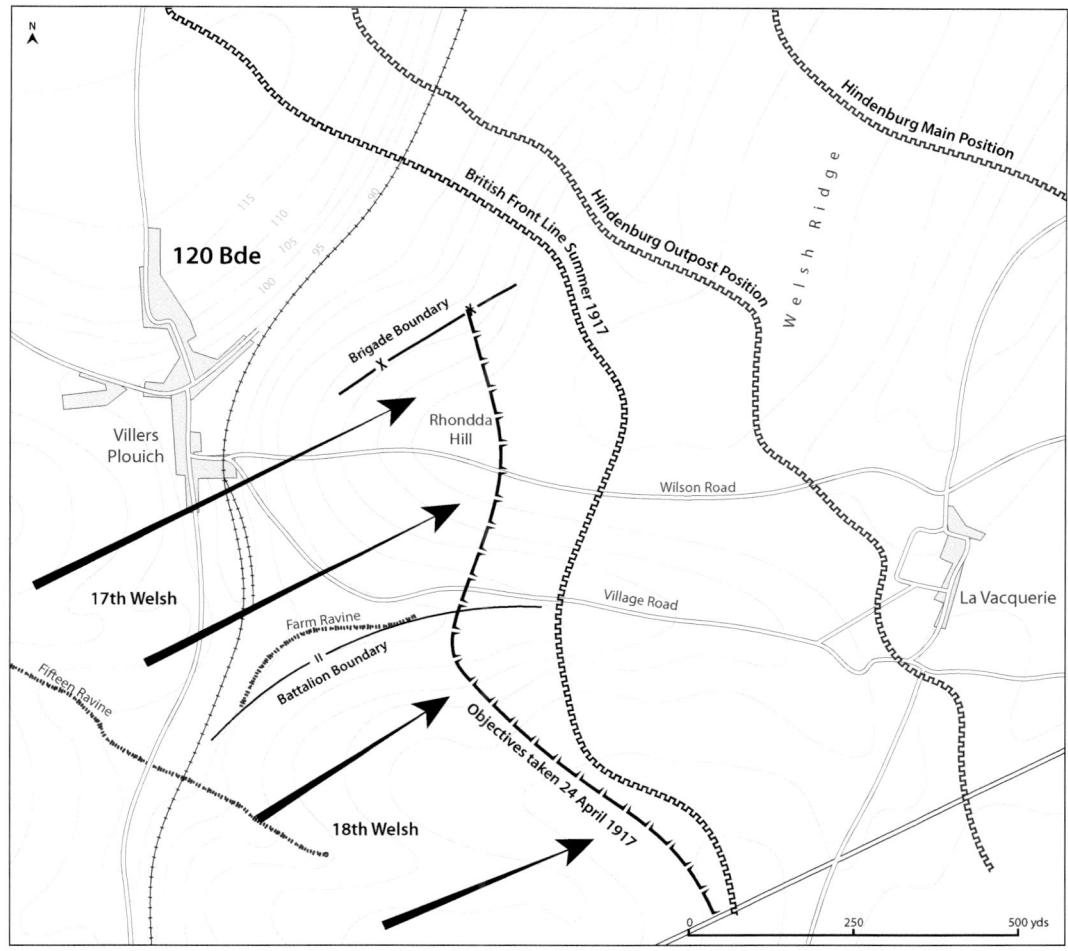

Map 3 Villers Plouich, 24 April 1917.

'suffered heavily' in the attack of 24 April.[77] The *Official History* was also more kind, referring to XV Corps' 'remarkable operations' and noting that the 'new' German divisions 'contained unexpectedly good material'.[78] Crozier's congratulatory message to his troops stressed the cooperation involved and their steadiness under the barrage.[79]

---

77 Intelligence Section of the General Staff, American Expeditionary Forces, *Histories of the Two Hundred and Fifty-One Divisions of the German Army Which Participated in the War 1914-1918* (London: London Stamp Exchange, 1989 reprint of 1920 edition), p.727.
78 Falls, *Military Operations France and Belgium 1917,* Vol. 1, p.531.
79 TNA WO 95/2607: War Diary 17th Welsh, Special Order of the Day 25 April 1917: 'GOC 119th Infantry Brigade wishes to thank all ranks of the Brigade which he has the honour to command on the success of their operations on 21st and 24th April 1917 and to congratulate them on the valour displayed. The gaining of all the objectives and the retaining of same was only made possible by the unlimited cooperation of all and the support of the 8th Divisional artillery. The advance under the barrage was on every occasion as steady as a parade ground movement. The exchange of communications left nothing to be desired throughout the operations'.

XV Corps intended to continue the steady advance of Fourth Army up to the Hindenburg Line by seizing the village of La Vacquerie which acted as an outpost just 500 metres from the German front line.[80] Orders were issued by 40th Division on 3 May for an attack to take place on the night of 5 May but this did not proceed as planned. Fourth Army was scaling back its operations as plans were developed to support the French offensives on the Aisne by British attacks in Flanders. The seizure of La Vacquerie in advance of an assault on the Hindenburg Line was now not required. Instead, orders were issued by 40th Division on 4 May for an 'extensive raid' on the village based on the original attack plan. At 7.00 p.m. that day Crozier met with the COs of the infantry, MGC and TMB to explain the scheme of attack. While 119 Brigade attacked the south of the village, 121 Brigade would attack the north. The 8th Division would raid Sonnet Farm, on the right flank of the attack, at the same time as the raid. The 12th SWB and 17th Welsh would be 119 Brigade's assault battalions while the 19th RWF formed brigade support and the 18th Welsh the reserve. Each assaulting battalion had two companies in front in line of columns of platoons and a company in close support in the same formation. One company would form the battalion reserve. The 19th RWF would supply moppers-up armed with clubs, revolvers and 'P' bombs (phosphorus bombs) for the assaulting battalions. The support companies would man a line just outside the German wire and cover the withdrawal. All the wire cutters in the brigade were given to the men of the assaulting battalions.[81] Major Richard John Andrews MC, 17th Welsh, was placed in command of the forward operations and would supervise the withdrawal.[82]

Lt-Col Richard John Andrews. (Jill Blackmore)

The brigade applied the tested tactics of April by forming up in no man's land parallel to the enemy line just before the barrage and following it to the objective. Zero was 11.00 p.m. and the withdrawal was planned for 1.00 a.m. The raiders were slowed by uncut wire and found that much of the village was also thickly wired. From 11.15 p.m. the German retaliatory barrage was intense. Some Germans were killed or captured but progress was slow. The attack of 121 Brigade on the left was halted outside the German wire and the 17th Welsh on the left of the 119 Brigade attack had to form a defensive flank. On the right the 12th SWB were also subjected to enfilade fire as the 8th Division raid was also held up. Both the 12th SWB and the 17th Welsh reached their objectives. The delay, though, meant that there was little time for accompanying RE parties to demolish the enemy infrastructure although two dugouts were demolished and several houses

---

80 The village would be fully incorporated into the Hindenburg Line over the summer of 1917.
81 TNA WO 95/ 2604 War Diary: 119 Brigade HQ GS.
82 Richard John Andrews (1887-1923). See Appendix VI.

badly damaged. The brigade's casualties were four officers and 101 other ranks. Eight prisoners were taken.[83] Second-Lieutenant W. Pollock, 12th SWB, wrote:

> We went on fairly well until we came to the wire in front of his [the German] 1st line. This was only cut in places and of course it was too difficult to find the gaps so we started to climb over and through it. Just then fire was opened on us from the trench and quite a number of our men got hit. Eventually when I got over the wire there were only about ten men with me and these got hit when about 25 yards from the trench … finding I was alone I dashed back to the 3rd and 4th waves (we went over in 4 waves) to get more men … then one of our Lewis guns opened fire at the Bosch and just as suddenly the fire from the trench stopped. At this time everything was mixed up, that is to say there were a few of A Coy, some C Coy, some 2nd Middlesex [8th Division], moppers up [from] 19th RWF and even one man of the 17th Welsh though goodness knows how he got there. We got to the trench and then the men got excited and started bombing like hell with the result that some of us who had jumped into the trench got hit … the original garrison must have been between 25 and 30. It had been arranged that the moppers up should take back our wounded and dead whilst we held on but they were in the hell of a hurry to get back and only made one journey … we had to leave the dead … The experience of this show impresses on me that men can never have too much training in advancing at night and keeping proper interval and line, for they will persistently bunch, no matter how much you shout at them … It has also showed me that 25 or 30 men with rapid fire can cause a large number of casualties to an attacking force.[84]

119 Brigade had gained its objectives despite being under-strength and its troops had demonstrated skill in keeping close to the barrage and adaptability in dealing with strongpoints and unexpected developments such a lack of flank support. They had also displayed commitment to the attack and personal valour. However, as Pollock's comments show, they needed more training and experience. Given the proximity of the Hindenburg Line and the ferocity of the German bombardment they were undoubtedly lucky that the original plan to seize and hold La Vacquerie had been abandoned.

Consolidation and Development

The brigade spent five months in the vicinity of Villers-Plouich initially consolidating and developing the new British front line and its supporting infrastructure but also integrating new drafts and new COs.

On 8 May Major John Richardson Heelis MC took command of the 18th Welsh.[85] He was already known to Crozier:

> [He] had been a subaltern with me [in the Manchester Regiment], and was just junior to me in days gone by at Aldershot … I was delighted to see him … he had been adjutant of the regiment, and in 1914 had been wounded. Having stayed at home till 1917 … and having been a brigade-major in a home service brigade … he was of course unfamiliar with modern war … but I was willing to make every allowance … I explained all sorts of details to him, after

---

83 TNA WO 95/2604: War Diary 119 Brigade HQ GS.
84 RRW Museum: Whitworth Memoir, pp.428 – 429. Transcript of letter from Pollock to Whitworth, 31 May 1917.
85 John Richardson Heelis (1880-1962). See Appendix VI.

lunch, on the day of his arrival, but alas! My efforts were in vain … I tolerated a good deal in the hopes of improvement … but he had to go, as he could not assimilate modern conditions. The SOS went up one night without a cause, the first and last time such a thing happened in the old brigade.[86]

The brigade's war diary records an SOS signal from the front line in response to a German raid on 4 June 1917, although the 18th Welsh war diary mentions only a German rocket signalling a raid and the 12th SWB (the other front line battalion) makes no mention of it.[87] There was a SOS signal fired from the front line on 30 June but the 18th Welsh war diary says that the 'right battalion' (ie the 12th SWB) fired it in response to a German raid. Acting Lieutenant-Colonel Heelis reported sick on 9 July and did not return to the battalion.[88] Crozier's description once again diminishes the capability of a CO and is certainly inaccurate in the detail (or lack of it) of Heelis' wartime record. It is difficult not to agree with Charles Messenger's conclusion that Heelis was removed because he would have known about elements of Crozier's rather dubious pre-war career.[89] How Crozier managed to justify his removal to his superiors so quickly is not known but a very poor report on Heelis' command ability must have been involved unless his sickness simply provided a fortuitous opportunity to replace him.[90]

Heelis' replacement was Major William Kennedy MC who had arrived as 2iC 12th SWB on 4 June 1917.[91] On 11 June Kennedy took command of the 18th Welsh while Heelis was on leave and became its 2iC on Heelis' return on 24 June. Kennedy took command of the battalion on 11 July.[92] He had transferred to 119 Brigade from the 18th HLI, 106 Brigade, 35th Division. That division and the 40th Division had, from 2 June, come under the command of III Corps (GOC Sir William Pulteney) indicating a corps-level input to transfers and promotions.

Downes-Powell, OC 19th RWF, had been replaced by Major A.C. White DSO, 7th KOYLI, 20th Division, on 14th May (both the 40th and 20th Division were still in XV Corps at his time, again indicating a corps role in transfers) but White was quickly replaced on 2 June by the returning Lieutenant-Colonel B.J. Jones (wounded in January 1917).[93] Jones was the last of the 'pre-Crozier' COs. On 6 August 1917 he relinquished command and handed over to 'the legendary Freddy Plunkett'.[94] Plunkett's career was remarkable.[95] A pre-war regular soldier he had been part of the original BEF, been promoted from the ranks and was one of only four men (other than aviators) to receive five British gallantry awards during the war.[96] He had joined 40th Division before it left for France and, while 2iC 12th Suffolk Regiment, had briefly deputised for the sick CO of the 21st Middlesex in June 1917 and then, in July, for the CO of the 20th Middlesex who was on leave. His diary records his impressions on arrival at the 19th RWF: 'I found that the last CO had been sent home, this appearing to be quite a common occurrence in this brigade as a few more were sent home later … I found the material of the 19th RWF, both in officers and men, excellent,

---

86   Crozier, *Impressions,* pp.192-193.
87   TNA WO 95/2604; WO 95/2606; WO 95/2607.
88   TNA WO 95/2606: War Diary 18th Welsh.
89   Messenger, *Broken Sword*, p.78.
90   Heelis appears to have been denied another field command during the war.
91   William Kennedy (1885–1917) was an unlikely soldier see Appendix VI.
92   TNA WO 95/2606: War Diary 12th SWB; WO 95/2606 War Diary 18th Welsh.
93   Arthur Charles White. See Appendix VI.
94   Richard Holmes, *Tommy: The British Soldier on the Western Front 1914-1918* (London: Harper Collins, 2004), p.206; TNA WO 95/2607: War Diary 19th RWF.
95   James Frederick Plunkett (1878 – 1953) see Appendix VI.
96   A.D. Harvey, 'A Good War: Wartime Officers who Rose to Command Level in the First World War', *RUSI: Royal United Services Institute Journal*, 153:1 (April 2006), pp.76 – 80.

but discipline bad. Discipline was soon much improved'.⁹⁷

After the raid on La Vacquerie training recommenced on 27 May 'according to programme' and included close order drill and musketry while Lewis gunners and bombers 'received special training under their respective specialist officers' at the reopened brigade schools.⁹⁸ The brigade moved back into the line on the night of 3 June. During tours over the next four months the battalions raided or attempted to raid the enemy lines on fifteen occasions (successfully six times), carried out 'vigorous patrolling' or 'active patrolling' on most nights and met enemy patrols or drove off German raids on eight occasions.⁹⁹

A raid planned for the night of 28/29 July clearly demonstrates how the art of raiding had evolved in a year and demonstrates the increased ability of the troops to undertake a complex operation. The raiding party of two groups of 24 and 20 men of the 17th Welsh with one and two officers respectively was to approach and pass through gaps in the German wire under cover of a creeping barrage. There would be a standing barrage on key trench junctions and approaches and a rolling barrage passing back and forth across key areas. 40th Division asked III Corps for an additional allocation of 4,000 rounds of 18-pounder shells and 700 rounds for the 4.5' howitzers, this request was duly passed from Corps to Third Army. When the raid was cancelled because 'the enemy has registered his front trenches' III Corps was not pleased: 'Corps Commander [Pulteney] considers it undesirable that the raid in question should be cancelled unless another one can be is prepared and can take place with little delay. It is most necessary that the enemy should receive a rebuff. If all raids are cancelled on the grounds mentioned in your minute, one will seldom take place.' The raiders would wear 'raiding order' equipment and a senior officer of the 17th Welsh would command. The firepower involved in this moderate sized operation, the involvement of corps and army staff in the preparations, the evolution of 'raiding order' equipment, and the presence of a senior officer are in marked contrast to the raids of the previous summer. The raid did not go ahead but the 12th SWB and 18th Welsh raided three days later.¹⁰⁰

During the summer of 1917 the battalions in reserve and support were digging and improving the trenches and roads in the sector. They seem to have done a good job. In October 1917 Captain Geoffrey Dugdale MC (Brigade Intelligence Officer, 60 Brigade, 20th (Light) Division wrote that he was 'lost in admiration … The trenches, beautifully planned to give an excellent field of fire, were built up with sandbags, supported with wire netting in the fire bays and round the trenches. The whole of the system was duck-boarded; it was the most perfect system of trenches I saw during the time I was in France'.¹⁰¹ However good the trenches, the Spring's attacks and subsequent raids

Lt-Col William Kennedy.
(*Glasgow High School Roll of Honour*)

---

97 NAM 1994/05/398/1: 'Diary of the War – by J.F. Plunkett'.
98 TNA WO 95/2604: War Diary 119 Brigade.
99 Ibid.
100 Ibid.
101 Geoffrey Dugdale, *'Langemarck' and 'Cambrai': A War Narrative, 1914-1918* (Shrewsbury: Wilding & Son, 1932), p.95. Dugdale also observed that the trench's occupants were operating a 'live and let live'

and shelling had taken its toll on the brigade's four battalions. On 6 August, for example, the 19th RWF had entered the line with just 452 men of all ranks and it was time to top up with new drafts organised by the Infantry Base Depots. The 19th RWF received two drafts in September 1917 totalling 156 men. The 18th Welsh had received fifty-seven ORs in June, a further 183 in four drafts in September, thirty-three in October and a final unlucky forty-two in November just before the attack on Bourlon Wood. The 12th SWB received thirteen ORs in June, just three in August and 118 in September.[102] The war diary of the 17th Welsh does not contain records of drafts in the summer of 1917 but it is unlikely that they did not occur as from this time a new type of soldier starts to appear in the lists of those killed in the brigade's units, men with Territorial Force six-digit numbers.[103] From August onwards the percentage of these men in the fatalities of 17th Welsh is 11%; 18th Welsh 11%; 19th RWF 19% and 12th SWB 4%. What impact did this have on the battalions? It seems not much because the IBDs sent replacements from the same regiments or recruiting areas as the battalions' own. The majority of men arriving at the 17th Welsh came from the 4th Welsh; those at the 18th Welsh from the 7th, 4th and 6th Welsh; those at the 19th RWF from the 4th and 6th RWF while those at the 12th SWB came from the Monmouthshire Regiment.[104]

On 13 June Crozier and Goodliffe met Ruggles-Brise and his GSO2 at the Brigade School at Nurlu where they watched a demonstration by the bombing and trench mortar classes. Brigade training again took place from 21 – 26 June and included musketry on the thirty yard range and a field day to demonstrate contact work with the RFC. Brigade sports were held on 26 June. The brigade major (Goodliffe) attended a demonstration 'of the fighting platoon in action' at the III Corps School on 23 July.[105] The brigade school at Nurlu was visited by Crozier on 5 October to see a demonstration of a raid that was carried out that same night by men of the 18th Welsh. Training was now a regular feature of the brigade's cycle of activities. Crozier wrote later that 'by September 1917 the brigade was at the top of its form … it had become well-seasoned.'[106] It had also escaped the large scale turnover of personnel that Mark Connelly has noted has 'the potential to disrupt internal cohesion and efficiency'.[107]

The longest and most intensive period of training undertaken by 119 Brigade was between 12 October and 15 November. Before this a new GOC was appointed to 40th Division. On 24 August 1917 Major-General Sir Reginald Pinney (GOC 33rd Division) noted in his diary that he had been told that 'Gen[era]ls Snow, Cuthbert, Ruggles-Brise and Ross have been selected for work at home'.[108] The arrival of John Ponsonby from 2 Guards Brigade does not seem to have been the

---

understanding. It is tempting to identify the perpetrators as 120 Brigade, which 60 Brigade relieved on 5 October 1917, but the dates and perhaps therefore other details in Dugdale's memoir are inaccurate.

102 Abstracted from the battalion war diaries TNA WO 95/2606 and WO 95/2607.
103 This renumbering of TF infantrymen took effect on 1 March 1917. The first one to appear in 119 Brigade fatalities is on 19 August 1917.
104 Data obtained by cross referencing fatalities with entries in the First World War Medal Rolls TNA WO329 available at <http://www.ancestry.co.uk>.
105 TNA WO 95/2604: War Diary 119 Brigade.
106 Crozier, *Impressions*, p.196.
107 Mark Connelly, *Steady the Buffs! A Regiment, a Region & the Great War* (Oxford: Oxford University Press, 2006), p.28.
108 IWM: Documents 66/257/1, Papers of Major-General R. Pinney. 'Selected for work at home' seems to imply a planned decision rather than a rushed clearout of poor commanders although Cuthbert and Ross were not up to the job. Significantly, given the increasing importance of training, Ivor Maxse noted that Cuthbert 'had little or no conception of training methods'. Ross 'left his brigadiers a free hand to go their way' and, although there is no evidence of criticism of Ruggles-Brise in this respect, it might have been the 'free hand' that Crozier noted that was his downfall too. (I am indebted to Professor John Bourne for the information on Ross and Cuthbert). Pinney's information was wrong about Thomas D'Oyly Snow who stayed on as

cause of any upheavals within the division, divisional and brigade staffs were unaffected.[109] Like Ruggles-Brise, Ponsonby was a Guardsman (although Coldstream in this case) who, like his predecessor, supposedly gave Crozier an 'entirely free hand'.[110] Crozier wrote 'I think there were times when … John Ponsonby may not have approved of me, or at least my methods' and he described him as amusing but prone to suffer fools too gladly in contrast to himself who was 'so engrossed in war that I could not tolerate anything or anybody I thought might clog the wheels of victory'.[111]

The training that took place in October / November was guided by *SS152 Instructions for the Training of the British Armies in France* which was first printed in June 1917. Jonathan Boff has examined the application of *SS152* in the Third Army and found a lack of consistency across different units.[112] In this case the syllabus as laid down seems to have been followed. The 119 Brigade war diary states that on 18th October (one week into the training period) training commenced 'in accordance with *SS152 Appendix XIII*'.[113] On 23 October there was 'a Brigade Instructional Scheme for [an] attack on enemy position' which was repeated next day 'with slight modifications'. The divisional commander visited to discuss training on 2 November and again on 5 November to 'discuss tactical schemes to be carried out'. His interest in training impressed his new ADC, Harry Graham: 'we went to watch another field-day, and I was enormously struck by his competence. He is charming to all the COs etc. but his criticisms struck the bull's eye every time; he sees every weak spot but can appreciate good work better than anyone – a perfect leader of men, I think'.[114] A week later Graham wrote: 'I am acquiring a perfect passion for J.P. I can't tell you what his usefulness and thoughtfulness are like. He keeps the whole thing going here … anyone so much beloved by all ranks, and so deserving of that affection I never met'.[115]

Training 'for the attack' is recorded on no less than eight days. On 5 November Crozier and Goodliffe watched the 17th Welsh and 19th RWF practising attacks and Crozier watched the 17th Welsh do it again next day when the battalion COs and brigade staff also met for a tactical ride. Brigade officers provided umpires on 8 November when the 18th Welsh were attached to 121 Brigade for an attack 'under divisional arrangements'.[116] On 9 November the 19th RWF and 12th SWB led a practice attack on the Bois de Robermont and established posts on its northern edge while the 17th Welsh passed through and 'captured' the village of Brevillers. The 18th Welsh threw out a right defensive flank in the Foret de Lucheux. The divisional staff was present on 12 November when 119 Brigade practised another attack through wooded country: 'the 19th RWF and 119 TMB formed rearguards in the Foret de Lucheux, 18th Welsh attacking and 17th Welsh passing through the 18th Welsh as soon as the wood was captured'.[117] The exercise was repeated three days later. H. Turner (119 Machine Gun Company) remembered one day when training

---

the commander of VII Corps. Gerald James Cuthbert (GOC 39th Division) was given command of 72nd Division; Charles Ross (GOC 6th Division) was given 69th Division and Ruggles-Brise the 73rd Division. Crozier states (*Impressions*, p.197) that Ruggles-Brise 'had gone home to England for a well-earned rest'.

109 John Ponsonby (1866–1952). See Appendix VI.
110 Crozier, *Impressions*, p.199.
111 Ibid.
112 Jonathan Boff, *Winning and Losing on the Western Front: The British Third Army and the Defeat of Germany in 1918* (Cambridge: Cambridge University Press, 2012), pp.59-64.
113 TNA WO 95/2605 War Diary 119 Brigade. On 1 November training was guided by *SS135* as suggested in *SS152 Appendix XIII*. Most afternoons were given over to sports which *SS152* suggests is guided by *SS137* [Recreational Training], while *SS143* is cited for platoon training.
114 IWM: Documents 66/298/1, Papers of Captain H.J.C. (Harry) Graham. Letter to his wife, 3 November 1917.
115 Ibid. Letter to his wife, 12 November 1917.
116 TNA WO 95/2605: War Diary 119 Brigade.
117 Ibid.

was 'ruled a wash-out by the Brigadier. We had to make another attempt a few days later and put more vim into it. This attempt passed as a success and the Brigadier was well pleased'.[118] Freddy Plunkett recalled:

> During our rest near Beaumetz from late in Oct to [the] 3rd week in Novr we had quite a good time with training, shooting and sports. We had some very good training in [a] wood about 4 miles from our billets called Lacheux [Lucheux] Wood. It was large and fairly thick with undergrowth. At the time little did we think how we would benefit by this training. At first we took an enormous amount of time to carry out an attack on a wood but gradually that 'stickiness' was replaced by 'dash' and 'getting there' without paying too much attention that beautiful line of formation which one reads so much in attack formation, our principle of training being 'those ahead assist those held up'.[119]

The GOC division was present at a 119 Brigade scheme on 24 October and on 14 November Douglas Haig watched a tactical exercise (involving 120 Brigade) noting that: 'the men (though many 'Bantams' amongst them), seemed quick and alert, and cleaner than when I last saw this division. Ponsonby has only had the Division 3 months and will, I am sure, quickly remedy the defects I noticed'.[120]

At about this time, commenting on the state of training of 51st Division, Lieutenant-Colonel Edward Speirs noted: 'The advance in tactical instruction in [this] and other divisions since the Somme was extraordinary'.[121] Given what was to come at Cambrai, the extent of the training described above is an indication that 40th Division was also a beneficiary of this advance.

Bourlon Wood

The genesis of the battle of Cambrai has been described elsewhere and will only be outlined here.[122] At the end of April 1917 the Cambrai area had been identified as the possible site of a joint French and British operation with the French enveloping St. Quentin and the British attacking the Hindenburg line near Havrincourt. The resulting plan, developed by III Corps, was not submitted until 19 June and GHQ ordered preparations to be made. At the same time, senior officers of the Tank Corps were seeking a suitable project with which to vindicate their faith in their much-abused weapon. In mid-June Lieutenant-Colonel J.F.C. Fuller (GSO1 Tank Corps) had suggested that the country between Cambrai and St. Quentin was ideal for the operation of tanks, being firm and not cratered by artillery bombardment. The idea got no further than Kiggell, Haig's Chief of Staff, but was revised and submitted to GHQ on 4 August. At this stage, no more than a tank 'raid' supported by aircraft in a ground attack role, it attracted the interest of Brigadier-General J.H. Davidson, Chief of the Operations Section at GHQ. Colonel J. Hardress Lloyd (CO III Tank Brigade) then took the idea to Byng (Lieutenant-General Julian Byng, GOC Third Army)

---

118 H. Gregory, *Never Again: A Diary of the Great War* (London: Arthur H. Stockwell, 1934), p.68.
119 NAM 1994/05/398/1 'Diary of the War – by J.F. Plunkett'. *SS152* places no particular emphasis on training in fighting through woods.
120 Gary Sheffield and John Bourne (eds.), *Douglas Haig: War Diaries and Letters, 1914-1918* (London: Weidenfeld & Nicolson, 2005), p.342.
121 Quoted in Bryn Hammond, *Cambrai 1917: The Myth of the First Great Tank Battle* (London: Weidenfeld & Nicolson, 2008), p.62. 'Speirs' was changed to 'Spears' in 1918.
122 For example: Hammond, *Cambrai*; W. Miles, *Military Operations France and Belgium 1917*, Vol. 3 (London: HMSO, 1948), pp.1-31.

and the idea of a major tank action became incorporated in the planned attack on the Third Army front. Byng himself presented the concept to GHQ but it was shelved – although this allowed a final element to be added. Brigadier-General H.H. Tudor, the commander of 9th Division's artillery, had developed the idea of a surprise attack by a limited number of troops supported by a sudden and intense barrage from guns which had not previously given away their intention by using registering shots on enemy positions. This found favour with Lieutenant-General Sir C.L. Woolcombe (GOC IV Corps), who forwarded it the Third Army on 23 August. The suitability of the ground was confirmed by the Tank Corps who suggested an enlargement of the attack. The essential elements of the attack were now identified: infantry supported by tanks; ground attack aircraft; and unregistered artillery bombardment.

By the 16 September, Byng was ready to put detailed plans for the operation to Haig who promised him the Canadian Corps (which was then briefly assigned to Third Army before its transfer to Passchendaele) but a final decision on a date was postponed as Third Ypres was still not concluded. Haig wrote on 15 October 1917:

> General Byng came to lunch and afterwards went into his proposals for an operation on his front. I had already discussed the matter twice before with him. It was now a question of getting him some troops … I was able to arrange for Byng to have 4 divisions to start training at once. Viz. the 8th, the 12th, 29th and 51st, the three latter are now in the Third Army. I promised before the operation is launched to concentrate a Reserve, if possible Cavan's XIV Corps including the Guards.[123]

Third Army's reserve had, from 11 October, included 40th Division. Byng briefed his own corps commanders and their staff on 26 October about the coming battle and issued a modified plan on 13 November. The object of operation 'GY', as the attack was called, was '… to break the enemy's defensive system by a coup de main; with the assistance of tanks to pass the cavalry corps through the break thus made: to seize Cambrai, Bourlon Wood, and the passages over the Sensée River and to cut off the troops holding the German front line between Havrincourt and that river'.[124] The bulk of the fighting would fall to III Corps to the south, which would press on to secure the crossings of the St. Quentin Canal, and to IV Corps in the north, which would secure the key high ground at Flesquières and then at Bourlon Wood. The plan stressed that 'It is very important that Bourlon Wood be captured by us on Z-day'.[125] Staff had estimated that it would take the Germans forty-eight hours to bring in substantial reserves and the CinC, not wishing further casualties in a protracted campaign, as at Third Ypres, placed a forty-eight hour time limit on the operation.

On 17 November Crozier, with his brigade staff, attended a conference at division and he met with his own COs, 2iCs and adjutants the next day 'to discuss the attack to be launched at an early date'.[126] There is no evidence that details of the offensive were shared earlier than that date.

The main attack was launched on 20 November and a conference at 40th Division HQ that afternoon heard that the 'attack was proceeding satisfactorily and that V Corps would be wanted shortly. In the event of Bourlon being captured [by IV Corps] the V Corps were to follow the cavalry and capture the crossings of the Canal de la Sensée as 1st objective. 40th Division to be on the right with 119th and 121st Infantry Brigades in front and 120 Brigade in Reserve'.[127] Crozier later recalled a conference at Lucheux:

---

123 Sheffield and Bourne (eds.), *Douglas Haig*, p.337.
124 Miles, *Military Operations 1917*, Vol. 3, p.306.
125 Ibid., p.307.
126 TNA WO 95/2605: War Diary 119 Brigade.
127 TNA WO 95/2608: War Diary 120 Brigade.

some days, or perhaps weeks before the battle [when] I was given the possibility of one of three tasks, namely (1) an attack on Bourlon (which actually fell to our lot), (2) the taking up of an outpost position some ten miles further east, or (3) an advance-guard scheme still further east <u>covered by a cavalry screen</u> [his emphasis]. The carrying out of the latter tasks would have meant that a very considerable breach had been effected in the enemy lines.[128]

If this conference did indeed take place at Lucheux it must have been before the division moved out on 16 November and it is more likely that Crozier was actually describing the divisional conference of 17 November. The note of the next day's brigade conference makes it clear that the planned objective was the high ground on the north side of the Canal de la Sensée some *seventeen kilometres north* of Bourlon Wood (see Appendix II).[129] This note does not suggest any alternative plans for the deployment of 40th Division.

The implication that 40th Division would be advancing as part of V Corps came to nothing. Despite notable success on the first day, due to innovative artillery tactics and the first massed use of tanks, progress in the northern sector was stalled by resistance at Flesquières. The attacking divisions of IV Corps did not arrive at the foot of the Bourlon Ridge until evening on 21 November. The operations of III Corps in the southern battle were then closed down but, with the dominating high ground of Bourlon so close, and the possibility of a cavalry breakthrough after its capture, Haig decided that operations would continue in the northern area.[130] Verbal orders to that effect were passed by telephone from Third Amy to IV Corps at 10.45 p.m.[131] By that time 62nd (West Riding) Division was in front of the southern edge of Bourlon Wood and 51st (Highland) Division had captured the village of Fontaine although it would be lost again next day.[132]

At 9.45 a.m. on 21 November 40th Division had been ordered to start a move to Hermies to bring it closer to the battle. At 8.00 p.m. the division was placed at the disposal of IV Corps.[133] Writing much later, Hugo De Pree, who had been BGGS, IV Corps during the battle, expressed his opinion that if the 40th and Guards Divisions 'had been brought close up beforehand or even brought up in lorries on Y/Z night …they would have accomplished very much more on Z day than they did three or four days later'.[134] At divisional HQ at 1.30 p.m. on 22 November it was announced that 40th Division had been tasked with the attack and capture of Bourlon Wood and village on the following day.[135] The original IV Corps Operational Orders had had not anticipated the use of 40th Division but envisaged 62nd Division taking Bourlon Village in the west while 51st Division took Fontaine-Notre-Dame to the east. The two divisions would bypass the wood

---

128 Crozier, *Impressions*, p.200.
129 TNA WO 95/2605: War Diary 119 Brigade, Notes on a Conference at Brigade HQ, 18 November 1917. This note is fully reproduced in Appendix II.
130 Haig's reasons for continuing the fight in the north are given, after the fact, in his Cambrai despatch dated 20 February 1918 in *The London Gazette (Supplement)*, 4 March 1918, pp.2721-2722.
131 Miles, *Cambrai*, p.120.
132 Bourlon Wood occupies part of a ridge trending roughly east to west rising over thirty metres from the Bapaume to Cambrai road and presenting a one-in-twenty gradient on its southern approaches. The shoulders of the ridge are anchored on the villages of Fontaine-Notre-Dame (approximately 5.5km west of Cambrai) in the east and Bourlon – 3km further to the north-west and slightly behind the spur that forms the western end of the ridge. The area between the two villages was (and is) occupied by the irregular mass of Bourlon Wood with close stands of mature trees and dense undergrowth cut by a few key rides – the two most important of which ran east/west (and slightly sunken in parts) and north/south – breaking the wood into four unequal parts.
133 Ibid., p.127.
134 Article in the *Journal of the Royal Artillery* (July 1928) quoted in Gary Sheffield (ed.), *In Haig's Shadow: The Letters of Major-General Hugo De Pree and Field Marshal Sir Douglas Haig* (Barnsley: Greenhill Books, 2019), p.48.
135 TNA WO 95/2608: War Diary 120 Brigade.

and link up behind it.[136] Given the dominating position of the wood and the possibility of flanking fire from its garrison it is clear why the plan was not implemented.

It is tempting to assume that the training of 119 Brigade in fighting through woodland was preparation for an attack on Bourlon but there is no evidence for this. Bourlon was originally the objective of 62nd Division which, after two days fighting and an advance of eight kilometres was deemed to need relief. Of 40th Division's three brigades only 119 Brigade seems to have undergone training in woodland fighting.[137]

> It was one of the most extraordinarily fortunate things that, quite by chance, we had those field days in the woods, and the wood which we were attacking was very similar to the one we had been practising on.[138]

While the experience gained by 119 Brigade in the Foret du Lucheux was certainly fortuitous, it was not planned in anticipation of action at Bourlon. The abandoned plan to attack across the Canal de la Sensée involved the occupation and defence of a wood called La Garenne and it is likely that the thoughts developed for this operation were applied to the very fast planning for Bourlon.[139] When the brigade went into action, it attacked on the right of the divisional front – as it had in the April actions. It appears that a familiar tried and tested formula was being applied and the position of the brigade opposite Bourlon was the result.

When 119 Brigade moved into position facing Bourlon Wood its men had marched 35 kilometres over two nights and one day in poor weather, on roads that had been cut up previously by the men, guns and supplies needed for the Cambrai battle. The relief of the 62nd Division was completed between 4.00 p.m. on 22 November and midnight. At 4.00 a.m. the brigade issued its orders for the attack.[140] Zero was 10.30 a.m. While 121 brigade seized Bourlon Village, the objective of 119 Brigade:

> will be the high ground to the N. of BOURLON WOOD (Coupez Mill which will be consolidated).
> The 19th Royal Welsh Fusiliers will attack on the right, and the 12th South Wales Borderers on the left.
> 17th Welsh will be in Brigade Support in proximity of CEMETERY at E.30.c.
> 18th Welsh Regt will be in Brigade Reserve under cover about K.6.b …
> … Battalions will attack on a 2 company front in depth and will maintain artillery formation throughout so long as situation allows of same.
> Infantry will keep from 100 to 200 yards in rear of tanks.
> Support Battalion will be in readiness to either reinforce assaulting battalions or throw out a right defensive flank to the East of BOURLON WOOD.
> Assaulting troops will be in position at minus 15 minutes.[141]

---

136 TNA WO 158/381: IV Corps Cambrai: Havrincourt – Bourlon Wood; Operations, Orders and Instructions November 10-27 [1917].
137 The war diaries of 120 and 121 Brigades make no mention of woods during the intense training of October / November 1917.
138 *Western Mail*, 23 March 1918. It is very likely that the writer was P.F. Hone, 119 Brigade's staff captain.
139 TNA WO 95/2605: War Diary 119 Brigade, Notes on a Conference at Brigade HQ, 18 November 1917. See Appendix II for full transcription.
140 TNA WO 95/2605: War Diary 119 Brigade, 119 Infantry Brigade Order No. 128. See Appendix III for full transcription.
141 Ibid.

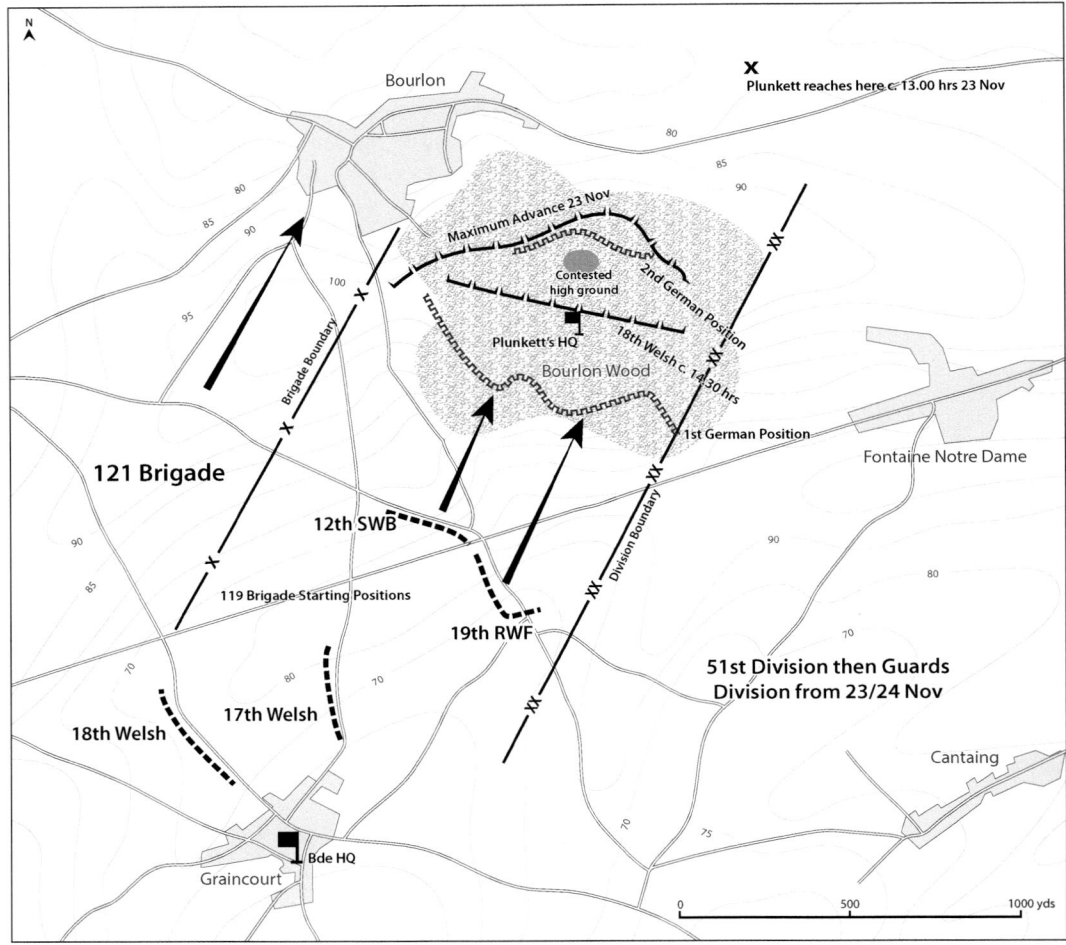

Map 4 Bourlon Wood, 23 November 1917.

The attack was to be supported by twelve tanks:

> 3 tanks will proceed along the road at the western edge of the wood.
> 3 tanks will proceed up the ride in F.20.a and splay out as the situation may demand.
> 6 tanks will crush the wire and cover the ground in between (a) and (b) and act as the situation may demand.
> These tanks will pass through the infantry advanced line at zero.

The 12th SWB war diary notes that 'tanks went in advance of our left company but there were none in front of our right company'.[142] They were the recipients of 'some tanks' from D Battalion, Royal Tank Corps who were assisting 121 Brigade to their left. The tanks of G Battalion, allocated

---

142 TNA WO 95/2606: War Diary 12th SWB.

to 119 Brigade were 'not able to arrive until after zero'.[143] The deployment of the tanks was disrupted because their petrol supply was delayed in the congested back area. Freddy Plunkett, CO 19th RWF, noted: 'I was now looking anxiously for my tanks but just then [10.15 a.m.] received a message to say that they would be late'.[144] He does not mention tanks again despite the *Official History* reporting that '[after about midday] the tanks of G Battalion were now in evidence and did good work' and 'of 16 tanks, 13 reached the northern edge of the wood'.[145] None of the four infantry battalions' war dairies mention tanks again.[146] The tanks were an important but ultimately ineffective component of the assaults on Bourlon village (121 Brigade) and on Fontaine-Notre-Dame to the east, but their importance to the attackers of Bourlon Wood seems debateable. The wood was not good terrain for tank operations and by the end of the day 'it had been established that in so thick a growth tanks could not force a way through'.[147] The tank crews had no time to make a reconnaissance and, crucially, no time to establish contact with the infantry with whom they were to cooperate. Neither had 119 Brigade (or the other two brigades of 40th Division) undertaken any training with tanks. Crozier anticipated problems and issued additional instructions to accompany the attack order: 'TANKS are a luxury. This must be impressed upon all ranks. If a tank breaks down, Infantry must push on at all costs unless particularly asked for help.[148] Most of the infantry were probably too occupied to notice what the tanks were up to.

The same traffic congestion that delayed the petrol prevented the arrival of the smoke shells that were to cover tanks and infantry as they advanced over the open ground south of the wood. Nevertheless, at 10.30 a.m. the artillery barrage hit the southern edge of the wood and the leading companies of the 19th RWF and 12th SWB moved off. The next three days were one of intense, close-quarter fighting during which attacks and counter attacks pushed the battle line backwards and forwards between the central east – west ride and the northern edge of the wood.

The details of the battle for Bourlon Wood have been extensively described in other books and are not duplicated here.[149] Instead, accounts of the battle will be examined and key points high-

---

143 TNA WO 95/110: War Diary D Battalion, Tank Corps. Report on Operations by D Battalion Tank Corps, 23 November 1917.
144 NAM: Plunkett – Diary of the War.
145 Miles, *Cambrai*, p.120. A similar remark appears in TNA WO 158/388 'Report on Operations Carried Out by 40th Division During the Period November 21st-28th 1917'. This acknowledges the lack of information on the operation of tanks in the wood but suggests that '… but for them the Infantry could not have progressed as well as they did'; TNA WO 95/100/1. *A Brief Battle-History of the 7th Tank Battalion* notes that the G Battalion tanks were delayed but 'passed the infantry inside the wood and succeeded in enabling them to get further forward …'
146 There is one other mention in the war diary of the 12th SWB which notes that a company was extricated from the outskirts of Bourlon village with the assistance of a (presumably D Battalion) tank on the afternoon of the first day's fighting. Having overshot its objective, the company was safely withdrawn after 24115 Lance-Sergeant H. A. Hampton made his way alone through the enemy, found a tank and guided it back. Hampton was awarded the DCM for his action. See TNA WO 95/2593: War Diary 40th Division General Staff. Report on Operations carried out by 40th Division Between November 20th and November 23rd, 1917. Including the Capture of the Bourlon Position.
147 J.C. MacIntosh, 'The Tanks at Cambrai' in John Buchan (ed.), *The Long Road to Victory* (London: Thomas Nelson and Sons, 1920), p.197.
148 TNA WO 95/2605 War Diary 119 Brigade. Instructions to accompany 119th Infantry Brigade Order No. 128. See Appendix III.
149 For example: Sidney Allinson, *The Bantams: The Untold Story of World War 1*(London: Howard Baker, 1981), pp.249-276; Crozier, *Brass Hat*, pp.176-190; Crozier, *Impressions*, pp.200-205; Bryn Hammond, *Cambrai 1917: The Myth of the First Great Tank Battle* (London: Weidenfeld & Nicolson, 2008), pp.249-302; Jack Horsfall and Nigel Cave, *Bourlon Wood* (Barnsley: Leo Cooper, 2002); Messenger, *Broken Sword*, pp.83-89; Miles, *Cambrai*, pp.129-149; William Moore, *A Wood Called Bourlon: The Cover-up After Cambrai* (London: Leo Cooper, 1988); Whitton, *History of the 40th Division*, pp.86-152.

lighted. In outline, the successful attack by the leading battalions was reinforced, initially by the 17th Welsh and in mid-afternoon by the 18th Welsh. As night fell the wood (and the high ground within it) was secure but in need of further reinforcement in anticipation of further counter attacks. The brigade works company and the salvage and burial sections were sent forward as were two companies of the 14th A&SH (from 120 Brigade in reserve). Overnight the remaining two companies of the A&SH moved up as did the dismounted 15th Hussars. During 24 November several determined counter attacks by the Germans were driven off with heavy losses to both sides and more reinforcements were received overnight in the form of two companies of the 11th King's Own (120 Brigade) and 2nd Scots Guards who had responded to 'an urgent message received from the GOC 119th Infantry Brigade to the effect that [the] position in Bourlon Wood was critical'. The message was received at 8.30 p.m. and the battalion was in position with three companies along the central ride and one in reserve, by 11.00 p.m.[150] There is some evidence that the defence was creaking. Captain Wilfred Ewart, Scots Guards later wrote:

> Down the centre of the ride … hurried a small body of men, shouting and talking excitedly … their faces were chalky white, they seemed incoherent and distraught. 'Retire!' they were crying. 'The Germans have broken through. They're coming down through the wood. Get back! Get back!' … Others – and these shattered, nerveless men whose human nature had been tried past endurance – now came surging back in twos and threes … Especially memory recalls the drawn, haggard face of an officer who was making rather pathetic attempts to reform these twos and threes … He kept trying to pull himself together but kept wandering off again. 'The bay'net!' he kept repeating, 'that's the thing for them. Show them the bay'net, get at them with the bay'net and they'll run … I've been fighting all day,' he went on. 'Everybody's killed, everybody. I'm the only one left.'[151]

The Scots Guards dug in. Next morning a short general advance collided with an incoming German attack. This and further attacks were driven off 'with difficulty'.[152] On the night of 25/26 November the exhausted and much depleted 40th Division and its reinforcements were relieved by the returning 62nd Division and the defence of the hard-won ground in Bourlon Wood passed to 186 Brigade (Brigadier-General R.B. Bradford VC, who was killed on 30 November). 119 Brigade had captured the wood but neither Bourlon village (though partly gained by 121 Brigade and reinforced by 120 Brigade and dismounted cavalry) nor Fontaine-Notre-Dame (51st Division, then the Guards Division) had been secured. 119 Brigade had retained the wood for three days despite having its flanks in the air. Further attacks took place after the departure of 40th Division but neither flank was secured and the wood was given up when the Germans counter attacked across the whole area on 30 November.

How did 119 Brigade manage to take and hold Bourlon Wood? Firstly, there was a reconnaissance of sorts. Crozier and Plunkett have both left accounts of the mounted dash to see the ground in front of Bourlon Wood before night fell on 22 November.[153] 'The trees were very close, and the wire on the southern end appeared thick, but by means of glasses I could see that there were diagonal lanes through the wire which decided me to advance in lines of platoons in the

---

150 TNA WO 95/1223/4: War Diary 2nd Scots Guards.
151 Wilfred Ewart, *When Armageddon Came* (London: Rich & Cowan Ltd, 1933), p.101. Crozier, *Brasshat*, p.180, also mentions 'A few men with flagging energy and less staying power than the rest' who bolted and were only stopped by an officer's revolver and a Lewis gun although, as he was not in the wood, he would not have seen any incident at first hand.
152 Miles, *Cambrai*, p.146.
153 Crozier, *Impressions*, p.201; Crozier, *Brass Hat*, pp.177-178; NAM: Plunkett – Diary of the War.

attack and not in an extended line.'¹⁵⁴ Secondly, in the spirit of the 18 November brigade conference, there was a briefing: 'we went through the idea of attack with all officers and NCOs'.¹⁵⁵ Thirdly, the attackers were determined and passed through the German counter-barrage despite the absence of covering smoke and the support of most of the tanks: 'Although never doubting them I watched the platoons approaching the Boche barrage but, although suffering many casualties, they never faltered. On reaching the wood (our artillery now having lifted 200 yards) the wire was encountered but platoon Comdrs soon found the lanes I had told them about, passed through them, and were in the wood'.¹⁵⁶ Fourthly, capable senior officers were in the wood with their men to organise defence and counter attack as appropriate but the attrition rate was correspondingly high. Plunkett (CO, 19th RWF) moved down into the wood and took charge before the first counter attack. Robert Benzie (CO, 12th SWB) was also on the spot and was placed in command of all the forces in the wood by Crozier on the evening of the first day. When the 17th and then the 18th Welsh moved up Richard Andrews (CO, 17th Welsh) went with them (and was severely wounded on the second day), as did William Kennedy (CO, 18th Welsh) who led his men across to the wood on horseback and was killed shortly afterwards. The 2iC, 19th RWF, Major Cole, was wounded before the advance started and two other 2iCs became casualties in the wood: Major C.C. Dowding, 18th Welsh, was wounded on the first day and Major W.E. Brown, 12th SWB, was wounded on the morning of the second day.¹⁵⁷ Losses in captains and junior officers were also high. Fifth, the tactics for attack and defence were appropriate and had been rehearsed. In attack: 'the enemy had a series of posts but these were overcome by rounding [*sic*] and getting in with the bayonet'.¹⁵⁸ '[I] ordered the whole line to attack. It did and used the bayonet to such purpose that the position was taken with a large number of prisoners. Our line reorganised and again moved forward, encountering machine guns in single prepared positions. By using 2 of our Lewis guns, one from either flank of a located machine gun, the latter was invariably put out of action.'¹⁵⁹ In defence: 'I now consolidated our position … on high ground pushing forward couples to [the] edge of [the] wood'.¹⁶⁰ At the end of the first day the 100 metre contour provided the site for 'two lines of posts at intervals of 150 yards on this line'.¹⁶¹ '[On the second day] the enemy attacked very heavily, coming on in droves, without any particular formation. We waited until they were about 150 yards away and then opened rapid fire with rifles and Lewis guns. They melted away completely and not a single German reached our line.'¹⁶² The 19th RWF and the 12th SWB also had two Vickers heavy machine guns attached to each battalion which added massively to the firepower available to their defence of the wood. The training received by the brigade had paid dividends. Finally, three other factors contributed to success in the wood: firstly, despite wires being cut by German shells visual signals contact was maintained between the wood and brigade HQ via a signals hub in the cemetery between Anneux and Graincourt which would have allowed timely situation reporting and requests for reinforcement; secondly, the signals facilitated protective fire from the artillery of 40th Division and elements of 62nd Division artillery that had been left in place; thirdly, there was a degree of confusion in the wood at the time of the opening attack which interrupted a relief,

---

154 NAM: Plunkett – Diary of the War. Ibid.
155 Ibid.
156 Ibid.
157 The creation of an advanced brigade HQ within the wood luckily came to nothing. See Whitton, *History of the 40th Division*, p.130. The HQs of both 119 Brigade and 121 Brigade remained in the catacombs beneath Graincourt Church.
158 TNA WO 95/2607: War Diary 19th RWF.
159 NAM: Plunkett – Diary of the War.
160 Ibid.
161 TNA WO 95/2605 War Diary 119 Brigade, first day summary by brigade intelligence officer.
162 TNA WO 95/2606 War Diary 12th SWB.

leaving the tired *3rd Battalion IR50 (214th Division)* in the southern part of the wood to face the first attack and the newly arrived *1st and 3rd Battalions Lehr IR (3rd Guards Division)* on unfamiliar ground in the north and west along with elements of other units.[163]

How did Crozier perform during the action? There is very little evidence other than the successful outcome. Harry Graham records 'I shall never forget that visit to Graincourt – I dived underground about 30 feet to find a wild-eyed Brigadier and a pale Bde Major who urged me to return immediately and say that unless they were reinforced at once they would be absolutely done in. 'Men, more men!' was their cry' – which is not the sort of image that Crozier would have wished circulated.[164] More to his taste would have been the description of 'the brigadier, a daredevil little warrior, setting an example to his men which none who followed him will forget'.[165] Back in Cardiff, as if to emphasise the brigade's continuing Welsh connections a laudatory article appeared in the *Western Mail*. A slightly abridged version reads:

> Private narratives which have reached the Western Mail ascribe the capture of Bourlon Wood to their dauntless courage and heroism. While at present details of battle formations etc cannot be entered into, sufficient material is gathered from letters to hand to throw light upon the admirable fighting qualities of the Welsh troops…. As our men went deeper A[ndrews] had to be called upon for assistance. He had his men lined across the middle of the wood and down either flank … by 12.30 we had reached the edge of the wood on the other side of the hill and our objectives were gained. In fact S[ymes, captain, 12th SWB] with some of his men had got into the village beyond which was not our objective … at 3.30 the situation became very critical and K[ennedy] taking half his battalion, rode into the wood, dismounted when he was half way through, deployed his men and met the Bosches just as they were launching a counter attack. He charged leading his men, and his fine spirit gave his men such confidence that they not only drove back the counter attack but captured 80 prisoners. K[ennedy] was killed but we still held the whole of the ridge and some of the slopes beyond … We dug in hard that night on the crest of the hill. C[rozier] had his work cut out at our headquarters, and he did splendidly. He has been magnificent all through. B[enzie] was wonderful, calm and collected all through. P[lunkett] was a perfect tiger and had a charmed life. He was everywhere bullets were thickest, beating off counter attacks and driving home local attacks; he was almost superhuman, as he never ceased until he came out of the line… A[Andrews] got hit in the morning. He was carried down on a stretcher to an advanced dressing station where he was able to draw on a map our exact dispositions … our men all fought like heroes. Of those you know, L[loyd?] had his hand almost off … he behaved most gallantly as also did D[unn?] who is missing. B[rown] was wounded but did awfully well.[166]

'Our Div. is frightfully bucked with itself about the share we took in the fighting, and congratulations are pouring in from every side. But it is a bloody business'.[167] 40th Division casualties were 172 officers and 3191 other ranks. 119 Brigade casualties in the infantry battalions were 60 officers and

---

163 Jack Sheldon, *The German Army at Cambrai* (Barnsley: Pen and Sword, 2009), p.161. The *214th Division* was rated 'good' and *3rd Guard Division* 'one of the best' according to the AEF, *Histories of the Two Hundred and Fifty-One Divisions of the German Army*.
164 IWM: Graham Papers, letter dated 7 December 1917. The 121 Brigade HQ was also in the catacombs beneath Graincourt church.
165 Arthur Conan Doyle, *The British Campaign in France and Flanders 1917* (London: Hodder and Stoughton, 1919), p.260.
166 *Western Mail*, 28 December 1917. This account is likely to have come from Percy Hone, Staff Captain, 119 Brigade.
167 IWM: Graham Papers, letter dated 29 November 1917.

1473 other ranks: 17th Welsh – 13 officers and 240 other ranks; 18th Welsh – 13 officers and 400 other ranks; 19th RWF – 16 officers 443 other ranks; 12th SWB – 18 officers and 390 other ranks.[168]

> We had not got the highest possible reputation before J[ohn Ponsonby] took over – chiefly by bad luck, for we never had a chance of showing our mettle – and it is surprising that we should have been given the hardest nut of all to crack. After it was over, the C-in-C ingenuously said to J.P: 'I can't understand how you got the 40th D to do it!' To which J.P. replied: For the simple reason that the 40th D was the best in the British Army! (I believe the betting at GHQ was 12 to 1 against the nut being cracked!).[169]

Congratulations came from Douglas Haig: 'who wished all ranks of the 40th Division to be congratulated on their recent success. Great credit is due not only to Infantry Brigades who gave proof of fine fighting qualities and endurance'; from the GOC, Third Army: 'The capture of Bourlon Wood to my mind stands out amongst all the other splendid actions of our infantry … and in years to come I shall remember with unqualified satisfaction that it was performed by the splendid division with which I have now been associated for some time'; and from division: 'The GOC wishes to especially congratulate you and your Brigade, also the A&SH and 15th Hussars attached to you'. Crozier's own Special Order of the Day pointed out that 'the valour and endurance displayed were beyond all praise. A most important tactical position … was assaulted and taken … and held against countless counter attacks and ceaseless pressure until handed over, consolidated and intact …The flanks were kept secure against abnormal difficulties.'[170] Freddy Plunkett observed:

> I have fought with many regiments in this war but the achievement of the 19th [RWF] and [the] remainder of 119 Infy Bde in taking Bourlon Wood on 23rd Novr 1917, with no assistance from tanks, smoke barrages, etc, and only a few minutes preliminary artillery bombardment, capturing at least 500 prisoners with many machine guns, then repelling counter-attacks for 3 days without sleep, subsisting on iron ration food only, handing over the wood intact, marching 15 miles to the rear, after the Brigade had suffered 75% casualties both in officers and men, and finishing the last mile of the march in high spirits, I place second to none of any other performance in the war.[171]

---

168 TNA WO 95/2594: War Diary 40th Division HQ A&Q, Casualties to date, 1 December 1917. The battalion war diaries give different figures: 119 Brigade total 73 officers, 1270 ORs; 17th Welsh 18 officers, 301 ORs; 18th Welsh 15 officers, 262 ORs; 19th RWF 18 officers, 343 ORs; 12th SWB 22 officers, 364 ORs. If the battalions did, as suggested at the 18 November brigade conference, put 500 men into action, the figures are appalling – no matter which figures are regarded as the most accurate. 80% of those killed have no known grave.
169 IWM: Graham Papers, letter dated 30 November 1917.
170 Congratulatory messages as compiled in TNA WO 95/2605 W:ar Diary 119 Brigade. Douglas Haig congratulated the men in person as they marched away on 26 November. 'There is only one word which can describe Sir Douglas Haig as he appeared to me on that occasion – 'fine' … A cavalry soldier he looked every inch of one with steel helmet and box respirator at the 'alert', 'sitting' his charger as only a British Light Cavalry Soldier can … he looked down upon and uttered words of encouragement, congratulation and thanks to my little Welshmen as they passed … 'Well done, well done', repeated the great Field-Marshal, over and over again for five minutes as the 'remnants' march by.' – Crozier, *Impressions*, p.206. 'What a great man he was' – *Impressions*, p.239. Contrast those remarks with Crozier's words on 10 May 1936 when he published an article in *Reynolds News* headed 'Fact is that Haig was no Soldier' and in 1937 when his allegiance to the cause of peace was total: '… they [the high command] were all branded with the same mark – incompetence and self-satisfaction. Haig, in latter days, thought that the mantle of the Almighty had fallen on him …' See F.P. Crozier, *The Men I Killed* (London, Michael Joseph, 1937), p.88.
171 NAM: Plunkett – Diary of the War.

5

Reorganisation, Destruction and Reconstruction

So far we have examined in detail the founding of the brigade and its development up to the fight for Bourlon Wood where it suffered the most substantial losses from its original establishment since arriving at the front eighteen months earlier. In contrast to this period of relative stability, 1918 was a year of constant change for 119 Brigade with structural reform and repeated major rebuilding testing the capabilities of its GOC. New units, new officers and new men gave the brigade a different character and structure on two occasions – resulting in a formation whose make up was in sharp contrast to that of the 'Welsh Bantam Brigade'. This chapter will cover the brigade's two episodes of restructuring, its actions during the German Spring Offensives of 1918 and its chequered history thereafter. It will show how in the hands of capable HQ staff the 'building block' of the brigade is capable of handling major change while delivering effective 'on the job' training – even when the raw materials are not of the best quality.

End of the Old Brigade

Crozier wrote of Bourlon that "nine months toil [was] wiped out in three days".[1] The tired and depleted units of 119 Brigade might have legitimately expected some rest after their exertions at Bourlon Wood but they would be disappointed. After settling into billets in villages south-west of Arras, the brigade spent just one day cleaning up before learning that it would relieve the 16th (Irish) Division in the line near Bullecourt on 3 December, but the relief was brought forward.[2] Crozier implies that this was because the 16th Division was needed to help check the German counter attack at Cambrai.[3] His opinion is supported by the war diary of the 2nd Royal Irish

---

1 F.P. Crozier, *A Brass Hat in No Man's Land* (London: Jonathan Cape, 1930), p.184.
2 The 16th Division had suffered very badly at Frezenberg Ridge and Langemarck in the Ypres salient earlier in the year and had moved to the Bapaume-Miraumont sector (VI Corps, Third Army) at the end of August. On 20 November, as a diversion from the Cambrai attack, 16th and 3rd Divisions had successfully attacked and held Tunnel Trench, a part of the Hindenburg Line south of Fontaine les Croisilles, killing 500 Germans and capturing 718. When it left the trenches in December it was 'desperately in need of rest and training'. See Terence Denman, *Ireland's Unknown Soldiers: The 16th (Irish) Division in the Great War* (Dublin: Irish Academic Press, 2008).
3 Crozier, *Brass Hat*, p.185. The British success at Cambrai had created a salient fourteen kilometres wide and six deep. The German counter-attack started on the morning of 30 November. After losing newly-won ground, particularly in the south of the battlefield, a general withdrawal of British forces took place between 4-7 December. Bourlon Wood was given up and a new front line established for the winter on the Flesquières Ridge to the south-west. Flesquières itself was now in a salient (albeit a shallow one) and would prove a tempting objective for the Germans in the spring.

Regiment (49 Brigade, 16th (Irish) Division).[4] So, on the night of 2 December, the 17th Welsh and the 19th RWF moved into the battered, captured German position at Tunnel Trench just north of Bullecourt. Crozier says that he believed that the move into the line was "best for all, provided they send us men".[5] Some men did arrive. The 17th Welsh war diary records forty-seven officers joining or being loaned to the battalion in December 1917 followed by four in January 1918 but does not mention any drafts to the ranks. During December 1917 the 18th Welsh received twenty-eight officers and 308 men, followed in January by a further six officers and ninety-nine men. The 19th RWF war diary shows that the battalion received thirteen officers in December, followed by another two in January but records no drafts of men.[6] Freddy Plunkett recalled though that the battalion "was made up to 500 strong including many Territorial officers who had not seen service before", so it is likely that drafts were not always recorded in war diaries.[7] The 12th SWB received thirteen officers and thirty-six other ranks in December, followed by four officers and 213 other ranks in January.[8] By the end of January 1918 all four battalions were probably, like the 19th RWF, at least 500 strong.

Through the months of December and January the brigade worked hard to bring some sort of order to the chaotic landscape of smashed trenches in this part of the Hindenburg system. Many of the trenches opposite were lightly held and there were numerous concrete strongpoints to be investigated and/or destroyed during the regular offensive patrols that took place. For example, the 17th Welsh investigated the 'Vulcan' pill box and, with associated RE parties, destroyed 'Argus' pill box on 28 December, another (unnamed) on 30 December and a third, with a MG emplacement on top, on 8 January. One of its new officers, 2/Lt Victor Trevor Jones, came a cropper during the 30 December demolition:

> I was in Tunnel Trench and was ordered to bring a patrol of A Coy from Fag Alley to Post 19 in Tunnel Trench to join up with another party that was waiting to go out into No Man's Land. I brought the patrol along between our line of posts and our wire. When near Post 19 an enemy strong point was blown up and pieces of concrete were dropping around. I jumped into the post to take cover and in doing so came into contact with the point of a bayonet which penetrated the region of the crutch.[9]

---

4 TNA WO 95/1979/1: War Diary 2nd Royal Irish Regiment. This records that the battalion was relieved on 1 December by the 12th Suffolk (121 Brigade) and that '40th Division had been at Bourlon Wood and was rather 'tired'.' On 2 December the rumour among the 2nd Royal Irish was 'that we are going to Bourlon Wood to take an active part in the Battle of Cambrai'. On 3 December the battalion moved closer to the fighting but on 4 December a move towards Havrincourt was cancelled. Instead, the battalion moved south to the VII Corps, Fifth Army, sector east of Péronne to rest and rebuild.
5 Crozier, *Brass Hat*, p.186.
6 TNA WO/95 2607: War Diaries 17th Welsh, 18th Welsh and 19th RWF. 167 of the men for the 18th Welsh came from Number Six Infantry Base Depot (Rouen) and forty-six from the Divisional Depot Battalion.
7 National Army Museum, Chelsea: 1994/05/398/1 'Diary of the War – by J.F. Plunkett'.
8 TNA WO 95/2606: War Diary 12th SWB. 100 of these men came from the 6th SWB (Pioneers, 25th Division). One of the new officers was second-lieutenant Harold Jones. Jones had joined the Montgomery Yeomanry at the outbreak of war and had served in Egypt. After applying for a commission in January 1917, he joined the 12th SWB on 12 December: 'Men who had come from the support line led us to Bttn HQ and there in a dugout we found our CO, Colonel Benzies [sic], and his staff enjoying a fairly decent looking meal. We were greeted enthusiastically as the Bttn was very short of officers having lost heavily in the Bourlon Wood scrap and we were the first reinforcements. The CO immediately posted us to our companies and I was posted to B Coy. In less than half an hour I was following a guide up the support trench to my Coy HQ. Here I reported to the Skipper who also appeared glad to see me' – RRW Museum, Brecon: 2001.98/Diary 68, Harold Jones Memoir.
9 TNA WO 339/111373: Victor Trevor Jones personal file.

Above and right: 119 Brigade Christmas card, 1917. The galvanising effect of the appearance of an officer. (Author)

Poor Jones not only found himself in No 10 Red Cross Hospital at Le Treport with a bayonet wound in the perineum but an enquiry into his possible self-inflicted wound was instigated. His story was investigated and found to be corroborated.

Despite the reduced establishment and the arrival of new officers, 19th RWF carried out a major raid to improve its position, demonstrating just what the brigade's units could do:

> Between Valley Trench and our forward posts were nothing but shell holes half full of water, and in attempting to relieve my forward posts ... no less than 20 men were stuck in the mud next morning, some waist high. One man was stuck for 36 hours before being taken out and lost a toe from frostbite. I decided that these forward posts were impossible for the winter and asked to be allowed to take the Boche line or fall back on Valley Trench, sending in a scheme for the former. After a weeks delay I was told that I could attempt to take the Boche line. Night patrolling told us that the Boche held the line strongly at night so I selected 3pm to attack. As the Boche trench was a part of the renowned Tunnel Trench we knew that there would probably be a deep dugout about every 100 yards, so we took over 10 10lb mobile charges. On the 15th Decr at 3 pm two parties of 30 each, who had been assembled at our extreme left and right post respectively, accompanied by RE with the mobile charges, rushed forward and reached the Boche line with hardly a dozen shots being fired at them, and working inwards, killing the Boche sentries, about 10, [and] posted 2 men at [the] door of each dugout. As the Boche could be heard down the dugouts he was called upon to surrender but would not come up. The RE officer blew up 8 dugouts. Our casualties were 31. A Boche prisoner, wounded, stated, stated that they would not surrender as they had been told we killed all prisoners ... On this front the new Boche line was quite 300 yards away, so that, with the ground in such an awful state and winter weather, neither side could hope to do much in the line of operations, but the Bullecourt sector lived up to its name by every day shell fire.[10]

Afterwards Crozier wrote a note to Plunkett:

> My Dear Plunkett,
> Just a line to congratulate you and 'yr' battn on yr very fine effort of this afternoon.
>   Words cannot express in any reality [sic] what I and the rest of the Bde think of yr performance.
>   Yours
>   FP Crozier

But the raid marked the 'last hurrah' for the old brigade.

While receiving reinforcements, patrolling and trying to keep the trenches free of mud during snow and subsequent thaw, the brigade's battalions once again made time for training. Usually, where it is described, it consisted of close order drill, "platoon, section and arms drill" or simply "training according to programme".[11] The impression formed is of a brigade that is trying to get

---

10   NAM: 1994/05/398/1: 'Diary of the War – by J.F. Plunkett'. According to the battalion war diary, two attacking parties of two officers and 54 other ranks and two officers and 46 other ranks were used. It was estimated that 20 of the enemy were killed while the attackers had four killed and 19 wounded. Operations were often restricted by the weather but the units were experienced enough by now to know that patrols over snow in bright moonlight would be spotted and that muddy ground was too heavy for 'good and silent work'.
11   TNA WO 95/2607: War Diaries 17th Welsh, 18th Welsh, 19th RWF; WO/95 2606 War Diary 12th SWB. The 17th Welsh did get one company on to the firing range.

back into a routine, trying to promote 'business as usual'. Its efforts were to be thwarted by decisions made at the highest level. On 19 January 1918, 40th Division received notification that brigades were to be reorganised to have only three battalions.[12] The change would prove to be more drastic than the simple loss of one battalion. On 31 January, the 12th SWB received "a large batch of orders ... regarding impending disbanding [of the] battalion".[13] It would not be alone. Three of 119 Brigade's four battalions were to be disbanded.

The background to the major changes to the composition of divisions in the field is detailed in the Official History.[14] At a time when a large increase in German divisions and materiel on the Western Front was anticipated following the cessation of hostilities on the Eastern Front, it became clear that the BEF would be facing a crisis in its own manpower during 1918.[15] The matter had been referred to the scrutiny of a Cabinet Committee in December 1917 and its draft report was passed to the Army Council early in January. In trying to resolve a genuine paradox between the maintenance of the BEF and the sustainability of industries and services now crucial, not only to the British war effort, but also to that of the Allies, it felt unable to allocate more than 100,000 'A' class men for the BEF (compared with the 615,000 required by the CinC). Faced with the certainty of a major German offensive in the west, the military members of the Army Council objected without effect. The committee suggested that by reducing the number of battalions, the existing number of divisions could be maintained.[16] A list of 145 battalions for possible disbandment was sent to Douglas Haig on 10 January.[17] His selection was then compiled and reported to the War Office on 18 January.[18] "This reduction seriously interfered with the existing organisation of every division, and with the tactical handling of every brigade, while the breaking up of battalions was often bitterly resented by officers and men and tended to lower morale."[19] 116 battalions were broken up, two were converted to pioneers in their own divisions and a further five converted to pioneers and transferred. The resulting gaps were filled by moving twenty-two battalions between divisions and re-distributing a further thirty-two internally. In total, 114 battalions were lost to the

---

12 TNA WO 95/2594: War Diary 40th Division HQ A&Q. The following week the war diary records the approval of a change to the divisional sign recognising the fight at Bourlon Wood – 'the white diamond to be superimposed on a red gamecock with an acorn in the diamond'.
13 TNA WO 95/2606: War Diary 12th SWB.
14 James E. Edmonds, *Military Operations France and Belgium 1918, Vol.1: The German March Offensive and its Preliminaries* (London: Macmillan, 1935), pp.47-56. Also David Stevenson, *With Our Backs to the Wall: Victory and Defeat in 1918* (London: Allen Lane, 2011), pp.49-53 and Keith Grieves, *The Politics of Manpower, 1914-18* (Manchester: Manchester University Press, 1988), pp.181-183.
15 See J.M. Bourne, *Britain and the Great War 1914-1918* (London: Edward Arnold, 1989), pp.81-85 for a concise account of the situation on the eastern front and the threat to the western front.
16 The likely necessity of this in the face of diminishing manpower levels had been pointed out to the War Office by Douglas Haig in November 1917. See Edmonds, *Military Operations France and Belgium 1918,* Vol. 1, p.28. For an alternative view of the aim of the process of reduction see Bob Butcher, 'The Nine Battalion Controversy', *Stand To! The Journal of the Western Front Association,* 68 (September 2003), pp.47-49.
17 No Regular, First-line Territorial or Yeomanry battalions were included at this point. Dominion troops were also excluded from the exercise as they were the responsibility of their respective governments. Martin Samuels, *Command or Control?: Command, Training and Tactics in the British and German Armies, 1888-1918* (London: Frank Cass, 1995), p.249, describes the effect on 30th and 36th Divisions and regards the former as an 'urge for administrative neatness' in removing the highest numbered battalions of two regiments. The fact that men were generally sent to another battalion of their own regiment (even when it was in a different Corps or Army) indicates that the process was placed firmly within the regimental system. The only other unit from 40th Division to be disbanded was the 11th KORL, another bantam battalion.
18 A similar organisational change in the French Army was largely complete by the end of 1917. See Elizabeth Greenhalgh, *The French Army and the First World War* (Cambridge: Cambridge University Press, 2014), pp.251-252.
19 C.M.R.F. Crutwell, *A History of the Great War 1914-1918* (Oxford: Clarendon Press, 1934), p.501.

British Army.[20] Four battalions from 40th Division were disbanded, three of them in 119 Brigade which was one of just eight brigades to lose at least three battalions.[21] This time the national affiliation of the brigade worked against it as regiments from Territorial District Number Four (which consisted mainly of Wales) were instructed to disband sixteen of their fifty-three battalions (30%) – the highest level of disbandment on the Western Front.[22] The reasoning behind this was that "The number of Battalions composing certain regiments is greater than can be adequately maintained by the output in men of the Territorial District concerned. It is necessary, therefore, to reduce the liabilities of these Territorial Districts by reducing the number of Battalions to be maintained".[23] In the case of New Army battalions the last formed were to be targeted making the high-numbered battalions of 119 Brigade particularly vulnerable. Within this broad direction many of the decisions on which battalions to disband were made at divisional level.

Crozier wrote later: "they took away my Royal Welsh Fusiliers and South Wales Borderers (the best battalions in my command) and left me the choice of keeping the 17th or 18th Welsh. I decided on retaining the 18th as it had been slightly less knocked about …".[24] While Crozier's books suggest that he was rather sanguine about the change, Starrett recalls a somewhat different picture: "that was a blow that the General took hardly. But all his letters, and he wrote a few, and all his arguments, and he saw nearly every brass-hat near and far, availed nothing."[25] Crozier went on leave to England on 25 January and returned on 17 February to find a very different brigade waiting for him.[26] What happened to the Welsh units?

The 18th Welsh was the sole surviving battalion from the original brigade. On 5 February the battalion received 179 men and seven officers from the 17th Welsh followed by another four officers on 18 February.[27] By 17 February it was strong enough to supply a working party of eighteen officers and 600 men.[28] On 8 February the 17th Welsh sent another two officers and fifty men to the 2nd Welsh (1st Division, II Corps) and two officers and fifty men to the 9th Welsh (19th Division, V Corps).[29] On 15 February the remaining officers and men were merged into

---

20 The process is detailed in Simon Justice, 'Vanishing Battalions: The Nature, Impact and Implications of British Infantry Reorganization prior to the German Spring Offensives of 1918' in Michael LoCicero, et al (eds.), *A Military Transformed? Adaptation and Innovation in the British Military 1792-1945* (Solihull: Helion & Company, 2014), pp.157-173. Justice has analysed the process and created a 'dislocation index' in an attempt to quantify the impact of the reorganization. Both the 40th Division and the 34th Division are categorized as having a 'severe' level of dislocation. It proved unfortunate to say the least that both were occupying adjacent sectors to the left of the Portuguese 2nd Division during the Battle of the Lys in April 1918.
21 I am very grateful to Simon Justice for the information in this paragraph which is additional to that in his publication referenced above.
22 Crozier, Starrett and the divisional historian all blame the shortage of Welshmen to maintain the 38th (Welsh) Division as well as 119 Brigade units. T.O. Marden, *The History of the Welch Regiment 1914-1918* (Cardiff: Western Mail and Echo, 1932), p.436, is more specific: 'there were too few Welshmen to keep up the strengths of all the Welsh units, as the coal mines made heavy demands on the man power of the Principality'.
23 TNA WO 106/415: Divisions in France; Reorganization Jan/Feb, Lieutenant-General H.A. Lawrence *OB/1851/A* (23 January 1918).
24 F.P. Crozier, *Impressions and Recollections* (London: T. Werner Laurie, 1930), p.212. See also Crozier, *Brass Hat*, p.189. The 18th Welsh had fewer casualties at Bourlon than the 17th Welsh according to the battalion war diaries but not according to the 40th Division war diary. See Chapter 4 footnotes.
25 IWM: Documents 79/35/1 'Batman' by David Starrett, unpublished typescript.
26 TNA WO 95/2605: War Diary 119 Brigade.
27 TNA WO 95/2594: War Diary 40th Division HQ A&Q.
28 TNA WO/95/2606: War Diary 18th Welsh.
29 TNA WO 95/2594: War Diary 40th Division HQ A&Q.

the 9th Entrenching Battalion.³⁰ Next day the final war diary entry noted "This Bn (17th Welsh) ceased today to be an [*sic*] unit".³¹

The 19th RWF sent eight officers and 150 men from its D Company to the 2nd RWF (33rd Division, VIII Corps) on 6 February. It then amalgamated with the 10th RWF (76 Brigade, 3rd Division) to form the 8th Entrenching Battalion on 15 February. The battalion's last casualty was its CO. Freddy Plunkett had a heart attack on 8th February while marching his men out but he would return to the brigade later in the year.³²

The 12th SWB was still raiding the German trenches as late as 4 February but on 8 February, two officers and fifty men left for the 5th SWB (19th Division, V Corps), followed on 10 February by two drafts each of two officers and 100 men to the 1st SWB (1st Division, II Corps) and to the 2nd SWB (29th Division, VIII Corps). Before they left they heard letters from Sir Douglas Haig and John Ponsonby read on parade.³³ Ten officers went with the remains of the battalion to form the 9th Entrenching Battalion along with the remnants of the 17th Welsh and 11th KORL (the only battalion of 120 and 121 Brigades to be disbanded) and those remaining went "to the Base for posting".³⁴ "The curtain rings down on the Welsh Brigade, which fought its way to glory while it carried a whole division on its shoulders".³⁵

The New Brigade

On 1 February 1918 the first of the new battalions arrived. The 10th/11th HLI (46 Brigade, 15th Division) stayed with 119 Brigade for just two weeks before transferring to 120 Brigade to make it a wholly Scottish formation.³⁶ According to Crozier it had been decided that "as the Welsh brigade had done so well at Bourlon Wood, it was thought by some that it would be a good thing to have another National brigade in the Division with the result that a Highland brigade was formed". ³⁷ He remained sceptical about the effect, believing "that an alteration is not made in the ingredients of any mixture by merely altering the labels".³⁸

---

30   Entrenching battalions were created on several occasions during the Great War. Those formed in 1918 worked on creating defences in the rear areas but were also 'holding units' for surplus manpower and were short-lived.
31   TNA WO 95/2607: War Diary 17th Welsh.
32   TNA WO 95/2606: War Diary 19th RWF; WO 95/2594: War Diary 40th Division HQ A&Q. Freddy Plunkett had a long life for a man with poor health. He died in 1953. It is possible that his 'heart attack' was a different manifestation of months of stress.
33   Ponsonby's letter is in TNA WO 95/2594. He wrote: 'To all ranks … who are now leaving the 40th Division I wish to express my deep regret at the loss occasioned by myself personally and to the division as a whole by your departure. Although the battalion in which you have served so long in this country is to be broken up, the memory of its splendid achievements will never fade. The record of your past services, the fine fighting spirit that you have invariably displayed, and your constant determination to maintain the lofty traditions of your battalion, not only redound to your own credit and to that of the 40th Division, but will add still further to the glorious reputation of your Regiment … As your Divisional Commander I wish to thank all ranks for the active and unfailing support you have so readily afforded me during the last six months of fighting under the most trying conditions.'
34   TNA WO 95/2606: War Diary 12th SWB. C.T. Atkinson, *The History of the South Wales Borderers 1914-1918* (London: Medici Society, 1931), p.392 says that there were still 500 men on the strength on 31st March – this may be an error or it might refer to the strength of 9th Entrenching Battalion.
35   Crozier, *Brass Hat*, p.189. Crozier's claim of pre-eminence for 119 Brigade will be discussed later.
36   TNA WO 95/2594: War Diary 40th Division HQ A&Q.
37   Crozier, *Impressions*, pp.212-213. 120 Brigade now consisted of the 10th/11th HLI, 14th HLI and 14th A&SH. 121 Brigade was made up of the 12th Suffolk, 13th Yorks and 20th Middlesex.
38   Ibid.

The replacement battalion for the 10th/11th HLI arrived from 120 Brigade on 16 February. The 13th East Surrey (Lieutenant-Colonel Herbert Lawton Warden) had taken twenty-one officers and 602 other ranks into the second day of the attack against Bourlon village.[39] Its casualties were six officers and 223 other ranks.[40] Since then it had received a draft of nine officers and 192 other ranks from the 7th East Surrey (37 Brigade, 12th Division) which was disbanded.[41] The final battalion to make up the three-battalion brigade was the 21st Middlesex (Lieutenant-Colonel Herbert Charles Metcalfe) from 121 Brigade.[42] Its casualties at Bourlon had been comparatively light: nine officers (two killed) and 126 other ranks (twenty killed). Since the action it had received just ten new officers and seemingly no drafts of men.[43] On 5 January 1918 its effective strength was forty-three officers and 723 other ranks. One month later the battalion transferred to 119 Brigade and on 12 February received a draft of fifteen officers and 300 other ranks from the disbanded 17th Middlesex (6 Brigade, 2nd Division). Its effective strength on 16 February is recorded as fifty-six officers and 1016 other ranks.[44]

119 Brigade was now fully reformed and approximately up to strength. Crozier could have some confidence in the Welsh which he knew but the other battalions had let him down at Bourlon (or so he believed) and needed to be brought up to a higher standard:

> We received two battalions that were far below the requirements of modern war … when being put through their paces for two days we found them to be greatly wanting. They did nothing quick enough. Officers hesitated while, of course, other ranks followed suit. They lost their equipment and were deficient of vital items and failed to realize that the role of the infantry is to get to grips with the enemy with cold steel supported by fire of their own making aided by the fire of others … the Welsh, my stalwarts, were of quite a different stamp, which caused me to resort to the unpleasant necessity of making the two battalions stand by and watch everything the Welsh did in the field for several days, while I in addition lectured them myself.[45]

From the middle of February all three battalions were training and all received regular visits from Crozier at camp, in training, on the ranges and at larger scale training schemes.[46] Notable among these events were the lectures given by Crozier to all officers and NCOs of the brigade on 25 February;[47] the battalion counter attack demonstrated by the 18th Welsh on 26 February, advancing 1000 yards and deploying into artillery formation and then extended order, which was repeated next day under the gaze of the C-in-C;[48] the brigade practice attack of 6 March at which the 13th East Surrey and the 21st Middlesex provided the assaulting waves and the 18th Welsh provided two companies as moppers-up and another two as the reserve. Again, this was repeated next day with a contact aeroplane, a barrage marked by flags, gas represented by smoke and the

---

39 Herbert Lawton Warden (1877-1946). See Appendix VI.
40 TNA WO 95/2612: War Diary 13th East Surrey Regiment. 38 men were killed, 77 missing and 108 wounded.
41 Ibid.
42 Herbert Charles Metcalfe (1864-1940). See Appendix VI.
43 TNA WO 95/2615: War Diary 21st Middlesex.
44 TNA WO 95/2606: War Diary 21st Middlesex.
45 Crozier, *Impressions*, pp.213-214. Both battalions had been transferred to 40th Division as part of the making up process in February 1915. They were not bantam units, nor did they have the national affiliation of the units of the original 119 Brigade.
46 TNA WO 95/2605: War Diary 119 Brigade, for example 18, 24, 25, 28 February and 7 March 1917.
47 Ibid.
48 TNA WO 95/2606: War Diary 18th Welsh.

final assault by men wearing their box-respirators.[49] There were lectures on pigeon training for signallers, cooperation with aircraft and with tanks and anti-aircraft Lewis gunnery. The 18th Welsh marched companies for differing times wearing their box respirators and discovered that it was possible to march for eighty minutes.[50] The 13th East Surrey practised attacks on strongpoints on 18th March and progressed to attacking a succession of strongpoints next day.[51] The 21st Middlesex practised the attack in cooperation with tanks.[52] The battalions trained constantly through February and March with a few days given to moves and for church parades. They also supplied working parties for trench improvements and for burying signalling cables. The divisional armourer sergeant inspected all rifles, Lewis guns and bicycles. There were practice alarms and the men might have noticed their officers' regular excursions to reconnoitre the ground and select suitable places of assembly.[53] A divisional conference was held to discuss the use of tanks, barrages, machine-guns and communication with artillery (see Appendix IV).[54] The hectic training, the GOC's constant presence, the digging, the reconnaissance, the weapons inspections – the German attack was clearly imminent and certainly not unexpected.

119 Brigade and 'Michael'

Both GHQ and the French GQG were expecting a German offensive that would take place as the weather improved in spring 1918. Douglas Haig told his Army commanders in December 1917 that: "We must be prepared to meet a strong and sustained hostile offensive. It is therefore of first importance that [you] should give [your] immediate and personal attention to the organization of zones for defensive purposes and to the rest and training of [your] troops."[55] This was the context of the training and digging carried out by 119 Brigade.

The German decision to attack was made in November 1917 and several plans were developed but the first operation orders were not issued until 24 January.[56] The French and British armies both believed that their own front would be the target of the attack. The BEF was particularly vulnerable in the south, where Fifth Army extended its front to take over more line from the French in January, but GHQ believed that Third Army would bear the brunt of the attack as the Germans attempted to pinch out the salient to the west of Cambrai.[57] In the event, the length of the attack front was longer than anticipated and while Third Army was heavily engaged, it was Fifth Army's collapse in the south that has become the abiding image of the offensive.

The Third Army sector was formed by V Corps in the south, then IV, VI and finally VII Corps in the north. 59th, 34th and 3rd Divisions formed VI Corps' front line centred on and to the east of the village of Croisilles. 40th Division was in GHQ reserve. The letters of Harry Graham

---

49 TNA WO 95/2605: War Diary 119 Brigade. This second demonstration was watched by the Divisional Commander, John Ponsonby.
50 TNA WO 95/2606: War Diary 18th Welsh, 4 March 1918.
51 TNA WO 95/2606: War Diary 13th East Surrey.
52 TNA WO 95/2606: War Diary 21st Middlesex, 11 March 1918. It is not clear whether tanks were actually present.
53 TNA WO 95/2605: War Diary 119 Brigade; WO 95/2606: War Diary 18th Welsh; WO 95/2606: War Diary 13th East Surrey; WO 95/2606: War Diary 21st Middlesex.
54 'Notes on the conference held at 40th Division Headquarters, 6 March 1918' is included as Appendix IV.
55 Edmonds, *Military Operations France and Belgium 1918*, Vol.1, p.37.
56 For a detailed analysis of the planning and execution of the German offensives see David T. Zabecki, *The German 1918 Offensives: A Case Study in the Operational Level of War* (London: Routledge, 2006).
57 See Jim Beach, *Haig's Intelligence: GHQ and the German Army, 1916-1918* (Cambridge: Cambridge University Press, 2013), pp.265-267 for GHQ's perception of the threat.

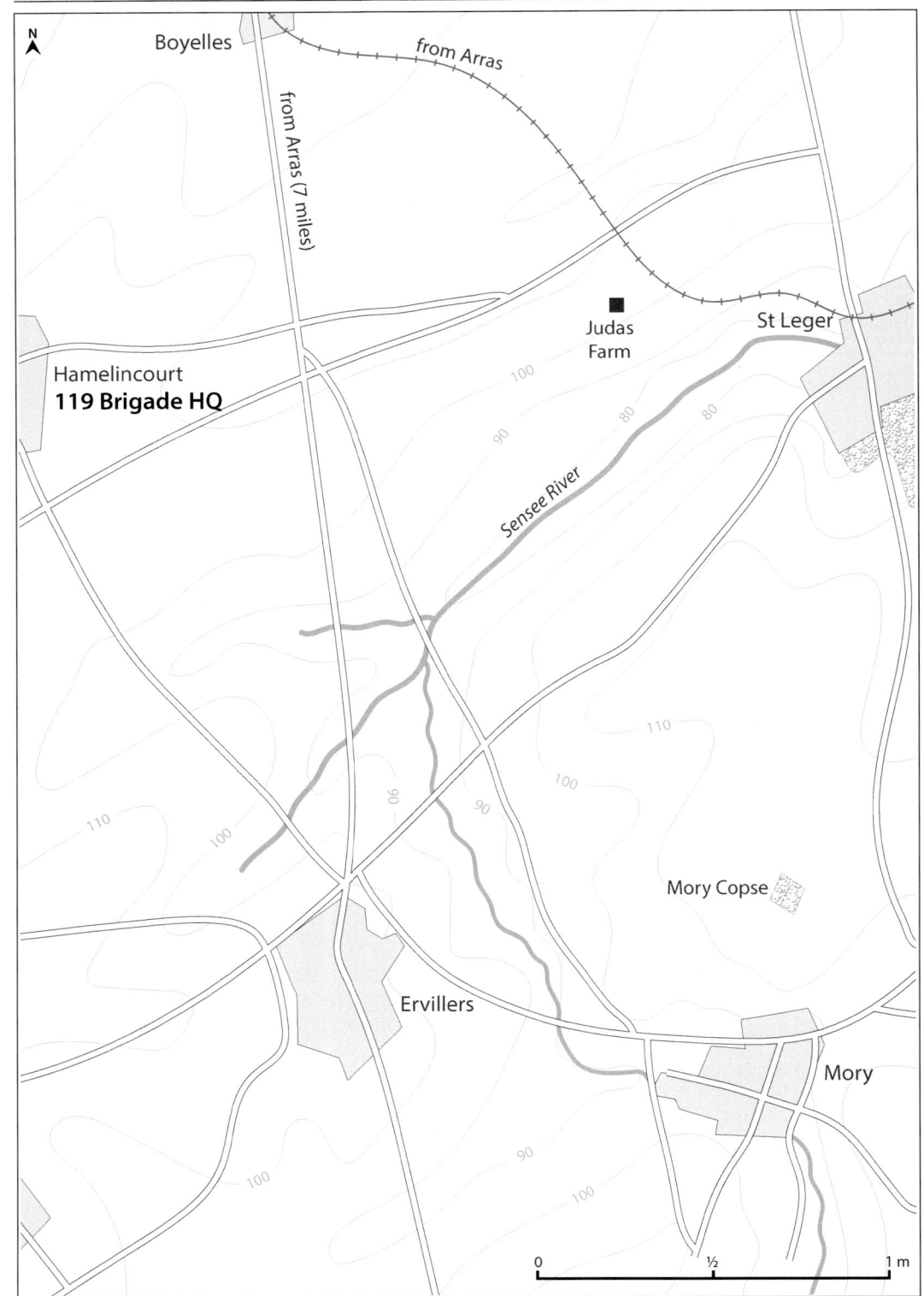

Map 5 Area of 119 Brigade actions, 22-24 March 1918.

(ADC to John Ponsonby, GOC 40th Division) demonstrate just how common speculation about the offensive had become: "the good *Daily Mail* tells us that the terrific Hun attack it has been so long prophesying should have started two days ago and is evidently disappointed by its unpunctuality. We can stand any number of such disappointments out here with perfect equanimity."[58] "Really, the English press is becoming intolerable. Not only do they insist upon the Hun making his onslaught at once, they also (*The Times* at any rate) urged him to choose that portion of the line where they must know I am. Tactless is hardly the word for it".[59] On 12 March 119 Brigade's units were notified that the attack on VI Corps' front was expected next day but the day passed without incident.[60] Harry Graham noted:

> I suppose, unless the whole thing is a gigantic bluff that the hun is bound to make his big attack this week …Things are <u>very</u> interesting out here now. I have been very busy making plans for all possible eventualities – and there are many – and have still more to make. Probably something will happen quite different to anything we've imagined. Anyhow, we're ready for them![61]

And on 15 March:

> Here we live in a continuous state of rumours. Hun prisoners and deserters tell us such cunning tales, giving dates of attack and all particulars, but nothing ever happens! I am beginning to believe that they are sent over to keep us nervous, and to make us waste millions of pounds worth of ammunition and that meanwhile Fritz is making off to Italy or Salonica or India or somewhere, and that the surprise will come when we least expect it. We have reached that condition of mind in which we singly pray for an attack, so that we may deal with it and get it over.[62]

The attack, codenamed '*Michael*', came on 21 March on an eighty kilometre front. In the south, where men and defences were sparse, the German advances gained momentum. In the north, where the defensive zones were more complete, things moved more slowly. The British defences were breached near Bullecourt by 11.30 a.m. but there was time enough to bring in reserves, including 40th Division. The events of the next few days demonstrate clearly the increased capability of the men of the "poor division" of a year before.

During the first day 119 Brigade was on half an hour's notice to move but, despite 120 and 121 Brigades moving forward in the middle of the day (when 40th Division passed from GHQ reserve to VI Corps reserve), the order did not arrive until the evening. The enemy was now advancing on Croisilles on the front line of the 'battle zone'.[63] After a false start the brigade moved off at 6.45

---

58 IWM: Documents 66/298/1. The Papers of Captain H.J.C. (Harry) Graham. Letter 18 February 1918.
59 Ibid. Letter 23 February 1918.
60 TNA WO 95/2606: War Diary 18th Welsh.
61 IWM: Graham Papers. Letter 12 March 1918.
62 Ibid. Letter 15 March 1918.
63 Croisilles was on the extreme right of the German offensive. To the north of Croisilles the only fighting was to protect the German right flank. The terminology of the newly introduced 'defence in depth' system does not seem to have been applied consistently or clearly. The rear of the 'Battle Zone' seems to have been the 'front line of the second system'. The 'Rear Zone' seems to have been largely non-existent in this area and represented by the 'Green Line' – a single trench and wire belts sited much too close to the 'Battle Zone'. See Edmonds, *Military Operations France and Belgium 1918*, Vol.1, pp.41-42 and Samuels, *Command or Control*, pp.214-229 for the background to this development and its flawed implementation.

p.m. eastward towards Henin Hill which was to be held "at all costs".[64] Despite chaos on the roads the brigade was in position by 10.30 p.m. with the 21st Middlesex in the "front line of the second system" with 13th East Surrey in support and the 18th Welsh in reserve. The brigade then had to cope (12.15 a.m.) with another night march to the south, acting as reserve to 34th Division which had been engaged since morning.

On 22 March, 119 Brigade started the day with 18th Welsh in the front line (the Sensée Switch) west of St Leger, the 13th East Surrey in support and the 21st Middlesex in reserve.[65] After conferring with the divisional commander, Crozier spent the morning visiting his battalion COs.[66] By 2.15 p.m. there were no British troops in front of the 18th Welsh. At about 6.00 p.m., in response to news that the Germans had taken St Leger, the 13th East Surrey was ordered to attack the village with the help of two tanks but, seizing an opportunity, the 18th Welsh commandeered the tanks "and by a brilliant counterstroke put a stop to the German advance and captured five enemy machine guns".[67] By nightfall 13th East Surrey was forming the brigade's left (northern) front just east of Judas Farm and facing east towards St Leger; the 18th Welsh formed the centre and the 21st Middlesex the right, facing north-east. The brigade frontage was approximately three and a half kilometres (4000 yards) and its right flank was about a kilometre north of the village of Mory. This was a very different form of warfare than that experienced in the confined spaces of Bourlon Wood just four months earlier.[68] Attackers had no option but to cross open spaces where they were subject to artillery, machine gun and concentrated rifle fire.

Early on 23 March the brigade was told of a crisis developing to the south where the enemy had broken through at Mory. The extension of the line of the 4 Guards Brigade, 31st Division, (on 119 Brigade's left flank) to the south allowed 119 Brigade to shift southwards. The 13th East Surrey was now on both sides of the Mory – Ervillers road facing Mory and effectively blocking the shallow valley. On its left the 21st Middlesex held the high ground while 18th Welsh formed the reserve. At 6.00 a.m. the 21st Middlesex received verbal orders from Crozier via the brigade major to attack Mory alongside the 13th East Surrey which it did at 9.00 a.m. British artillery fell short causing casualties but the attack continued "in short rushes, one section or Lewis gun team covering the advance of another" until it was halted by fire from a strongpoint in Mory Copse on the left and from machine-guns in Mory to the right.[69] "The troops carried out the attack in the best possible order and with magnificent dash, more as though they were on a field day than a battle".[70] However, "it was then realised that the amount of cooperation which the [13th] East Surrey were apparently able to afford would make it impracticable to press home the attack on Mory and at the same time comply with the instructions to keep touch with the Guards on our left".[71] The 21st Middlesex stopped and dug in on the high ground. "The Lewis gunners had an

---

64 TNA WO 95/2605: War Diary 119 Brigade.
65 The countryside in this area consists of broad, rolling uplands dissected by shallow valleys, the most prominent of which contains the headwaters of the Sensée river. This flows south to north from just east of Ervillers, turning north-eastward to St Leger and Croisilles. It is an obvious conduit for an attack. The importance of this and other similar valleys were recognised in the VI Corps Defence Scheme. See Edmonds, *Military Operations France and Belgium 1918*, Vol.1 (London: Macmillan, 1937), Appendix 15, pp.68-114.
66 TNA WO 95/2593: War Diary 40th Division HQ GS, A Short Account of the Part Played by 40th Division in the Operations Round Bapaume, March 21st-26th, 1918.
67 Ibid.
68 F.E. Whitton, *History of the 40th Division* (Aldershot: Gale & Polden, 1926) p.185 notes that the men of the 18th Welsh were twenty paces apart.
69 TNA WO 95/2606 War Diary 21 Middlesex, 'Narrative of Events During Operations in the Neighbourhood of Croisilles, St Leger, Mory and Ervillers From the 21st to 26th March, 1918'.
70 Ibid.
71 Ibid.

unlimited number of targets but he necessity of keeping a reserve of ammunition for any attack prevented the gunners from taking full advantage of them."[72]

The 13th East Surrey were held up by machine gun fire and it was probably at this point when Crozier supposedly made a call to press home the attack to "an officer" [unnamed but certainly Lieutenant-Colonel Warden] who told him that it could not be done:

> "What's that I hear", I say. "Can't!" "Don't understand the meaning of the word, I say. "Lead your men to the objective", I order, "or, if you 'can't', come back here … and you can be tried by court martial". He thinks twice and attacks, gaining much kudos thereby.[73]

In another version of events:

> I had to tell one senior officer over the telephone that if he could not see his way to carry out an attack instantly he not only would rue the day but might not live to see another.[74]

Warden "proceeded to the village himself to push on the main attack, reorganised three of his companies in the lower portion of the village, sent for the OC, Reserve Company and gave orders for his entire command to mop up the village and establish itself in the Army Line beyond. This attack commenced about 5.00 p.m. and proved entirely successful, the village being captured and great loss inflicted on the enemy".[75] Because of growing German numbers the village was quietly evacuated and when the enemy attacked in strength during the night, heavy Lewis gun and rifle fire was maintained on the village causing numerous German casualties. Advanced British troops were withdrawn at dawn on 24 March when it was clear that German troops were massing near Mory for an attack on Ervillers.

119 Brigade was now drawn up east of Ervillers and, when the German attack moved up the valley below, enfilade fire from the brigade and the adjacent 4 Guards Brigade aided by 40th Division's artillery ensured that the it was "completely wiped out."[76] However, by 6.00 p.m. the German forces had broken through from the direction of St Leger and were advancing up the Sensée Valley towards the rear of the two brigades. Crozier now had to practise what he preached about Spion Kop. Although the Guards Brigade was retiring, he "had received no orders to move. It is now dark. We wait … I send my own groom with a personal letter asking for instructions and point out the danger … 'if morning comes … and we are seen … we shall be wiped out' … My duty is clear. The lesson of Spion Kop is at my own feet! The words I burnt into the souls of my subalterns apply equally to me. 'Never give any excuse for retiring, don't retire unless you're ordered to' … At last the moment arrives. We may go!"[77] The 21st Middlesex were withdrawn, then the 18th Welsh and finally the 13th East Surrey, to a line on the north of Ervillers. On 25 March, the right of 40th Division was fending off repeated attacks from the south-east but was pushed north-westwards. 119 Brigade HQ moved from Gomiecourt to Courcelles. That evening

---

72 Ibid.
73 Crozier, *Brass Hat*, p.193. Warden received a bar to his DSO for the action at Mory. This tale might be another example of Crozier building his own reputation by diminishing another's but it would have been a dangerous thing to make up. When *Brass Hat* was published Warden was still alive and a prominent Edinburgh lawyer who could easily have resorted to litigation to defend a damaged reputation. The divisional history states that the original idea to attack was Warden's.
74 F.P. Crozier, *The Men I Killed* (London: Michael Joseph, 1937), pp.92-93.
75 TNA WO 95/2593: War Diary 40th Division HQ GS, 'A Short Account of the Part Played by 40th Division in the Operations Round Bapaume, March 21st-26th, 1918'.
76 Ibid.
77 Crozier, *Brass Hat*, pp.196-197.

the twice-postponed relief of the division by 42nd Division took place.⁷⁸ At 11.00 p.m. 119 Brigade marched from Courcelles to Bucquoy, only to move further back to Bienvillers the next day as the Germans kept up the pressure on the front line. In response to rumours about a break-in by German armoured cars, the 21st Middlesex, the only unit to have arrived at Bienvillers, took up a line on the ridge to the south, while, to the east, the 18th Welsh and 13th East Surrey formed the left flank of 40th Division "in battle formation" at Monchy-au-Bois. Crozier temporarily passed command of his brigade to the GOC 120 Brigade while he took command of, and inspected, the line and machine gun positions in front of Mochy-au-Bois. No attack came. In the evening, 40th Division was ordered out of the line. It had been a hard and confusing five days during which the new formation had done well in a fluid situation and despite a type of combat with which it was unfamiliar.⁷⁹ This recommendation by Crozier for a DSO for Lieutenant-Colonel W.E. Brown, 18th Welsh, gives a flavour of the nature of the fighting:

> For gallantry and good leadership and a fine example set in the retention of ground in front of Ervillers, etc, Lieut-Colonel Brown was in command of the battalion which on the 22nd March was holding Sensée Switch. On the evening of the 22ndMarch the enemy attempted to outflank this position in the vicinity of Judas Farm from St Leger. Lt Col Brown extended his left and held the railway bank and during this counter attack killed many Germans. He kept the situation well in hand and by bold counter strokes warded off the pressure. On being relieved in the Sensée Switch by the Guards, the Battalion returned to Brigade Reserve, and in this position for the remainder of the time the Brigade was in action up to March 26th, this officer was constantly reinforcing the other two battalions and heading off local and general attacks. Frequently his whole battalion HQ were in action at close range. This battalion was responsible for the observation of the enemy on the whole Brigade front and the information sent back was of the utmost use. Lieut-Colonel Brown's personal efforts and example under heavy fire for a long period cannot be over-estimated, and it is largely due to him that the Germans were held up for a time at Ervillers.⁸⁰

Likewise, the citation for the award of the DSO to H.C. Metcalfe, CO 21st Middlesex:

> At a critical moment this officer was ordered to take a portion of the army line. Advancing with his battalion, he was just in time to repel a formidable counter-attack by the enemy. He remained in the firing line throughout the day and during the next two days and the night he repelled furious attacks made on our positions. He personally led many counter-attacks, and his complete disregard of danger was a most inspiring [sic] example to his men, and his able leadership imbued all ranks with great confidence and a firm determination to hold up the enemy and save the line.⁸¹

---

78 42nd Division (Major-General A. Solly-Flood) had just been relieved from the First Army line north of Arras.
79 Harry Graham, ADC to John Ponsonby, wrote to his wife: 'we haven't taken our boots off since [the] 21st and have only snatched a few hours of sleep here and there. I don't think I've ever been so utterly tired out! The Division has done quite splendidly and if left to themselves would never have given away an inch. They are terribly disappointed that, owing to retirements on the right, they had to fall back too. It was us who re-took Mory and our machine-guns held on to Henning [sic] Ridge against astonishing odds as you have seen in the papers. Bourlon Wood was a mere play to this show.' – IWM: Graham Papers, letter, 25 March 1918.
80 Royal Regiment of Wales Museum, Brecon: 99.88 W.E. Brown Scrapbook.
81 *Edinburgh Gazette*, 18 September 1918.

Crozier later observed:

> Thanks to the lack of uniformity of training throughout the British Armies in France, we were a bad brigade just prior to the Somme battle in 1918, as the introduction of two new battalions to take the place of my best two ... spoilt the general level or standard. Fortune had, however, favoured us, as we came through the second Somme better than might have been expected. Though our casualties were heavy.[82]

The brigade casualty figures were less than those of the other two brigades of the division which had been heavily engaged to the right of 119 Brigade. The 13th East Surrey had 206 casualties of all ranks; the 18th Welsh 228 and the 21st Middlesex 268. The brigade total was 702 (52 killed) while that of 120 Brigade was 911 (76 killed) and that of 121 Brigade was 825 (77 killed).[83] On 30 March the 13th East Surrey still had a strength of 800.

Crozier's opinions on the two new COs that he inherited are interesting. The 13th East Surrey "deceived me, as I thought they were better than they were. Undoubtedly they could have been had they been better led".[84] Their CO, Lieutenant-Colonel Warden, embodied the failure to take Bourlon village as far as Crozier was concerned. He (Warden) had gone into the village with his battalion on 25 November and had assumed command of troops there after the death of Lieutenant-Colonel Battye (14th HLI, 120 Brigade). The battalion was the last to leave the village on 27 November, well after the rest of 40th Division had been relieved. But Warden had not completed the capture of the village and, according to Crozier, even though the 13th East Surreys retook Mory on 23 March 1918, it was "only after great 'pressure' on the telephone from Brigade Headquarters".[85] It is also possible that Crozier disliked the fact that Warden was an ex-TF officer. He seems to have regarded the regular army, or rather regular 'gentlemen', as his preferred source of COs, despite his positive experiences of men such as Benzie, Andrews and Kennedy and his own early association with volunteer and irregular units.[86] His comments about Metcalfe are in sharp contrast to those about Warden. Metcalfe had arrived as CO of the 21st Middlesex (which had also failed at Bourlon) on 18 December 1917 – and was not tainted by the earlier failure. Despite concern about Metcalfe's age (he was fifty-three – Crozier calls him "nearly sixty"), "despite the previous poor training of his men, despite their low morale and narrow outlook, despite all their other defects, [he] turned them into real 'Diehards' on the battlefield itself, by his own efforts, courage, leadership and example.".[87] "He held the line ... because of what was in him – blood and breeding."[88]

---

82 Crozier, *Impressions*, pp.216-217.
83 TNA WO 95/2594: War Diary 40th Division HQ A&Q.
84 Crozier, *Impressions*, p.215.
85 Ibid.
86 Crozier, *Brass Hat*, p.220 illustrates Crozier's aversion to men who were not clearly 'gentlemen' when recommending promotion: 'I never recommend men for commissions now, unless I see they are sahibs, without inserting on the form in the certificate "in accordance with the standard at present in vogue!"'. This is confirmed by the case of 16218 Sergeant W.H. Williams, 19th RWF, whose application as candidate for commission was endorsed by Crozier on 23 December 1916: '... he is up to the standard at present in vogue for Candidates for Commissions'. Williams was commissioned into the King's (Liverpool) Regiment and was killed in action on 22 March 1918 – TNA WO 339/94177: Personal File, William Henry Williams.
87 Crozier, *Impressions*, p.215. The nickname 'Diehards' had been coined for an antecedent regiment of the Middlesex when, at the Battle of Albuera (1811), the wounded Lieutenant-Colonel Inglis encouraged his men with the words 'Die hard 57th, die hard!' It had subsequently been inherited by the Middlesex Regiment.
88 Crozier, *Brass Hat*, p.192.

Warden did not last long after the March fighting. Crozier says that a Medical Officer reported that:

> 'Colonel Morden [Warden] should go down or go to a suitable rest house', he says; 'he's nearly off his head. I've doped him quite a lot but he wants an entire change.' 'Do what you like with him, Doctor,' I say. 'Last night he was found fighting under his bed with a pillow, swearing it was a Boche.' 'Poor devil,' I say, 'he's played out!'[89]

Lieutenant-Colonel Warden was admitted to hospital on 6 April 1918 and returned to his unit on 14 April.[90] During the next major action his battalion would be commanded by the 2iC, Major W.G. West.

The thanks of senior commanders were forwarded to 40th Division. The VI Corps Commander, J.A.L. Haldane, said that he could not speak too highly of the division: "They have made a magnificent defence and, tired as they must be with so prolonged a struggle, have stood like a stone wall between my right and the Germans".[91] Sir Julian Byng, GOC Third Army wrote: "they have broken up overwhelming attacks and prevented the enemy from gaining his object, viz: a decisive victory."[92]

Lt-Col H.C. Metcalfe. (*History of the Northamptonshire and Rutland Militia*)

Meanwhile, John Ponsonby thanked his division. He said presciently: "We shall no doubt be called upon again to fight for all we are worth".[93] He was right.

---

89 Ibid., p.200.
90 TNA WO 95/2606: War Diary 13th East Surrey. Warden wrote: 'I was so worn out that I was sent off for a week to sleep' – quoted in Paul McCue, *Wandsworth and Battersea Battalions in the Great War 1915-1918* (Barnsley: Pen and Sword, 2010), p.153.
91 TNA WO 95/2593: War Diary 40th Division GS.
92 Ibid.
93 'To all ranks of the 40th Division. I wish to thank the Division, one and all, for their splendid courage and behaviour. You know what the Commander-in-Chief and your Corps Commander think of you, and I can only say you have done your duty like British soldiers always do. We shall no doubt be called upon again to fight for all we are worth. We in the 40th Division, I know will be ready again, and I feel very proud to be the Divisional Commander of such a splendid body of men that you have proved to be. I thank you from the bottom of my heart and whatever may happen I feel complete confidence in the ultimate result with soldiers of such spirit and bravery under my command. John Ponsonby, Major-General, Commanding 40th Division, 28/3/18' – quoted in McCue, *Wandsworth and Battersea Battalions*, p.143. King George V visited the division on 30 March and 'was fully conversant with the work accomplished by the Division and while offering his sincere congratulations thereon he deplored the losses that have been incurred' – TNA WO 95/2593: War Diary 40th Division GS.

119 Brigade and 'Georgette'

40th Division moved north to join XV Corps, First Army, and entered the line on 2 April 1918.[94] It relieved 57th (2nd West Lancashire) Division in seven kilometres of the front line in a quiet sector south of the River Lys between Neuve Chapelle and Armentières.[95] On the evening of 6 April 119 Brigade moved from reserve into the line in its usual position on the right with 121 Brigade on the left.[96] On 119 Brigade's right was the Portuguese 2nd Division spread very thinly indeed over ten kilometres of front.[97]

As early as November 1917 the German army planners had identified the Portuguese sector as the weakest on the Western Front. One of several offensives developed for 1918 was aimed to smash through the line here and press on toward the important railway junction at Hazebrouck. Originally planned as a larger operation, '*Georg*', involving attacks towards Hazebrouck and against the Ypres salient, the operation was recast first as '*Klein-Georg*' and finally as '*Georgette*' – a follow-up to '*Michael*' – at very short notice.[98] The all-important artillery plan was put into place in just nine days. At GHQ it was thought that any attack in the sector was likely to be a feint, masking another strong attack in the vicinity of Arras and this belief persisted for several days after the start of the attack.[99] The British were aware of the vulnerability of the Portuguese sector. In December 1917 Douglas Haig had been told by Henry Horne (GOC, First Army) that "he did not think that the Portuguese Corps would stand against a German attack".[100] That view was also conveyed by General Smuts following a visit to the front in January 1918.[101] Haig believed that any break-in by the Germans could be contained by the adjacent British units throwing back defensive flanks to the line of the rivers Lawe and Lys which would also be defended by British troops.[102] Part of the Portuguese front was taken over by XV Corps in December but the lack of available divisions prevented further reduction in its length.[103] When the 1st Portuguese Division was

---

94 Harry Graham wrote: '[we are] only praying to be left in peace for a bit. But the worst of acquiring a reputation as a fighting Division is that directly there's trouble they shove you in again. They are busy reinforcing and reequipping us now at a great pace!' – IWM: Graham Papers, letter dated 3 April 1918.
95 Though the area had seen no significant fighting since 1915, in March 1918 this 'quiet' sector had still inflicted 39 killed and 238 wounded on 57th Division which also had 619 sick. It was moved south to army and then corps reserve behind the fronts of VI and IV Corps. 'All ranks were pleased to get out of the dull and damp country in Flanders and see the hills and pretty country of the Somme for the first time.' The division's artillery was left behind and did not rejoin the division until May – TNA WO 95/2967: War Diary 57th Division A&Q.
96 Crozier, *Brass Hat*, p.200 wrote that the brigade arrived on 7/8 April, thus heightening the drama of what followed.
97 Germany declared war on Portugal on 9 March 1916. Portuguese troops arrived on the western front in April 1917 and thereafter proved both a military and political problem for the CinC. By April 1918 they were under strength, under equipped and with low morale. Harry Graham noted 'I am not impressed by the Portuguese officers. They gallop their wretched horses about on the pavé streets and their appearance is more than squalid. I believe the men would be alright if properly led' – IWM: Graham Papers. Letter dated 'Easter Monday [1 April] 1918.
98 See Zabecki, *The German 1918 Offensives*, pp.174-186 for a full account of the planning and execution of '*Georgette*'.
99 See Beach, *Haig's Intelligence*, pp.292-295 for a description of intelligence issues surrounding he battle.
100 James E. Edmonds, *Military Operations France and Belgium 1918, Vol.2, March-April 1918: Continuation of the German Offensives* (London: Macmillan, 1937), p.147.
101 Ibid.
102 Ibid.
103 Crutwell, *A History of the Great War*, p.516, was scathing: 'These troops were undoubtedly the worst of any nation in the West and had always been regarded as practically worthless. The staff blunder that made …

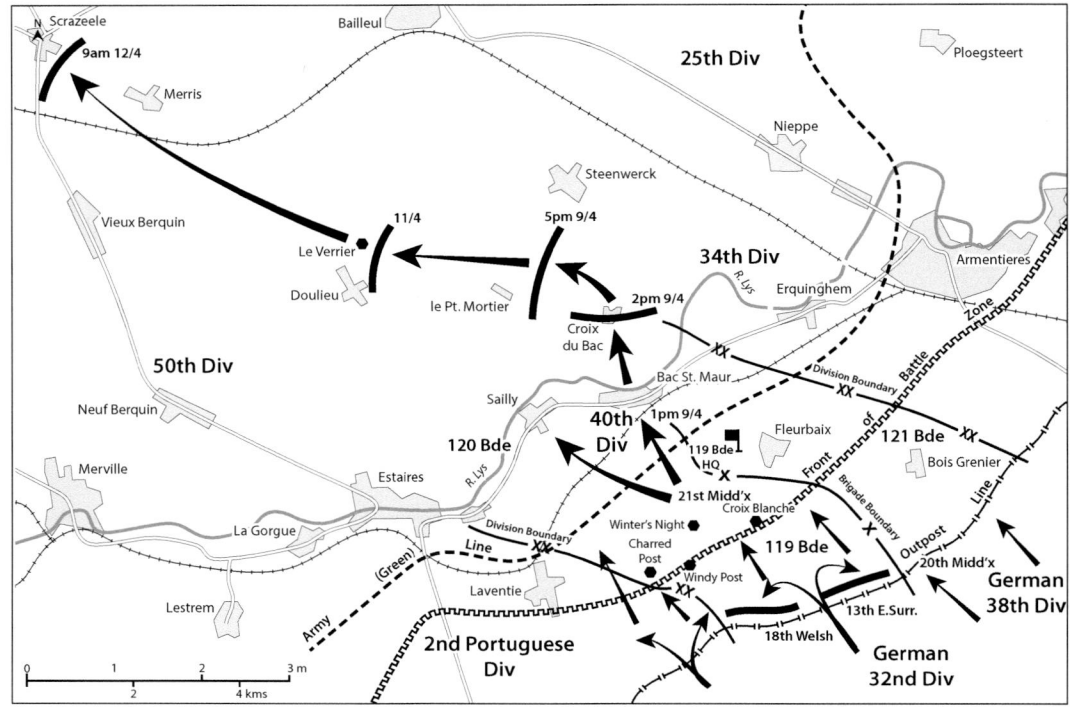

Map 6 119 Brigade positions, 9-12 April 1918.

finally withdrawn from the line on 5 April, the weak 2nd Portuguese Division simply extended its frontage to compensate.[104] Its relief by 51st (Highland) Division was overtaken by events.

Crozier too recognised the danger posed by the Portuguese on his right. On 3 April he had been visited by Lieutenant-General John Du Cane, GOC XV Corps, who no doubt pointed it out, but he later described "Our certainty that the Germans were going to attack owing to that 'trench sense' which we had acquired".[105] On 3 April the 21st Middlesex received orders to man a system of trenches on the right flank "in the event of the Brigade on the right (Portuguese) giving way".[106] On 4 April Crozier "reconnoitred the defensive flank to be manned in case of an enemy attack on the right flank which is held by Portuguese troops" and on 5 April he "reconnoitred the Bridgeheads of Estaires and La Gorgue with a view to defence in case of an attack on the Portuguese".[107] On 7 April while the Brigade Major visited the brigade's left battalion, the 13th East Surrey, Crozier visited the right, the 18th Welsh. Next day Crozier visited the left battalion while the Brigade Major took the right. The "various defensive positions" of the 21st Middlesex (in support) were also visited by Crozier.[108] He also records in *Brass Hat, Impressions*

---

them responsible for holding six important miles in an avowedly threatened area is one of the most grotesque of the war'.
104 By this time 2nd Portuguese Division was in need of 139 officers and just under 6,000 men to complete its strength.
105 TNA WO 95/2605: War Diary 119 Brigade. Includes letter from Crozier to Sir James Edmonds, 24 August 1927.
106 TNA WO 95/2606: War Diary 21st Middlesex.
107 TNA WO 95/2605: War Diary 119 Brigade.
108 Ibid.

and *The Men I Killed* how he visited the Portuguese front line only to find few sentries, men asleep without wearing boots or equipment, rusty rifles, jammed Lewis guns and insufficient wire.[109] He unsuccessfully requested that 40th Division's reserve brigade (120 Brigade) be put into the line immediately.[110] 119 Brigade patrols on the nights of 6, 7 and 8 April reported all quiet and made no contact with the enemy.

At 4.15 a.m. on 9 April the German bombardment opened in thick fog.[111] While trench mortars targeted forward positions, the heavier artillery deluged strongpoints, HQs, villages, and crossroads with high explosive and poison gas. Four German divisions faced the Portuguese with another three ready to reinforce.[112] German troops were in the Portuguese front line of the forward zone by 7.00 a.m. The main infantry attack swept in at 8.45 a.m. and the second line of the forward zone was occupied by 9.00 a.m. By 1.40 p.m. the Portuguese 2nd Division was in captivity or scattered beyond the fighting line. Chris Baker notes how "the sheer scale and speed of the Portuguese capitulation makes a coherent view of the battle difficult to compile".[113] The same could be said of the difficulties of following 119 Brigade's battle, driven as it was by the Portuguese collapse and rapid infiltration of the line.[114]

When the bombardment started, the 21st Middlesex 'stood to'. On receiving an 'SOS' signal from the 18th Welsh, they moved into their pre-arranged battle positions behind the right flank of the brigade, taking heavy casualties from shelling.[115] At 5.55 a.m. the 18th Welsh reported large numbers of Germans advancing on the Portuguese front as the barrage lifted onto the support line. Just a few minutes later they reported a German breakthrough between their left post and the first post manned by the 13th East Surrey.[116] Large numbers of the enemy advanced behind the battalion towards the support line. No men of the 18th Welsh appeared from the forward posts which were presumed lost. At 8.20 a.m. the right company of the 18th Welsh reported that it was surrounded but fighting on. No one from the company made it to the rear.[117] At 9.00 a.m. the left front of the battalion was pushed back and by 10.00 a.m. the Germans were within 100 metres of the battalion HQ. Lieutenant-Colonel Brown now led a fighting withdrawal, inflicting many casualties at point-blank range but also losing men.[118] Behind him, the 21st Middlesex had heard that the front line had been penetrated at 9.20 a.m. and by 10.00 a.m. had learned of the Portuguese collapse. By 11.00 a.m. they had lost their 2iC (killed) and their adjutant (wounded) and their battalion HQ had been forced

---

109 Crozier, *Brass Hat*, pp.200-201; *Impressions*, p.219; *The Men I Killed*, p.96.
110 TNA WO 95/2605: War Diary 119 Brigade. Includes letter from Crozier to Sir James Edmonds, 24 August 1927; Crozier, *The Men I Killed*, p.96.
111 For a detailed overview of the battle see Chris Baker, *The Battle for Flanders: German Defeat on the Lys, 1918* (Barnsley: Pen and Sword, 2011).
112 Ibid., p.28.
113 Ibid., p.32.
114 For a robust, if over-sympathetic, defence of Portuguese actions on the Lys see Jesse Pyles, 'The Portuguese Expeditionary Force in World War 1: From Inception to Combat Destruction, 1914-1918', MA Thesis, University of North Texas, May 2012. Pyles has recently followed up his thesis with 'Scapegoats No More': The Portuguese Expeditionary Corps, British Myths and Cover-ups, and the Battle of the Lys, PhD Thesis, Florida State University, 2015. The present author has not accessed this publication.
115 TNA WO 95/2606: War Diary 21st Middlesex.
116 TNA WO 95/2606: War Diary 18th Welsh. This is confirmed by the statement of Lieutenant J.S.G. Hackney, 18th Welsh – 'the enemy broke through on our left flank (right flank of East Surrey Regiment) and on right of A Coy (who were on our right flank) through the Portuguese lines' – TNA WO 339/46940: Personal File, Lieutenant J.S.G. Hackney.
117 TNA WO 95/2606: War Diary 18th Welsh.
118 Ibid., 'Narrative of Events 9th April – 14th April 1918'.

to move to a nearby trench.[119] Meanwhile Brown had led his remnants to Winters Night Post which was held by a detachment of the 21st Middlesex. Returning from seeking ammunition he found the post surrounded by Germans who were advancing towards the 21st Middlesex HQ. The post was all but wiped out by machine gun and shell fire. Brown, his signalling officer and just twenty men escaped.

"As I now had no troops to command I made my way to Bac St Maur [temporary Brigade HQ] hoping to find some of my men on the road to organise but I found none except a Lewis gun and two men …"[120]

The actions of the 13th East Surrey on the left of the brigade front would be the cause of persistent annoyance and resentment for Crozier who believed that they had surrendered because of "the cowardice of a battalion commander on the left, who surrendered his regiment [sic] without firing a shot because he was attacked in the rear instead of the anticipated front and his person was thereby endangered".[121] The CO, 13th East Surrey, Major West, wrote:

> My battalion was holding front line trenches on the left flank of Portuguese Corps. About 7.30am the enemy shelled our lines heavily with gas and high explosive causing heavy casualties to my battalion, after eight o'clock the enemy completely broke through the Portuguese front. No infantry attack occurred on my batt[alion] front at this time and no information as to what was happening reached me from any source. While endeavouring to get in touch with my Coy commanders, I was rushed and taken prisoner by a German 'mopping up' party which had worked along a road to my rear, coming from the right flank of my brigade.[122]

There does appear to have been some inertia on the part of the battalion HQ staff:

> It was stated in my hearing that the Germans had broken through the Welsh. Messages were also brought in to Major West which were also read by Capt. Ainger and Capt. Price but the other officers were not informed of their nature … I waited to receive orders from Major West as to his plan of action but received none … I heard no orders given by Major West and received none. Suddenly I heard a voice cry 'Heraus' [Come out] and Major West walked out of the dugout holding up his hands … Before going out Battalion Sergeant-Major Lee turned to me and said, 'Well Sir, we have held out to the last'. I was thoroughly disgusted at not having had a fight for it and replied, 'Yes and never fired a shot'.[123]

However, Crozier was too quick to place the blame. There had been resistance:

> I was on the extreme left flank. The enemy did not attack our direct front but there was a lot of movement going on in front of us in which we stopped a lot by sniping and Lewis gun fire. I tried but could not get any information as to what really had happened until about 9 o'clock when my Company Commander came up to my post and told me that we were being surrounded and we were to move back on to the Middlesex [20th Middlesex, 121 Brigade,

---

119 TNA WO 95/2606: War Diary 21st Middlesex. Captain R.C. Sheen, 21st Middlesex, survived. He noted that his company had been reduced to 70 rifles following the action at Mory where two of four Lewis guns had also been destroyed. Sheen says that he held out with a small group until almost dusk when they surrendered and were taken prisoner – TNA WO 339/28557: Personal File, Ronald Cross Sheen.
120 TNA WO 95/2606: War Diary 18th Welsh, 'Narrative of Events 9th April – 14th April 1918'.
121 Crozier, *The Men I Killed*, p.98.
122 TNA WO 339/27856: Personal File, Major William Gerald West.
123 TNA WO 339/49925: Personal File, Lieutenant William Henry Allason.

was on the left flank of the 13th East Surrey], when at the same time we were attacked from our right. I at once got my Lewis gun going which unfortunately broke down in the first magazine and I only had 8 rifles with me. We stood out until the enemy was within 50 yards of us and which outnumbered us by a 100, when I received a bad wound in my arm ... we got back to the next trench where we got more support and I handed my men over ... I went down to the dressing station and in the next minute the enemy was on us and we were forced to surrender.[124]

The 13th East Surrey was overwhelmed by the speed of the attack just as the 18th Welsh and the 21st Middlesex had been. The line consisted of posts linked by a (usually unmanned) breastwork. These posts were several hundred metres apart, easily within range of supporting fire from rifles and machine-guns in adjacent posts, but with visibility down to twenty to thirty metres at the start of the battle it is unsurprising that the line was quickly infiltrated.[125] This fight was in total contrast to that at Mory two weeks earlier where the open spaces allowed repeated opportunities to destroy attacks with bullets and shells. The 13th East Surrey was surrounded by about 9.30 a.m. Elsewhere, as we have seen, isolated groups held out or tried to fight their way back but the posts were surrounded and, as the fog lifted, retreating troops were easily killed or captured. By the middle of the day there was very little left of 119 Brigade.

Crozier had been woken by his batman Starrett as the artillery bombardment crashed down on his billet and brigade HQ:

> By the time I got to the signallers the General was away ... Back came Crozier, swearing dreadfully, to lead us or drive us in hurried retreat to Bac St Maur ... Our reserve battalion [21st Middlesex] did its best to put some guts into the Portuguese defence, and how the General managed to be with them and with us at the same time passes my understanding to this day. But there he was whipping us into some sort of order, and there he was steadying the reserve, with every bit of ground he trod torn to pieces by heavy stuff. My, his charmed life was being proved just then.[126]

Crozier was later critical of the "slowness of a brigade on the right".[127] 120 Brigade had started to move to support the Portuguese left at the start of the attack only to find that the left had gone and its own left flank was under attack. Steadily losing men it pulled back towards the River Lys.[128] Realising the need for support, early in the morning Crozier had ordered the OC the brigade school to bring forward the entire school to Bac St Maur.[129] He now fell back, forming a

---

124 TNA WO 339/100140: Personal File, Second-Lieutenant John Albert Victor Cant. Once the East Surrey had collapsed the Germans moved to envelop 20th Middlesex and the rest of 121 Brigade which from then fought what was in effect a separate battle on the left, pushed towards Fleurbaix, well away from 119 and 120 Brigades.
125 Posts were widely spaced. For example: 'My Coy [A] was right flank Coy of support Battn [21st Middlesex] of 119th Inf Bde holding three posts over about 800yds of the support line with a Coy HQ post 250 yds to the rear of the centre' – TNA WO 339/28557: Personal File, Captain Ronald Cross Sheen. 'The morning was very foggy and it was impossible to see more than 20 or 30 yards' – TNA WO 374/54354: Personal File, Lieutenant Louis William Pinnick. There was no frontal attack on the 13th East Surrey but it is clear that the line of the 18th Welsh had been outflanked on the right where the Portuguese had broken *and* on the left in the vicinity of the East Surreys.
126 IWM: Documents 79/35/1 David Starrett 'Batman', unpublished typescript, p.110.
127 Crozier, *The Men I Killed*, p.98.
128 Whitton, *History of the 40th Division*, p 222.
129 TNA WO 95/2605: War Diary 119 Brigade.

defensive line on the south bank of the river with such remnants as he could find, joined by the 12th Yorkshire (the divisional pioneers) and what remained of the brigade's units. Major Amery-Parkes (40th Battalion MGC) and 229 Field Company, RE held the bridges at Bac St Maur.[130] The troops on the south side of the river, including Crozier, withdrew over the bridges, probably between 1.00 p.m. and 2.00 p.m. Slightly further upstream, at Sailly, Metcalfe and his remnants (numbering about 400) crossed later at about 4.00 p.m.[131] The permanent bridge at Bac St Maur was then destroyed. There Crozier met the troops from the brigade school which he used as "a mobile reserve".[132] The Germans took possession of the houses on the south side of the river and opened heavy machine gun fire on the defenders of the north bank, preventing the destruction of the last pontoon bridge and forcing the defenders away from the bank. Crozier and the brigade HQ troops resisted until the German machine guns were 100 metres away, giving time for a position to be formed in their rear in front of Croix du Bac. The line was held there until about 5.00 p.m. when the division ordered a withdrawal to Le Petit Mortier, a farm two kilometres to the north-west, behind an existing trench called the Steenwerk Switch. About this time 74 Brigade (25th Division) passed through and attacked Croix du Bac but failed to push the Germans back over the river.[133] The remains of 119 and 120 Brigades were then reorganised into composite battalions. The 120 Brigade-battalion mustered 300 rifles. The 119 Brigade battalion was made up of 'details' and the brigade school troops.[134] If the story is not a fabrication, it was probably during this afternoon that Crozier shot a fleeing British subaltern on the Strazeele road.[135] This story appeared in 1937 at the height of Crozier's pacifism. It is designed to shock. It may be true. When challenged about the story, Crozier named David Starrett as a witness but Starrett did not make any public statement or mention the incident in his own writing.[136] Crozier claims to have shot the subaltern and a German behind him thus locating himself in among the action. He also mentions losing "two of the best and most valuable members" of his staff shortly before.[137] Both the machine gun officer and the signals officer were severely wounded (one later died) on 9 April. There are two other, less quoted, examples of Crozier administering summary justice in the pages of *The Men I Killed*. He claims to have shot a soldier who was harming a French woman during the April retreat and hints that he also killed the man who stole both his horses at Ervillers who "never stole another".[138] Neither of these incidents is mentioned elsewhere or corroborated. Crozier promoted the impression that he believed that men running away would be shot. The case for him actually carrying out the threat is not proven.

The composite battalions occupied the Steenwerk Switch during the night and were told to hold it at all costs. The trench was enfiladed and pressure from the Germans pushed back the flanks. The centre withdrew but then counter attacked, driving the advancing Germans back and reoccupying

---

130 Ibid. Douglas John Amery-Parkes (1897-1918). See Appendix VI.
131 Whitton, *History of the 40th Division*, p 232.
132 TNA WO 95/2605: War Diary 119 Brigade.
133 Baker, *Battle for Flanders*, p.57 quotes the CO of the 11th Lancashire Fusiliers, 74 Brigade as saying: 'The retiring Brigade had apparently melted away and it was only later that I met its Brigadier in a car when he had just got clear of Croix du Bac and was looking for his men'. It is inferred that the brigade was 119 Brigade and the Brigadier therefore Crozier. This is repeated by Messenger, *Broken Sword*, p.100. Whilst he *may* be referring to Crozier and 119 Brigade, the HQ of 120 Brigade was in the same area. No other source mentions Crozier using a car on that day and Starrett mentions travel on foot.
134 TNA WO 95/2605: War Diary 119 Brigade. 119 and 120 Brigades mustered a total of about 1,200 men at the start of the second day's fighting – TNA WO 95/2593: War Diary 40th Division GS.
135 Crozier, *The Men I Killed*, pp.54-55, 98 and 287.
136 *Daily Mail*, 9 August 1937.
137 Crozier, *The Men I Killed*, p.98.
138 Ibid., pp.103 and 139.

the Switch.[139] At about 5.30 p.m. 180 men of the RE were incorporated in the line and at about midnight Major Gough (18th Welsh) brought up 200 men.[140] At 10.30 a.m. on 11 April, John Ponsonby (GOC, 40th Division) visited the HQs of 119 and 120 Brigades and told them "that to hang on was what was expected of us".[141] Ponsonby wrote that "I found Crozier and Hobkirk [GOC, 120 Brigade], they both seemed tired out. All I could tell them was that divisions were coming up behind us and that we must all hang on as long as possible and stop the Bosch".[142] But, under pressure, the line withdrew for two kilometres by stages through the day, to a position in front of Le Verrier.[143] Late that night the brigade was relieved and marched back to Strazeele where it arrived between 9.00 a.m. and 10.00 a.m. the next morning.[144] 40th Division had suffered badly, worse than at Bourlon. Total casualties were 4,491 of which 3,020 were missing. 119 Brigade had 1,442 casualties, the highest in the division (Table 18).[145] 120 Brigade had a total of 1069 casualties and 121 Brigade 1227.

Overnight on 12/13 April, 40th Division's troops, acting as XV Corps reserve, dug in to protect Strazeele (and therefore Hazebrouck) from any further advance by German forces but their active involvement in the Battle of the Lys was over. John Ponsonby noted: "… it was a soldiers battle and impossible to direct matters from Head Quarters as the situation kept changing every minute".[146] By 15 April they were behind the lines "resting and reorganising".[147] On 17 April the formation was transferred to VIII Corps and training recommenced, aided by the arrival of specialist instructors in musketry, physical training, bayonet fighting and Lewis gunnery "rendering valuable assistance to battalion commanders in the training of the reinforcements recently arrived".[148] Harry Graham noted "They are reinforcing and re-equipping us as fast as possible – you can imagine what our losses have been in the last 3 weeks – and I suppose we will go in again as soon as we are ready, but the new material is untrained and necessarily inferior – I do think we deserve a bit of a rest".[149]

Table 18: 119 Brigade casualties Battle of the Lys (compiled to 23 April 1918)[150]

Unit	Killed		Wounded		Missing		Total
	Officers	OR	Officers	OR	Officers	OR	
13th East Surrey	1	7	–	56	18	428	510
18th Welsh	1	18	12	187	15	306	539
21st Middlesex	6	25	12	107	10	233	393

---

139 TNA WO 95/2605: War Diary 119 Brigade. Edmonds, *Military Operations France and Belgium 1918*, Vol.2, p.200 states that some 500 yards of the 1,500 yard withdrawal were regained; the 40th Division GS war diary says 600 yards. The possibility of a German advance caused 119 Brigade HQ to move twice during the day.
140 Harry Percy Bright Gough (1880-1918). He had previously served in the 17th Welsh, was severely wounded on 13 April while in command of details of the 13th East Surreys and DoW on 22 April. See Appendix VI.
141 TNA WO 95/2605: War Diary 119 Brigade.
142 TNA WO 95/2597: War Diary 40th Division GS, Ponsonby Diary, 11 April 1918. Clarence John Hobkirk (1869-1949) had taken command of 120 Brigade on 24 March 1918.
143 TNA WO 95/2606: War Diary 21st Middlesex. Lieutenant-Colonel Metcalfe received a serious leg wound during the day and command of the 21st Middlesex remnant passed to Captain Worthington.
144 TNA WO 95/2605: War Diary 119 Brigade.
145 TNA WO 95/2594: War Diary 40th Division A&Q.
146 TNA WO 95/2594: War Diary 40th Division GS. John Ponsonby Diary, 13 April 1918.
147 TNA WO 95/2594: War Diary 40th Division GS.
148 Ibid. 40th Division also found time on 19 April to discuss the lessons from the fighting. See Appendix V.
149 IWM: Graham Papers. Letter dated 18 April 1918.
150 TNA WO 95/2594: War Diary 40th Division GS.

Perhaps it was tiredness, overwork, stress or just bad judgement that caused Crozier to overstep the mark in correspondence with his old superior Major-General Oliver Nugent at this time. The incident was recounted to Wilfred Spender by his wife after a visit to Netley Hospital where Sergeant Russell, ex-9th RIRifles, was recuperating. According to Russell, Nugent had kept the Ulster Division in the line at Ham during the German March offensive "long after it was hopeless" and "according to him [Russell] Col. Crozier (now Brig.Gen.) wrote such a strong letter to O.N. on the subject that the latter was furious and made him apologise. That sounds highly probable!"[151]

The continuing need for reinforcements elsewhere now caused the division to be regarded as a source of manpower.[152] On 23 April, 119 and 120 Brigades were ordered to form one composite battalion each for work on the line.[153] The same day: "Information has been received that that the whole personnel of the Division, less Div., Brigade and Battalion Headquarters and a small staff of instructors are to be sent to the base".[154] Harry Graham wrote home:

> We are fighting for our existence. The lack of imagination in high places is absolutely incredible. There are endless divisions (or several at any rate) who have had no share in any fighting for months and months – but when one like ours survives 2 battles in 3 weeks, and by means of reinforcements etc is almost up to its old strength, they propose to break it up all together – thereby killing the esprit de corps that has taken months to build up, and thoroughly depressing hundreds of gallant men who are drafted away to fresh units for which they have no affection at all.[155]

And the next day:

> We are all sunk in the depths of depression. The fate of the 40th Div is sealed. We are to be broken up, so that nothing remains but a staff and a very small nucleus, and all our men sent to reinforce other Divisions. It is vain to fight against our doom. John [Ponsonby] went to GHQ, where they were very nice to him, told him how much they appreciated and recognised

---

151 PRONI D1633/1/2/865: Lilian to Wilfred Spender, 29 April 1918, quoted in Margaret Baguley (ed.), *World War One and the Question of Ulster: The Correspondence of Lilian and Wilfred Spender* (Dublin: Irish Manuscripts Commission, 2009)
152 The BEF casualties between 9-30 April 1918 were 82,040. See Edmonds, *Military Operations France and Belgium 1918*, Vol.2, p.493. Fighting continued to the end of the month and further German offensives were (correctly) anticipated.
153 Crozier, *Impressions*, p.222, wrote that working on the line 'was a come-down for a fighting brigade such as the 119th was'.
154 TNA WO 95/2593: War Diary 40th Division GS. Warning Order No. 157, 23 April 1918. Eight divisions (including 40th Division) with less than 3,500 infantrymen apiece had been selected by the C-in-C to be reduced to cadre strength – Edmonds, *Military Operations France and Belgium 1918, Vol.2*, p.7.
155 IWM: Graham Papers. Letter dated 23 April 1918. The congratulations on the division's recent exploits sound hollow: 'I wish to express my appreciation of the great bravery and endurance with which all ranks have fought and held out (during the last five days) against overwhelming numbers. It has been necessary to call for great exertions, and more must still be asked for, but I am confident that, at this critical period, when the existence of the British Empire is at stake, all ranks of the First Army will do their very best. [signed] H.S. Horne, Commanding First Army, 13 April 1918'; 'On you leaving the Corps, the Corps Commander directs me to convey to you his appreciation of the services rendered by you Division during the operations of 9th April – April 13th. [signed] H. Knox, BGGS, XV Corps, 16/4/18'; 'The Division has again been engaged in heavy fighting and all battalions have fought the enemy with great courage and determination in spite of having to face overwhelming odds. The same fighting spirit continues and I know will continue in the Division. I wish GOC Brigades to convey to the troops under their command my sincere congratulations and thanks for their gallant behaviour under trying circumstances. [signed] John Ponsonby, Major-General, Commanding 40th Division, 19/4/18.' – all copied in TNA WO 95/2593: War Diary 40th Division GS.

the way the Div had fought in the last two battles, but said that owing to the lamentable shortage of men all divisions that had sustained heavy losses must be broken up instead of being remade. They promised that if ever any men turned up, we should be the first to be reinforced. So the poor old Div. is reduced to about 500 men and if ever we can make it up again it will be a totally <u>new</u> Div (whatever one calls it), composed of men who have never heard of Bourlon, of Armentieres or Bapaume, and the esprit de corps will have to be built-up again <u>ab initio</u>. All this is very depressing. Meanwhile we have nothing to do though I believe we may be employed training Yanks or Irish conscripts or even (save the word!) Portuguese.[156]

On 25 April:

I have come to the conclusion that it's no use being depressed at the breaking up of the division. The 40th can never die. They may take away all the officers and men, but they can't take away all the traditions and the reputation; and these we shall have to instil into whatever type of conscript we eventually get to fill us up. After all, why is one Division ever different to another? Why for instance, have we seen the – Div. actually stampeded, while we (made of the same material) held on? Simply, I think, John – and the 3 Brigadiers – one of them a perfect little tiger to fight, absolutely fearless, not much liked, but a splendid man in a tight place [Crozier]; the second a 'strong decent man', quiet and reliable [Hobkirk]; the third … fairly capable and resolute and cheerful and brave [Campbell] – we shall be all right, and we can rebuild the new division on the old lines and be ourselves again ere long. Several divisions, in our plight as far as casualties are concerned, have been done away with altogether.[157]

On 27 April:

All orders for our breaking-up are cancelled, and it is assumed that with the remnants of men who have not yet left us (and of course we have had <u>no</u> reinforcements – they having been directed elsewhere!) we are to form composite units of some kind to go and dig or hold or do something to a line somewhere in front! All this is very disturbing and depressing, for it seems that we don't know where we are. After the farewells are said, bands playing at stations and John waving goodbye to his troops, we find ourselves still a division (of a sort), all mixed up under new leaders and without an interval of a few days to coordinate and train the units together. I know what John fears is that those in authority will say to themselves 'Oh, it's all right – such and such a bit of the line is held by the 40th!' whereas it isn't the 40th at all that will hold – it's a mixed remnant of the 40th, jumbled together hurriedly and having been so badgered about with contradictory orders during the last fortnight that that it is doubtful whether the esprit de corps that once sustained them is left.[158]

The situation was obviously very confused for the men on the receiving end of GHQ's decisions and it continued to be so. On 1 May "Instructions were received from GHQ that 'circumstances demand the immediate withdrawal for drafting purposes of all available Infantry and Machine Gun Corps personnel'".[159] Next day the division transferred from VIII to VII Corps: "I think the fate of the Division is settled at last, and that we are to train B1 men who can <u>fight</u> but can't march

---

156   Ibid., Letter dated 24 April 1918.
157   Ibid., Letter dated 25 April 1918.
158   Ibid., Letter dated 27 April 1918.
159   TNA WO 95/2593: War Diary 40th Division GS.

far, owing to veins or feet or whatnot – old soldiers I believe, and well disciplined … Thank God we have left the Corps we were in a day or so ago, and can hope to be treated with some common sense".[160] 'Common sense' was apparently in short supply.

Orders for the disbandment of battalions were received by 119 Brigade on 3 May. On 4 and 5 May, the MGC troops and the men of 119 Brigade and the 12th Yorks (the division's pioneers) left for the base or for Calais after Crozier had visited each battalion. On 6 May, 120 Brigade sent four officers and 578 other ranks to the base while 121 Brigade sent 36 officers and 1666 other ranks. By now Harry Graham was despairing, especially when news was received about the Portuguese version of events on the Lys:

> You will hardly believe it possible, but all our orders to move are cancelled again last night, and now we are to stay here (with no men) and superintend the digging of another line. By the way, our oldest allies have sent in an official report of their wonderful stand on the Lys … they say that they would have hung on even longer (time enough to boil an egg perhaps) if the Division on their left hadn't broken!!! Pretty good isn't it when you recall my experiences with them that morning and how we waited on till afternoon until almost surrounded? The Corps we were in at that time is much upset by this, and it undoubtedly accounts for the fact that, although sent in for mention, GHQ took no notice thereof – to describe how we held out would have been to give the lie to the Blue Monkeys, an impossible thought truly! It is not worth bothering about now, especially as we don't really exist now except on paper.[161]

> So now a Major-General, three Brigadiers and the united staff of the whole Division are concentrating their minds on the digging (by Chinamen) of a new line. Such a waste of time to many of us who have nothing on earth to do for the moment, and might better be at home.[162]

119 Brigade Reformed

Crozier spent most of May 1918 looking over the ground and laying out the line of defences to be created by RE, Chinese Labour Corps and Labour Corps units. The brigade war diary records that he was out, usually with his Brigade Major, on almost every day from 10 May until the end of the month. There had been some changes in the brigade staff. After Bourlon, Percy Hone had taken over as Acting Brigade Major when Goodliffe left to go on a course. His upward move left a vacancy for Staff Captain and Lieutenant R.W. May, 18th Welsh, the brigade's intelligence officer, stepped up, also on an acting basis.[163] A vacancy for a permanent post was created when Goodliffe was promoted to GSO2, XVIII Corps, on 4 April. The new BM was Captain Anthony John Muirhead MC, Oxfordshire Yeomanry, who arrived on 25 April.[164] Both Hone and May had done good work during the fighting in March and April.[165] Hone was awarded a second bar to his DSO and given command of a battalion. May was confirmed as Staff Captain.

---

160 IWM: Graham Papers. Letter dated 3 May 1918.
161 Ibid., Letter dated 5 May 1918.
162 Ibid., Letter dated 6 May 1918.
163 Reginald Walter May (1896-1969) see Appendix VI.
164 Anthony John Muirhead (1890–1939) see Appendix VI.
165 Hone was appointed DAAG, 62nd Division on 12 January 1918 but declined the appointment out of loyalty to Crozier (Crozier, *Impressions*, pp.209-211). Crozier claims that the appointment was made without the knowledge of 40th Division HQ. This seems likely because after the announcement on 17 January that

119 Bde Staff late 1918. Front row L to R: Lt-Col James Frederick Plunkett; Brig-Gen Frank Percy Crozier; Capt Anthony John Muirhead, Brigade Major; Lt Reggie May, Staff Captain.
(*A Brass Hat In No Man's Land*)

Crozier wrote that during the construction of the new defence lines he took four days "local recreation at the base" and spent time at Paris Plage.[166] Charles Messenger has pointed out that neither the divisional nor brigade war diaries mention this.[167] The episode may be a plot device, providing a break from descriptions of fighting and life at the front, but there are no references to his presence in the brigade war diary from 7 – 10 June, so he may have gone away as he said. Away or not, he received notice that he was "to form a new brigade which has to be in action within a month ... Into the line again, three new battalions once more, thank goodness I have a good staff".[168]

Hone would remain as Staff Captain (his BM role was in an acting capacity), 40th Division A&Q noted: 'Instructions regarding recommendations for advancement of staff and other officers [were] revised' – TNA WO 95/2594: War Diary 40th Division HQ A&Q. Hone was awarded a second bar to his MC, was promoted Lieutenant-Colonel, 21st Middlesex, May-October 1918 and took the battalion back to the UK. He was posted to command the 13th DLI (74 Brigade, 25th Division) in the final weeks of the War and was badly wounded on 24 October. Reggie May had 'entirely lost the use of his legs for two days at the end of the March battle, owing to fatigue' – Crozier, *Brass Hat*, p.198.
166 Crozier, *Brass Hat*, pp.207, 209-212.
167 Messenger, *Broken Sword*, p.104.
168 Crozier, *Brass Hat*, p.210. Crozier's staff teams – the pairings of Goodliffe/Hone, Hone/May and Muirhead/May – provided continuity and seem to have operated efficiently and effectively. There is no evidence of the decline in standard of brigade majors or definite improvement of staff captains as the war progressed

"A growing feature of the supply of military manpower was the use of Category 'B1' men for front line service".[169] On 8 June notification was given to brigades "of the raising of infantry Garrison Guard Battalions composed of men of category lower than 'A'. These units to be posted in the first instance to the cadres of 40th and 59th Divisions as a temporary measure".[170] The need for men for defence was such that in April Labour Corps guard companies were brigaded to take over part of the line south-west of Arras and by the end of May the Labour Corps units were being scoured for category B1 men who had previously served in the infantry.[171] Twenty-four 'Garrison Guard' Companies were quickly assembled to form numbers 6 to 11 Garrison Guard Battalions. Three of these units would form the 'new' 119 Brigade and the 'temporary measure' would become permanent.[172]

The Category B Men

On 10 June 1918 the HQ of the six Garrison Guard battalions arrived at 120 Brigade. And on 12 June the battalion designations were amended to reflect the move from Labour Corps to infantry. Numbers 7, 8 and 11 Garrison Battalions became the 13th Garrison Battalion Royal Inniskilling Fusiliers, 13th Garrison Battalion East Lancashire Regiment and the 12th Garrison Battalion North Staffordshire Regiment respectively.[173] These battalion HQ transferred to 119 Brigade on 15 June and the four companies of the 12th North Staffords arrived the same day. The men of the 13th RIF and 13th East Lancs followed the next day.[174] Freddy Plunkett returned to command the 13th RIF "by pure chance" according to Crozier in one book but in another, having arrived in France and seen the commandant of the base camp, "insisted on being sent" rather than taking a soft job.[175] Plunkett simply says that he was "given command".[176] His comment on his new unit was: "When they marched in my heart sank to the lowest as they straggled badly, looked old and weary, with not the slightest sign of discipline in them. These remarks apply to both officers and men."[177]

---

  suggested by W.N. Nicholson (GSO 1, 51st (Highland) Division and later AA&QMG, 17th (Northern) Division) as quoted in Aimée E. Fox, 'Military administration and the Role of Brigade Staff, 1916-1918', University of Birmingham, MA Thesis, 2010, p.51.
169 Grieves, *The Politics of Manpower*, p.196. Grieves does not specifically mention the use of Labour Corps men of this category but focuses on men from Home Service divisions in Britain.
170 TNA WO 95/2605: War Diary 120 Brigade.
171 See Charles Messenger, *Call to Arms: The British Army 1914-18* (London: Cassell, 2005), pp.521-522 for definitions of medical categories. B1 men were classified fit for service abroad in Garrison or Provisional units, but not for general service.
172 John Starling and Ivor Lee, *No Labour, No Battle: Military Labour During the First World War* (Stroud: Spellmount, 2009), pp.146-147. Harry Graham's comments (quoted earlier) about training B1 men were then ultimately correct but the whole division had indeed been close to being permanently disbanded. Douglas Haig came under pressure from Ferdinand Foch (appointed during the March crisis as Allied CinC) who had 'protested very strongly against the reduction of any divisions'. By the end of June six of eight threatened divisions had been reconstituted, five with 'B' men (including 40th Division). See Edmonds, *Military Operations France and Belgium 1918*, Vol. 3, pp.5-6.
173 Orders for the elimination of the 'Garrison' designation were received on 13 July and duly implemented.
174 TNA WO 95/2605: War Diary 119 Brigade.
175 Crozier, *Impressions*, p.226; *Brasshat*, p.215.
176 NAM: 'Diary of the War – by J.F. Plunkett'.
177 Ibid.

Table 19: Background of 119 Brigade troops 1918[178]

	12th North Staffords (72)	13th Royal Inniskilling Fusiliers (76)	13th East Lancs (81)
Place of Residence/Birth given	97% (70)	95% (72)	85% (69)
Place of Residence/Birth*	Lancs 20% (14)	Lancs 17% (12)	Yorks 18% (15)
	London 14% (10)	London 15% (11)	Lancs 17% (12)
	Yorks 10% (7)	Lanarkshire 11% (8)	
		Yorks 10% (7)	
Total 'counties' represented**	22	22	26
Previous service given	94% (68)	95% (72)	81% (66)
Number of Regiments/Corps represented by previous service	36	40	39
Ages present in sample	64% (46)	57% (43)	54% (44)
Youngest/Oldest	19 / 43	19 / 45	19 / 42
Average / Median	28 / 25	30 / 31	27 / 25

*Only locations making up 10% or more of the battalion total are specified
**includes 'Ireland' and the Channel Isles

Data compiled from *Soldiers Died in the Great War* and the online database of the Commonwealth War Graves Commission has been used as a sample of the men of the three battalions (see Table 19). In summary, compared with the recruits that made up the original 'Welsh' brigade in 1915/17, these men were older, with previous service in other regiments or corps and from a wider range of localities in the UK and beyond. The majority had no geographical affiliation to the regiments in which they now found themselves.[179] Most came from the industrial areas of the north, particularly Lancashire and Yorkshire with (for reasons unknown) men from Lanarkshire providing a significant part of the 13th RIF. London is prominent in the figures for two battalions but not (again for reasons unknown) the 13th East Lancs. If the Labour Corps 'pool' was homogenous, one would expect all three battalions to have had approximately the same composition. 44820 Private August William Cooper, 12th North Staffords, was typical of the new men if rather at the younger end of their age-range. The twenty-year-old miner's son from Houghton le Spring, County Durham first joined the Durham Light Infantry, transferred to the 5th West Yorks in France and finally the 88th Company, Labour Corps before a final transfer to the 12th North Staffords.[180]

---

178 Data extracted primarily from *Soldiers Died in the Great War 1914-1919*, CD-ROM, Naval and Military Press, 1998 supplemented by information from the CWGC extracted with 'Geoff's 1914-1921 DB Search Engine' at the *Hut Six* <http://www.hut-six.co.uk/cgi-bin/search1421.php> (Accessed 5 February 2016).
179 For example, just one man from North Staffordshire has been found in the sample of the 12th North Staffords.
180 Data compiled from <http://ancestry.co.uk>. Cooper was discharged in September 1919 and applied unsuccessfully for a pension citing the effects of gas. He died in 1980.

Men of the 12th North Staffordshire Regiment, 1918, wearing 40th Division patches. On right 44820 Pte August William Cooper, age 20, who had previously served with the DLI, W. Yorks and Labour Corps. (Ian Cooper)

The Officers

David Starrett noted: "we sorted out officers and men, especially the officers, who always made the General's greatest problem. Some were old men – as were some of the men – from Dunkirk and La [sic] Havre where they had cushy jobs, sheltered by their own, or their superior's red tape".[181] Freddy Plunkett said of his officers: "The only officer of my battn staff who had previous experience in his appointment was Lt Petrie my Signalling Officer. Capt Fleming, my Adjutant, had never worked in an orderly room, and my QtMaster had never worked in a QtMaster's stores (later

---

181 IWM: Starrett, '*Batman*', p.117.

I had to get rid of him)".[182] Data on the officers is sparse but a small sample has been compiled.[183] Twenty-three of the files are of officers of the 13th RIF, eight of the 13th East Lancs and just two from the 12th North Staffords. Ten of these had come from the Labour Corps or a Garrison Battalion, nine had been posted from their regiment's reserve battalion and three had come from TF units.[184] Twenty-three (70%) had been promoted from the ranks and twenty-one of these had been commissioned from an OCB (18) or OTC unit (3). Six had received their first commission in 1914, four in 1915, one in 1916, fifteen (50%) in 1917 and just four in 1918. The majority (22) had been born between 1890 and 1900. Of the twenty-nine records noting civilian occupation ten (34%) were clerks or civil servants and six (21%) were schoolmasters or students – a similar picture to that outlined in Chapter 2 for an earlier stage of the war. It is doubtful, however, whether the boilermaker's apprentice and the machine cutler represented in this sample would have received commissions in 1915.

Training

Major Sidney Tabor, 13th East Lancs, noted: "[as] a number of officers and men had not been in the line for some time, and a great many never had, it was necessary that they be put into strict training".[185] "The Division will be required to hold a quiet sector of the line and all efforts are to be concentrated on training with this object" was how the division phrased it.[186] Plunkett was practical: "the Brigadier informed me that I could settle down to three months steady training so I treated all as recruits, except that after a week I fired ball cartridge and threw live bombs to try and improve the nerves of the men, and most of them required improving badly".[187] The battalion war diaries give little detail of the training programme but the 13th East Lancs war diary is used as a source here to describe it in outline (Table 20); it was certainly 'back to basics'.

Table 20: Training carried out by the 13th East Lancs June-August 1918[188]

Date	Training Activity
18 June	Squad drill, musketry, specialist training
19	Squad drill, platoon drill, musketry. A Company on range, grouping practice; B Company firing stopped when Chinese Labour refused to work in vicinity
21	GOC lecture to all officers in evening
22	Brigade route march, five miles
24	Gas drill, platoon drill, musketry

---

182 NAM: 'Diary of the War – by J.F. Plunkett'. Captain Fleming is David Pinkerton Fleming (1877-1944), see Appendix VI.
183 Just thirty-three officer files have been traced and examined (compared with 156 of the four Welsh battalions). The low number may be due to a higher proportion of officers from this last year of the war staying with the army into the 1920s and their files not yet being in the public domain. Files of officers with TF commissions seem largely absent from the files at TNA. Note that some of the sample arrived at the brigade after June 1918.
184 A list of 19 officers posted to the 13th East Lancs in June and July 1918 shows a similar make up. Eight came from Garrison Battalions or the Labour Corps, six were attached from other East Lancs battalions or the Lancashire Fusiliers (2), two came from Special Reserve battalions and three from TF units – *London Gazette*, 2 October 1918.
185 TNA WO 95/2606: War Diary 13th East Lancs, 'History of 13th Bn The East Lancashire Regiment'.
186 TNA WO 95/2594: War Diary 40th Division GS, 14 June 1918.
187 NAM: 'Diary of the War – by J.F. Plunkett'.
188 Extracted from TNA WO 95/2606: War Diary 13th East Lancs and WO 95/2605: War Diary 119 Brigade.

Date	Training Activity
26	Musketry, rapid loading, outposts, small schemes, specialist training
27	Musketry, platoon drill, outposts, small schemes, specialist training
28	Musketry, platoon drill, outposts, PT
29	Musketry, platoon drill, outposts, route march (D Company)
30	Football, Brigade HQ v E. Lancs (result 3-2)
1 July	Musketry, platoon drill, PT, lecture on Gas (to all senior officers and company COs in brigade)
2	Saluting and box respirator drill. Lecture on outposts to all officers by CO
3	Gas drill, marching in masks, musketry, platoon drill and handling of arms, PT
4	PT, musketry, identification of targets, rapid loading, platoon drill, handling of arms
5	Gas drill, musketry, PT, platoon drill, specialist training, short route march in fighting order
6	Company training (B, C and D Companies – A Company working creating new range)
7 – 11	Manning East Hazebrouck Line for instruction in trench duties
13	Battalion saluting, gas drill
14	Range (two companies), gas test
15	Practice concentration West Hazebrouck Line
16	Range (two companies), gas drill, PT and bayonet training, musketry, company drill, specialist training, Lewis guns on range
1 August	Range
2	Range, PT and bayonet fighting (two companies), bombing (two companies)
3	Bombing (two companies)
5	Range, Battalion through lachrymatory chamber, Brigade Intelligence Officer lecture on SOS (Sniping, Observation, Scouting)
6	Company training, training under specialist officers
7	Battalion training, recreational training p.m.
8	Battalion training
9	Battalion training – the battalion in the attack. CO attends lecture on 'Infantry Training' by Sir Ivor Maxse and watches platoon demonstration by XVIII Corps School students[189]
10	Battalion sports
12	Battalion moves to Second Army School of Musketry
13	Companies practising attack. Ranges p.m.
14	Companies practising attack. Ranges p.m.
15	Ranges – rapid fire and snap shooting. ("Companies as a whole showed great improvement". CO and company COs attend demonstration in fire discipline and control by School students.
16	Battle practice all companies – "on the whole fairly good for the first time"
17	Brigade sports
19	Company training. Platoons and companies practising attack, PT and bayonet fighting, gas and close order drill
20	Brigade field day – East Lancs defend attack by 12th N Staffords and 13th RIF. GOC Division present.

---

189 Maxse had been in command of XVIII Corps until his appointment as Inspector General of Training in July 1918.

Some weeding out of unfit men took place. On 24 June a visit from the Medical Inspector of Drafts from GHQ to inspect the brigade's battalions resulted in forty-four other ranks from the 12th North Staffords "of category less than B1 [being] sent to Labour Group Base" followed on 6 July by "a certain number" from the 12th North Staffords and 13th East Lancs. The ADMS visited the 12th North Staffords on 9 July "to enquire into their sick wastage as it had been reported that many men are on light duty daily". Sadly, the brigade's war diaries give few other details but the ADMS noted that in July a divisional total of twelve officers and 200 ORs who had not improved through training was sent to base while also noting "great improvement in general physique and morale". A further two officers and eight ORs out of twenty 'unfits' of the 12th North Staffs were despatched to base on 6 August.[190] While there was obviously a problem, Crozier's later claim of fifty per cent of men being rejected seems exaggerated.[191]

The GOC 40th Division, John Ponsonby, inspected the brigade on 16 June just after its arrival and this was followed by an inspection by the DAG on 19 June.[192] On 24 June the CinC inspected one battalion of each brigade. The 13th RIF represented 119 Brigade:

> I saw some at drill, others musketry, one whole battalion was on parade in open order. The latter presented arms and handled their rifles well. I was greatly surprised and pleased with the class of men in the ranks. They can shoot and will hold a position but cannot march very far, say, 5 miles slowly is the normal ... I think that these divisions of old veterans will be a very great strength to us as they can hold 'Support lines', and if the front becomes quiet can relieve a division (for training) in the line.[193]

Plunkett recalled that Haig "said he was astonished to see them [the men of 13th RIF] looking so wonderfully well. In a conversation he told me that it was not intended to make first line troops of the B1 Battns but they would simply be used in the event of the Boche breaking through. He asked COs to make it known to the men".[194] Crozier said that he ignored an order to do just that but Ilana Bet-El is wrong when she writes that he "specifically disregarded an order that B grade men should not be employed in offensive action".[195]

---

190 TNA WO 95/2605 War Diary 12th North Staffords and WO 95/2597-1: War Diary ADMS 40th Division.
191 Crozier, *Brass Hat*, p.215. On 17 June 119 Brigade strength was noted as 2500 rifles – WO 95/2594: 40th Division GS, Division Order 170. When B Company, 12th North Staffords, went to the range on 29 June it had four officers and 120 OR – WO 95/2605 War Diary. In mid-July Freddy Plunkett noted that he 'had 2 Battns of the brigade at my disposal of about 450 bayonets each' – 'Diary of the War – by J.F. Plunkett'.
192 There are nine DAGs in the *Army List* for August 1918.
193 Gary Sheffield and John Bourne (eds), *Douglas Haig: War Diaries and Letters, 1914 – 1918* (London: Weidenfeld and Nicolson, 2005), p.423.
194 NAM: 'Diary of the War – by J.F. Plunkett'. In the event, the brigade was used for more than 'line holding' in a quiet sector although this was the original intention. One of the items on the agenda for a 40th Division conference on 21 June was 'Is it advisable for Commanding Officers to explain to the men the probable role of the Division in future as regards their duty in active operations' – WO 95/2608: War Diary 120 Brigade. The conference agreed that 'Battalion commanders should explain to the men under their command the role which the Division has been called upon to fill and that the enrolment of Class B men in fighting units is necessitated by the shortage of manpower' – WO 95/2611: War Diary 11th Cameron Highlanders, 120 Brigade. Crozier writes that he ignored an order from the C-in-C to explain to the men that they would only be used in a quiet sector and not put into offensive action – Crozier, *Impressions*, p.226.
195 Ilana R. Bet-El, *Conscripts: Forgotten Men of the Great War* (Stroud, Sutton, 1999), p.35. Crozier actually wrote that he ignored an order from the C-in-C to explain to the men that they would only be used in a quiet sector and not put into offensive action – which is not the same thing – Crozier, *Impressions*, p.226. Grieves, *Politics of Manpower*, p.198, recounts Crozier's account at face value.

On 2 July, the day before Ponsonby's departure to command 5th Division, 40th Division's brigades were inspected by Field-Marshal HRH The Duke of Connaught, ADC to King George V, with Sir Herbert Plumer, commanding Second Army, and Sir H. de Beauvoir De Lisle, commanding XV Corps, in attendance.[196] Crozier wrote of later: "We were not slow to seize upon the useful Royal lesson of disinterested service brought before us by the presence of the Royal Field-Marshal in our midst, which we passed on to 'the old and the bold', as they liked to call themselves".[197] He summed up the training process: "We 'electrified' our 'B' men into activity by a simple process … We got them all to play games, take part in sports, take a pride in their new regiments, march, shoot and forget about their ills – real or imaginary".[198] Was this positive development reflected in the number of trials by FGCM of men from 119 Brigade?

Table 21: Field General Courts Martial, 119 Brigade, July 1918 – June 1919

	12th N. Staffords	13th E. Lancs	13th Royal Inn. Fus	Total
July 1918	1	1	–	2
Aug	3	3	4	10
Sept	3	2	4	9
Oct	8	2	10	20
Nov	5	4	10	19
Dec	2	1	1	4
Total	22	13	29	64
Jan 1919	2	3	2	7
Feb	2	1	–	3
Mar	5	1	–	6
Apr	1	1	1	3
May	–	–	–	0
June	–	1	–	1
Total	10	7	3	20
Overall	32	20	32	84

Source: TNA: WO213/23-29

The figures (Table 21) clearly show that there was an issue. In 1917 fifty-four men of the original brigade were sent for trial while in just six months of 1918 sixty-four men were tried. The highest number of offenders came from the 13th RIF perhaps indicating that the ex-RSM, now CO, Plunkett enforced a stricter regime. The 12th North Staffords suffered from an initial high turnover of COs and this may have contributed to the battalion having the second highest total of FGCMs. The arrival of an ex-Grenadier Guardsman, Major E.R. O'Connor (see below) as CO in October may account for the rise in numbers of trials at that time although it is notable that the higher monthly figures correspond to periods when the brigade was in action. This is in contrast to the record of the Welsh bantams which showed an increase when the brigade came out of the line. The command of the 13th East Lancs was stable through the summer of 1918 and this may be a factor in the lower number of FGCM cases from this battalion.

---

196 This appears to have been an exercise in public relations designed to confirm the place of the new battalions within the BEF and the men's identification with their new regiments.
197 Crozier, *Impressions*, p.228.
198 Ibid., pp.227-228.

Table 22: Offences tried by Field General Courts Martial, 119 Brigade, July 1918 – June 1919 (Instances of offence in brackets)

Offence	119 Brigade
Absence	39% (36)
Desertion	21% (19)
Insubordination	5% (5)
Disobedience	7% (6)
Drunkenness	2% (2)
Desertion Quitting post / Sleeping	1% (1)
Striking	2% (2)
Miscellaneous Military Offences	20% (18)
Self-inflicted Wound	3% (3)
Total Offences	92

Source: TNA WO213/23-29

The ex-Labour Corps men of the new brigade brought a different culture with them. Having believed that they would not find themselves in the front line it is not surprising to see that 50% of offences were absence or desertion (Table 22). The low figure for drunkenness might indicate that the offence was dealt with by the CO rather than being indicative of a high level of sobriety. Although three cases involving self-inflicted wounds are specifically recorded it is known that this offence was also categorised under 'miscellaneous' and it is almost certainly under-represented in the figures. Despite the problems with absence and desertion the sentencing regime remained broadly the same as earlier in the war with a very similar percentage of offences punished by hard labour, penal servitude or field punishment number one (Table 23). Twenty-one of thirty-five sentences of hard labour or penal servitude were remitted or commuted and eleven were suspended – as was the only death sentence (for desertion, August 1918) which was commuted to five years penal servitude and suspended. The drop in the most severe sentences after the armistice is marked.

Table 23: Sentences of Field General Courts Martial, 119 Brigade, July 1918 – June 1919

Sentence	Instances in 119 Brigade	
	July-December 1918	January-June 1919
Field Punishment No1	37% (31)	–
Field Punishment No2	6% (5)	50% (10)
Imprisonment	1% (1)	–
Penal Servitude	13% (11)	–
Hard Labour	29% (24)	35% (7)
Death	1% (1)	–
Reduction in Rank	6% (5)	–
Stoppages/Fine	1% (1)	5% (1)
Discharge with Ignominy	5% (4)	–
Not Guilty / Quashed	1% (1)	10% (2)
Total Sentences	84	20

Source: TNA WO213/23-29

Commanding Officers

What of the battalion COs? Crozier had confidence in "the old warrior" Freddy Plunkett in the 13th RIF but the others were unknown to him, sent from what Crozier called the 'CO's pool'.[199] The 13th East Lancs were commanded from 17 June by Australian-born Lieutenant-Colonel R.I.B. Johnson DSO, RWF.[200] He seems to have performed satisfactorily until 7 October when Crozier (apparently unofficially) gave his command to the newly-returned Richard Andrews who had turned up (also unofficially) while Johnson was away.[201] "Of course 'the Base' made a dreadful fuss when they found out what had happened, but ... 'what we have we hold'" was Crozier's comment.[202] So, the command of two battalions was relatively stable but Plunkett noted that not all was well with the 12th North Staffords which "had no less than three Battn Comdrs in a month ... I had the doubtful honour of being the only CO who lasted three months. Brig Genl Crozier our commander, who was a thorough fighter, had no sentiment".[203] Plunkett implies that the turnover in COs was driven by Crozier. While Crozier had no say as to who was posted from the 'CO's pool', he clearly had some say in who stayed and who was posted elsewhere. The first CO of the 12th North Staffords was Lieutenant-Colonel G.M. Grogan DSO, Royal Irish Regiment who stayed from 10-19 June.[204] He was replaced by Major T. K. Pardoe DSO, Worcestershire Regiment who stayed for four days.[205] He was followed by Lieutenant-Colonel H.S. Tew CMG, East Surrey Regiment, who remained until 26 July.[206] Next to arrive was Lieutenant-Colonel C.H. Kitching DSO, KRRC, who stayed until October 1918.[207] The final CO of the battalion was Major E.R. O'Connor who arrived at the 13th RIF as 2iC on 5 August.[208] He had a totally different background from the others having risen through the ranks of the Grenadier Guards and commissioned in 1915. Crozier was impressed and he was put in charge of the 13th East Lancs when Johnson left, only to be removed when Andrews arrived. Crozier says that, in seeking a replacement for a colonel, he "was afraid to apply to the base for one lest I should get a 'dud' from 'the pool' ... I spotted O'Connor ... and to his great surprise told him to take command of the North Staffords. He 'electrified' that battalion and really transformed it within ten days".[209] In another version Crozier "told" the staff captain to post O'Connor to command the battalion.[210] In this case Crozier seems to have had the authority to deal with a vacancy without upsetting the base. Peter Hodgkinson notes how, despite the attrition of COs in the German March Offensive, battalion disbandments ensured there was no shortage of replacements.[211] Yet none of the officers noted in the preceding paragraphs came from that source. All, except O'Connor, were above (in some cases well above) the average age of a battalion CO in the Hundred Days of thirty-four years and eleven

---

199 Ibid., p.227. Actually the Commanding Officers' Pool at Étaples – Hodgkinson, *Battalion Commanders*, p.188.
200 Robert Ingelow Bradshaw Johnson (1874-1955). See Appendix VI.
201 It may not be coincidence that on 20 September, division had asked for submission of names of battalion COs and 2iCs for three months leave. Johnson went on leave on 28 September and officially remained CO until 26 November. Andrews took command of the 13th East Lancs on 7 October.
202 Crozier, *Impressions*, p.227.
203 NAM: 'Diary of the War – by J.F. Plunkett'
204 George Meredyth Grogan (1867-1942). See Appendix VI.
205 Thomas Kenyon Pardoe (1873-1946). See Appendix VI.
206 Harold Stuart Tew (1869-1945). See Appendix VI.
207 Charles Henry Kitching (1881-1952). See Appendix VI.
208 Ernest Robert O'Connor: (1886-1970). See Appendix VI.
209 Crozier, *Impressions*, p.232. The *London Gazette* entry gives the date of O'Connor's promotion as 24 October 1918.
210 Crozier, *Brass Hat,* p.225.
211 Hodgkinson, *Battalion Commanders*, p.188.

months.²¹² At this point in the war forty per cent of battalion COs were professional soldiers. In 119 Brigade at the end of August 1918 all three were regulars (Plunkett, Kitchen, Johnson) but by November the appearance of Richard Andrews had reduced that number to two (Plunkett and O'Connor). This reconstituted brigade was an unusual formation in more ways than one.²¹³

What of Crozier's own promotion prospects? Brigadier-General John Campbell who had commanded 121 Brigade since October 1915 had been promoted to command 31st Division in May 1918.²¹⁴ Given Crozier's successful record he might also have expected promotion. He acted as divisional commander during Sir William Peyton's (see below) brief absence in August 1918 and, while attending a memorial service and a corps conference, met a figure from his past service with the UVF and the 36th (Ulster) Division. Wilfred Spender reported to his wife:

> I saw Crozier – looking rather too fat a Brigadier – who seemed pleased to see me at first but shied violently when I talked of our rebellious days etc and he sheered off. Considering I got him his first step at a deal of fuss with O[liver] N[ugent] I think perhaps_____but that is probably why.²¹⁵

> Little Crozier was at the powwow as Acting Divisional Comm[ande]r! I cannot get over the amusement at this nor at his evident desire to leave behind the associations of which I am most proud.²¹⁶

If Spender was correct, it seems that Crozier was being very careful to guard his reputation at this time by avoiding mentions of one element of his irregular career path.

Just as John Ponsonby was leaving the 40th Division he supposedly told Crozier that he had recommended him for "command of a Division, which, however, came too late to be of use to me, as the war was over just as I was about to be appointed".²¹⁷ Was this wishful thinking on Crozier's part? There is no evidence of a recommendation from Ponsonby. Ponsonby's replacement was Major-General Sir William Peyton KCB KCVO DSO who, Crozier acknowledged, "knew something about me".²¹⁸ Peyton had served in Thorneycroft's Mounted Infantry from May to October 1900, knew Alexander Thorneycroft (Crozier's step-father) and may well have known something of Crozier's dishonourable early career. If he did not, his long spell as Military Secretary at GHQ should have ensured that he (or his staff) accessed Crozier's personal file. Yet, on 29 November, Peyton confirmed that Crozier's name had indeed "been submitted for advancement to the command of a Division".²¹⁹ It was unfortunate for Crozier that the GOC Second Army, Sir Herbert Plumer, also knew something about him, having "owing to friendship with my mother" helped "to get oil poured on troubled waters" around the time of Crozier's resignation and bankruptcy in 1909.²²⁰ Peyton's replacement as Military Secretary at GCQ was none other than Harold Ruggles-Brise who would also have had access to

---

212 Ibid., p.63.
213 The make-up of formations rebuilt from cadres in mid-1918 and the performance of category B men in general would repay further study.
214 John Campbell (1871-1941). See Appendix VI.
215 PRONI D1633/1/1/1172: Wilfred Spender to his wife, 5 August 1918, quoted in Baguley (ed.), *World War One and the Question of Ulster*, p.429.
216 PRONI D1633/1/1/1155: Wilfred Spender to his wife, 6 August 1918, quoted in Baguley (ed.), *World War One and the Question of Ulster*, p.431.
217 Crozier, *Impressions*, p.228.
218 William Elliot Peyton (1866 – 1931) see Appendix VI.
219 TNA WO 374/16997: Personal File F.P. Crozier. Memorandum from Sir William Peyton to HQ XV Corps, 29 November 1918.
220 Crozier, *Impressions*, p.136.

Crozier's personal file although, as he seems to have remained a friend of Crozier, he may not have read it.[221] Either these senior officers did not know at this time about Crozier's past misdemeanours or they chose to overlook them in the light of his recent record. Crozier did not get his division. With formations being reduced or disbanded after the end of hostilities it was too late.[222] His aggressive style was not suited to peacetime soldiering and had won him few friends. In late 1917 he had been warned by Sir Oliver Nugent that he "was in the wrong shop; [he had] cut off too many heads to be popular".[223] There is no evidence that Crozier was 'just about to be appointed' as the war ended.

Defence to Offence: July-November 1918

The evidence clearly shows that the perceived role of the reconstituted 40th Division was defensive. Indeed, through June and July it was regarded by the CinC as being incapable of anything else. In mid-June orders were issued "In case of an enemy attack on the Second Army Front 40th Division ... will be required to man the West Hazebrouck Line ... units must be prepared to act ... at short notice".[224] The division front was 13,000 yards (11.8 kilometres) and it needed support from additional Labour Corps and Royal Engineer units that, for example, increased the strength of 119 Brigade from (a probably notional) 2500 rifles to 4500 rifles.[225] The line was to be held "in accordance with the principles set down in *SS210 The Division in Defence*.[226] It was to be "clearly impressed on the troops that they are to hold the line in which they are posted ... to the last man and the last round of ammunition. No withdrawal of troops will take place, even from the line of Observation until orders are issued from Divisional Headquarters to do so".[227] Clearly someone was very worried. From April to July GHQ expected the German army to attack the BEF in Flanders again, despite the obvious build-up of their forces against the French further south. There was indeed a German plan for a new attack in Flanders (codename *Hagen*) that would press north-west and west to the north of the Lys to take Hazebrouck and Ypres. Plans were completed in June but the offensive was first delayed and then abandoned on 20 July as German divisions and artillery were moved south in response to the allied counter-offensive on the Marne.[228] By the beginning of August GHQ had confirmed the cancellation, although Second Army remained cautious.[229] A change of outlook can be seen expressed in the training programme (Table 15, above) where 'the battalion/company/platoon in the attack' appears several times after 9 August. By then, of course, the bigger picture had changed for the better and the BEF had started on its advance in Picardy with Fourth Army's success at Amiens on 8 August. Second Army's advance in Flanders started on 18 August.

---

221 Ruggles-Brise became Military Secretary on 22 March 1918. In December he endorsed the recommendation for a divisional command and forwarded to the War Office 'for such consideration as it may be possible to give'. TNA WO 374/16997: Personal File F.P. Crozier. Memorandum from Military Secretary to War Office, 8 December 1918.
222 See later comments regarding Crozier's applications for retention in the army and his personal file.
223 Crozier, *Impressions*, p.207.
224 TNA WO 95/2594: War Diary 40th Division GS, 15 June 1918.
225 TNA WO 95/2594: War Diary 40th Division GS, Divisional Order 170, 17 June 1918.
226 *SS 210* was issued in May 1918 and was regarded as 'too little, too late'. See Jim Beach, 'Issued by the General Staff: Doctrine Writing at British GHQ, 1917-1918', *War in History*, 19:4 (2012), pp.464-491, particularly pp.473-474, for the genesis of this publication.
227 TNA WO 95/2594: War Diary 40th Division GS, Divisional Order 167, 15 June 1918. The swift loss of the outpost zone in April 1918 probably accounts for the reference to 'no withdrawal'.
228 Zabecki, *The German 1918 Offensives*, pp.280-307.
229 See Beach, *Haig's Intelligence*, pp.295-301.

The B men of 40th Division had to learn fast. In addition to the practice manning of the West Hazebrouck Line, in July every battalion of each brigade had a four day tour in the East Hazebrouck Line. This enabled the induction of the men into trench routine well away from the front line.[230] More realistic conditions were provided for 119 Brigade on 18 July when it relieved 87 Brigade (29th Division) in the front line where it was attached to 1st Australian Division.[231] Next day the new formation suffered its first casualty from shell fire. The 13th RIF were in the front line which consisted of posts "of about platoon strength with intervals of from 70 to 200 yards between".[232] The 13th East Lancs were in support and the 12th North Staffords provided the reserve.[233] The East Lancs relieved the RIF on 22 July and were relieved in turn by the North Staffords on 26 July. Despite their lack of recent experience and what must have been a strange new context for warfare, the battalions all patrolled actively and all brought in prisoners of the *98th RIR* during the tour.[234] Freddy Plunkett recalled that on the night his men took their first prisoners: "From this night the men became a fighting force".[235] On the night of 21/22 July a patrol of the 13th RIF found no enemy and no obstacles on their front and managed to advance their line by an unspecified distance and establish new posts.[236] But there were setbacks. On the previous night, when a 13th RIF patrol was engaged by machine guns, a flanking party of one sergeant and eight other ranks was sent to "get round the guns". They failed to return.[237] Second-Lieutenant J.N. Robinson, 13th East Lancs was killed during a patrol on 23 July and on the night of 25/6 July a patrol of one officer and twelve men was forced to withdraw by flanking fire from German machine guns. It withdrew without loss but an Australian officer and corporal were killed while they watched the patrol. During the tour the adjacent Australian 1st Division placed one officer and four NCOs with each front line company: "they were invaluable in instructing both officers and men in their duties".[238] The CO of the 13th East Lancs was "on the whole satisfied" with the battalion's tour "but pointed out certain faults which steps are to be taken to remedy", including not paying enough attention to improving the posts and to wiring.[239] The brigade was relieved on

---

230 11th Cameron Highlanders (120 Brigade) were supported by three officers and six NCOs from 31st Division's troops during this exercise and it is probable that all battalions were so treated – TNA WO 95/2611: War Diary 11th Cameron Highlanders.
231 At this date XV Corps was made up of 9th, 29th, 31st and 1st Australian Divisions. 40th Division was Corps Reserve.
232 TNA WO 95/6505: War Diary 12th North Staffords. The 13th East Lancs war diary mentions seven posts in the front line.
233 TNA WO 95/2605: War Diary 119 Brigade.
234 The 13th RIF captured two prisoners on the same night that they took over the position; the 13th East Lancs captured two on 25 July; the 12th North Staffords captured one on 28 July and three on 30 July – TNA WO 95/2605: battalion war diaries. Crozier had promised £5 for the first prisoner and £1 for each thereafter for a fixed period. He says he paid up 'over £15' – Crozier, *Impressions*, p.231. The incentive is confirmed in the Plunkett Diary.
235 IWM: Plunkett Diary.
236 This may have been the night that Plunkett describes: 'the Australians decided to try and take Merris, a commanding position on the Outiersteen [sic] Ridge. The attack was to take place at dawn and I was asked to conform so as to connect up with their right if [the] attack was successful. Instead of waiting for dawn I moved forward during the night and had my left waiting for the Australians. They attacked successfully next day but were rather surprised to find us already in position as, knowing we were a B1 division, they had not much faith in us.' But Plunkett must have been mistaken about Merris which was captured on 29/30 July when 13th RIF were out of the line.
237 TNA WO 95/2605: War Diary 119 Brigade. Plunkett regarded the incident as 'a good fight both sides losing about 10 men' – NAM: Plunkett Diary.
238 TNA WO 95/2606: War Diary 13th East Lancs.
239 Ibid. 119 Brigade casualties for this tour were 2 officers killed, 1 officer wounded, 13 OR killed, 33 OR wounded and 5 missing.

31 July and continued its training programme until 21 August when the B men of 40th Division were ordered to relieve 31st Division in the front line.[240] The principle of using category B men for defence had lasted just eight weeks.

XV Corps' contribution to Second Army's advance in Flanders had a successful opening on 18 August when the 9th, supported by 29th, Division had captured the Outtersteene Ridge.[241] On the night of 22/23 August 120 Brigade (already in the front line) sidestepped to the left and 119 Brigade entered the line taking over part of the 120 Brigade front and relieving 94 Brigade (31st Division). The 13th RIF and the 13th East Lancs manned the forward positions with 12th North Staffords in support. At this time of likely offensive action Crozier went on leave to the UK from 23 August to 8 September. This turn of events seems very strange but on 28 August his wife Ethel appeared in court and was certified insane and ordered to be detained in a private asylum.[242] He is not mentioned in the account of her trial but it is likely that he was called back deal with this family crisis. Command of 119 Brigade passed to Lieutenant-Colonel Johnson. While Crozier was away the brigade carried out its first serious offensive scheme. Freddy Plunkett had come up with a plan:

> On the 24th Aug the brigade on my right attempted to take Rue Pruvost [sic] and the ground immediately north of it. They failed and suffered fairly heavily. I watched the fight and came to the conclusion that my Battn, by swinging my left flank round southwards during the night, I could attack at dawn … thereby compelling the Boche to give up Rue Pruvost. I gave my scheme to my Divnl Comdr Sir W E Peyton and he approved.[243]

Remarkably, at this late stage in the war, Sir William Peyton sent the plan to the Corps commander, Beauvoir de Lisle, who returned it on the same day with four changes.[244] Orders were issued by division on 25 August for the attack to take place on 27 August. The left flank would be sealed by a standing barrage from heavy artillery – which also targeted roads, cross roads and buildings – while the right flank was protected by a 4.5 inch howitzer barrage. Troops would advance behind a creeping barrage from fifty-four 18-pounder guns. Strangely, Freddy Plunkett gives the wrong zero hour (it was 10.00a.m. in division orders and the after action report) but his account gives a good

---

240 TNA WO 95/2594: War Diary 40th Division GS. Division Order 186, 21 August 1918. XV Corps lost the 1st Australian Division early in August in the build up to the Fourth Army offensive at Amiens. The corps now consisted of 9th, 29th, 31st and 40th Divisions. On 11 September 9th and 29th Division were transferred north to II Corps on Second Army's left flank leaving VX Corps with just the 31st and 40th Divisions. These were reinforced by the arrival of 14th Division at the end of September. 31st Division moved to II Corps on 25 October. From September 40th Division was the right (southernmost) flank of Second Army.
241 For a detailed account of Second Army's offensive and its military and political context see Dennis Williams, 'British Second Army and Coalition Warfare in Flanders in the Hundred Days, 1918', MPhil Thesis, University of Birmingham, 2015.
242 *The Globe*, 28 August 1918. Mrs Crozier, who was described as 'independent' was charged with causing a disturbance at the War Office by using threatening words and behaviour when persistently demanding to see Mr Ian Macpherson, the Under Secretary of State for War. She had previously thrown a brick through the window of his Epsom home and sent him a shillelagh marked 'From Errin'.
243 NAM: Plunkett Diary. The hamlet of Rue Provost sat within a small salient that projected westward into the British Line. The salient was approximately 3 kilometres wide and 1.4 kilometres deep.
244 TNA WO 95/2594: War Diary 40th Division GS. His suggestions included getting 'supplies of Stokes and Rifle grenades in place to go forward with troops and assist the advance' and that 'mopping up parties to be at least equal to the probable garrison, 2 or 3 companies'. Eminently sensible though these suggestions are, why did a corps commander need to make them?

picture of this type of engagement and of the importance of German machine guns and artillery in countering incursions like this:

> Zero hour was 5am on 27th Aug. I was in position about 4am, my Hdqts being in a hole 3' deep on [the] assembly line. About 4.30am a Boche plane came over us flying very low but I dare not fire at him as I would give the situation away. He went back to his lines and shortly afterwards a Boche observation balloon went up. Needless to say as 5am approached I was a bit anxious but somehow I felt that both officers and men would play the game. Exactly at 5am we went forward under a creeping artillery barrage 3 minutes to 100 yards. The Boche machine guns opened a heavy fire and in the first 300 yards my four Coy Comdrs were casualties, Captain Summerhayes killed leading his men, Captains White, Moss and Roxburgh being wounded. I at once placed the senior officers of each Coy in command and the advance continued. House to house fighting took place on the left and Lieut Smiles who had taken command of his coy handled his men wonderfully, so that in less than an hour he was at Bishops Corner consolidating posts. The two Coys on the right were not so well led, so I went forward with them and by 7am we had taken the whole of the objective. We consolidated the line by means of small posts on a 2000 yards front under heavy MG fire. I noted Rue Pruvost [sic] was strongly held by the Boche and sent word for our artillery to concentrate on it, but before our artillery opened the Boche counter-attacked my right from Rue Pruvost. He paid dearly and had to retire as he was practically enfiladed from 3 of my Lewis guns at Bishops Corner. Shortly afterwards our artillery opened on Rue Pruvost with I am afraid disastrous results to the Boche. By 9am I was enabled to send by messenger (all wires had been cut by Boche shell fire) to Brigade that we had completed consolidation. I then went to my hole of a Headqtrs and got a devil of a time. The Boche balloon must have spotted it by messengers going to and fro. For 3 hours without a break he concentrated on us rooting up the ground all round, one gun in particular landed his shots within 20 yards of us. We got quite accustomed to this gun and from the sound knew exactly when to expect one from him. I wanted to send a message to our artillery to retaliate but had no orderlies near as they had very sensibly moved some distance away, but I had a messenger dog with me. I placed a message on him but every time I pushed him out he came back with the first fall of a shell. I cannot speak too highly of the conduct of all ranks in this engagement. When I think of what they were like on 10th June, and then this performance after a little over 2 months training it only proves what the Britisher will do when put to it. One weak lad took 6 prisoners in a house.[245]

This colourful account contains several important points: Plunkett was close enough to the fight to intervene personally (he received a second bar to his DSO for this action); casualties amongst junior officers were high; responses from German machine guns were heavy, accurate and immediate; the German response was quickly followed by counter attack; German artillery fire could still be heavy and accurate; consolidation was by means of posts not trench lines; the category B men had impressed an old stager like Plunkett. What he did not mention was that the response from machine-guns and artillery had stopped a flanking attack by 121 Brigade troops and that the final objective was not reached. The official after-action report noted that the barrage had been good and that the men had kept up with it; that German machine gunners put up stout resistance until their positions *were turned* by troops on their flanks; that the enemy held out at one position until rushed from three sides; that enfilading machine guns were the cause of failure. The men taking part carried just two Mills bombs each, clearly demonstrating the effectiveness of rifle

---

245 NAM: Plunkett Diary.

grenades, Stokes mortars and Lewis guns in destroying or suppressing the opposition. German casualties were fifty killed (counted on the ground) and thirty-two prisoners; two heavy and three light machine guns and three Lewis guns were captured. 119 brigade casualties were two officers killed and nine wounded, and fifteen ORs killed and sixty wounded.[246] The northern half of the salient had been captured but the southern half was taken by 120 Brigade on the afternoon of 29 August after night patrols had failed to do so.

On 30 August, morning patrols were "500 yards in front of the old line moving east".[247] 40th Division reported "all indications point to the enemy being in retreat in front of us".[248] This was followed at 11.15 p.m. that day by "the 40th Division will continue its advance tomorrow".[249] An advanced guard was formed consisting of 121 Brigade, two batteries of 18-pounders, one section of 4.5 inch howitzers, one company of a machine gun battalion and one company of XV Corps cyclists. Brigadier-General W. B. Garnett DSO who had followed John Campbell as GOC 121 Brigade was in command.[250] 119 Brigade was left to man the old divisional front temporarily while "the advance guard troops will attack the enemy where and when located".[251] Over the next week the advanced guard pressed the German forces as they slowly pulled back eastwards across the old Lys battlefield. The 121 Brigade war diary records the German use of machine guns to guard the flanks of the retreating forces, "considerable opposition" and "considerable machine gun opposition". The potential for serious error was obviously very great and the relatively inexperienced officers needed careful supervision. Things went badly wrong for 121 Brigade on 5 September when B Company, 8th Royal Irish Regiment, advanced through Pont de Nieppe, suffered many casualties to heavy artillery fire and lost communication with battalion and brigade HQ. Those not killed were captured.[252] The brigade was relieved next day and the GOC Division 'conferred' with Brigadier-General Garnett twice on 7 September. Reports on the events of the day were submitted to Division on 9 September and it is unlikely to be a coincidence that Garnett was replaced on 17 September. Immediately after the incident 40th Division told its brigades: "The situation regarding reinforcements for the Division, particularly Infantry Reinforcements, is not, at the moment entirely satisfactory. Hence it becomes more than ever necessary to conserve as far as possible officers and men. The Divisional Commander looks to unit commanders for their wholehearted cooperation in this."[253] Suggested methods to minimise wastage included the avoidance of unnecessary movement, the use of cover and appropriate use of steel helmets and box respirators. On 6 September 119 Brigade relieved 121 Brigade as advanced guard and the 13th East Lancs occupied the whole brigade front of 5,000 yards (4.5 kilometres) with its fighting strength of 369 men. The next day the battalion was ordered to capture Pont de Nieppe and establish posts beyond. Zero was at 10.00 a.m. and all went well at first but a strong counter-attack by sixty to seventy of the enemy forced the attacking company out of the village and back to its start line.[254] This reverse

---

246 TNA WO 95/2594: War Diary 40th Division GS, 'Account of the attack on Bishops Corner by 119th Infantry Brigade … on the 27th August, 1918'.
247 TNA WO 95/2594: War Diary 40th Division GS.
248 Ibid., Division Order 195.
249 Ibid., Division Order 196.
250 William Brooksbank Garnett (1875-1946) see Appendix VI.
251 TNA WO 95/2594: War Diary 40th Division GS. Division Order 196.
252 TNA WO 95/2613: War Diary 121 Brigade. According to Plunkett, 'Diary of the War', the lost company consisted of 3 Officers and 80 men. The village of Pont de Nieppe is on the west bank of the Lys, opposite and to the west of, Armentières.
253 40th Division Instruction 23(a), 6 September 1918. Quoted in Williams, 'British Second Army', p.131.
254 TNA WO 95/2605: War Diary 119 Brigade; WO 95/2606: War Diary 13th East Lancs. Total strength of the two companies involved was 105 – 'History of 13th Bn The East Lancashire Regiment'.

would have done nothing to enhance Lieutenant-Colonel Johnston's reputation as advanced guard commander. Next day, 8 September, Crozier returned from leave and took command. On the night of 10/11 September patrols found the village of Pont de Nieppe empty and the 12th North Staffords moved forward to occupy the village with 13th RIF in support. Plunkett recalled that he:

> Found that the Staffords had gained an entry into Pont de Nieppe but had made no move to reach the river which was the natural obstacle to prevent a Boche counterattack from Armentieres. As I could not find their CO I took command of those in Pont de Nieppe and with a few casualties pushed forward until the whole town and left bank of the river to [the] S of the town was in our hands and then placed out a line of posts and consolidated.[255]

The enemy tried to regain the village and was successfully beaten off by the North Staffords but attempts by the battalion get patrols across the River Lys that night were thwarted by the destroyed bridges and a river in flood.[256] 119 Brigade was relieved next day. The 12th North Staffords had two officers wounded, fifteen ORs killed, thirty-five wounded and thirty-five missing in the week as advanced guard.[257] The 13th East Lancs had one officer wounded, three ORs killed, twenty-nine wounded and ten missing.[258] These are tiny figures compared with those of the major battles of 1917 and spring 1918 but, as 40th Division had pointed out, the depleted battalions could not afford to lose more men.

During the next ten days 'rest', although some working parties were provided for road improvements, the brigade's units set once again to training. The 13th East Lancs recorded 'saluting drill without arms' before breakfast as well as the 'standards' of arms drill, gas drill, musketry and platoon drill. On two days 'tactical schemes for companies' were carried out and A Company managed to use a miniature range.[259] The 12th North Staffords carried out bombing and Lewis gun training and, even after the unit had moved up into reserve, carried on with Lewis gun training in which "the whole battalion was engaged".[260] Clearly, great importance was now attached to the Lewis gun as an essential tactical weapon and a boost to depleted firepower. The 12th North Staffords received a draft of one officer and seventy-seven ORs on 29 September just before it moved back into the line but there are no other references by battalions to drafts around this time.[261]

On 28 September three bridges had been thrown across the Warnave River which, although little more than a large drainage channel, effectively blocked the northern approach towards Armentières. The 13th East Lancs pushed patrols across the bridges but these were driven back across the river by strong opposition. On the next night, posts were established on the German side and held despite strong counter-attacks. Robert O'Connor, acting CO 13th East Lancs, was

---

255 IWM: Plunkett, 'Diary of the War'. The war diaries of the 13th East Lancs and the 12th North Staffords do not mention this detail.
256 TNA WO 95/2606: War Diary 12th North Staffords.
257 Ibid.
258 TNA WO 95/2606: War Diary 13th East Lancs. There are no figures in the 13th RIF War Diary which has the least information of the three battalion diaries.
259 Ibid.
260 TNA WO 95/2606: War Diary 12th North Staffords.
261 Ibid. The manpower shortage was an ongoing problem. On 28 September 40th Division had decided that 'as there are surplus pioneer officers, they may be cross posted to ordinary battalions who are short of officers'. On 5 October the division responded to a request for a list of agricultural labourers in the division by stating that if agricultural labourers were withdrawn 'the division will be reduced to a non-fighting capacity' – TNA WO 95/2594: War Diary 40th Division A&Q.

awarded the MC for this action which he led from the front.²⁶² The next obstacle, the village of Le Bizet, was taken by the 13th RIF. "The open ground to the NW of Le Bizet rendered a direct assault ... inadvisable. It was therefore decided to capture it by an encircling movement during the night."²⁶³ Freddy Plunkett described the attack and the subsequent action:

> I tried to find out if Le Bizet was occupied and had 3 officers and a few men wounded in the effort. I now received orders for what appeared to be a most daring movement. I had to 'take Le Bizet, find or make a crossing over the River Lys, mop up Houplines and occupy the old British front line from the river to 2000 yards frontage.' Simultaneously another brigade would move through Armentieres and occupy 2000 yards of [the] old British front line on my right as far south as the railway. The whole time both my flanks would be in the air unless 31st divn on my left moved forward, and once I had taken Le Bizet nobody would be within a mile of my right. At dawn on 30th Sept I took Le Bizet with little opposition and beating down machine gun fire. I reached the Lys eventually finding a place where it was possible to bridge. On [the] night of 1st Oct the Engineers constructed a one man bridge and the battn crossed. Just after dawn on the 2nd we took Houplines but no sign of the brigade which was to connect up with my right appeared. Reorganising at Houplines I made up my mind to take and hold the 4000 yards of old British front line from the right bank of the river to the railway. I sent 12 platoons forward, operating 300 yards apart, holding one coy in reserve. Only MG fire was encountered on the N[orthern] 2000 yard front and my batt objective in [the] old British front line was taken by 3 p.m. On the southern 2000 yard front more opposition was encountered but the platoons pushed on until they had taken the old British front line and consolidated. During the night the Boche attacked the left of my line but Lieut Foulds with his platoon gave them a hot time, the upshot being that they left 8 prisoners in his hands. Next day we were relieved.²⁶⁴

A brigade consisting of category B men, having had intense training in a short period was now, with aggressive leadership, conducting large encircling operations and river crossings at night.

With Houplines taken, the north and north-east of Armentières were secure and the Germans evacuated the town.²⁶⁵ The 12th North Staffords took nine prisoners during mopping up of the captured ground on 4 October. The brigade continued its forward moves through October but saw little action. What it did see plenty of was training and more training. The war diaries of the 13th East Lancs and the 13th RIF both record fourteen days devoted to training in October while the 12th North Staffords record ten days training. In addition to the usual entries for musketry, platoon and company drill, close and open order drill, bayonet fighting and physical training appear: "all ranks who had not fired [rifle] grenades were practised and all ranks instructed how to fire and load the Lewis gun"; "practise with smoke and rifle grenades on a strong point"; "all companies practised the attack, each company demonstrating with a platoon under the CO [Andrews]";

---

262 *London Gazette,* 1 February 1919. 'While acting in command of a battalion ... he led his men forward under heavy fire and established a line of posts east of Warnave. Throughout the night, which was very dark, he moved from post to post, visiting them all, and improving their tactical positions, under continuous fire of all descriptions.'
263 TNA WO 95/2605: War Diary 119 Brigade.
264 NAM: Plunkett, 'Diary of the War'.
265 It was during this period that the BM, Anthony Muirhead, won a bar to his MC: 'near Armentieres, between 29th September and 6th October 1918, in carrying out many daring reconnaissances, always under fire and exposed to danger, in order that the situation might be kept in hand. The enemy rearguard of machine gunners and snipers were all over the country. This officer did the work entirely on his own initiative, and the results were very valuable'. *London Gazette*, 1 February 1919.

a platoon demonstrated before the GOC [Crozier] the use of grenades 27 [phosphorus] and 36 [Mills]"; "demonstration by CO of new formation of the platoon in the attack"; "CO lectures all officers on *FSR Part 1*" and lecture to all officers on *FSR Part 1*" by Crozier.[266] The 12th North Staffords' C Company also demonstrated the use of rifle grenades for the GOC. Even on the march training was carried out. When the 13th East Lancs were acting as the brigade's advance guard on the march to Bondues "an attack was carried out against the town. This was done as an exercise".[267] The 12th North Staffords used the same occasion to "carry out an advanced guard scheme".[268] The brigade advanced eastward:

> After a couple of days rest we advanced through Mouveaux to Roubaix on to Wattrelos. The inhabitants of Roubaix gave us a great reception, masses of flags being in evidence. Their faces told us what they had been through during the last 4 years under the heel of the Hun. There now being a brigade in front of us, we rested for some days at Wattrelos. Here my battn had a knock. I had taken my battn … N of Wattrelos for live rifle grenade and bombing practice. The morning went off without anything of note happening. We were out again at 2pm for bombing practice. After about ¼ hour practice the Brigadier sent for me so that Capt Fleming who was there, my 2nd in Comd, carried on. While talking with the Brigadier at Brigade Hdqrs about ½ mile from the bombing ground we heard a terrific explosion which smashed all the glass in Brigade Headqrs. We were under the impression that a plane was bombing us. I returned to the bombing ground about 4pm and found that a Boche delayed mine had blown up where we were bombing. 3 of my officers were killed including Lieut Foulds who had just been awarded the MC. Capt Fleming had been thrown some yards and stunned but not seriously hurt. 6 men were killed and a dozen injured.[269]

Despite the setback, training continued as did the eastward advance towards the next major obstacle, the River Scheldt (also called the Escault).

On the night of 4/5 November 119 Brigade took over the division's front line at around Pecq on the west bank of the Scheldt with 12th North Staffords on the right and 13th East Lancs on the left.[270] The weather was wet and the permanent bridges had been demolished. There was a single plank footbridge on the ruins of the old bridge but this was submerged knee deep during the height of the flood. On the east bank was a low lying flood plain overlooked by higher ground and crossed from Pecq bridge by a narrow causeway. Both battalions pushed out daylight patrols across the river on 5 and 6 November but these were driven back by heavy machine gun fire and trench mortars.[271] On 8 November patrols again came under heavy machine gun fire but two RA officers had crossed behind them and quickly brought down artillery fire on to the German defences.[272] These patrols reported signs of impending evacuation and at 8.30 p.m. the battalions started to cross the river. "The Brigadier, determined to be first of the Army across the river, used artillery, and after slight resistance the Boche retired, with our brigade after him."[273] By 2.00 a.m.

---

266 TNA WO 95/2606: War Diary 13th East Lancs. It is interesting to note the continuing relevance/importance of *FSR*.
267 Ibid. Bondues is just north of the modern suburbs of Lille.
268 TNA WO 95/2606: War Diary 12th North Staffords.
269 NAM: Plunkett, 'Diary of the War'. Wattrelos is north-east of Lille and the adjacent town of Roubaix.
270 There is no evidence to support Crozier's assertion that the brigade 'was specially put back into the line out of their turn' – Crozier, *Brass Hat*, p.227. The 121 Brigade had formed the advance guard from 14 October and 120 Brigade from 6 October – WO 95/2594: War Diary 40th Division GS.
271 TNA WO 95/2605: War Diary 119 Brigade.
272 TNA WO 95/2606: War Diary 13th East Lancs.
273 NAM: Plunkett, 'Diary of the War'.

on 9 November they were safely across and Herrines, to the north of Pecq on the opposite bank, was occupied.[274] Through the 9 November the battalions pushed east onto the high ground. A mounted German patrol was driven off with three killed by the 13th East Lancs and by evening the battalions were as far as La Bacotterie and Clipet. By 2.00 p.m. on the 10th, patrols had pushed forward to the high ground around Haut Rejet, eleven kilometres from Pecq (as the crow flies) and corps cyclists attached to the brigade pushed on for another six kilometres.[275] From here, once contact had been made with 29th Division to the north and 69th Division to the south, the brigade, along with the rest of 40th Division, was withdrawn from the narrowing battlefront. When the armistice came into effect the brigade's units were in billets east of the Scheldt.[276]

After the Armistice

On 16 November 1918 119 Brigade retired to the town of Croix "and killed time there until coming home as a cadre in June 1919".[277] There would be no glorious march to Germany and the formation withered as men were demobilized.[278] Time was passed in training and sports and even in January 1919 bayonet fighting and physical training were being conducted by the 12th North Staffords.[279] On 18 November 12th North Staffords' officers, warrant officers and NCOs instituted a series of educational classes in French, elementary mathematics, motor engineering, agricultural science, poultry keeping, shorthand, business methods, accountancy, building construction, music and singing, magnetism and electricity, farming, carpentry and freehand drawing in the afternoon on four days per week.[280] Men not attending had arms drill. The last military gathering of the brigade was on 21 January when King's colours were presented to the three battalions in the square of Roubaix by the XV Corps Commander (De Lisle). 40th Division noted "rapid demobilization" in February.[281] On 7 March seventy-six men and ten officers of the 13th East Lancs left for the 1st East Lancs and fifty-six men and two officers left the 13th RIF for the 7th/8th RIF on 16 March. On 28 March 1919 all men of the 12th North Staffords, except the cadre (cadre strength in May was just thirty-six), left to join POW Companies at Calais and Dunkirk and on 4 June the cadre moved to Bordon, Hampshire for dispersal.[282]

There were still war-related casualties. Richard Andrews seems to have had a breakdown, telling his men in robust terms what he thought about the value of educational training and the GOC Division who encouraged it. When his behaviour was reported to Crozier, Andrews confronted his officers, seeking the informant, and had to be disarmed and arrested. Crozier says that he managed to get "matters fixed up satisfactorily" by speaking to the CO of the hospital where Andrews

---

274 TNA WO 95/2605: War Diary 119 Brigade.
275 'From Pecq the battalion had advanced 17 kilometres [sic] to furthest outpost without a casualty, keeping in touch with the enemy the whole time' – War Diary 13th East Lancs. The total distance advanced since the end of August to Pecq (in a straight line) is approximately 54 kilometres.
276 13th East Lancs in Herrines; 12th North Staffords in Chemin Vert; 13th RIF in Bois de Chin.
277 NAM: Plunkett, 'Diary of the War'. Croix is a suburb south-west of Roubaix and north-east of Lille.
278 Second Army advanced to the German frontier by 2 December. It consisted of II, III and XXII Corps, the Canadian Corps and Cavalry Corps (less one division). 40th Division and the rest of XV Corps passed *in situ* to Fifth Army on 16 November 1918. Neither 119 Brigade's war diary nor those of its battalions give figures for the progress of demobilization.
279 TNA WO 95/2606: War Diary 12th North Staffords.
280 Ibid. The war diaries of the 13th East Lancs and the 13th RIF stop at the end of March and April respectively.
281 TNA WO 95/2594: War Diary 40th Division GS.
282 TNA 95/WO 95/2606: War Diary 12th North Staffords.

was detained.²⁸³ Another victim of the mental trauma caused by war was Second-Lieutenant Eric Wetherall, 12th North Staffords. While Andrews had been more at home in the fighting than in a classroom, Wetherall certainly was not. A twenty-three year old civil servant at the Admiralty, he had been conscripted in January 1917 and was commissioned into the Labour Corps from the Artists Rifles in June. On 27 December 1918, having seen that his latest confidential report contained the phase "is not a good officer under fire", he protested to the adjutant and the CO (O'Connor) and then went to his room and shot himself.²⁸⁴ He was the brigade's final casualty overseas.

With the prospect of having no brigade to command, what was Crozier going to do? His prospects for divisional command have been discussed above. He evidently wrote to his old commander Harold Ruggles-Brise (Military Secretary, GHQ, since March 1918) to enquire about employment with the Army of Occupation. Ruggles-Brise replied:

> Many thanks for your letter. I hope you are all flourishing. If anything comes along in Germany, I will think of you. But what will the 119th Infantry Brigade do without you? ... I hear you and your men did wonders.²⁸⁵

On 26 November Crozier requested to be retained in the army at demobilization and the associated paperwork sheds some light on his reputation at the time. His request for retention was strongly supported by Peyton:

> General Crozier's services during the present campaign have been such as to bring him continuously to notice as a leader of marked ability with great capacity for the administration and training of troops, and his name has, with every confidence, been submitted for advancement to command of a Division.²⁸⁶

This note was endorsed by Lieutenant-General Beauvoir de Lisle, GOC XV Corps, on 1 December: "Brig-General Crozier is an excellent Brigade Commander in the field".²⁸⁷ The request must have been passed on by Fifth Army as it was also endorsed by Harold Ruggles-Brise, with a hint of realism: "Forwarded for such consideration as it may be possible to give. Brig-General Crozier is an excellent Brigade Commander and has proved himself a most efficient soldier".²⁸⁸ It was too late. Whether these officers knew about Crozier's early record is not certain but a note in Crozier's personal file dated 11 December indicates that someone in the Military Secretary's section at the

---

283 Crozier, *Impressions*, p.234. According to Andrews' personal file he left his unit on 24 December and embarked for the UK on 31 December, 'sick, post influenza' – TNA WO 339/59109: Personal file, Richard John Andrews. Crozier's claims to have had him released into doctor's care on medical grounds may still be true. Major H.W.D. Cox assumed command of the 13th East Lancs on 24 December. The CO 13th East Lancs gave a lecture to troops on 7 December and this may be the date of the incident – WO 95/2606: War Diary 13th East Lancs. Henry William Darling Cox DSO (1894–1970) was seconded from the 175th Battalion Canadian Expeditionary Force.
284 TNA WO 339/107802: Personal file, Eric Francis Cecil Wetherall. His captain, A.R.D. Rawlins said at the inquiry into his death, 'I considered him an unsatisfactory platoon officer in the line'. Wetherall had returned to his unit on 14 December after being invalided home with influenza on 4 November. His last letter to his mother said, 'I have no future before me with such a war record'.
285 Quoted in Grace Crozier, *Guns and God*, undated typescript biography of her husband, Frank Crozier (author's collection), p.101. The letter is undated but is likely from November 1918.
286 TNA WO 374/16997: Personal file, Frank Percy Crozier. Memorandum from Sir William Peyton to HQ XV Corps, 29 November 1918.
287 Ibid., Memorandum from GOC XV Corps to HQ Fifth Army, 1 December 1918.
288 Ibid., Memorandum from MS, GHQ to Secretary, War Office, 8 December 1918.

War Office had seen the paperwork relating to dishonoured cheques, Crozier's resignation from the Special Reserve in 1909 and his barring from the Reserve of Officers.[289] A diplomatic rejection of the application followed on 14 December. It acknowledged Crozier's good service but pointed out that there were many regular majors with equally good service records already seeking employment.[290] It did not mention past misdemeanours.

Crozier did not give up his search for employment. In February 1919 he wrote that "while in London recently" (he was on leave from 1-18 December) he had applied for employment with the Colonial Office, the Foreign Office and the Office of the First Lord of the Treasury. As he had heard nothing so far he attempted to speed things up with another letter enclosing "various reports that have been made upon me".[291] One of these was a copy of Peyton's latest report on Crozier:

> Pre-eminently a fighting leader with sound knowledge, energy and determination. The efficiency of his Brigade in all details testifies to his high power of command and organisation. It will be a great loss to the Army if he is not retained with rank and position consistent with his age and attainments.[292]

The latest application was also endorsed by the C-in-C (signed on his behalf by one of the assistant military secretaries, Lieutenant-Colonel the Honourable Eustace Vesey DSO): "in view of the circumstances set forth in the attached application and of the valuable services rendered by this officer during the war, I trust that every consideration will be afforded to his request for employment in the capacity stated."[293]

Once again he was unsuccessful. In March 1919 he assumed command of the 40th Division cadre and in April handed over to Freddy Plunkett. He returned to assume temporary command of the 3rd Welsh (the previous CO was Alexander Pope, late 12th SWB, who had died on 9 April). Crozier's file notes that he had "refused a battalion on the Rhine which was offered to him. His reason for refusing it was that he hopes to obtain an appointment in Palestine".[294] He was indeed "anxious to get to Palestine as it is a country possessing opportunities suitable to my temperament".[295] Crozier stayed with the 3rd Welsh until July. He was thwarted in his attempts to find a niche until appointed 'Inspector General' in the Lithuanian army in September.[296]

The comments on Crozier's ability quoted above also shed a little light on the reputation of 119 Brigade which was not often remarked on. John Ponsonby, writing to Crozier on 5 May 1918, wrote "I can't help feeling that whatever credit has been due to the Division has been mainly brought about by the very fine fighting spirit that has invariably existed in your Brigade".[297] As we have seen, Crozier also claimed pre-eminence for his brigade and his view receives some support

---

289 Ibid. ms annotation to file, initialled (but illegibly), 11 December 1918. For the background to Crozier's resignation see Charles Messenger, *Broken Sword: The Tumultuous Life of General Frank Crozier 1879-1937* (Barnsley: Pen and Sword, 2013), pp.35-44.
290 Ibid. Copy letter from Lieutenant-General Francis Davis, MS, War Office to C-in-C, GHQ, France, 14 December 1918.
291 Ibid. Letter from Crozier to HQ 40th Division, 5 February 1919.
292 Ibid. 'Copy of Confidential Report, Jany 1st 1919'.
293 TNA WO 374/16997: Personal file, Frank Percy Crozier. Letter from C-in-C, British Armies in France, to Secretary, War Office, 20th February, 1919.
294 Ibid. File note dated 16 April 1919. Presumably this was through the good offices of Ruggles-Brise but there is no other evidence of the offer.
295 Ibid., Letter from Crozier to HQ Western Reserve Brigade, 16 May 1919.
296 For more information on this episode (which Crozier called 'a ghastly failure') and Crozier's later life, see Messenger, *Broken Sword*.
297 RRW Museum: 99.88 W.E. Brown Scrapbook.

from the list of 'Honours and Rewards' kept for 40th Division. This bound ledger was started in 1916 and records all awards, including mentions in dispatches, mentions in divisional routine orders, brevet promotions, British and foreign honours and medals for all ranks and all divisional troops including HQ, RA, ASC and RE units.[298] There are 1,658 entries and 1,024 of these are to men of the three infantry brigades. Of these, 528 (52%) are to men of 119 Brigade, 159 (16%) are to 120 Brigade and 337 (33%) are to 121 Brigade. While some awards may have been regarded as 'coming up with the rations', and other factors such as some commanders' tendency to be generous (or not) with their recommendations for awards must be recognised, the army had instructions which should have provided for equal and fair consideration of awards.[299] The marked disparity in the scale of recognition of achievement between the three brigades is significant. This adds some support to Crozier's claims about his brigade. In the matter of awards the brigade did indeed "carry a whole division on its shoulders".[300]

---

298 NAM: 1980-02-40-33 Ruggles-Brise Papers, '40th Division Honours and Rewards'. The volume is embossed with the title and 'From Capt. A.H. Bathurst, France 1916'. Bathurst was the division's DAA&QMG.
299 See for example Military Secretary's Branch, GHQ, *Instructions Regarding Recommendations for Honours and Awards 1918* (Reprint, Naval and Military Press, no date).
300 Crozier, *Brass Hat*, p.189.

Conclusion

This study set out to investigate aspects of one of the least known formations of the British army in the Great War and to answer particular questions about 119 Brigade and the brigadier-general who commanded it from November 1916 until its disbanding in 1919. In pursuing these questions it has been necessary to establish exactly how and when the brigade and its constituent battalions came into being and what part they played in events on the Western Front from embarkation in June 1916 until the armistice in November 1918. By looking at the social background of officers and ORs it has been possible to develop a picture of the type(s) of men making up the brigade and, particularly for those units that Brigadier-General Frank Percy Crozier inherited, make an informed judgement regarding their national identity and potential *esprit de corps*. In examining the brigade in action it is possible to see key elements of how it carried out its role at the tactical level and, in particular, how these tactics were moulded by the training it carried out.

The origins of the brigade were established in Chapter 1 as part of the failed attempt to create a Welsh Army Corps of at least two divisions envisaged by David Lloyd George in September 1914. The National Executive Committee enthusiastically and very quickly took up the idea of forming bantam battalions as pioneered in Birkenhead by Alfred Bigland. The creation of more units to make a bantam brigade commenced after approval in Wales in January 1915 but was not officially sanctioned by the War Office until May. The four Welsh battalions created were the product of the pragmatic expansion of recruiting to include men of modest stature who had previously been excluded and of the ambition to create a distinct national force that embodied the Welsh (or at least Lloyd George's) view of Wales as a nation of freedom-fighters with a proven record of martial achievement in the face of larger, aggressive nations. The evidence presented in Chapter 1 demonstrates that, although the proportion of non-Welsh recruits and Welsh-speakers varied from unit to unit, the brigade can certainly be confidently regarded as 'Welsh'. This contrasts with the other brigades of 40th Division where there was no national identity and consequently less potential *esprit*.[1] These Welsh units were composed of volunteers from the labouring classes (predominantly colliers) commanded by junior officers who were students and teachers, clerks and civil servants in civilian life. Senior officers were initially selected because of their connections locally or with Wales more generally but as the war progressed COs were brought in without such connections. When the creation of a second Welsh division failed, the brigade was eventually incorporated into 40th Division where it retained its distinct identity. This was expressed by the continuing use of the term 'Welsh Bantam Brigade' and by the repeated use of 'Welshmen' or 'little Welshmen' by senior officers when referring to the brigade long after the formation left the control of the NEC. The reported reaction of the NEC Secretary to the lack of Welsh representation at the royal inspection in May 1916 attests to the clear national identity of the brigade and, as if to confirm its continuing 'Welshness', Crozier wrote to David Lloyd George in December 1917 describing the fight at Bourlon Wood.[2]

---

1 120 Brigade was briefly made up of Scottish units in spring 1918. See Chapter 5.
2 Crozier's letter is now lost but Lloyd George's reply is reproduced in Crozier, *Brass Hat*, opposite p.182.

The history of the brigade shows that it did evolve through time: both tactically, as it became more experienced and received more training, and organisationally as brigadier-generals and COs were replaced. This evolution was interrupted by two periods of sudden 'mutation' in February and June 1918 when new units were introduced. Crozier's leadership and the training carried out following his arrival produced a formation that, having spent the summer of 1916 carrying out no action larger than a trench raid, successfully captured Fifteen Ravine and the ground east of Villers-Plouich in April 1917 and raided the Hindenburg Line outpost village of La Vacquerie with some (albeit limited) success in May. The brigade that captured Bourlon Wood and held it for three days in November was substantially the original Welsh bantam brigade that Crozier had inherited one year previously. Its depleted battalions had only just been made up to strength when the February 1918 reform of divisional structures removed all but one of the original battalions from the brigade and introduced one from each of 120 and 121 Brigades. The training of these units was curtailed by the German Spring Offensives but as described in Chapter 5, they played a positive role in slowing the enemy advance in the north of the Third Army sector in March 1918. The much reduced battalions had no time for the induction of any new drafts they had received before they faced the full force of the German attack on the Lys just three weeks later. Faced with the sudden collapse of the front, some units fought on while others were quickly captured. Reserves were caught in the wrong place by the speed of the German break-in but the remnants of the brigade fought to stem the tide over three days with scratch formations. The losses on the Lys were such that 40th Division (along with others) was not deemed to be viable by GHQ and its units were disbanded or relocated. After it was reconstituted with category B men in June 1918 the brigade provides a case study of the importance of training in creating troops that can achieve the tasks demanded of them. These new units lacked local, regional or national identity and had been pulled together for a particular purpose. Originally formed for a strictly defensive role, the units of 'ex-non-combatant' men from the Labour Corps carried out attacks in conditions of open warfare from late August until the armistice and dealt with a succession of enemy rearguards using sophisticated tactics. They embody the positive evolution that the brigade had undergone.

The assessment of the quality of the brigade is a difficult task. There is certainly no doubt that 40th Division was not amongst the elite formations of the BEF.[3] Having arrived as the last New Army division to reach France it did little for six months and was undoubtedly looked upon as poor. Chapter 2 examined the issues surrounding the performance of the 35th Division's bantams during the Somme battle and developed the view that their performance did impact on the deployment of 40th Division. It also suggested that there were many elements contributing to the poor performance of 35th Division and that the perceived poor performance of that division was not directly attributable to bantam men *per se* but rather to a complex combination of factors including poor quality recruits and poor use of the division on the battlefield. The men of 119 Brigade were not given the chance to demonstrate their potential during the summer of 1916. They had been under the command of an artilleryman who was learning the basics of commanding an infantry formation and the appointment of Crozier as GOC can be seen as the deliberate introduction of energy and drive to the command of the 'bad brigade' described to Crozier on his arrival by the GSO1, 40th Division.

The perception of the performance of the brigade by the C-in-C in the following spring described in Chapter 4 was almost certainly still influenced by the negative views of the previous year. The successful actions of April were unfairly attributed to the presence of 'new' German divisions

---

3 See Paddy Griffith, *Battle Tactics of the Western Front: The British Army's Art of Attack* (London: Yale University Press, 1994), pp.79-83; Peter Simkins, 'British Divisions in the "Hundred Days", 1918' in Paddy Griffith (ed.), *British Fighting Methods in the Great War* (London: Frank Cass, 1996), pp.50-69.

that would not stand and it was not until the appointment of John Ponsonby as GOC 40th Division that Haig acknowledged that the division was 'coming on'. After Bourlon he acknowledged their 'fine fighting qualities and endurance', their 'gallant service' was mentioned in his Cambrai despatch and he was there to thank them as they marched back from the front line.[4] The evidence presented does not support Paddy Griffith's dismissive description of "the whole pathetic Bantam phenomenon" which was apparently based on his reading of Allinson's *The Bantams*.[5] Griffith also noted that 40th Division "seems to have been so little trusted that it was committed [to action] only 9 times".[6] This statement is the result of an assessment of the capability of BEF divisions by counting the number of times that each was engaged in an official operation as listed by Becke in the *Order of Battle of Divisions*.[7] Whilst this may give a broad picture of activity it is questionable whether in itself it supports the "unavoidable conclusion that the high command observed an informal 'pecking order' of divisions" as proposed by Griffith.[8] It does not include a qualitative assessment of performance in these actions, ignores actions not included by Becke and makes no allowance for heavy losses curtailing active involvement in further actions. Neither does it allow for the time actually spent in France.[9] Griffith's other conclusion, that the pecking order was based on "little more than prejudice, hearsay and the cut of the division commander's jaw", receives some support from the contrast between the negative comments made by Douglas Haig referred to above and the performance of 119 Brigade in action in 1917 and 1918.[10]

In an attempt to introduce a qualitative element into the assessment of 119 Brigade's performance 40th Division's honours and awards were analysed (Chapter 5). The possible drawbacks of this are identified but within the Division the level of recognition of achievement is considered to be an indicator of the relative success of the division's brigades. While acknowledging that all awards may not have been subjected to the same standard of rigour by battalion, brigade or divisional HQ, the difference in numbers between 119 Brigade's awards (56%) and those of the other two brigades (33% and 16%) is clearly significant. It has not been possible to extend the exercise beyond the 40th Division as a comparable and compatible dataset has not been located.

How crucial was Crozier's leadership to the development of the brigade? There is no doubt that there were other competent brigadier-generals in the British army who could have taken on the role successfully – but Crozier was there for a reason. His conduct as CO of 9th RIRifles and his action on the first day of the Somme merited recognition and this was supported by his immediate superiors. His promotion to brigadier-general and the award of the DSO were the result. His posting to command the brigade, part of a formation that had accomplished little in its first six months in France, was certainly related to the skills that he had demonstrated as a battalion commander, particularly leadership under fire, and a thirst for discipline and efficiency. His role was, in his words, 'to electrify' the brigade. The relatively poor archive of contemporary documents and memoirs left by his subordinates sheds a little light on how he achieved his goals but many of them were written after (in some cases well after) the publication of Crozier's books in the 1930s and the consequent self-destruction of his public image. All these sources must be read with this

---

4   *London Gazette*, 4 March 1918, p.2721.
5   Griffith, *Battle Tactics*, p.236, fn.72; Sidney Allinson, *The Bantams: The Untold Story of World War 1* (London: Howard Baker, 1981).
6   Griffith, *Battle Tactics*, p.81.
7   A.F. Becke, *Order of Battle of Divisions, Parts 1-4* (London: HMSO, 1934-1945).
8   Griffith, *Battle Tactics*, p.82.
9   For comparison the 41st Division, which arrived in France one month before the 40th Division, was in action fourteen times according to Becke. Two of these were during the 1916 Somme battles when the 40th Division was being ignored on account of its bantam status. Three were during Operation '*Michael*' – compared with 40th Division's two – when the 41st division was able to continue longer in the front line.
10 Griffith, *Battle Tactics*, p.82.

in mind and used carefully. Chapter 3 described how and why Crozier's books were produced and examined their impact on his reputation and their use as (un)reliable sources.

As we have seen, Crozier projected an image of himself as a hard man with extreme views on discipline. He certainly believed in the efficacy of the death penalty as a deterrent to others and argued later against its removal.[11] Yet, despite the regular association of his name with one execution by authors, it was the only execution that occurred during his command of the 9th RIRifles and there were none at all during his command of 119 Brigade. His attitude seems to have been more flexible in matters of discipline than has been recognised. He turned a blind eye in the case of Captain George Gaffikin, 9th RIRifles, on receipt of a promise of sobriety and he "tore up" the request by a CO for the trial by court martial on a capital charge of an un-named "little Welshman", recognising that the man's evacuation of a front line post (that he later reoccupied) during a sudden bombardment was common sense, not cowardice.[12] His apparent addiction to summary justice as a way of keeping men to the task in hand perhaps has a core of truth. Crozier seems to have made it clear to his men that in fleeing they risked death from his and other officer's pistols but such a standpoint was not uncommon among BEF officers – we have seen in Chapter 3 how Major-General Nugent implied as much in his address to the officers of the Ulster Division.[13] Crozier's mantra of 'if you run, I will shoot' repeated within the pages of his books might be interpreted as just another device to emphasise the horror of war. Yet the incident on the road to Strazeele as described by Crozier leaves the impression that it did take place in a moment of extreme stress and 'in hot blood'. This event and the other examples cited in Chapter 5, may actually have occurred but will probably remain 'not proven'. Crozier's view on the matter of summary justice may have been more nuanced than it appears. In one book he states clearly (and apparently without realising that it contradicted his stated position) that "I did not and do not think positions can be held by using threats".[14] As an efficient soldier with a need to get the job done, he surely recognised that summary execution "destroyed the element of trust which lay at the heart of the officer-man relationship".[15] It is going too far to use Crozier as representative of "a tiny handful of officers [who] did make a practice of summary execution" without qualifying the statement.[16]

Crozier's style could certainly be brusque. He called a spade a spade. In Chapter 4 we read how Wilfred Spender commented on the roughness and ruthless way that Crozier handled the men of the 9th RIRifles while acknowledging his courage and leadership. One of his staff officers told him long after the war that "he disliked the way I handled and treated the divisional staff above me".[17] Harry Graham also noted from his own position as ADC to John Ponsonby, GOC 40th Division, that Crozier "was not well liked". Yet he also inspired loyalty. We saw how Captain Montgomery, 9th RIRifles, respected him, how Crozier tried to help Montgomery by requesting his services, how two of his COs, Plunkett and Andrews, came back after illness and wounds to serve under him and how Lieutenant Lamb thought him 'awfully nice'. Starrett stayed with him throughout the war and helped Crozier afterwards. An ex-soldier from 121 Brigade noted how "he was always

---

11 *Daily Mirror*, 31 March 1930, p.3. Crozier argued for the retention of the death penalty for cowardice but its abolition in cases of treachery and mutiny. See also F.P. Crozier, *Impressions and Recollections* (London: Werner Laurie, 1930), pp.170-171 for his views on the death sentence.
12 F.P. Crozier, *A Brass Hat in No Man's Land* (London: Jonathan Cape, 1930), pp.68-73; F.P. Crozier, *The Men I Killed* (London: Michael Joseph, 1937), p.181.
13 See Gary Sheffield, *Leadership in the Trenches: Officer-Man Relations, Morale and Discipline in the British Army in the Era of the First World War* (London: Macmillan, 2000), p.149, for other examples.
14 Crozier, *Impressions*, p.219.
15 Sheffield, *Leadership*, p.149.
16 Ibid.
17 Crozier, *The Men I Killed*, p.66.

looked upon as someone a little different from the old school of Brass Hats".[18] Crozier was a strong-willed individual. The origins of his willpower and drive to succeed may lie in his small stature and the adoration of his flawed soldier father but such speculation needs to be informed by psychological expertise. One manifestation of his willpower was his abstinence from alcohol from 1910 until his death – a remarkable achievement through times of great stress. If anyone doubted the truth of this, in 1925 Sir William Peyton confirmed (for reasons unknown) that "I know as an absolute fact that from the commencement of the war until the present time he [Crozier] has been a strict teetotaller".[19] Captain Eric Whitworth's observation that Crozier was a 'hustler' (Chapter 4) unintentionally confirms his energy and drive but the use of a term with such negative connotations was influenced by Whitworth's own background as a well-educated young man (Radley; Trinity College, Cambridge) and a volunteer.[20] After the previous more 'gentlemanly' brigadier-generals that Whitworth had encountered, Crozier would have appeared blunt and driven but he did, as Whitworth grudgingly acknowledged, get things done.

There is no doubt that he set an example by his own physical courage. We have read in earlier chapters how both David Starrett and Malcolm McKee comment on it in their accounts of the first day of the Somme. To McKee Crozier was a 'tiger' while later to Freddy Plunkett he was a 'thorough fighter' with 'no sentiment'. To Harry Graham he was also a tiger and 'absolutely fearless', a 'splendid man in a tight place'. Robert Graves quotes an ex-19th RWF sergeant who called Crozier reverently "a mad gentlemen", going on to explain that this was a compliment.[21] An annotation in his personal file states "a fighting brigadier" and a transcription of a memorandum from Sir R.D. Whigham includes "his record as a fighting soldier is excellent".[22] The fact that he remained in command of his brigade for over two years indicates that courage was just one facet of his character. Gary Sheffield notes that there are two functions in leadership: the creation and sustaining of unit cohesion (a broadly managerial function) and the moulding of the cohesive group as part of the greater organisation.[23] Crozier has been seen to have carried out both functions. While he was assisted in the organisational aspects of brigade command by a succession of staff officers that he could rely on, it is revealing to note the comments (Chapter 5) by Sir William Peyton. Acknowledging Crozier's leadership skills, Peyton highlights his "great capacity for the administration and training of troops" and "his high power of command and organisation". These are crucial aspects which have been overshadowed by the image of Crozier as Stewart-Moore's

---

18 C.G. Gardiner, late 12th Suffolks, 121 Brigade, quoted in Grace Crozier, *Guns and God*, undated typescript biography of her husband, Frank Crozier (author's collection), p.155. In one letter Crozier called himself a 'Bashi Bazook' [sic]. *Bashi Bazouk* was originally a Turkish appellation for a mercenary with poor discipline and came to mean a bandit – Liddell Hart Archive: LH 1/207/5. Letter from Crozier to Liddell Hart, 29 August 1932.
19 TNA: WO 374/16997: Personal File F.P. Crozier. Memorandum from Military Secretary, Sir William Peyton, to unnamed Parliamentary Under Secretary, 21 November 1925.
20 The term 'hustle' has developed greater negative connotations since the Great War when its meaning was to push on or jostle. Whitworth's usage of the term is negative none the less.
21 Robert Graves, 'A Brass Hat in No Man's Land Reviewed by Robert Graves', *Now and Then* (Summer 1930), pp.5-7. '"He was a mad gentleman" said Sergeant H ----- reverently. This was praise usually applied only to young platoon commanders and it surprised me. "Gentleman" meant a man who was not too much on his dignity with the troops under his command and expected nothing from them that he would not do himself. "Mad", a term still in use in the RAF, meant "recklessly brave".' When a platoon had a mad gentleman in command it responded by relaxing its own dignity … and by proving that it could be as reckless as he'.
22 TNA: WO 374/16997: Personal File F.P. Crozier. Transcribed memorandum from Whigham, 13 November 1925. Robert Dundas Whigham (1865-1950) was GOC VII Corps, April – June 1918 and had been appointed Adjutant-General to the Forces in 1923.
23 Sheffield, *Leadership*, pp.42-43.

'callous and overbearing martinet'. This evidence in this book shows that he was not simply lucky to remain in post; he was an effective and efficient commander.

Does Crozier's claim to have removed a brigade major, a brigade signalling officer, nearly a dozen commanding officers, a few seconds in command, three adjutants, several doctors, quartermasters and transport officers and one or two sergeant majors stand up to scrutiny? There was a certainly a significant turnover of battalion COs in 119 Brigade. Plunkett's comment that he "had the doubtful honour of being the only CO who lasted three months" in summer 1918 indicates that the turnover was a recognised phenomenon. Oliver Nugent told Crozier that he "had cut off too many heads". Yet it remains unclear exactly how he did this. The selection and posting of new COs was not within his remit (Crozier acknowledges the role of the COs 'Pool') and was the responsibility of the Military Secretary at GHQ.[24] While it was apparently possible for a divisional commander to exercise some influence over postings – as seen in the case of John Ponsonby and H.C. Metcalfe (Chapter 5) – it is not likely that a brigadier-general could operate in a similar fashion. Crozier had to work with the material that he was given. He believed that "Four good colonels, *well backed up* [his emphasis], make a good brigade".[25] If the CO was not efficient and effective in Crozier's eyes he implies that he removed them. Even if, as he asserts, two of the divisional commanders under whom he served gave him a 'free hand' it is not likely that his authority extended to the removal of battalion COs. It is probable that a bad report from Crozier to higher authority would result in the replacement of a CO and that this might be accomplished quickly as, for example, in the case of Lieutenant-Colonel C.B. Hore, OC 17th Welsh, in January 1917 following the surge in cases of trench foot in the battalion. Sometimes, however, Crozier has not been accurate in reporting the timescale or circumstances of a CO's departure as seen in the case of Lieutenant-Colonel Alan Bryant, Hore's replacement. Here Crozier's description of events is shown to be at odds with the facts and was likely constructed to boost his own image as an efficient and effective commander and diminish that of a subordinate. In the case of Arthur Soames, the Brigade Major, posting to a training course (presumably on Crozier's recommendation) was the method used to remove him from his appointment. Unfortunately, there is no evidence to confirm the removal of the other officers and WOs as claimed by Crozier. In the case of the COs matters are clearer. With the exception of the appointment of Lieutenant-Colonel Andrews as OC 12th North Staffords at the end of the war, when Crozier deliberately ignored the role of 'the Base', there was a turnover which was initiated by Crozier although he exaggerated his part in the decision making process.

The results of evolution by Crozier's selection were three successive generations of the brigade, starting with the Welsh Bantam Brigade in 1917 and then the reorganised three-battalion brigade of February 1918 that did not have the chance to develop its full potential and finally, the new brigade of June 1918 composed of category B men. This book has concentrated on aspects of the first of these because of its unique origin as a part of the WAC and its bantam composition and yet it is the creation of the last that clearly demonstrates that Crozier's ability was beyond simply that of a man who was good in a fight.

To modern historians Crozier remains "not an easy man to like".[26] Some at least of the men who served with him had another view: "I had the privilege of serving under General Crozier and I think that all who did so … agree with me in that we knew him as a very fine General, a wonderful

---

24 The details of the operation of the Military Secretary's department at GHQ remain unknown and are being investigated at the time of writing – Professor J.M. Bourne personal correspondence.
25 Crozier, *Impressions*, p.161.
26 Brian Bond, *Survivors of a Kind: Memoirs of the Western Front* (London: Continuum, 2008), p.129.

soldier and a very brave man. If any suggests otherwise – they are wrong."[27] Basil Liddell Hart noted that "some who had wide experience considered that he was the best brigade commander they saw in action and quote his share in the capture of Bourlon Wood as an epic feat of arms."[28] Was 119 Infantry Brigade a 'bad brigade'? The evidence demonstrates that it was not.

---

[27] Lieutenant-Colonel G.F.P. Worthington, letter written in 1937, quoted in Grace Crozier, *Guns and God*, undated typescript biography of her husband, Frank Crozier (author's collection), p.154. As a captain, Worthington had been temporarily promoted to command the 21st Middlesex during the Lys battles.

[28] *The Times*, 4 September 1937.

Postscript

Remembrance

There is no memorial to the 119 Infantry Brigade. In April 1919, prompted by the formation of the War Office Battle Exploits Memorial Committee, the *Western Mail* called for the urgent formation of 'an influential and representative working committee' to formulate an application for a memorial in Bourlon Wood which had the 'most enthusiastic support' of Brigadier-General Crozier.[1] Whether the committee was formed and an application submitted is not known but, if it was, it was not among the 93 proposals approved by May 1921.[2] Bourlon Wood now contains one of the memorials to Canadian forces to mark their capture of the wood in 1918. The only battalion of the original brigade to have its own memorial is the 17th Welsh. Originally intended as a memorial to Lieutenant-Colonel Wilkie, who was killed in action in 1916, the idea was first proposed in December 1916 by Major Gilbert and quickly approved by Wilkie's widow. The design work would be carried out by Alice Meredith Williams, the very capable wife of Lieutenant Morris Meredith Williams, late of the 17th Welsh, and would take the form of a stained-glass window and associated plaques in St Basil's Church, Bassaleg, Monmouthshire close to the Wilkies' home.[3] The slow development of the scheme allowed it to be modified before completion to form a memorial to all the casualties of the now disbanded battalion. It was finally unveiled on 19 February 1921 by Crozier (having just resigned from his post with the ADRIC) who made a speech praising the battalion's record, in the presence of several officers of the battalion including Richard Andrews and Percy Hone.[4]

The single surviving relic of the 18th Welsh, the King's Colour presented by the Prince of Wales in France in 1918, is displayed framed in All Saints Church, Porthcawl where it was laid up in June 1919. Another flag with tentative links to the brigade via Lieutenant-Colonel Pope is the much-battered red dragon flag of the 3rd Welsh laid up in St Mary's Church, Stratton, Dorset above the memorial plaque to Pope and his brother-in-law A.R. Haig-Brown. The flag was passed to Pope's father by Crozier who was CO of the battalion briefly in 1919. He wrote: 'You are entitled to it by the laws of merit. It is the flag of the 3rd Welch, which flew at their Quarter Guard from August 4/14 to July 20/19 and must have been saluted daily at Retreat by your son, both at the

---

1   *Western Mail*, 3 April 1919. The Battle Exploits Memorial Committee was formed in April 1919 to allocate memorial sites for British, Indian and Dominion forces in consultation with the IWGC to avoid competition and duplication. Memorials were meant to mark 'significant engagements that contributed to victory'. The committee hoped that 'as a rule' proposals from divisions and higher formations would be forthcoming but at least six brigades and forty-two 'lesser formations' applied. *The Scotsman*, 28 August 1919.
2   *Army and Navy Gazette*, 7 May 1921.
3   Phyllida Shaw, *Undaunted Spirit: The Art and Craft of Gertrude Alice Meredith Williams* (Independent Publishing Network, 2018).
4   *Western Mail*, 21 February 1919.

very beginning of the war, and in '17, '18 and '19 when he was in command'.[5] None of the replacement battalions of the brigade were marked by a specific memorial until, in 1964, the 13th East Surrey was finally given its own memorial in the form of a plaque in the grounds of Wandsworth Town Hall.

The 40th Division's memorial is the altar at Bourlon Church which was dedicated on 27 May (Whit Sunday) 1928 'in memory of those of the Division that fell in Bourlon Wood in November 1917'.[6] The memory of Bourlon and the division's history were also perpetuated through the meetings of the 40th Division Dinner Club which met in various London restaurants, including the Café Royal and Savoy, from 1921 to 1938 on the anniversary of the battle at Bourlon Wood. Crozier does not appear in any of the lists of guests attending. The event was advertised and reported in *The Times* and only officers attended.[7] Other divisional troops also held regular reunions. The 40th Divisional Artillery were still meeting in 1938 (at the Trocadero, London in this instance) and the Divisional Signal Company R.E. met for its rather more inclusive Annual Parade and Reunion at the 'Danum Estaminet' (the Danum Hotel), Doncaster, where a memorial plaque to the 40th Divisional RE had been installed in the Mansion House in 1920.[8] The officers of the 17th Welsh met in Cardiff for their second reunion dinner on the day of the unveiling of the Bassaleg memorial and there exists in the Imperial War Museum collections an address list for the 18th Welsh Officers' Association but whether it ever met is not known.[9] The 19th RWF were still holding their annual reunion dinner at the War Memorial Club Wrexham in 1937.[10] Of the 'new' battalions the officers of the 13th East Surrey held their 16th reunion dinner at Gatti's Restaurant, London in April 1937.[11]

The largest number of the brigade's dead are found inscribed on the memorial to the missing of the battle of Cambrai at Louverval where the eighty percent of the brigade's Bourlon fatalities that have no known grave are commemorated. Those same names and many others appear on war memorials, gravestones and family memorials across the length and breadth of the United Kingdom and particularly in South Wales. When Frank Crozier died at the height of the controversy over his final book, his low-key cremation on 3 September 1937 at Woking Crematorium was protected by a special police guard in case of demonstrations.[12] His ashes were interred in the garden of his last home in Walton on Thames but his wife, who did not stay there for long after his death, hoped that they might one day be laid at the side of the memorial to his distant ancestor Sir Harry Burrard Neale (1765-1840) at Lymington, Hampshire.[13] The ultimate fate of his remains is unknown and there is no memorial to the most well-known and most controversial commander of 119 Brigade.

---

5 Quoted in *Stratton Dorset War Memorial* <http://www.strattondorset.com/war-memorial-pope-e.htm> (accessed 20 February 2021).
6 *Yorkshire Post*, 5 May 1928 and Web Matters Carte de Route First World War <http://www.webmatters.net/index.php?id=674> (accessed 20 February 2021).
7 For example, *The Times*, 26 November 1937.
8 Menu cards 40th Divisional Artillery, 12 November 1938 and 40th Divisional Signals Company RE, 4 February 1928. Author's collection.
9 *Western Mail*, 21 February 1919; IWM 72/11/1: Papers of Captain B.D. Gibbs, 18th Welsh.
10 *Staffordshire Sentinel*, 4 September 1937.
11 *The Times*, 30 April 1935.
12 *Sunderland Daily Echo*, 3 September 1937.
13 Grace Crozier, *Guns and God*, unpublished typescript, p.214. The illustrious Admiral Burrard (later Burrard Neale) was the uncle of Crozier's paternal grandmother.

Appendix I

Bourlon and Mametz: A brief comparison

[Bourlon] was the second occasion in the war when a splendid piece of woodland fighting was carried through by the men of the Principality, and even Mametz was not a finer performance than Bourlon."[1]

The attacks of the 38th (Welsh) Division at Mametz Wood in July 1916 have, as was shown by the scale of the centenary commemorations, become part of the national identity of Wales. The evocative writing of Llewelyn Wyn Griffith in *Up to Mametz*, the epic poem *In Parenthesis* by David Jones and mentions in the novels of Graves and Sassoon have given a few days of ferocious woodland fighting a cultural importance well beyond their military significance but the attack at Mametz Wood continues to generate publications.[2] So much so that the fight has become a "proxy for the Welsh experience" of the war. This situation has been challenged in recent years by Chris Williams who has published a more measured and impartial appraisal of the battle and of 38th (Welsh) Division.[3] Williams believes that Mametz Wood "should not act as a surrogate for the war-time efforts of all Welsh soldiers and points out that the "Welsh experience of the war clearly neither began nor ended at Mametz Wood". It is hoped that this brief note about Mametz and Bourlon will help to promote that assessment.

Fourth Army regarded the capture of Mametz Wood, along with the village of Contalmaison to its west, as an essential first step in securing a line from which to assault the German second position in that part of the Somme battlefield. Mametz Wood is smaller than Bourlon Wood (approximately 1.64 square kilometres compared with 2.93 square kilometres) and is elongated along its north/south axis. Like Bourlon, it was divided by a central north/south ride and there were two significant cross rides dividing the wood into six unequal parts. The western flank was protected by a fortified re-entrant valley which was itself flanked by Contalmaison. On the south east corner an irregular projection of the wood known as the 'Hammerhead' flanked its southern edge and was in turn flanked by Flatiron and Sabot Copses which were in German hands. The land sloped gently from the open ground on the south and continued rising through the wood

---

[1] Arthur Conan Doyle, *The British Campaign in France and Flanders 1917* (London: Hodder and Stoughton, 1919), p.260.

[2] Llewelyn Wyn Griffith, *Up To Mametz* (London: Faber, 1931); David Jones, *In Parenthesis* (London: Faber, 1937); Robert Graves, *Goodbye To All That* (London: Cape, 1929); Frank Richards, *Old Soldiers Never Die* (London: Faber, 1933); Siegfried Sassoon, *Memoirs of an Infantry Officer* (London: Faber, 1930); Jonathon Riley, *Ghosts of Old Companions: Lloyd George's Welsh Army, The Kaiser's Reichsheer and the Battle for Mametz Wood, 1914-1916* (Warwick: Helion and Company, 2019).

[3] Chris Williams, 'A Question of 'Legitimate Pride'? The 38th (Welsh) Division at the Battle of Mametz Wood, July 1916', *Welsh History Review/Cylchgrawn Hanes Cymru*, 28:4 (2017), pp.723-752.

to its northern edge. The trees were dense and two years of growth had produced a thick mass of shrubs and brambles beneath them.

The task of taking the wood was given to XV Corps whose 17th and 38th Divisions would attack the left and right flanks of the wood respectively. It would be 38th Division's first offensive action. A preliminary assault on the left was driven off and a second attack went in on the morning of 7 July 1916 while the 38th Division attacked westwards across open ground towards the 'Hammerhead'. Originally planned by Brigadier-General H.J. Evans (115 Brigade) as an attack by two battalions on a one battalion front, it was (for reasons that remain unclear) extended to a two battalion front. This pushed the right flank much closer to enfilading German machine guns in the copses. Zero was at 8.30 a.m. A planned smoke barrage was not delivered and the totally exposed attacking battalions never reached the wood. "It would be difficult to imagine a more suicidal direction of attack than that chosen by XV Corps for the 115th Brigade."[4] Further artillery support was at first refused by XV Corps which remained convinced that two battalions were sufficient for the task. When a renewed barrage materialised it fell short. In the afternoon the failure was reinforced as a third battalion was fed in. Further attack plans were abandoned in the evening. There were over 400 casualties among the three attacking battalions for no gain.[5]

On 8/9 July another attack on the western edge of the wood was preceded by confusion over the scale of the action which led to it being called off. Next day Major-General Sir Ivor Philipps was removed from command of 38th Division (Major-General T.D. Pilcher, GOC 17th Division followed on 11 July) and was replaced temporarily by Major-General H.E. Watts, GOC 7th Division. Watts immediately put in place plans for a much larger attack by the two brigades of 38th Division that had not been involved on 7 July, supported by the depleted 115 Brigade. East of the central ride 114 Brigade attacked on a two-battalion front while to the west the 113 Brigade attacked into a narrower space on a one-battalion front. Zero was 4.15 a.m. and this time the barrage contained covering smoke. Despite setbacks, the wood was entered and by 5.00 a.m. the first objective (the first cross-ride) was reached. Fighting within the wood was confused and at close quarters. Problems were caused by the British barrage falling short at times and communications with the rear were dependent on runners and were consequently very slow. The barrage did not stop German reinforcements arriving but by evening the wood was cleared to within forty metres of its northern edge despite some shaky moments when panic spread amongst groups within the wood. By now Contalmaison and the western re-entrant had also fallen to 23rd and 17th Divisions respectively. Overnight a line 200 metres from the northern edge of the wood was consolidated. No major counter attacks had taken place. Next day the wood was almost cleared but, as troops approached the northern edge, they became visible from the German second position and withdrew to the 200 metre position once more. The exhausted troops were relieved on the morning of 12 July 1916 by 62 Brigade (21st Division) who completed the capture of the wood. The Welsh had taken more than 400 German prisoners and thirteen guns. Casualties were almost 4,000 all ranks including seven battalion commanders.[6] Douglas Haig wrote "What effect on the division has a good commander!"[7]

---

4 Colin Hughes, *Mametz: Lloyd George's 'Welsh Army' at the Battle of the Somme* (London: Gliddon Books, 1990), p.92.
5 Hughes, *Mametz*; Michael Renshaw, *Mametz Wood* (Barnsley: Pen and Sword, 2006); Jonathan Hicks, *The Welsh at Mametz Wood: The Somme 1916* (Talybont: Y Lolfa, 2016); Wilfred Miles, *Military Operations France and Belgium 1916*, Vol. 2 (London: Macmillan, 1938).
6 Miles, *Military Operations, 1916,* Vol. II, p.54.
7 Haig Ms Diary quoted in Hughes, *Mametz*, p.116.

> The terrain [was] a defender's dream. In such conditions it was extremely difficult to maintain control over troops. Visibility was very restricted, many officers (the only ones with compasses) had become casualties in the initial assault, and it was no easy matter for troops to work out in which direction they should be heading or where the enemy might be hiding. Telephone lines were easily cut and communications became reliant on runners, themselves often caught in artillery barrages. Soldiers from different units became jumbled together, there were casualties from artillery and small-arms 'friendly fire'.[8]

This description by Chris Williams is of Mametz Wood. It could just as easily be Bourlon. In Chapter One we saw how 119 Brigade shared a common ancestry with 38th Division and both formations had a strong national identity. The attacks at Mametz and Bourlon by Welsh units have some common features but some significant differences. Both woods were dense and difficult to traverse; both were on rising ground (though Bourlon was a steeper climb); both were subdivided by rides and both were flanked by strongpoints – the copses and Contalmaison in the case of Mametz and the villages of Fontaine and Bourlon in the case of Bourlon Wood. It took five days for 38th Division to capture Mametz and just one day for 119 Brigade to capture Bourlon. Both actions were planned at short notice but at Mametz a number of factors combined to produce a failure at the first attempt: poor planning; no smoke screen; inexperience; inadequate and inaccurate artillery fire and confusion caused by interference from XV Corps which dictated inappropriate tactics. At Bourlon, artillery fire was (mainly) accurate and visual signalling facilitated reasonable response times. Despite the lack of smoke the more experienced troops of 119 Brigade pressed home their attack. The ultimate success of the action at Mametz was due largely to the weight of numbers used which surprised the Germans and prevented serious counter attack. At Bourlon, the wood was taken by one brigade rather than a whole division but the problem then was how to hold it with limited reinforcements against repeated, aggressive counter attacks.

The most significant difference between these two attacks, separated by just fifteen months, was in the level of training and experience of the troops at all levels.[9] Mametz was at the start of the BEF's learning process while Bourlon was some way into it. Brigade staffs were inexperienced and internal communication was poor in July 1916.[10] In the opinion of G.P.L. Drake-Brockman, one of Major-General Watts' staff, Ivor Philipps' wish that attacks should not be continued in the face of machine gun fire also undermined discipline and morale and led to half-hearted attacks.[11] In the aftermath of Mametz there was said to be a widespread belief that the 38th Division had 'bolted'.[12] 113 Brigade COs were told later "that the word 'retire' is not to be used and that any man using it is likely to be shot on the spot. Officers must deal with all cases of indiscipline of this nature which can only be stamped out by the most drastic action."[13] Despite its significant achievements in 1917 and 1918, the reputation of 38th Division took some time to recover from Mametz while 119 Brigade's was enhanced by the success at Bourlon but it is the former battle that still attracts the most attention. The valour of Welsh troops in both actions is worthy of wider recognition.

---

8   Williams, 'A Question of 'Legitimate Pride', p.732.
9   Henry Horne, GOC XV Corps, wrote about 38th Division on 13 July 1916 after the capture of Mametz Wood: 'this division is not yet sufficiently trained to take part in an attack' – Horne to Fourth Army quoted in Simon Robbins, *British Generalship in the Great War: The Military Career of Sir Henry Horne (1861-1929)* (London: Ashgate, 2010), p.118.
10 Hughes, *Mametz*, p.134.
11 Ibid. p.138.
12 Ibid. p.139.
13 Ibid. p.136. Quoting WO/95 2552 War Diary 113 Brigade, message dated 16 July 1916.

Appendix II

40th Division Cambrai – Original Plan for Advance to the Sensée River

Secret 119th Inf. Bde. No.39/249/G.L.

NOTES ON CONFERENCE AT BRIGADE H.Q. SUNDAY NOV. 18TH. 1917

1. <u>Shell Fire</u> There will no doubt be a lot of shell fire. The Boche has got a lot of guns. Men must be impressed with the fact that shell fire cannot be accepted as an excuse for not going on. Rifle fire at close range may stop people but shell fire must not.
Men must go on irrespective of what fire there is.

2. The Best flank is his most vulnerable flank.

3. <u>Discipline</u> The whole of our success for this show depends upon the fitness of the men when they reach a certain point. Men must be as fresh as possible. Marching, fighting and digging all the same day. Men must be told later on and the whole thing explained to them. COs to lecture the Battalion on this subject so that he knows every man has been told.
Units must not parade before necessary.

4. Packs and equipment to be taken off at halts.

5. At least 10 officers must be left behind, but at least 21 officers must be taken.

6. Battalions are to be not less than 500 strong. Officers, NCOs on leave, courses and men at the Depot Bn. may be included in those left behind, so that if the GOC wants 'A' or 'B' Battalion, he knows there are 500 men there.

7. 2nds in Command and Coy Commanders must proceed with the Battalion. COs should make the greatest use of his [sic] 2nd i/c. He is to be at Bn HQ when the CO is not there. He is useful for finding out information.

8. Mounted officers to be told that they must make the utmost use of their horses. They do not do so at present.
A Coy Commander following up an attack will keep his horse moderately close under cover. He can use his horse if necessary.

9. Blankets, greatcoats and haversacks will be dumped at Brigade dump. Men will carry cardigan, jerkin, 2 iron rations and unexpired portion of the day's ration, also at least one spare pair of socks.
    GOC Division wants an inspection of this equipment to be carried out most rigidly by Battalion Commanders.

10. 120 rounds SAA to be carried. No unauthorised stuff, presents or souvenirs to be carried.
    The whole success of the operation depends on the condition of the men when they arrive at their place. If they arrive done, they will be done.
    Waterproof sheet to be carried under the flap so that it can be got at.
    Bombs, SAA, etc., will be equally divided among 4 limber wagons. 2 of these will form Echelon 'A'.
    The Staff Captain will go into this matter with COs and see what adjustments will be necessary.

11. Flares are going to be WHITE. This is the Corps colour. They will <u>not</u> be issued at the rate of 2 per man. 1500 are being issued per Brigade. There must be a careful re-adjustment of flares.
    A certain proportion are to be kept in reserve at Bn. HQ., as it is possible that men with flares will be knocked out.
    The method of carrying these will be as already laid [out].

12. <u>Stokes</u> 1 limber wagon will be detached from the DAC to each Brigade to carry 2 Stokes guns and 108 shells.
    Remainder of guns to be left at the dump in the Brigade Area. 2 Mortars will be in Brigade Reserve.

13. 110 long handled wire cutters will be issued to each Brigade. They are to be carried in the Battalion tool cart.

14. <u>Baggage</u> Officers baggage is to be cut down to 35lbs. All baggage wagons will be parked in the BAPAUME Area under Divisional arrangements. Officers are to be warned that they may not see their kits for about 3 days.

15. <u>Water</u> Water is scarce. Water tins will be issued to Units and carried empty on the carts.

16. The policy is to let civilians remain where they are. Arrangements can be made to send them away later.
    If they want to get away, warn the Brigade.

17. Battalion Commander, 2nd i/c, Adjutant, Intelligence Officer and Signalling Officer, remainder to make up to 21.

18. As regards Lewis Gunners and people at Schools these are to be counted out.

19. Part II Infantry Training is to be thoroughly gone into. Instructions impressed upon all officers.

20. We go tomorrow night to ROCQUIGNY which is close to YTRES.

NOTES ON OPERATIONS

1. The chief element of this operation is one of absolute surprise. No gossiping. Ample time if Coy Commanders are told tomorrow.

2. The attack itself is going to begin from GONNELIEU South to CROISELLE in the north. The north performance will be bluff but no gas will be discharged. The main idea is to break through from GONNELIEU to north of HAVRINCOURT WOOD on a 2 Corps front. This sector is quieter than ever.

3. On that front 350 tanks are going to be employed to cut wire. The 2 Corps that are in the line will follow up.

4. Zero will be within the next 2 or 3 days.

5. Cavalry are to push on and isolate CAMBRAI and seize bridgeheads over the Canal running East and West North of CAMBRAI.
   The 36 Division do not go forward but the way is going to be cleared for them from SE to NE and when this cleared that Division will be used.
   The 29th Division are following up the people who go over first.
   We go up from ROCQUIGNY on 2 roads, BAPAUME – CAMBRAI Rd and the other running through DOIGNES – GRAINCOURT – LES HAVRINCOURT – ANNEUX – ST OLLE – SANCOURT.
   The objective of the Division is the high ground north of the canal already alluded to, the bridgeheads of which will be seized by the Cavalry.

6. It is not yet known which brigade goes on which road. The 120th Brigade will probably go on the BAPAUME – CAMBRAI RD.

7. Provided the Cavalry have already collared their Bridgeheads, the first task will be the occupation of the high ground the left of which is to the north of the village of BUGNIECOURT on the left, the high ground of the village of ERCHIN being held as an advanced post. It is very commandeering [sic] ground. There is a wood there which will have to be held called LA GARENNE.
   The Divisional Commander has not yet decided as to whether the rest of the high ground from FRESSAIN to WAVRECHAIN will be held, or whether we will hold in a more N.E. direction the high ground just north of MONCHECOURT running out into a spur north of EMERICOURT south of ANICHE.
   We have got the advantage of holding the north of the high ground farther away from the marshes.

8. You will see that this amounts approximately to a 2-brigade front, 1 in Divisional reserve somewhere on the left.
   Divisional mounted troops will be 2 squadrons of Cavalry and 2 companies of Cyclists. They will be withdrawn when they have done their work on the right of the South of the Canal.
   The Boche has on that front where the main attack will be pushed through, 2 Divisions whose morale is not very good, consequently it is hoped to get through. If he can bring reserves into CAMBRAI it will present another feature.

DOUAI is a place where concentrations can take place, and it is from that direction that a counter attack may be expected, this is the reason that the Brigade in Divisional reserve is somewhat on the left.

Orders will be issued to secure the high ground and to hold it at all costs.

9. Subalterns must therefore be told to be more particular than ever in the siting of their trenches and the matter is one which is one for them, as we have not enough supervision to go all round. They will dig for their lives.

If this Brigade is there, Battalions in reserve will be sent up to dig should the opportunity occur and the Works Coy will work under the RE.

10. The Brigade Transport Officer will have to be prepared if necessary to take up wire and short stakes.

When we started in April last the whole of the trenches were spoilt by undercutting.

11. Visual signalling must be established at all costs.

12. In the event of the bridges being destroyed, COs must let the GOC know the exact state of what they want and must look about for every expedient to crossing. In any case a thorough reconnaissance of the river is wanted.

Division are to let us have later on information regarding fords. It is not certain if there are any.

13. In all probability your right will be in the air and a strong flank guard probably need to be thrown out. Your left should be fairly secure.

It is possible that after the Bridgeheads and high grounds have been seized by the Cavalry, villages etc may hold out as strong points. On the other hand it is possible that you might have quite easy marching on the BAPAUME – CAMBRAI RD under peace conditions.

The idea is that CAMBRAI should not be entered for some time, except by selected people and that steps must be taken to see that it is not destroyed by fire.

There are 2 Div HQrs in CAMBRAI which is hoped to seize and 1 at EPINOY which may come into our operations.

14. The idea is to go up by steps and possibly we may have a few hours at DOIGNES. Major GOUGH is now there with some men putting in Soyer Stoves, where food will be dished out. You will see the object is to get the men up fresh.

There will possibly be a few hours halt a DOIGNES, and then go through. Men are to be rested as much as possible and hours of silence are to be in all camps. Everybody is to be sure of getting sleep.

The question of whether tents will be struck; it may be by day if it is fine. COs will find out from Town Majors re striking tents.

15. Orders will be of the briefest when we get to ROCQUIGNY, and as clear as possible. They must be acknowledged.

SDRs will be sent whenever necessary. There will be a lot of work to do afterwards and the men are to be saved as much as possible.

Brigade Signals to be made up by runners from Battalions.

Caps are to be stored in haversacks.

> Platoon Commanders are to be impressed with the fact that the censoring of letters is of more importance than ever.

November 18th 1917

[signed] G.V. Godliffe
Captain.
Brigade Major
119th Infantry Brigade.

[Pencil Annotation] To be destroyed before leaving Gommiecourt [*sic*]

Appendix III

Attack Orders – Bourlon Wood

SECRET **119 INFANTRY BRIGADE ORDER NO.128**

<u>Reference Map MOEUVRES 1/20,000</u>

1. (a) The 40th Div. assisted by tanks will attack BOURLON WOOD and Village today, 23rd November.
   (b) The 51st Division will attack FONTAINE-NOTRE-DAME on our right and the 36th Division QUARRY WOOD and INCHY on our left.
   (c) The 119th Infantry Brigade will attack on the right of the Divisional front, and the 121st Infantry Brigade on the left.

2. (a) The objective of the 119th Infantry Brigade will be the high ground to the N. of BOURLON
   WOOD (Coupez Mill which will be consolidated).
   (b) The 19th Royal Welsh Fusiliers will attack on the right, and the 12th South Wales Borders on the left.
   17th Welsh will be in Brigade Support in proximity of CEMETERY at E.30.c.
   18th Welsh Regt will be in Brigade Reserve under cover about K.6.b.

3. BOUNDARIES
   Right Divisional Boundary from F.20.c.6.0. through F.8.central and in prolongation.
   Inter-brigade boundary will be Crossroads E.24.a to about E.18.central inclusive, thence along west edge of BOURLON WOOD skirting the village in E.12.d.and b. to road junction E.12.b.9.9. thence along road to its junction with the railway at F.1.c.2.8. inclusive.
   Inter-battalion boundary will be the ride F.19.c.3.9. thence through the centre of wood through the <u>B</u> of <u>B</u>OURLON thence to F.1.b.9.1.

4. TANKS
   12 tanks 1st Tank Brigade will assist 119th Infantry Brigade as under:-
   (a) 3 tanks will proceed along the road at the western edge of the wood.
   (b) 3 tanks will proceed up the ride in F.20.a and splay out as the situation may demand.
   (c) 6 tanks will crush the wire and cover the ground in between (a) and (b) and act as the situation may demand. These tanks will pass through the infantry advanced line at zero.

5. INFANTRY PLAN
   Battalions will attack on a 2 company front in depth and will maintain artillery formation throughout so long as situation allows of same.
   Infantry will keep from 100 to 200 yards in rear of tanks.

Support Battalion will be in readiness to either reinforce assaulting battalions or throw out a right defensive flank to the East of BOURLON WOOD.

Assaulting troops will be in position at minus 15 minutes.

6. A shovel waved from the top of a tank signifies that the tank is out of action. Infantry desiring assistance from a tank will wave their helmets on their bayonets.

7. MACHINE GUNS

O.C. 119th Machine Gun Company will detail 3 Sections to be placed in echelon in the trenches in F.20.c. to protect the right flank. These sections will move forward in bounds conforming to the pace of the tanks.

Should the attack by the 51st Division be successful, these sections will eventually take up positions in F.2. and F.8.

1 subsection will be placed at the disposal of 19th RWF and 12th SWB to be used as the situation may demand.

O.C. 18th Welsh will detail a carrying party of 64 o.r. with a suitable proportion of NCOs as carrying party for M.G. Company.

O.C. 119th M.G. Company will remain at Brigade Headquarters.

8. TRENCH MORTAR BATTERY

O.C. 119th T.M.B. will hold 2 Stokes in readiness at Brigade Headquarters to move at short notice.

O.C. 119TH T.M.B. will remain at Brigade Headquarters.

9. WORKS COMPANY

O.C. 119TH Works Company will hold his men in readiness under cover in the neighbourhood of Brigade Headquarters to proceed at short notice. O.C. will remain at Brigade Headquarters.

10. 2nd Lieut T.G. DANIEL, 19th RWF will proceed with 4 selected ORs immediately in rear of assaulting Battalions and will from time to time report by runner direct to Brigade Headquarters regarding the situation.

11. ARTILLERY
    (a) The preliminary advance of the tanks will be covered by a smoke screen from Zero minus 40 to Zero plus 20.
    (b) The subsequent advance will be covered by H.E. and shrapnel barrage in lifts of 200 yards every 10 minutes finally forming a protective barrage on the line F.3. X.26. X.25.
    (c) The initial intense barrage will be put down from F.20.a.7.7. along the S. edge of the wood.

12. Tanks will not withdraw till the infantry has consolidated. Tank Commanders will consult with Infantry Commanders before withdrawing.

13. Assaulting Battalion Commanders will keep close touch with the formations operating on their flanks by means of patrols.

14. Zero hour will be 10.30. a.m.

15. When contact aeroplanes sound Claxon Horns or fire Very Lights, each section of Infantry will light a White Flare and endeavour to attract attention by movement.

16. Prisoners of War will be marched to Brigade Headquarters under escort as per instructions already issued.

17. Advanced Dressing Station will be established at the pond in Graincourt.
    On Bn. Headquarters moving forward R.A.Ps. will also move forward when original R.A.Ps. will be taken over by Medical Officer in charge of Advanced Dressing Station.

18. Assaulting Battalions will exchange liaison officers with the Battalions on their flanks.

19. O.C. Signal Section will arrange for synchronisation of watches prior to Zero minus 60.

20. Brigade Headquarters will be at the CHURCH, GRAINCOURT, to which all reports will be sent.

21. Acknowledge.
    Issued at 4-0. a.m.
    Nov. 23rd. 1917.
     [signed] G.V. Goodliffe
    Captain.
    Brigade Major.
    119th Infantry Brigade.

INSTRUCTIONS TO ACCOMPANY 119TH INFANTRY BRIGADE ORDER NO. 128.

1. <u>TANKS</u> are a luxury. This must be impressed upon all ranks. If a tank breaks down, Infantry must push on at all costs unless particularly asked for help.

2. The rendering of information, negative or otherwise, is the essence of the attack.
    This must be impressed on all ranks prior to moving off and every possible effort must be made by every means to get information back to Brigade H.Q.

3. All commanders must at all times have in their minds the possibility of counter attack, flanks must therefore be closely watched, and when the objective is gained, men must instantly dig in and all ranks must realise that rifle fire is the first line of defence of an Infantry soldier for this purpose.

4. It is most important that in debouching from a wood all ranks do so at the rush.

Appendix IV

Preparations for Defence March 1918

NOTES ON THE CONFERENCE HELD AT 40TH DIVISION HQ 6TH MARCH 1918

PART 1

Tanks Pace
Over good dry surface downhill, tanks go faster than infantry.
Over ground like that between the 2nd and 3rd Systems on the VI Corps front, allow 20 minutes per 1,000 yards.

Formation
(a)   Tanks work in groups of three.
(b)   Infantry move preferably in small columns, extending into line when nearing enemy.
(c)   Infantry should not follow tanks closely but should work more or less independently.

Gaps in Wire
When going through wire the two rear tanks close in and cross wire entanglements where the leading tank did so. Tanks do not cut gaps in wire they only crush it down. Infantry should pass through these places in file, being cautioned to be particularly careful not to kick up the wire, for if they do, it will spring up and form an obstacle again.

Tactics
When all three tanks cross the first enemy trench, the leading tank goes on as close to our barrage as possible; the other two work sideways and help leading wave of Infantry to kill the enemy.
When the next wave of infantry comes up, the tanks go on again to the next objective, followed by the Infantry detailed for the purpose.

NOTE: Owing to various reasons, it cannot be guaranteed that tanks will be available for counter-attacks and also that, if available, they will not break down. Infantry must therefore always be prepared to attack without tanks, even if arranged for.

Liaison
A Liaison Officer from the Tank Corps to be at Divisional and each attacking Brigade Headquarters during operations in conjunction with tanks.

Barrages

Our Artillery Barrage to be put down and worked on a pre-arranged timetable, not to be controlled by aeroplanes.

If our assaulting troops have to move far in order to get up to our initial barrage, this barrage could with advantage, at first be largely a smoke one, turning to shrapnel before the first lift.

When working over good ground the barrage to lift at 200 yards in eight minutes.

Barrages to be put down on the whole front of attack.

Practice Attacks

GOCs Infantry Brigades to arrange for dummy tanks for practising Infantry to work with tanks and communicate direct with OC No. 6 Battalion Tank Corps at WAILLY, for officers of the Tank Corps to be present at practices.

Aeroplanes

The question was raised of aeroplanes signalling to the artillery, when to commence and when to begin lifting the barrage.

It was decided that this was impracticable – owing to the dust and smoke it would be impossible for the aeroplane to see our Infantry, and also there would always be the chance of the aeroplane being brought down prematurely.

PART 2

1. Notes from the Corps Conference were read out regarding probability of an early German attack.

2. The difficulty of communicating with Artillery of Divisions already in the line and of their cooperating was discussed.
   This difficulty would also probably be found with Machine Guns of other Divisions.
   A counter-attack would therefore probably have to rely chiefly on its own Artillery only for support.

3. Machine Guns
   Two sections of Machine Guns would probably be attached to each attacking Brigade for close cooperation and the remainder being employed on barrage work if practicable.

4. It has been found in another Division, that many box-respirators of men employed on working and carrying parties have become damaged.
   The box-respirators of RA, RE, Infantry and Pioneers are all to be examined accordingly, and all damaged ones replaced at once.

5. Brigadiers to consider the various counter-attacks which they may have to carry out and to work out one or more with battalion commanders, and then select a piece of ground and practice with troops.

6. If the Division is moved to another area by rail, all surplus kits to be taken; but if the Division is marched up for counter-attack in this neighbourhood, all surplus kits to be left behind.
   All formations and units to arrange for storing their kits locally, and to inform 'Q' of arrangements they make.

Appendix V

40th Division Lessons of the Recent Fighting, April 1918

NOTES ON THE CONFERENCE HELD AT DIVL. HQ 19/4/18

1. Lessons of the recent fighting which had been brought to notice in GHQ memoranda were discussed and Brigadiers were directed to go into them categorically with their subordinate commanders.

2. The following points were agreed upon:
   (a) Every opportunity should be taken for giving instructions to Lewis Gunners on lines laid down in No. 3 'Notes on Recent Fighting'. In the attack Lewis Guns should be pushed up boldly in order to give supporting fire to the advancing infantry in the same manner that German Light Machine Guns do, and in the Defence they should be employed to counteract the tactics of the German Light Machine Gunner by occupying advanced posts in front of the main line of resistance in any particular zone.
   (b) When making a defensive line, a series of defended localities arranged chequer-wise to afford one another mutual support is preferable to successive long trench lines which cannot be garrisoned throughout.
   (c) Obstacles should first be erected between those Defended Localities rather than covering the localities themselves with a view to the continuity of the hostile advancing line being broken up and the enemy troops held under enfilade fire from the defended localities.
   (d) If a withdrawal becomes necessary it should be carried out on the principle laid down in FSR for rearguard actions, ie a proportion of troops should be left out in the original positions as a covering force while the remainder are withdrawn quietly and systematically to a selected position in rear. When the new position is established then only should covering troops be drawn back on to it as rapidly as is found possible or desirable.
   (e) The best means of preventing the turning of flanks is the organisation of the Defence in depth and the maintenance of adequate local reserves to deal with unforeseen situations as they arise.
   (f) The dispositions of MGs should not be made separately from those of the Infantry but in strictest coordination with them. To enable this to be done the MG Commanders act in consultation and mutual agreement with Infantry Commanders.
   (g) The organisation and delivery of local counter attacks must be carried out by the subordinate infantry commanders on the spot. All subordinate commanders, therefore, should be trained and encouraged to act on their own initiative and responsibility. Such action on their part should never be allowed to pass without commendation or acknowledgement.
   (h) During a fight, all Brigadiers should have at their HQrs selected liaison officers from each Battalion who should be freely used for personal reconnaissances whenever necessary.

HQrs should be organised into two echelons so that during movement, forward or backward, control is never lost or communication cut.

(i) Arrangements for the collection and disposal of battle stragglers must be made at all times by whatever formation may be in general or local reserve.

20/4/18

[signed] Black Lieut. Col.
General Staff, 40th Division

Appendix VI

Biographies

The key sources for all of the entries below are the *Army List* and *The London Gazette*. Additional sources are provided at the end of each entry as appropriate.

John Amery-Parkes (1897-1918): educated Wellington School; joined 2nd Battalion Middlesex Regiment from RMC Sandhurst, June 1915; posted to 23 Coy Machine Gun Corps [MGC], January 1916; lieutenant, November 1916; 2iC 121 Coy MGC, February 1917; CO 119 Coy MGC, July 1917; captain, August 1917; major, February 1918; wounded, 9 April 1918; died 30 April; MC, April 1918.

Richard John Andrews (1887-1923): born Hackney (not "a Scot" as stated by Crozier, *Brass Hat*, p. 142); educated City of London School; poulterer; lance-sergeant 128th Company (Westminster Dragoons), Imperial Yeomanry, South Africa; Queen's South Africa Medal; engineering staff, Antofagasta and Bolivian Railway (no evidence of service in Chilean Amy – see obit. *The Times*, 19 January 1923 probably by Crozier); arrived Liverpool from Chile 13 January 1915, listed as 'civil engineer'; enlisted 14th Battalion Royal Fusiliers (London Scottish), 18 January 1915; second-lieutenant, 2nd Battalion Devonshire Regiment, 1 May 1916; part of battalion's battle reserve 1 July 1916; acting captain 2 July 1916; MC August 1916; acting Major and 2iC, 17th Battalion Welsh Regiment, 18 April 1917; DSO June 1917 for work at La Vacquerie; acting lieutenant-colonel, July 1917; lieutenant-colonel, October 1917; wounded at Bourlon Wood, November 1917; CO 13th Battalion East Lancashire Regiment, October-November 1918; Chief Liaison Officer, Onega River Column, North Russian Expeditionary Force, April-July 1919; prisoner July 1919-April 1920; relinquished commission October 1920; CO G Company, Auxiliary Division, Royal Irish Constabulary, October 1920-January 1921. Starrett's description of Andrews in *Batman* was "a machine that never ran down".
  Personal File TNA WO 339/59109.

Digby Appleby (1880-1945): son of a Co. Durham ship broker; educated Uppingham and Pembroke College, Cambridge; became ship broker at Cardiff; lieutenant then captain 17th Welsh, January 1915; major, January 1916; to Aldershot October 1916 for 10-week course in duties of a CO; returned January 1917; MiD, January 1917; temporary CO 17th Welsh, February 1917 and June 1917; temporary CO 12th SWB, also February 1917; last mentioned in 17th Welsh war diary 28 October 1917; attached to regular battalion Welsh Regiment, 22 November 1917; CO 3rd Welsh by April 1919 when he attended Lt-Colonel Pope's funeral; 'B' class Mention in Secretary of State's List, date not found; relinquishes commission December 1920. An enthusiastic golfer. Along with Major Gilbert a promoter of the memorial to Lt-Colonel Wilkie.
  Western Mail, 15 December 1917 and 15 April 1919; G.V. Carey (ed.), *The War List of the University of Cambridge* (CUP, 1921); Personal File TNA WO 374/1974.

Herbert Clifford Bernard (1865-1916): was educated at Llandovery School and Derby Grammar School; graduated from the Royal Military College and was gazetted into the Hampshire Regiment in 1884. He transferred to the Indian Army the next year and saw active service in the Burmese Expedition 1885-89, the Burmese War 1889-92 and the Chinuk Expedition 1901. CO Rattray's Sikhs from 1909-1914 when he retired from the Indian Army. CO 10th Royal Irish Rifles, October 1914 – July 1916.
Short obituaries in the *Belfast News-Letter*, 7 July 1916 and 13 July 1916.

Robert Benzie DSO** (1874-1930): of Methlick, Aberdeenshire; served an apprenticeship with Alan S. Weir, Chemist, Kemnay, Aberdeenshire; occupation 'Merchant'; sailed for Ceylon February 1899; by 1914 Second-Lieutenant, F Company, Ceylon Planters Rifle Corps; captain CPRC by 1916; served at Gallipoli; captain Scottish Rifles, June 1916; major 12th Battalion South Wales Borderers, April 1917; lieutenant-colonel 12th South Wales Borderers, May 1917; DSO January 1918; bar to DSO February 1918; second bar to DSO July 1918; relinquished commission March 1919; sailed for Ceylon August 1926. Returned to farm in Aberdeenshire. W.R. Birdwood, *Khaki and Gown* (London: Ward Locke, 1941), p. 244, describes how the CPRC was made up of keen and well-educated men and how he obtained commissions for all of them except one.
Short obituary *Aberdeen Press and Journal*, 8 February 1930.

William Ernest Brown (1882-1949): chartered surveyor; second-lieutenant, 12th SWB, June 1915; lieutenant, September 1915; captain and adjutant, 12th SWB, February 1916; understudying BM 119 Infantry Brigade, January–April 1917; MiD, June 1917; acting major, July 1917; wounded Bourlon Wood, returned to duty 31 December 1917; bar to MC, December 1917; MC gazetted January 1918; acting lieutenant-colonel, 18th Welsh, March 1918; DSO, May 1918; relinquishes commission June 1919. Clerk to the Governors, Queens School, Chester, 1930s.

Alan Bryant (1869-1917): educated Marlborough and was gazetted second-lieutenant, Gloucestershire Regiment March 1890 from the Royal Military College; lieutenant, 1891; captain, February 1900; major, October 1911; South African War, Queen's Medal (3 clasps). In 1902 he was "seconded whilst a student at the Staff College". Between 1904 and 1907 he acted as Brigade Major, 12 Brigade, 6th Division and BM, 8 Brigade, 4th Division, Southern Command; from July 1908-July1912 he was GSO2 Coastal Defences, Eastern Command; from November 1912 he was GSO2, Military College of Canada. In December 1914 he was appointed GSO2 and, in December 1915, GSO1, 18th Division until September 1916 although his last signature in the war diary is in June. From October-December 1916 he was GSO1, 56th (1st London) Division. He was MiD January 1916; DSO, January 1917. His medal card states that he first landed in France in October 1916 but this is clearly incorrect. After commanding the 17th Battalion Welsh Regiment he took command of 9th Battalion Northumberland Fusiliers in the Ypres Salient on 2 October 1917. On 17 October 1917 his HQ dugout was hit by a shell killing him, his adjutant, medical officer and intelligence officer.
Gloucester Echo, 1 November 1899 and 23 October 1917.

Philip Thomas Buston CB CMG DSO (1853-1938): of Tilstock Lodge, Whitchurch, Shropshire, had retired from the Royal Engineers with the honorary rank of Brigadier-General in 1910. He had seen active service in Afghanistan, the Hazara expeditions and in the Second Boer War. He was a member of the Shropshire T.F. Association Committee and was appointed to the staff of Western Command in November 1914.
Western Mail, 15 July 1915; *England and Wales National Probate Calendar* <http://www.ancestry.co.uk>

John Campbell (1871-1941): was educated Haileybury College, RMC; second-lieutenant 1st Cameron Highlanders, 1892; lieutenant 1893; captain 1898; served Sudan, 1898 (MiD, brevet-major); South Africa, 1900-1; DSO, 1901; Staff College, 1902-3; staff captain, 1904-5; BM Aldershot, 1905-8; School of Musketry, Hythe, 1909-13; CO 2nd Battalion Cameron Highlanders, January-May 1915 (wounded Hooge); GOC 121 Brigade, October 1915-May 1918; CMG, 1915; GOC 31st Division, May 1918-1919; CB, 1918; GOC 11 Brigade, 1919-1921; retired, 1921.
Professor John Bourne personal communication.

Thomas Astley Cubitt (1871-1939): was commissioned into the Royal Artillery in 1891 and served in West Africa and Northern Nigeria where he was Crozier's CO for a period. He was one of the witnesses at Crozier's second (public) wedding. The start of the Great War found him in Somaliland where he served until transferring to the Western Front in 1916, rising to command 38th (Welsh) Division from May 1918. His final appointment was as Governor of Bermuda.
Who Was Who.

Ernest William Parry Davies (1891-1964): educated at Wycliffe College. Applied for a temporary commission on 6 May 1915; lieutenant; transferred from the ASC (40th Divisional Train) to the 18th Welsh (attached 40th Divisional HQ) on 6 Dec 1917 (which is the likely date of his involvement the 'The Gamecocks') and was posted to the 24th Welsh on 25 May 1918 on the reduction of the Division. He contributed a photograph of 'The Gamecocks' and one of himself in female costume to Sir Ernest Swinton, *Twenty Years After: The Battlefields of 1914-18, Then and Now* (London: George Newnes, no date), Volume One, p.436.
Personal File TNA WO 339/1403.

Maurice Fitzmaurice Day (1878-1952): educated at Oakham School and Pembroke College, Cambridge; private Suffolk Regiment (Cambridge Volunteers) South Africa 1900-1; second-lieutenant KOYLI, July 1901; lieutenant, December 1905; adjutant, 2nd Battalion King's Own Yorkshire Light Infantry, April 1911; captain, January 1912; seconded to staff appointment, August 1914; major, May 1915; MC, June 1915; BM 107 Brigade, 36th (Ulster) Division). In 1917 he went on to the American Military Mission for the duration of the war and remained as Military Attaché at the British Embassy in Washington. GSO2 and lieutenant-colonel October 1927. He was also an Irish tennis international.
Cambridge Independent Press, 10 May 1901.

James Henry Richard Downes-Powell (c.1874-1958): a solicitor and Welsh-speaker. He was admitted to the Middle Temple in 1911 and in July 1914 was selected as the unionist candidate to contest East Denbighshire at the next General Election. In September 1914 as "late Lt. Imperial Yeomanry" he was commissioned lieutenant, Glamorgan Yeomanry; captain, Glamorgan Yeomanry, November 1914; seconded as a staff captain (formation unknown) July 1915; major and 2iC 19th Battalion Royal Welsh Fusiliers, October 1916; CO 19th RWF January-May 1917. After being replaced as CO he was seconded and by November 1918 was Director for Wales and Monmouthshire of the Appointments Department, Ministry of Labour. He relinquished his commission in July 1919, was granted the rank of lieutenant-colonel and went on to be Chairman of Bevan & Co., Cardiff; a successful dog breeder, JP and Chair of Penarth Urban District Council.
Western Mail, 3 November 1945.

Cyril Bentham Falls CBE (1888-1971): joined the 11th Battalion Royal Inniskilling Fusiliers and served on 36th Division's General Staff. He became a military historian and journalist, military

correspondent for *The Times*, 1939-53, and Chichele Professor of Military History at All Souls College, Oxford, 1946-53.
Oxford Dictionary of National Biography.

David Pinkerton Fleming (1877-1944): educated at Glasgow High School and the University of Glasgow; admitted to Faculty of Advocates 1902; second-lieutenant 1st Volunteer Battalion Highland Light Infantry, 1899; resigned his commission as lieutenant, 1904; captain 5th Battalion Cameronians (Scottish Rifles), February 1915; staff captain formation unknown, August 1915 – May 1916; adjutant 13th Royal Inniskilling Fusiliers, June 1918 – October 1918; acting major and 2iC, October 1918; MC gazetted December 1918 most likely for the action on 27th August – "For conspicuous gallantry and initiative. Owing to casualties among the company commanders he assisted officers with but little experience to carry out their instructions, and, when the position was captured, he personally supervised the consolidation"; resigned commission as captain, December 1920; Solicitor General for Scotland, 1922; MP for Dunbartonshire, 1924 – 1926; elected to Scottish Bench as Lord Fleming, 1925; Hon LLD, University of Glasgow 1938; Hon Bencher, Middle Temple, 1940; Private Home Guard, 1940; Chairman of committee that authored the influential *Report on Public Schools and the General Education System* (London: HMSO, 1944).
Personal File TNA WO 374/24595; *Oxford Dictionary of National Biography.*

William Brooksbank Garnett (1875-1946): educated at Charterhouse; joined Inland Revenue; second-lieutenant 24th Battalion Middlesex Regiment (Post Office Rifles), 1895; lieutenant, 1897; second-lieutenant 1st Battalion Royal Welsh Fusiliers, 1900; to half pay (ill health), 1908; captain and adjutant, April 1913; CO 20th Battalion Royal Fusiliers, August 1916 – February 1917; CO 2nd Battalion Royal Welsh Fusiliers, October – December 1917 and January-April 1918; GOC 121 Brigade, May – September 1918; retired 1927; High Sheriff County Tyrone, 1941. According to Siegfried Sassoon he was "indulgent and conciliatory" and "greater aggressiveness would have been preferred" – quoted in Hodgkinson, *Battalion Commanders*, p. 136.

Edmund Harry St George Gilbert (1863-1947): born Calcutta; son of Captain (later Major) Edward Kerr Otho Gilbert, 27th Native Infantry; educated at United Services College, Westward Ho!, Devon; second-lieutenant 3rd Welsh, 1880; lieutenant, 1881; to Reserve of Officers, 1884; by 1888 an actor with the stage name Frank Atherley and appeared in provincial, London and New York productions; married actresses Katie Marian Bell (1891, divorced 1896) and Jessie Tenniel; captain, 9th Welsh, September 1914; transferred to 17th Welsh, March 1915; major, March 1915; Town Major Les Brebis, August 1916; Commandant First Army Rest Camp Boulogne, September 1916; returned to battalion November 1916; appointed Area Commandant XV Corps (Chipilly Area), December 1916; Commandant Frise Bend District, March 1917; major, General List, while employed with Chinese Labour Corps (33 Chinese Labour Coy), July 1917; acting lieutenant-colonel CLC, May 1918; demobilized September 1919; awarded Order of Wen Hu 4th Class, Feb 1920. Resumed acting; collapsed on stage September 1926. Film credits for *Carry On* (1927), *Sexton Blake, Gambler* (1928), *Betrayal* (1932) and *Trouble* (1933).
Personal File TNA WO 339/23024; *The Stage*; TNA WO95/2594 40th Division HQ, A&Q.

Guy Vernon Goodliffe (1883-1963): educated at Charterhouse and Magdalen College, Oxford; played first-class cricket for Oxford University and minor counties cricket for Berkshire; played soccer for Oxford University 1902-3; second-lieutenant, 1st Battalion Royal Fusiliers, 1906; lieutenant, 1st Battalion R F, November 1909; captain, 1st Battalion RF, December 1914; acting major, August 1916; MC, January 1917; BM, 119 Brigade, February 1917 to April 1918; GSO2, VIII Corps, April 1918; MiD December 1917 and May 1918; brevet major, Reserve of Officers,

June 1918; restored to establishment February 1920; "Instructor of English at a French Military School", November 1920 – November 1923; Officer of A Coy Gentlemen Cadets, Royal Military College, September 1926; major, January 1927; retired, September 1930. Took up farming at Birdstown, Co. Donegal. Appointed Military Member County Antrim Territorial Army and Air Force Association November 1939; lieutenant-colonel commanding Army Cadet Force Londonderry 1943-1947. Relinquished commission in Territorial Army Reserve of Officers "having exceeded the age limit", July 1948. Goodliffe's account of the 2nd Battalion Royal Fusiliers' attack at Beaumont Hamel on 1st July 1916 is in TNA: CAB 45/189 and is quoted in Paul Kendall, *Somme 1916: Success and Failure on the First Day of the Battle of the Somme* (Barnsley: Frontline, 2015), p.171.

Yorkshire Post, 6 September 1939; *Ballymena Telegraph,* 3 November 1939; Obituary *Belfast Telegraph,* 30 May 1963.

Harry Percy Bright Gough (1880-1918): educated at Llandovery College and Sidney Sussex College, Cambridge; taught at Neuenhein College, Heidelberg for two years; Science Master at Lancaster Royal Grammar School (7 years) and then Oakham School from 1911; rugby player and sportsman; CO Oakham School OTC; gazetted second-lieutenant, OTC, October 1914; second-lieutenant, 17th Welsh, February 1915; lieutenant, June1915; captain, July 1915; adjutant 17th Welsh to September 1916; to 40th Division HQ as learner in staff duties, January 1917; MC, June 1917, for action at Welsh Ridge; acting major, October 1916; acting lieutenant-colonel, 9-27 December 1917; bar to MC, January 1918, for actions in Bourlon Wood; on disbandment of 17th Welsh posted to 9th Entrenching Battalion then to 18th Welsh, February 1918; severely wounded by shellfire 13 April 1918 while commanding details of 13th East Surreys; DoW 22 April 1918; buried at Arneke Military Cemetery. Second-Lieutenant M.M. Williams, 17th Welsh, thought him a "dull little man".

'Cambridge University Alumni, 1261-1900' <http://www.ancestry.co.uk>; Personal File TNA WO339/25014; Williams Papers.

Jocelyn Henry Clive 'Harry' Graham (1874-1936): actor, author, lyricist, screenwriter and wit. Educated at Eton and the Royal Military College; second-lieutenant Coldstream Guards, 1895; lieutenant 1898; seconded as ADC to Lord Minto, Governor General of Canada 1899 and again in 1903; South Africa 1901-1902 (QSA medal, three clasps); supernumerary captain 1901; captain 1902; retired 1904 and was Private Secretary to Lord Rosebery; re-joined regiment in 1914; ADC to John Ponsonby, October 1917; relinquished appointment, February 1919. Best known today as the author (under the pseudonym Col. D. Streamer) of *Ruthless Rhymes for Heartless Homes* (London: Edward Arnold, 1899) and *Perverted Proverbs: A Manual of Immorals for the Many* (New York: R.H. Russell, 1903). His output of musical comedy and operetta was prolific. He wrote the lyrics for one of the Great War's most popular stage shows *The Maid of the Mountains* (1917), translated the lyrics of Franz Lehar's *You are my heart's delight* (from *The Land of Smiles,* 1929) which was recorded and made famous by Richard Tauber in 1936. *Goodbye* (from *White Horse Inn,* 1931) was the hit song of the show and was later recorded by tenor Joseph Locke (1947). Graham was almost certainly the anonymous author of *The Lies Book: Lies Within Lies* (London: War Narratives Publishing Company for Private Circulation, 1919) a collection of outrageous and humorous claims by members of and visitors to the 40th Divisional Mess during John Ponsonby's tenure as GOC and probably copied from a manuscript kept in the mess.

Obituary *The Times,* 31 October 1936; *Who Was Who; Oxford Dictionary of National Biography;* private papers in IWM; Personal File TNA WO 374/28451.

Hugh Gilbert Gregorie (1878-1928): son of Charles Frederick Gregorie (1834-1918; major-general 1890, Colonel in Chief, Royal Irish Regiment 1897). Gregorie served briefly with TMI in South Africa, transferred to the Imperial Light Infantry and was gazetted second-lieutenant Royal Irish Regiment on 26 October 1900. He was Mentioned in Despatches 9 November 1900; gazetted lieutenant 1903; captain 1908; major 1915; lieutenant-colonel 1916 and brigadier-general November 1917.

George Meredyth Grogan (1867-1942): second-lieutenant 1st Battalion Royal Irish Regiment (from 5th Battalion Royal Dublin Fusiliers, Militia), July 1890,; lieutenant, August 1891; captain, May 1899; adjutant 5th Royal Irish Regiment (militia), July 1906; major, 1907; retired, August 1909; Railway Transport Officer, August 1914; CO 5th Battalion Royal Irish Regiment (Pioneers), January 1916-May 1918, service in Gallipoli and Salonika; DSO, January 1917; briefly CO 12th North Staffords, June 1918.

Alan Roderick Haig-Brown (1877-1918): the son of the Head Master of Charterhouse School; educated Oxford Preparatory School, Charterhouse and Pembroke College, Cambridge; author, footballer and field sportsman; played amateur soccer for Old Carthusians, Brighton and Hove Albion, Worthing, Shoreham, Clapton Orient and Tottenham Hotspur (1901-03); appointed Assistant Master at Lancing College, 1899; lieutenant 2nd (Volunteer) Battalion Royal Sussex Regiment, 1906; captain and CO Lancing College OTC, 1908; commission transferred to TF, 1908; major and 2iC 23rd Middlesex Regiment, January 1916; lieutenant-colonel and CO 23rd Middlesex, September 1916; MiD May 1917 and May 1918; DSO June 1917; kia 25 March 1918 in a rearguard action that also claimed the life of one of his captains, Walter Tull. Buried Achiet le Grand Communal Cemetery Extension.
  Personal File TNA WO 339/51862; Lancing College War Memorial web pages at <http://www.hambo.org/lancing/view_man.php?id=132>, accessed December 2020.

John Richardson Heelis (1880-1962): was educated at Dover College and Clare College, Cambridge; second-lieutenant, 5th Battalion Manchester Regiment, May 1900; transferred to 1st Manchester, May 1901; lieutenant, December 1901; West African Frontier Force, 1907-9; in India 1911; captain, 1912; to France 28 August 1914 as captain and adjutant, 1st Battalion Manchester Regiment; wounded; MC June 1915; BM, 182 Infantry Brigade, 61st Division, October 1915 to April 1917; CO 18th Battalion Welsh Regiment, May-July 1917; MiD three times; served post-war in Iraq and India; lieutenant-colonel, 2nd Battalion Manchester Regiment, November 1925; retired May 1930.
  Personal File TNA WO 76/207/42; 1901 Census at <http://www.ancestry.co.uk>

Percy Frederick Hone (1878-1940): educated at Blackheath School and Downing College Cambridge; Private, Cambridge University Rifles Volunteers 1898-1900; Trooper Southern Rhodesia Volunteers 1900-1902; Mines Dept, British South Africa Company's Civil Service, S. Rhodesia 1900-1905; author *Southern Rhodesia* (London: George Bell, 1909); "Secretary for Viscount Rhondda's American Interests", pre-1914; private, Cardiff Exchange Volunteers, August 1914; lieutenant, 17th Battalion Welsh Regiment, 12 January 1915; captain 17th Welsh, 16 January 1915; staff captain 119 Brigade, 5 October 1915; brigade major, 119 Brigade, 13 December 1917; lieutenant-colonel 21st Battalion Middlesex Regiment, May 1918; lieutenant-colonel, 13th Battalion Durham Light Infantry, 16-26 October 1918, when seriously wounded; MiD, May 1917 and June 1920; MC January 1918; bar to MC, February 1918; second bar to MC, September 1918; DSO, January 1919; bar to DSO, February 1919; relinquished commission due to ill-health caused

by wounds, December 1919; Commissioner National Savings Committee, 1919-38. Head ARP Warden, West Horsley 1939-40. Died 19 April 1940 by an accidental fall into a chalk-pit.
Personal File TNA WO 339/22723. Report of inquest, *Surrey Advertiser*, 27 April 1940.

Charles Beauman Hore (1879-1965): was given command of the 17th Battalion Welsh Regiment after Lieutenant-Colonel Wilkie was killed by a shell in October 1916; educated Shrewsbury School; second-lieutenant Royal Warwickshire Regiment (RWR) 'from the militia' April 1900; lieutenant RWR August 1900, captain RWR July 1908; adjutant Special Reserve May 1912; served South Africa 1899-1901, Queen's S.A. Medal (4 clasps); major RWR September 1915; 2iC 12th Battalion South Wales Borderers, December 1915; temp CO 10th Battalion Royal Welsh Fusiliers, 4 Oct 1916; CO 17th Battalion Welsh Regiment, 27 October 1916; Acting Lieutenant-Colonel 2nd Battalion Royal Welsh Fusiliers, March – September 1917; Company Commander No. 5 Officers Instructional School December 1918; major RWR, retired pay November 1926.

Robert Ingelow Bradshaw Johnson (1874 – 1955): educated All Saints College, Bathurst, Sydney; second-lieutenant New South Wales Defence Force 2nd Regiment, 1895; transferred to UK to Loyal North Lancashire Regiment, June 1896; transferred to 2nd Battalion Royal Welsh Fusiliers, September 1896; lieutenant, August 1898; served Crete (1898), China (1901-2), India and Burma (1902-14); captain, June 1905; retired, December 1913; major 8th Battalion Royal Welsh Fusiliers, September 1914; lieutenant-colonel 8th Battalion Welsh Regiment (Pioneers), November 1915-November 1917; served at Gallipoli and in Mesopotamia; MiD and DSO 1917; CO 13th Battalion East Lancashire Regiment, June-November 1918; killed in car collision with a train in New Zealand, 1955.
Personal File TNA WO 76/230/31.

James Gwyther Jones (1887-1965): a commercial traveller/draper from Swansea. He enlisted in the Glamorgan Yeomanry as a private in September 1914 but was recommended for commission by Grant-Thorold; second-lieutenant, 18th Welsh, March 1915; lieutenant, June 1915; captain, August 1915; MiD, June 1916; wounded at Bourlon Wood, November 1917 and left the army in March 1919.
Personal File TNA WO 339/27676.

Bryan John Jones (1874-1918): a grandson of Sir Theophilus Shepstone and the son of a Royal Artillery officer, after a private education Jones was gazetted second-lieutenant (1894); lieutenant (1896); captain (1900); major (1915); lieutenant-colonel (November 1915). He was awarded the Queen's South Africa Medal (3 clasps) and the King's Medal (2 clasps), mentioned in despatches for his Great War service twice (London Gazettes, 14 January 1916 and 25 May 1917) and awarded the DSO (*London Gazette*, 14 January 1916) and Bar (*London Gazette*, 10 March 1919). He took command of the 6th Battalion Leinster Regiment on 28 August 1918 just before their disbandment, then took over the 15th Battalion Royal Irish Rifles and was killed in action on 22 October 1918. His second wound probably occurred during Second Ypres when the 1st Leinsters were heavily engaged but the battalion war diary is sparse for this period. According to Beynon Davies (*Ar Orwell Pell*, p. 35) Jones was respected and was an authority on Marlborough's wars.
De Ruvigny's Roll of Honour, 1914-1919, Volume 5, p.94.

William Kennedy (1885–1917): an unlikely soldier; son of a Lanarkshire textile manufacturer; educated at the High School of Glasgow and Glasgow University. He shone academically, winning prizes at school and university; graduated MA, 1907; First-Class Honours Economic Science, 1909; research student London School of Economics, 1910; DSc (Econ) London University; studied in

Germany 1913; taught at Wren's College and the LSE 1914; Inns of Court OTC, December 1914; captain, 18th Battalion Highland Light Infantry, April 1915; MC October 1916 for action near Longueval – "He handled his company with great skill in the defence of his part of the line. He organised men from various regiments who were retiring before a counter-attack. Though himself wounded, he remained at his post, and was mainly responsible for repulsing a counter-attack"; major, February 1917; acting lieutenant-colonel 18th Welsh, July 1917; killed at Bourlon Wood, 23 November 1917.
Glasgow University Roll of Honour <http://www.universitystory.gla.ac.uk/ww1-biography/?id=478> Personal File TNA WO 339/29287.

Charles Henry Kitching (1881-1952): commissioned from the Royal Military College as second-lieutenant, Worcestershire Regiment, January 1901; lieutenant, 1902; captain, 1910; resigned commission February, 1912; major, 15th Battalion Hampshire Regiment, March 1916; CO (as major) 12th (Reserve) Battalion East Surrey Regiment, September-October 1916; lieutenant-colonel 18th Battalion King's Royal Rifle Corps, December 1916-September 1917; DSO, June 1917; 2iC Officer Cadet Unit (unidentified), March-April 1918; CO 12th Battalion North Staffordshire Regiment, July-August 1918; CO 4th (Extra Reserve) Battalion West Yorkshire Regiment, October-November 1918; Commandant Reception Camp, November 1918.

Charles Reginald Knowles (1868-1950): born in Leeds he was a highly accomplished and popular vocalist both before and after the Great War. He was Farrier Sergeant Major, 2nd County of London Yeomanry in Egypt, 1915; second-lieutenant, 3/2nd County of London Yeomanry, July 1916; seconded to the Labour Corps, August 1917; lieutenant, January 1918; temporary Captain, 13th East Lancs, July 1918; brigade Transport Officer, November 1918; unemployed list February 1919; retired June 1921.

Rowland Broughton Mainwaring CMG (1850-1926): of Park Hall, Longton, Staffs, had an active career with the Royal Welsh Fusiliers, serving in the Ashanti, Burmese and Hazara campaigns and the Second Boer War and was the author of *Historical Record of the Royal Welch Fusiliers ...* (London: Hatchlands, 1889). He retired with the rank of colonel in 1905 but found employment as GOC 68th (Welsh) Division from January-November 1915. He was declared bankrupt in July 1916.

Reginald Walter May (1896-1969): educated at Towcester Grammar School and Westminster College; second-lieutenant, 12th Battalion Suffolk Regiment, August 1915; transferred to 18th Battalion Welsh Regiment, April 1916; lieutenant, March 1917; 119 Brigade Acting Intelligence Officer, April 1917; 119 Brigade Intelligence Officer, June 1917; MC, January 1918; MiD; Acting Staff Captain 119 Brigade, February 1918; Staff Captain, 119 Brigade, May 1918; dismissed the service by sentence of a General Court-Martial found guilty of 'scandalous conduct', October 1928.
TNA WO 90/8 Register of General Courts Martial. *Northampton Mercury*, 11 January 1918.

Herbert Charles Metcalfe (1864-1940): RMC Sandhurst 1884-85; lieutenant, 2nd Battalion Northamptonshire Regiment 1885; ADC to Governor of Hong Kong, 1886-87; seconded as lieutenant 1st Perak Sikhs (an 'armed police force' in NW Malaya), 1892-1895; Deputy Commissioner, Perak Police to 1897; captain, Northamptonshire Regiment 1894; District Inspector of Musketry, Scottish Command, 1899; District Inspector of Musketry, Irish Command, 1900; retired, November 1902; Chief Constable of West Suffolk, 1902; Chief Constable of West Riding of Yorkshire, 1905; Chief Constable of Somerset, 1908; major, 3rd Battalion Northamptonshire

Regiment, December 1914; Staff Officer, Musketry, 1st Thames and Medway Special Reserve Brigade, July 1915; duty on lines of communication, France, August 1917; CO 20 Infantry Base Depot, Etaples, September-December 1917; CO 21st Battalion Middlesex Regiment, 18 December 1917; seriously wounded 11 April 1918; DSO, May 1918; Bar to DSO, May 1918; MiD November 1918; CO 3rd Battalion Northamptonshire Regiment, November 1918; demobilised, May 1919; King's Police Medal, 1931; Deputy Lieutenant, Somerset, 1932; retired as Chief Constable of Somerset, 1939.

Metcalfe had tried to get a command early in the war when he wrote to Sir Ian Hamilton "Dear Sir Ian – You may not remember me as Asst D.I.M. to Congreve at Aldershot in 1898 when my name was submitted to you for a musketry appointment. I left the service in 1902, after holding two such appointments, to take up a County Chief Constableship because being then 13th on the list of Captains in my Regiment with 17½ years service I saw no chance of ever commanding a battn. In response to the enclosed WO letter I have offered my services and have said that I would be glad to take up a musketry staff or other staff billet. Forgive me for troubling you when I know you must be busy, but if you have a chance, will you very kindly say a word for me. The county authorities have given me leave to take up a military duty if I am wanted. I send you copies of my testimonials. Yours v. truly, H.C. Metcalfe – PS, General Chapman, Cmdr Scottish District, gave me a very good 'chit'. It is now at the WO with my offer. [signed] HCM" – Kings College, London: Liddell Hart Archive: Hamilton Correspondence, letter, 25 October 1914. Hamilton replied "I shall be glad to take an early opportunity of reminding people of your existence. Personally I am purely a Training and Operations man for Territorials and have no patronage at my disposal. Hoping you will get something suitable in due course". – Hamilton Correspondence, letter 26 October 1914. Metcalfe's eventual arrival at 119 Brigade seems to be due entirely to John Ponsonby: "Metcalfe from the Base who was on my staff at Chatham has joined me. I wrote for him to come out and command a battalion – I hope he will be able to stick it. He is a hard nut, but as he is now well over 50, it will be a bit of a trial for him, but he is just the right sort that I want" – TNA WO 95/2594: War diary 40th Division GS, Ponsonby Diary, 13 Decembers 1917.

TNA WO 95/2615: War Diary 21st Middlesex; Obituary, *Somerset County Gazette*, 20 January 1940.

Seton James Montgomery (1889-1966): Tentatively identified as J.S. Montgomery, second-lieutenant 15th Royal Scots, 1915, but there seems to be some confusion about his initials in the *London Gazette*. Educated George Heriots School; captain, June 1915; acting BM, 119 Brigade December 1916-February 1917. He became briefly 2iC 17th then 18th Welsh in April 1917 but was evacuated to the UK in May due to 'debility and neurasthenia'; married July 1917 in Edinburgh while at Craiglockhart Hospital, occupation given as 'marine engineer, Major 18th Welsh'; given as attached captain 1st or 2nd Welsh in August 1918 Army list; relinquished commission September 1921; emigrated to Halifax, Nova Scotia and became Professor of Engineering.

The Hydra, 21 July 1917; Personal File TNA WO 339/54957.

David Watts Morgan (1867-1933): a Welsh-speaking miners' leader and politician active in the Rhondda Labour and Liberal Association. He was a Glamorgan County Councillor from 1903 and a magistrate from 1914. Served six years as private and corporal in the Glamorgan Artillery Volunteers. Attested 18 September 1914, private, 10th Welsh (1st Rhondda); he recruited energetically for the battalion; applied for commission October 1914; discharged to commission January 1915; transferred to the 17th Welsh in March 1915 but remained active in promoting recruiting to South Wales battalions; captain May 1915; 'relieved' from 17th Welsh to concentrate on recruiting September 1915; transferred to a Works Battalion King's Liverpool Regiment, May 1916; major November 1916; to 80th Labour Company April 1917; DSO 1918 for actions during the German counter-attack at Cambrai; MiD three times; discharged March 1919. He became a MP in 1918; CBE 1920 for recruiting work in South Wales. See *Oxford Dictionary of National Biography*: Morgan, David Watts. Personal File TNA WO 339/21978.

Anthony John Muirhead (1890–1939): educated at Eton and Magdalen College, Oxford; University of Oxford OTC; second-lieutenant, Oxfordshire Yeomanry, August 1914; lieutenant, Oxfordshire Yeomanry, March 1915; ADC to Major-General R. Fanshawe, 48th (South Midland Division), October 1915; lieutenant, June 1916; captain, May 1917; MC, June 1917; GSO3, 48th Division, September 1917; BM, 119 Brigade, April 1918; bar to MC, February 1919; MiD three times; brevet major, January 1919; 'Chief of Staff' with Crozier, Lithuania, 1919-20; appointed to DAA & QMG's Department, TF, April 1920; major, 100 Field Brigade, RA, Territorial Army, December 1924; elected MP for Wells, 1929; Parliamentary Private Secretary to Minister of Agriculture, 1931-35; Parliamentary Secretary to Minister of Labour, 1935; lieutenant-colonel, 100 Field Brigade, RA, August 1936; Under-Secretary of State for Air, 1937-38; transferred as Lieutenant-Colonel to 53 Anti-Tank Regiment, TA, November 1938; Under-Secretary of State for India and Burma, 1938-39; committed suicide, 29 October 1939.

Obituary, *The Times*, 30 October 1939.

Ernest Robert O'Connor (1886-1970): started the war as 9089 CSM 2nd Battalion Grenadier Guards; after fourteen years and 119 days in the ranks, second-lieutenant Manchester Regiment, January 1915; lieutenant, June 1915; adjutant 11th Manchester Regiment, January 1916; captain (supernumerary) Royal Munster Fusiliers, July 1916; acting major/Chief Instructor, Musketry Corps Reinforcement Camp, September 1917 – June 1918; acting major/2iC 13th Battalion Royal Inniskilling Fusiliers, 19 August 1918; acting lieutenant-colonel 12th Battalion North Staffordshire Regiment, 24 October 1918 – 23 June 1919; MC, October 1918; captain and adjutant 3rd (Reserve) Battalion Royal Munster Fusiliers, August 1919-June 1922. As captain King's Own (Royal Lancaster Regiment) seconded as an adjutant Auxiliary Force, India December 1922; major King's Own, May 1931; as lieutenant-colonel reached age limit for Reserve of Officers June 1945.

Thomas Kenyon Pardoe (1873-1946): second-lieutenant 2nd (Volunteer) Battalion Worcestershire Regiment, 1899; South Africa (Queen's Medal 3 clasps, King's Medal 2 clasps); second-lieutenant 1st Battalion Worcestershire Regiment from 2nd (Volunteer) Battalion, 1901; seconded as Adjutant of Indian volunteers, June 1907; captain, September 1908; BEF, November 1914; wounded Neuve Chapelle, March 1915; major, September 1915; Assistant Embarkation Staff Officer, January 1916; CO 2nd Battalion Worcestershire Regiment from June 1916 – July 1917 (wounded) and again from April – June 1918 (wounded); CO 12th Battalion North Staffordshire Regiment, June 1918; Assistant Embarkation Staff Officer, December 1918; Embarkation Staff Officer, January 1919; Assistant Embarkation Staff Officer, July 1919; retired, 1920; lieutenant-colonel Movement Control Staff March 1924; no longer eligible for recall, 1928.

William Elliot Peyton (1866–1931): educated Brighton College; enlisted 7th Dragoon Guards, 1885; second-lieutenant, 1887; lieutenant, 1892; adjutant, 1892-96; captain 15th Hussars, 1896, Egyptian Army, 1896-1898; Dongola Expedition, 1896; MiD, 1896; Nile Expeditions, 1897 (wounded) and 1898; DSO, 1898; Special Service Officer, South Africa 1900; MiD, 1901; brevet lieutenant-colonel, 1905; colonel, 1907; AQMG, HQ India, 1907-8; CO Meerut Cavalry Brigade, 1908-12; Military Secretary to C-in-C India, 1912-14; GSO1 1st Mounted Yeomanry, TF, Home Defence, 1914; CO 2nd Mounted Division, Gallipoli, 1915; MiD twice, 1915; GOC Western Frontier Force, Egypt, 1916; Military Secretary GHQ BEF, May 1916-April 1918; KCB, 1917;

GOC Reserve Army; April-July 1918; GOC 40th Division, July 1918-March 1919; later served Rhine Army, India and again as Military Secretary; lieutenant-general, 1921; full general, 1927; GOC Scottish Command to retirement, 1930.

James Frederick Plunkett (1878–1953): the son and grandson of rankers; probably joined Royal Irish Regiment as drummer boy c.1891; attended Kneller Hall (proficiency as cornet player 'good'), left October 1893; RSM, 2nd Battalion, Royal Irish Regiment by 1914; DCM, December 1914; MC, January 1915; second-lieutenant, Royal Irish Regiment, June 1915; captain, Middlesex Regiment, February 1916; major, Suffolk Regiment, October 1916; lieutenant-colonel, Royal Welsh Fusiliers, August 1917; DSO, January 1918; bar to DSO; February 1918; second bar to DSO, July 1918; lieutenant-colonel, Royal Inniskilling Fusiliers, June 1918; MiD ten times 1914-18; brevet major, June 1919; captain and brevet major, East Lancashire Regiment, October 1920; to half pay list on account of ill-health, November 1922; retired December 1922; Military Knight of Windsor, May 1930.

Information on Plunkett at Kneller Hall from Stephen Mason, personal communication.

John Ponsonby (1866–1952): educated Eton; second-lieutenant, Royal Irish Rifles from 3rd Battalion Sherwood Foresters (Derby Regiment), 1887; second-lieutenant, Coldstream Guards, 1888; lieutenant, 1891, captain, 1898; major 1904; lieutenant-colonel, 1st Battalion Coldstream Guards, October 1913; brigadier-general 2nd Guards Brigade, August 1915; GOC 1st Thames and Medway Reserve Brigade, December 1916; GOC 21st Brigade, 30th Division 8-18 March 1917; GOC 2nd Guards Brigade, 21 March 1917; GOC 40th Division, 24 August 1917; GOC 5th Division, July 1918; GOC Madras District, 1922-26; colonel, Suffolk Regiment, 1925-1939; CO 7th Cumberland Battalion Home Guard, 1940-41; Uganda, 1888-89; Matabeleland, 1893-94; South Africa 1889-1902; DSO, 1900; CMG, 1915, KCB, 1927.

Robert Emile Shepherd Prentice CB CMG DSO (1872-1953): a professional soldier. He was commissioned into the Highland Light Infantry from Sandhurst in 1892, served on India's North West Frontier 1897-98 and as a major was Staff Captain, Eastern Counties Regimental District, 1905-8, and No.9 District Eastern Command, 1908-9. After his service with 119 Brigade he commanded 2nd Battalion Highland Light Infantry until 16 July 1916 when he left to be GOC 1st Naval Brigade (later 188 Brigade), 63rd Royal Naval Division, until 15 December 1917. He retired from the army in 1928.

The Scotsman, 20 February 1915.

Charles Stewart Prichard (1861-1942): for his work in South Africa Prichard was awarded the Queen's Medal (4 clasps) and the King's Medal (2 clasps). His DSO was gazetted on 26 June 1902. He was promoted to major Northamptonshire Regiment, 1901, lieutenant-colonel, 1911 and colonel in December 1914. GOC 119 Infantry Brigade, May-August 1916. After his service with 119 Brigade he was briefly placed on the half-pay list before being 'Attached to Hd-Qtr Units' on 18 September 1916 – presumably within Northern Command as he was fined nineteen guineas for having an unshaded light on an air-raid night on 13 October 1916 at Patrington, East Yorkshire (*Flight*, 19 October 1916, p.10). On 22 May 1918 he was placed in command of No. 9 District, Eastern Command until 7 November that year when he reverted to half-pay.

Buckinghamshire Herald, 26 June 1942.

Sidney Walter Pugh (1883-1943): born in Talgarth, Brecon and emigrated to Canada in 1903, passed through the Canadian Military School in 1908 and was lieutenant in the 90th Winnipeg Rifles. He returned to Wales before the start of the war and acted as Canadian Government

Special Representative for Wales and European Inspector of Canadian Government Agents. He was invalided back from France in July 1917, presumably returned to Canada and made at least one more trip to the UK in August 1918. He returned to Canada with his family in February 1923.

Brecon and Radnor Express, 17 January 1918 and 'Canadian Ocean Arrivals, 1919-24' at <http://www.ancestry.com>

Harry Leslie Reed (1885-1969): educated Clare College, Cambridge; author of *Problem Papers for Upper and Middle Forms* (London: Alston Rivers, 1909); schoolmaster, Westminster School; second-lieutenant, Westminster School Contingent, OTC, October 1909; lieutenant, January 1913; captain, Middlesex Regiment from Unattached List, TF, December 1915; adjutant 20th Middlesex, May 1916; temporary BM, 119 Infantry Brigade January – February 1917; major, March 1917; staff captain (formation unknown), June 1918; relinquished commission, February 1920.

Personal File TNA WO339/50096.

Henry Charles Rees (1883-1916): accountant; "all-round sportsman"; rugby captain London Welsh 4th Team, 1906; holder of Men's Doubles Championship of Egypt; returned from Egypt on S.S. *Kaisar-I-Hind*, December 1914; lieutenant 10th Bedfordshire Regiment, January 1915; transferred at own request to 12th SWB, May 1915; captain, June 1915; major w.e.f. 7 July 1916 but not gazetted until November 1916, after his death; kia 5 August 1915; buried Loos British Cemetery.

Personal File TNA WO 339/30682; *The Referee*, 6 May 1906; 'Incoming Passenger Lists' <http://www.ancestry.com>; *Middlesex Chronicle*, 12 August 1916.

John Edward Bernard Seely (1868-1947): educated at Harrow and Trinity College Cambridge. Joined Hampshire Yeomanry and served for eighteen months in South Africa. "His remarkable courage, although it occasionally brought him into conflict with authority, won him distinction and several decorations". Elected MP for Isle of Wight in 1900. DSO 1900. Lieutenant-Colonel Hampshire Yeomanry 1907. Appointed Secretary of State for War 1912 and resigned the office following his poor handling of the Curragh Mutiny. Brigadier-General 1915. Commanded Canadian Cavalry Brigade 1915-1918. Major-General July 1918. CB 1916; CMG 1918. Resigned from the Army 1923. Created first Baron Mottistone, 1933.

Oxford Dictionary of National Biography: Seely, John Edward Bernard, first Baron Mottistone (1868-1947).

Henry Nathaniel Sheppard (1877-1952): Unionist Agent for the Rhondda Parliamentary Division, 1914 (later agent for the Ogmore Division, 1921); involved in South Wales recruiting campaigns along with David Watts Morgan, autumn 1914; second-lieutenant then lieutenant, 17th Welsh, January 1915; captain, CO 'D' Company, 17th Welsh, September 1915; 'wounded', 9 July 1916; dismissed the service by sentence of a General Court-martial, December 1916. An 'eloquent platform speaker'.

Western Mail various dates; Personal File TNA WO339/19229.

Arthur Granville Soames OBE (1886-1962): after his time as Brigade Major 119 Brigade he served as a GSO2 (unit unknown) and Brigade Major, No.2 Training (Reserve) Brigade. OBE June 1919. He retired on grounds of ill-health on 3 December 1919. Sheriff of Buckinghamshire in 1926 and 1927. Divorced twice and married three times. His son Arthur Christopher John Soames (1920-1987) was a prominent Conservative politician (later Baron Soames) who married Mary, youngest daughter of Sir Winston Churchill, in 1947. Their son Nicholas (1948-) was an active Member of Parliament from 1983-2019.

Oxford Dictionary of National Biography: Soames (Arthur) Christopher John, Baron Soames (1920-1977).

Harold Stuart Tew (1869-1945): educated at Clifton; second-lieutenant, East Surrey Regiment, March, 1889; lieutenant, June 1891; captain, June 1896; South Africa (Queen's Medal 5 clasps, King's Medal 2 clasps), MiD, February 1901; brevet major, October 1901; adjutant, 1st Surrey Rifle Volunteers, July 1902; transferred from 2nd East Surrey (India) to 1st East Surrey (Plymouth), February 1909; BEF, August 1914, wounded at Le Cateau; OC 1st Battalion East Surrey Regiment (as Major), September-October 1914; brevet lieutenant-colonel, February 1915; lieutenant-colonel 1st Battalion East Surrey Regiment, June 1915-June 1916; CMG, January 1916; CO 9th Battalion East Surrey Regiment, September-October 1916 (invalided); CO of a Yeomanry Cyclists Battalion (unidentified), October 1917 – February 1918; CO 3rd (Special Reserve) Battalion East Surrey Regiment, February-July 1918; CO 12th Battalion North Staffordshire Regiment, June – July 1918; (remainder of career not traced); reached age limit and ceased to belong to Reserve of Officers, February 1924.

Herbert Lawton Warden (1877-1946): educated at George Heriot's School, Edinburgh 1889-92; second–lieutenant, Queen's Rifle Volunteer Brigade, the Royal Scots, 1903; lieutenant, 1905; captain 1907; Signalling Officer, Lothian Territorial Infantry Brigade, 1908-10; resigned commission, 4th Battalion Royal Scots, TF, 1912; major, 16th Battalion Royal Scots, December 1914; lieutenant-colonel while Commandant, Divisional School, October 1916 – January 1917; CO 25th Battalion Northumberland Fusiliers, July 1917; CO 13th Battalion East Surrey Regiment, August 1917; DSO, February 1918; Bar to DSO September 1918; MiD three times; relinquished commission, March 1919; Regional Director, War Pensions 1919-25; CBE 1924; Deputy Lieutenant, County of Edinburgh, 1942; solicitor; freemason.
TNA WO 339/18296. *The Scotsman*, 28 November 1942.

Eric Edward Allen Whitworth MC (1889-1971): left Radley School in 1908, graduated MA, Cambridge (Trinity College) 1912; Assistant Master at Rugby School, 1913-28; CO of the school OTC from 1919-28; Headmaster of Bradfield College, 1928-39 and Headmaster of Tonbridge School, 1939-49.
Obituary, *The Times*, 8 January 1971.

Charles Joseph Wilkie (1869-1916): born in Australia 8 January 1869 but his mother had Welsh connections and he married into a Welsh family; educated at Brighton and at Owen's College, Manchester; commissioned from the 3rd Battalion Sherwood Foresters (Derbyshire Regiment) as second-lieutenant in the Oxfordshire and Buckinghamshire Light Infantry in 1892; Lt. 1893; Capt. 1894; Tirah Expeditionary Force 1897-8; Commandant Convalescent Depot, Commandant Discharge Depot; Station Staff Officer; Acting Bn. Quartermaster for two years; invalided home with malaria and dysentery 1899; OC Details Limmerick and Buttevant; OC mixed troops Buttevant 1900; Adjutant 6th Provisional Bn Ox & Bucks Light Infantry, Fermoy 1901; Brigade Major Cork District for 1901 manoeuvres; Adjutant South Middlesex Volunteers and 26th Middlesex (Cyclists) 1902; retired 1907 to Reserve of Officers; Brigade Major South Wales Infantry Brigade (TF) 1908; 1909-14 Secretary Glamorgan TF Association; Major 9th Battalion Welsh Regiment, 8 October 1914; Lieutenant-Colonel 17th Battalion Welsh Regiment, 26 November 1914; KiA 18 October 1916.
De Ruvigny's Roll of Honour, 1914-1919, Volume 3, p.285.

Morris Meredith Williams (1881-1973): illustrator and painter; educated Slade School of Fine Art; studied in Florence and Paris; married Gertrude Alice Williams, artist and sculptor, 1906; Art Master Fettes College, Edinburgh; second-lieutenant 17th Welsh, April 1915; acting captain 17th Welsh, February-March 1917; lieutenant, July 1917; acting captain, Labour Corps, February 1918; transferred to Royal Engineers, Special Works Park (Camouflage), February 1918; discharged March 1919. Among many artistic projects, he collaborated with his wife on aspects of the Scottish National War Memorial, Edinburgh Castle, notably the bronze frieze in the Shrine.
Personal File TNA WO339/30375; Shaw, *An Artist's War*.

Arthur Charles White: second-lieutenant, 7th Battalion King's Own Yorkshire Light Infantry, September 1914; captain, December 1914; acting lieutenant-colonel, 7th KOYLI, October – November 1916 (invalided); DSO, January 1917; acting lieutenant-colonel, 18th Battalion Welsh Regiment, May–June 1917; major, KOYLI "from a service battalion", December 1917; relinquished commission on grounds of ill-health, August 1918.

Hugh Reginald Wood (1880-1958): was by 1914 a Valuer and Boundary Surveyor, Irish Civil Service. He was gazetted second–lieutenant, 18th Battalion Welsh Regiment, April 1915; lieutenant, June 1915; captain, August 1915; major, September 1915; MiD, April 1917; DSO, June 1917. He was replaced as CO 18th Battalion Welsh Regiment in May 1917 and reverted to 2iC. Just a month later he was wounded and lost his right eye. After his time with the 18th Welsh he was major in the Training Reserve, May 1918 and relinquished his commission in August 1919. In the Second World War he was Lieutenant-Colonel, 26th Battalion Sussex Home Guard and received the OBE.
Western Mail, 24 May 1917.

Bibliography

Unpublished Sources

Blair Archives, Blair Castle, Perthshire
Blair Papers, Bundle 880, Correspondence of Sir Harold Goodeve Ruggles-Brise

The Imperial War Museum, Department of Documents
01/9/01, H.A.J. Lamb, Lieutenant RE, Diary 1915-18
07/63/1, C.L. Morgan. Lieutenant, 21st Middlesex. Account written 1972
07/12/1, C.M. Dunn, Captain 17th Welsh. Account of his death at Bourlon written 1918
66/257/1, Papers of Major-General R. Pinney
66/298/1, Papers of Captain H.J.C. (Harry) Graham
72/11/1, B.D. Gibbs, Captain 18th Welsh. Letters to his sweetheart and ephemera including list of names and addresses for 18th Welsh Officers Association, 1919
79/35/1, D. Starrett, 'Batman' – unpublished typescript of his time as Crozier's Batman, 1914-1918
80/28/1, Wolff, C.H., Brigade Major, 120th Infantry Brigade. Desk diary Jan – Oct 1915
83/23/1, F. Turner. Account of sniper attached to 119th Brigade then 19th RWF, written in 1982
94/46/1, K. Fraser. 94 ms and ts letters from surviving 'bantams' or their families. 1980s
99/58/1, A.L. Bonsey, 13th East Surrey Regiment – ms account written in 1923

The Imperial War Museum, Sound Archive
AC4581, Oral History of Ronald Mallone, recorded January 1980

Liddell Hart Centre for Military Archives, King's College, London
Hamilton: 6/3, Letter from H.C. Metcalfe to General Sir Ian Hamilton requesting employment with the army
Liddell Hart: LH1/207, Correspondence with Frank Percy Crozier

Liddle Collection, University of Leeds
Lieutenant F. Hargrave, 19th Royal Welsh Fusiliers, photo album

London School of Economics Archives
M3383 Coll. Misc. 1155, Papers from F.P. Crozier including draft of a political pamphlet

The National Archives, Kew
CAB 45, Historical Section, drafts and correspondence relating to the Official History
WO 71/450, James Crozier, Court Martial papers
WO 86, Judge Advocate General's Office: District Courts Martial Registers
WO 95/100, War Diary 7th [G] Tank Battalion, Tank Corps
WO 95/110, War Diary D Battalion, Tank Corps
WO 95/1223-4, War Diary 2nd Scots Guards
WO 95/1857, War Diary 8th Royal Fusiliers
WO 95/1979, War Diary 2nd Royal Irish Regiment

WO 95/2468, War Diary 35th Division HQ General Staff
WO 95/2503, War Diary 9th Royal Irish Rifles
WO 95/2491, War Diary 36th (Ulster) Division HQ General Staff
WO 95/2539, War Diary 38th (Welsh) Division HQ General Staff
WO/95 2552, War Diary 113 Brigade HQ
WO 95/2592, War Diary 40th Division HQ General Staff
WO 95/2594, War Diary 40th Division HQ, A&Q
WO 95/2597-1, War Diary 40th Division, ADMS
WO 95/2604-5, War Diary 119th Infantry Brigade HQ
WO 95/2606, War Diary 12th South Wales Borderers, June 1916 – Jan 1918
WO 95/2606, War Diary 21st Middlesex, February-June 1918; War Diary 13th East Surrey, February –July 1918; War Diary 12th North Staffordshire, June 1918 – June 1919; War Diary 13th East Lancashire, June 1918 – April 1919; War Diary 13th Royal Inniskilling Fusiliers, June 1918 – April 1919
WO 95/2607, War Diary 17th Welsh, June 1916 – February 1919; War Diary 18th Welsh, June 1916 – June 1919; War Diary 19th Royal Welsh Fusiliers, June 1916 – February 1919; War Diary 119th Machine Gun Company; War Diary 119th Trench Mortar Battery
WO 95/2608-10, War Diaries 120th Infantry Brigade
WO 95/2611, War Diary 11th Cameron Highlanders
WO 95/2612, War Diary 13th East Surrey, June 1916 – January 1918
WO 95/2613-16, War Diaries 121st Infantry Brigade
WO 95/2615, War Diary 21st Middlesex, June 1916 – January 1918
WO 95/2617, War Diary 41st Division HQ General Staff
WO 95/2746, War diary 48th Division HQ General Staff
WO 95/2967, War Diary 57th Division HQ A&Q
WO 95/5460, War Diary 13th East Surrey, August 1918
WO 114/26-27, Weekly Return of the British Army (exclusive of Territorial Force) and Dominion contingents at home
WO 158/388, Report on Operations Carried Out by 40th Division During the Period November 21st-28th 1917
WO 213, Judge Advocate General's Office: Field General Courts Martial and Military Courts Registers.
WO 339, Personal Files Officers
WO 374, Personal Files Officers (includes 374/16997, F.P. Crozier)
WO 394, Statistical abstracts of information regarding the armies at home and abroad

The National Army Museum, Chelsea
1994-05-398, 'Diary of the war by J.F. Plunkett. Copied from my rough notes taken in the field'
6306-69, Sir John Ponsonby. Documents and maps relating to his command of 2nd Guards Brigade and 40th Division on the Western Front, 1917-18
8002-40, Harold Ruggles-Brise. Ms account 'Some records of the 40th Division prior to arriving in France' and ledger inscribed '40th Division Honours and Rewards', 1916-1919

The National Library of Scotland, Edinburgh
Haig Papers. Douglas Haig Manuscript Diary

Random House Archive, Rushden
Correspondence and contracts with F.P. Crozier

National Library of Wales, Aberystwyth
Records of the Executive Committee, Welsh Army Corps

Public Record Office of Northern Ireland, Belfast
D2794, Montgomery Family Papers, Correspondence of Captain William Montgomery
T 3217, J.L. Stewart-Moore, 'Random Recollections'
D 3835, Farren Connell Papers [Contain the correspondence of Sir Oliver Nugent]

University of Oxford, Bodleian Library
Lugard MSS 9/7, Papers of Lord Lugard
C679/147, Ponsonby Papers

Royal Regiment of Wales Museum, Brecon [Now the Royal Welsh Regimental Museum]
Papers of W.E. Brown, 12th SWB
Memoir Harold Jones
Diary of Captain J. Gwyther-Jones, 18th Welsh
Memoir Captain E.E.A Whitworth, 12th SWB

University of Reading, Jonathan Cape Archive
MS 2446, Sales ledgers

Author's Collection
Platoon Roll Book, 16 Platoon, 17th Welsh (digital copy)
Guns and God, copy of unpublished (incomplete) typescript by Grace Crozier c.1939

Published Sources

Books
Sidney Allinson, *The Bantams: The Untold Story of World War 1* (London: Howard Baker Press, 1981)
Anon, *A Book of Remembrance: being a short summary of the Service and Sacrifice rendered to the Empire during the Great War by one of the many Patriotic Families of Wessex, the Popes of Wrackleford, Co. Dorset* (London: Chiswick Press, 1919), privately printed
Anon, *History of the 50th Infantry Brigade, 1914-1919* (London: 1919)
Anon, *Soldiers Died in the Great War 1914-1919* (London: HMSO, 1921)
Anon, *A Short History of the Welch Regiment* (Aldershot: Gale & Polden, 1929)
Anon, *The Great War 1914-1918: Ulster Greets Her Brave and Faithful Sons and Remembers Her Glorious Dead* (Belfast: Books Ulster, 2015, first published 1919)
Anon, *The Welch Regiment 1719-1960* (London: Malcolm Page, 1960)
Tony Ashworth, *Trench Warfare 1914-1918: The Live and Let Live System* (London: Macmillan, 1980)
C.T. Atkinson, *The History of the South Wales Borderers 1914-1918* (London: The Medici Society, 1931)
Anthony Babington, *For the Sake of Example: Capital Courts Martial 1914-18, the Truth* (London: Leo Cooper, 1983)
Margaret Baguley, (ed.), *World War One and the Question of Ulster: The Correspondence of Lilian and Wilfred Spender* (Dublin: Irish Manuscripts Commission, 2009)
Chris Baker, *The Battle for Flanders: German defeat on the Lys 1918* (Barnsley: Pen & Sword, 2011)

Robin Barlow, *Wales and the First World War* (Cardiff: University of Wales Press, 2006)
Robin Barlow, *Wales and World War One* (Llandysul: Gomer Press, 2014)
Nick Baron, *King of Karelia: Col. P.J. Woods and the British Intervention in North Russia 1918 – 1919* (London: Francis Boutle, 2007)
Jim Beach, *Haig's Intelligence: GHQ and the German Army, 1916-1918* (Cambridge: Cambridge University Press, 2013)
A.F. Becke, *Order of Battle of Divisions, 4 Parts* (London: HMSO, 1934, 1938 and 1945)
R. Bennett, *The Black and Tans* (Stroud: Spellmount, 2006, first published 1959)
Ilana R. Bet-El, *Conscripts: Forgotten Men of the Great War* (Stroud, Sutton, 1999)
David Bilton, *Hull Pals: A History of 92 Infantry Brigade, 31st Division* (Barnsley: Pen and Sword, 1999)
David Bilton, *The Badges of Kitchener's Army – Infantry* (Barnsley: Pen and Sword, 2018)
Jonathan Boff, *Winning and Losing on the Western Front: The British Third Army and the Defeat of Germany in 1918* (Cambridge: Cambridge University Press, 2012)
Brian Bond, *Survivors of a Kind* (London: Continuum, 2008)
J.H. Boraston, (ed.) *Sir Douglas Haig's Despatches (December 1915 – April 1919)* (London: Dent, 1979 first published 1919)
J.M. Bourne, *Britain and the Great War 1914-1918* (London: Edward Arnold, 1989)
J.M. Bourne, 'A New Army Battalion at Gallipoli: The 7th Battalion The Prince of Wales's (North Staffordshire) Regiment' in Rhys Crawley and Michael LoCicero (eds.), *Gallipoli: New Perspectives on the Mediterranean Expeditionary Force, 1915-16* (Warwick: Helion, 2018), pp. 507-530
Timothy Bowman, *Irish Regiments in the Great War: Discipline and Morale* (Manchester: Manchester University Press, 2003)
Timothy Bowman, *Carson's Army* (Manchester: Manchester University Press, 2007)
Henry Brinton, *The Peace Army* (London: Williams and Norgate, 1932)
Malcolm Brown, *Tommy Goes to War* (London: Dent, 1978)
P. Buitenhuis, *The Great War of Words: Literature as Propaganda, 1914-18 and After* (London: Batsford, 1989)
Bruce Cherry, *They Didn't Want to Die Virgins: Sex and Morale in the British Army on the Western Front 1914-1918* (Solihull: Helion, 2016)
Brendan Clifford, *The Men I Killed: A Selection from the Writings of General F.P. Crozier* (Belfast: Athol Books, 2002)
Arthur Conan Doyle, *The British Campaign in France and Flanders 1917* (London: Hodder and Stoughton, 1919)
Mark Connelly, *Steady the Buffs! A Regiment, a Region & the Great War* (Oxford: Oxford University Press, 2006)
H.C. Cook, *The North Staffordshire Regiment* (London: Leo Cooper, 1970)
Cathryn Corns, and John Hughes-Wilson, *Blindfold and Alone: British Military Executions in the Great War* (London: Cassell, 2001)
A. Crookenden, *History of the Cheshire Regiment in the Great War* (Chester: W.H. Evans, 1939)
Frank Percy Crozier, *A Brass Hat in No Man's Land* (London: Jonathan Cape, 1930)
Frank Percy Crozier, *Impressions and Recollections* (London: T. Werner Laurie, 1930)
Frank Percy Crozier, *A Word to Gandhi: The Lessons of Ireland* (London: Williams and Norgate, 1931)
Frank Percy Crozier, *Ireland for Ever* (London: Jonathan Cape, 1932)
Frank Percy Crozier, *Five Years Hard* (London: Jonathan Cape, 1932)
Frank Percy Crozier, *Angels on Horseback* (London: Jonathan Cape, 1932)
Frank Percy Crozier, *The Men I Killed* (London: Michael Joseph, 1937)

C.M.R.F. Crutwell, *A History of the Great War 1914-1918* (Oxford: Clarendon Press, 1934)
Gloden Dallas and Douglas Gill, *The Unknown Army* (London: Verso, 1985)
Evan Beynon Davies, *E Ar Orwel Pell* (Llandysul: Gomer Press, 1965)
H.M. Davson, *The History of the 35th Division in the Great War* (London: Sifton, Praed & Co., 1926)
E.M. Delafield, *Diary of a Provincial Lady* (London: Howard Baker, 1930)
Terence Denman, *Ireland's Unknown Soldiers: The 16th (Irish) Division in the Great War* (Dublin: Irish Academic Press, 2008)
Marquis De Ruvigny, *De Ruvigny's Roll of Honour 1914 – 1918* (London: Naval and Military Press reprint of 1922 edition)
C.H. Dudley Ward, *Regimental Records of the Royal Welsh Fusiliers (Late the 23rd Foot), Volume 3, 1914-1918, France and Flanders* (London: Forster, Groom & Co., 1928)
Geoffrey Dugdale,*'Langemarck' and 'Cambrai': A War Narrative, 1914-1918* (Shrewsbury: Wilding and Son, 1932)
Myles Dungan, *Irish Voices from the Great War* (Dublin: Irish Academic Press, 1995)
James E. Edmonds, *Military Operations: France and Belgium 1916,* Vol.1 (London: HMSO, 1932)
James E. Edmonds, *Military Operations: France and Belgium 1918,* Vol. 1 (London: Macmillan, 1935)
James E. Edmonds, *Military Operations: France and Belgium 1918,* Vol. 2 (London: Macmillan, 1937)
James E. Edmonds, *Military Operations: France and Belgium 1918,* Vol. 4 (London: HMSO, 1947)
James E. Edmonds, *Military Operations: France and Belgium 1918,* Vol. 5 (London: HMSO, 1947)
Richard van Emden, *Boy Soldiers of the Great War* (London: Bloomsbury, 2012)
Wilfred Ewart, *When Armageddon Came* (London: Rich & Cowan Ltd, 1933)
John Ewing, *The History of the 9th (Scottish) Division 1914-1919* (London: John Murray, 1921)
Cyril Falls, *The History of the 36th (Ulster) Division* (London: Constable, 1922)
Cyril Falls, *War Books* (London: Greenhill Books, 1989. First published 1930)
Cyril Falls, *Military Operations: France and Belgium 1917 Vol. 1* (London: Macmillan, 1940)
A.H. Farrar-Hockley, *The Somme* (London: Batsford, 1964)
F. Fox, *The Royal Inniskilling Fusiliers in the World War* (London: Constable, 1928)
J.G. Fuller, *Troop Morale and Popular Culture in the British and Dominion Armies, 1914-1918* (Oxford: Clarendon Press, 1990)
GHQ, *Instructions Regarding Recommendations for Honours and Awards 1918* (Reprint, Naval and Military Press, no date)
General Staff, *Field Service Regulations Part 1, Operations* (London: HMSO, 1909, Reprinted with Amendments 1914)
General Staff, *SS107 Notes on Minor Enterprises* (March 1916)
General Staff, *SS135 Instructions for the Training of Divisions for Offensive Action* (December 1916)
General Staff, *SS137 Recreational Training* (January 1917)
General Staff, *SS143 Instructions for the Training of Platoons for Offensive Action* (February 1917)
General Staff, *SS152 Instructions for the Training of the British Armies in France* (June 1917)
General Staff, *SS210 The Division in Defence* (May 1918)
Craig Gibson, *Behind the Front: British Soldiers and French Civilians, 1914-18* (Cambridge: Cambridge University Press, 2014)
Robert Graves, *Goodbye To All That* (London: Cape, 1929)
Richard Grayson, *Belfast Boys: How Unionists and Nationalists Fought and Died Together in the First World War* (London: Continuum, 2009)
Elizabeth Greenhalgh, *The French Army and the First World War* (Cambridge: Cambridge University Press, 2014)

Keith Grieves, *The Politics of Manpower, 1914-18* (Manchester: Manchester University Press, 1988)
Paddy Griffith, *Battle Tactics of the Western Front: The British Army's Art of Attack 1916-18* (London: Yale University Press, 1994)
Paddy Griffith (ed.), *British Fighting Methods in the Great War* (London: Frank Cass, 1996)
Llewelyn Wyn Griffith, *Up To Mametz* (London: Faber, 1931)
Alan Isaac Grint, *A Sturdy Race of Men: 149th Brigade – A History of the Northumberland Fusiliers Territorial Battalions in The Great War* (Barnsley: Pen and Sword, 2018)
H. Gregory, *Never Again: A Diary of the Great War* (London: Arthur H. Stockwell, 1934)
J. Hammerton (ed.), *The Great War, I Was There* (London: Amalgamated Press, 1938-9)
Bryn Hammond, *Cambrai 1917: The Myth of the First Great Tank Battle* (London: Weidenfeld & Nicolson, 2008)
Peter Hart, *The Somme* (London: Cassell, 2005)
A. D. Harvey, *A Muse of Fire: Literature, Art and War* (London: The Hambledon Press, 1998)
L.E. Henry, *Napoleon's War Maxims* (London: Gale and Polden, 1899)
Jonathan Hicks, *The Welsh at Mametz Wood: The Somme 1916* (Talybont: Y Lolfa, 2016)
Peter E. Hodgkinson, *British Infantry Battalion Commanders in the First World War* (Farnham: Ashgate, 2015)
Peter E. Hodgkinson, *'Glum Heroes': Hardship, Fear and Death – Resilience and Coping in the British Army on the Western Front 1914-1918* (Wolverhampton: Helion, 2016)
Richaed Holmes, *Tommy: The British Soldier on the Western Front 1914-1918* (London: Harper Collins, 2004)
Percy F. Hone, *Southern Rhodesia* (London: George Bell, 1909)
Jack Horsfall and Nigel Cave, *Battleground Europe: Bourlon Wood* (Barnsley: Pen & Sword, 2002)
Clive Hughes, 'The New Armies' in Ian F.W. Beckett and Keith Simpson (eds.), *A Nation in Arms: the British Army in the First World War* (Manchester: Manchester University Press, 1985)
Clive Hughes, *'Arm to save your Native Land': Army Recruiting in North-West Wales, 1914-1916* (Llanwrst: Gwasg Carreg Gwalch, 2015)
Colin Hughes, *Mametz: Lloyd George's 'Welsh Army' at the Battle of the Somme* (Norwich: Gliddon Books, 2nd Edition, 1990)
Intelligence Section of the General Staff, American Expeditionary Forces, *Histories of the Two Hundred and Fifty-One Divisions of the German Army Which Participated in the War 1914 – 1918* (London: London Stamp Exchange, 1989 reprint of 1920 edition)
E.A. James, *British Regiments 1914-1918* (Dallington: Naval and Military Press, 1998 reprint of 1929 edition)
H.L. James (ed.), *Sixteenth, Seventeenth, Eighteenth, Nineteenth Battalions, the Manchester Regiment: A Record 1914-1918* (Manchester: Sherratt and Hughes, 1923)
Robert Rhodes James, *Gallipoli* (London: Pan, 1984)
Douglas Jerrold, *The Lie about the War* (London: Faber and Faber, 1930)
Davis Johnson, *Executed at Dawn: British Firing Squads on the Western Front 1914-1918* (Stroud: Spellmount, 2015)
David Jones, *In Parenthesis* (London: Faber, 1937)
Mair Saunders Jones, Ned Thomas and Harri Pritchard Jones (eds.), *Letters to Margaret Gilcreist* (Cardiff: University of Wales Press, 1993)
Peter Jones, *He did his Bit: The Stories Behind the Shirt Collection of Welsh Rugby Legend Charlie Pritchard* (Llandysul: Gomer, 2020)
Simon M. Justice, 'Vanishing Battalions: The Nature, Impact and Implications of British Infantry Reorganization prior to the German Spring Offensives of 1918' in LoCicero, M. et al (eds.), *A Military Transformed? Adaptation and Innovation in the British Military 1792-1945* (Solihull: Helion & Company, 2014)

J. Keating and F. Lavery, *Irish Heroes in the War: The Story of the Tyneside Irish Brigade* (London: Everett, 1917)

Paul Kendall, *Somme 1916: Success and Failure on the First Day of the Battle of the Somme* (Barnsley: Frontline, 2015)

Martin Kitchen, *The German Offensives of 1918* (Stroud: Tempus, 2005)

John Laffin, *Damn the Dardanelles* (Stroud: Sutton, 1989)

David M. Leeson, *The Black & Tans: British Police and Auxiliaries in the Irish War of Independence, 1920-1921* (Oxford: Oxford University Press, 2011)

Edward G. Lengel, *World War 1 Memories: An Annotated Bibliography of Personal Accounts Published in English Since 1919* (Oxford: Scarecrow Press, 2004)

Ron Lock, *Hill of Squandered Valour: The Battle for Spion Kop, 1900* (Newbury: Casemate, 2011)

J.C. MacIntosh, 'The Tanks at Cambrai' in Buchan, John (ed.), *The Long Road to Victory* (London: Thomas Nelson and Sons, 1920)

Ernest McCall, *Tudor's Toughs* (Newtonards: Red Coat Publishing, 2010)

Paul McCue, *Wandsworth and Battersea Battalions in the Great War 1915-1918* (Barnsley: Pen and Sword, 2010)

Stephen McGreal, *Cheshire Bantams: the 15th, 16th and 17th Battalions of the Cheshire Regiment* (Barnsley: Pen and Sword, 2006)

R.B. Mainwaring, *Historical Record of the Royal Welch Fusiliers* (London: Hatchlands, 1889)

T.O. Marden, *The History of the Welch Regiment, Part 2 1914-1918* (Cardiff: Western Mail and Echo, 1932)

'Mark VII' (Max Plowman), *A Subaltern on the Somme* (London: Dent, 1927)

Charles Messenger, *Call to Arms: The British Army 1914-18* (London: Cassell, 2005)

Charles Messenger, *Broken Sword: The Tumultuous Life of General Frank Crozier 1879-1937* (Barnsley: Praetorian Press, 2013)

Martin Middlebrook, *The First Day on the Somme, 1 July 1916* (London: Allan Lane, 1971)

Wilfred Miles, *Military Operations France and Belgium, 1916, Vol. II, 2nd July 1916 to the End of the Battle of the Somme* (London: Macmillan, 1938)

Wilfred Miles, *Military Operations: France and Belgium 1917, Vol III, The Battle of Cambrai* (London: HMSO, 1948)

K.W. Mitchinson, *Villers Plouich and the Five Ridges* (Barnsley: Leo Cooper, 1999)

William Moore, *The Thin Yellow Line* (London: Leo Cooper, 1974)

William Moore, *A Wood Called Bourlon: The Cover-up After Cambrai, 1917* (London: Leo Cooper, 1988)

C.L. Mowat, *Britain Between the Wars, 1918-1940* (London: Methuen, 1955)

J.E. Munby (ed.), *A History of the 38th (Welsh) Division* (London: Hugh Rees Ltd, 1920)

National Executive Committee, *Welsh Army Corps 1914-1919, Report of the ExecutiveCommittee* (Cardiff: Western Mail Ltd, 1921)

L. Nicholson, and T. McMullen, *History of the East Lancashire Regiment in the Great War 1914-1918* (Liverpool: Littlebury Brothers, 1936)

Padraic O'Farrell, *Who's Who in the Irish War of Independence and Civil War 1916-1923* (Dublin: Lilliput Press, 1997)

Gerald Oram, *Death Sentences Passed by Military Courts of the British Army 1914-1924* (London: Francis Boutle, 1998)

Philip Orr, *The Road to the Somme: Men of the Ulster Division Tell Their Story* (Belfast: The Blackstaff Press, 1987)

David R. Orr, and David Truesdale, *"Ulster Will Fight…": Volume 2, The 36th (Ulster) Division From Formation to the Armistice* (Solihull: Helion, 2016)

H.W. Pearse and H.S. Sloman, *History of the East Surrey Regiment 1914-1919* (London: The Medici Society, 1934)
Nicholas Perry, 'Politics and Command: General Nugent, the Ulster Division and Relations with Ulster Unionism 1915-17' in Bond, Brian et al, *'Look to your Front': Studies in the First World War by the British Commission for Military History* (Staplehurst: Spellmount, 1999)
Nicholas Perry (ed.), *Major-General Oliver Nugent and the Ulster Division 1915-1918* (Stroud: Sutton, for the Army Records Society, 2007)
Nicholas Perry, *Major-General Oliver Nugent: The Irishman Who Led The Ulster Division In The Great War* (Belfast: Ulster Historical Foundation, 2020)
William Philpott, *Bloody Victory: The Sacrifice on the Somme and the Making of the Twentieth Century* (London: Little Brown, 2009)
William Philpott, *Attrition: Fighting the First World War* (London: Little Brown, 2014)
David A. Pretty, *Farmer, Soldier and Politician: The Life of Brigadier-General Sir Owen Thomas, MP, Father of the 'Welsh Army Corps'* (Wrexham: Bridge Books, 2011)
Julian Putkowski, *British Army Mutineers 1914-1922* (London: Francis Boudle, 1998)
Kenneth Radley, *On the Dangerous Edge: British and Canadian Trench Raiding on the Western Front* (Warwick: Helion, 2018)
Andrew Rawson, *The Cambrai Campaign* (Barnsley: Pen & Sword, 2017)
Michael Renshaw, *Mametz Wood* (Barnsley: Pen and Sword, 2006)
Frank Richards, *Old Soldiers Never Die* (London: Faber, 1933)
John Richards (ed.), *Wales on the Western Front* (Cardiff: University of Wales Press, 1994)
Jonathon Riley, *Ghosts of Old Companions: Lloyd George's Welsh Army, The Kaiser's Reichsheer and the Battle for Mametz Wood, 1914-1916* (Warwick: Helion and Company, 2019)
Simon Robbins, *British Generalship on the Western Front 1914-18: Defeat into Victory* (London: Routledge, 2005)
Simon Robbins, *British Generalship on the Western Front 1914-18: The Military Career of Sir Henry Horne (1861-1929)* (London: Ashgate, 2010)
E.W.J. Rowan, *The 54th Infantry Brigade, 1914-1918: Some Records of Battle and Laughter in France* (Aldershot: Gale and Polden, 1919)
Martin Samuels, *Command or Control? Command, Training and Tactics in the British and German Armies, 1888-1918* (London: Frank Cass, 1995)
Siegfried Sassoon, *Memoirs of an Infantry Officer* (London: Faber, 1930)
Anthony Saunders, *Dominating the Enemy: War in the Trenches 1914-1918* (Stroud: Sutton, 2000)
Anthony Saunders, *Raiding on the Western Front* (Barnsley: Pen and Sword, 2012)
Caroline Scott, *The Manchester Bantams: The Story of a Pals Battalion and a City at War; 23rd (Service) Battalion The Manchester Regiment (8th City)* (Barnsley: Pen & Sword, 2016)
Michael Senior, *Haking – a Dutiful Soldier: A Study in Corps Command* (Barnsley: Pen and Sword, 2012)
Phyllida Shaw, *An Artist's War: The Art and Letters of Morris and Alice Meredith Williams* (Stroud: The History Press, 2017)
Phyllida Shaw, *Undaunted Spirit: The Art and Craft of Gertrude Alice Meredith Williams* (Independent Publishing Network, 2018)
J. Sheen, *Tyneside Irish: A History of the Tyneside Irish Brigade Raised in the North East in World War One* (Barnley: Pen and Sword, 1998)
G.D. Sheffield (ed.), *Leadership and Command: The Anglo-American Military Experience since 1861* (London: Brassey's, 1997)
G.D. Sheffield, *In Haig's Shadow: The Letters of Major-General Hugo De Pree and Field Marshal Sir Douglas Haig* (Barnsley: Greenhill Books, 2019)

G.D. Sheffield, *Leadership in the Trenches: Officer-Man Relations, Morale and Discipline in the British Army in the Era of the First World War* (London: Macmillan, 2000)
G.D. Sheffield, *The Somme* (London: Cassell, 2003)
G.D. Sheffield, *Douglas Haig: From the Somme to Victory* (London: Aurum Press, 2016)
G.D. Sheffield and J.M. Bourne (eds.), *Douglas Haig, War Diaries and Letters, 1914-1918* (London: Weidenfeld and Nicolson, 2005)
G.D. Sheffield and Dan Todman (eds.), *Command and Control on the Western Front: The British Army's Experience 1914-18* (Staplehurst: Spellmount, 2004)
Jack Sheldon, *The German Army at Cambrai* (Barnsley: Pen and Sword, 2009)
H.R.L. Sheppard, *We Say No: The Plain Man's Guide to Pacifism* (London: 1935)
Peter Simkins, *Kitchener's Army: The Raising of the New Armies 1914-1916* (Manchester: Manchester University Press, 1988)
Peter Simkins, 'British Divisions in the 'Hundred Days', 1918' in Paddy Griffith (ed.), *British Fighting Methods in the Great War* (London: Frank Cass, 1996), pp. 50-69
Peter Simkins, 'Building Blocks: Aspects of Command and Control at Brigade Level in the BEF's Offensive Operations, 1916-1918' in Gary Sheffield and Dan Todman (eds.) *Command and Control on the Western Front: The British Army's Experience1914-18* (Staplehurst: Spellmount, 2004)
Peter Simkins, '"Each One a Pocket Hercules": The Bantam Experiment and the Case of the Thirty-fifth Division' in Sanders Marble (ed.), *Scraping the Barrel: The Military Use of Sub-Standard Manpower* (New York: Fordham University Press, 2012), pp. 79-104
Andy Simpson, *Directing Operations: British Corps Command on the Western Front, 1914-18* (Stroud: Spellmount, 2006)
Keith Simpson, 'The Officers' in Ian F. W. Beckett and Keith Simpson (eds.), *A Nation in Arms: The British Army in the First World War* (Manchester: Manchester University Press, 1985), pp. 63 – 96
F.C. Stanley, *The History of the 89th Brigade* (Liverpool: Daily Post, 1919)
John Starling and Ivor Lee, *No Labour, No Battle: Military Labour During the First World War* (Stroud: Spellmount, 2009)
Michael Stedman, *Manchester Pals, 16th, 17th, 18th, 19th, 20th, 21st, 22nd and 23rd Battalions of the Manchester Regiment: A History of the Two Manchester Brigades* (London: Leo Cooper, 1994)
Michael Stedman, *Battleground Europe, Somme: Thiepval* (Barnsley: Pen and Sword, 2005)
David Stevenson, *With Our Backs to the Wall: Victory and Defeat in 1918* (London: Allen Lane, 2011)
G. Stewart and J. Sheen, *Tyneside Scottish: A History of the Tyneside Scottish Brigade Raised in the North East in World War One* (Barnsley: Pen and Sword, 1999)
Colin Taylor, *'I Wish They'd Killed You in A Decent Show': The Struggle for the Hindenburg Line between Croisilles and Fontaine-les-Croisilles, March 1917 to August 1918* (Brighton: Reveille Press, 2014)
D.G. Tendulkar, *Mahatma: Life of Mohandas Karamchand Gandhi. Volume 3, 1930-1934* (Bombay: Jhaveri and Tendulkar, 1952)
T. Ternan, *The Story of the Tyneside Scottish* (Newcastle: Northumberland Press, 1919)
H. Thomas, *The History of the Royal Welsh Fusiliers late the Twenty Third Regiment* (London: T. Fisher Unwin, 1916)
Charles Townsend, *The British Campaign in Ireland 1919-1921* (London: OUP, 1975)
AlexanderTurner, *Cambrai 1917: The Birth of Armoured Warfare* (Oxford: Osprey Publishing, 2007)
Stephen Walker, *Forgotten Soldiers: the Irishmen Shot at Dawn* (Dublin: Gill and Macmillan, 2007)

War Office, *Infantry Training* (London: HMSO, 1914)
Alexander Watson, *Enduring the Great War: Combat, Morale and Collapse in the German and British Armies, 1914-1918* (Cambridge: Cambridge University Press, 2008)
Chris Williams, 'Taffs in the Trenches: identity and military service 1914-1915' in Matthew Cragoe and Chris Williams (eds.), *Wales and War: Society, Politics and Religion in the Nineteenth and Twentieth Centuries* (Cardiff: University of Wales, 2007), pp. 126-164
Denis Winter, *Death's Men* (London: Allen Lane, 1978)
F.E. Whitton, *History of the 40th Division* (Aldershot: Gale and Polden, 1926)
E. Wyrall, *The Die-Hards in the Great War* (London: Harrison and Sons, 1926-1930)
David T. Zabecki, *The German 1918 Offensives: A Case Study in the Operational Level of War* (London: Routledge, 2006)

Journals and Periodicals

Jim Beach, 'Issued by the General Staff: Doctrine Writing at British GHQ, 1917-1918', *War in History*, 19:4 (2012), pp. 464-491
Timothy Bowman, 'Officering Kitchener's Armies: a case study of the 36th (Ulster) Division', *War in History*, 16:2 (2009), pp. 189-212
Timothy Bowman, 'Review of Broken Sword by Charles Messenger', *History Ireland*, 22 (July/August 2014), p. 63
Bob Butcher, 'The Nine Battalion Controversy', *Stand To! The Journal of the Western Front Association*, 68 (2003), pp. 47-49
Robert Graves, 'Review of A Brass Hat in No Man's Land', *Then and Now* (Summer 1930), p. 5
Lesley A. Hall, 'Impotent ghosts from no man's land, flappers' boyfriends, or crypto-patriarchs? Men, sex and social change in 1920s Britain', *Social History*, 21 (1996), pp. 54-70
Yuval Noah Harari, 'Martial Illusions: War and Disillusionment in Twentieth-Century and Renaissance Military Memoirs', *The Journal of Military History*, 69 (2005), pp. 43-72
A. D. Harvey, 'A Good War: Wartime Officers who Rose to Command Level in the First World War', *RUSI: Royal United Services Institute Journal*, 153:1 (April 2006), pp. 76-80
Clive Hughes, 'The Welsh Army Corps, 1914-15: shortages of khaki and basic equipment promote a 'national' uniform', *Imperial War Museum Review*, No.1, 1986, pp. 91-100
Brooke Maury, 'Review of The Men I Killed', *The Field Artillery Journal*, May/June 1938, p.252
Gerard Oram, 'Pious Perjury: Discipline and Morale in the British Force in Italy, 1917-1918', *War in History*, 9:4 (2002), p. 412-430
Gervase Phillips, 'Dai Bach y Soldiwr', *Llafur*, 6:2 (1993), pp. 93-105
M. Pittock, 'Max Plowman and the Literature of the First World War', *Cambridge Quarterly*, 33 (2004), pp. 217-243
H. Senior, 'Review of Richard Bennett, The Black and Tans', *Irish Historical Review*, 47 (March 1961), pp. 277-280
Martin G. Staunton, 'Soldiers Died in the Great War 1914-19 as historical source material', *Stand To! The Journal of the Western Front Association*, 27 (1989), pp. 6-8
Chris Williams, 'A Question of 'Legitimate Pride'? The 38th (Welsh) Division at the Battle of Mametz Wood, July 1916', *Welsh History Review / Cylchgrawn Hanes Cymru*, 28:4 (2017), pp. 723-752

Theses

Aimée E. Fox, 'Military administration and the role of brigade staff, 1916-1918', MA Thesis, University of Birmingham, 2010
Trevor Gordon Harvey, '"An Army of Brigadiers": British Brigade Commanders at the Battle of Arras 1917', PhD Thesis, University of Birmingham, 2015
Clive Hughes, 'Army Recruitment in Gwynedd, 1914-1916', MA Thesis, University of Wales, Bangor, 1983
Jesse Pyles, 'The Portuguese Expeditionary Force in World War I: From Inception to Combat Destruction, 1914-1918', MA Dissertation, University of North Texas, 2012
Dennis Williams, 'British Second Army and Coalition Warfare in Flanders in the Hundred Days, 1918', MPhil Thesis, University of Birmingham, 2015

Newspapers

Aberdeen Journal; Belfast Telegraph;Brecon and Radnor Express; Buckinghamshire Herald; Colwyn Bay News; Cambria Daily Leader; Cambridge Daily News; Daily Express; Daily Mirror; Daily Sketch;Daily Telegraph; Edinburgh Evening Dispatch; Edinburgh Gazette; Evening Standard; Glamorgan Gazette; Gloucester Journal; Irish Times; Larne Times; Liverpool Daily Post; Liverpool Evening Express; London Gazette; Manchester Guardian; Monmouthshire Evening Post; Morning Post; New Statesman and Nation; New York Times; North Wales Chronicle; Nottingham Journal and Express; Peace News; South Wales Daily News; South Wales Echo; Sunday Dispatch; Sunday Express; The Cambrian News, Merioneth and Welsh Farmers Gazette; The Chronicle; The Globe; The Scotsman; The Spectator; The Times; Times Literary Supplement; Western Daily Press; Western Mail; Yorkshire Post and Leeds Intelligencer

Index

People

Andrews, Lieutenant-Colonel Richard, 117, 162, 179, 200, 208, 210–11, 217, 238
Appleby, Major Digby, 93, 238

Benzie, Lieutenant-Colonel Robert, 138-139, 161, 179, 239
Beynon Davies, Captain Evan, 52, 63-64, 66, 71, 244
Brown, Lieutenant-Colonel W.E., 130, 161, 178, 183-184, 239
Bryant, Lieutenant-Colonel Alan, 140-141, 219, 239

Campbell, Brigadier-General John, 189, 201, 206, 240
Chadwick, Lance-Corporal H., 45-46
Crozier, Brigadier-General Frank Percy, 102–32, 134–44, 149–50, 152–53, 155–56, 159–65, 170–72, 176–92, 197–98, 200–204, 209–19, 221–22, 238, 252–53
Crozier, Grace, 118, 211, 218, 220, 222, 254
Crozier, Rifleman James, 108, 126, 128
Cubitt, Major-General Thomas Astley, 105, 120, 240
Cunliffe-Owen, Brigadier-General Charles, 91–92, 96, 134, 136

Downes-Powell, Lieutenant-Colonel H.R., 138-139, 150, 240

Falls, Captain Cyril Bentham, 118, 121, 123-124, 240
Fitzgerald, Colonel Brinsley John Hamilton, 106
Fitzmaurice, ay, Major Maurice, 115, 240

Gaffikin, Captain George, 109–10, 217
Gandhi, Mohandas Karamchand, 119
Gibbs, Captain B.D., 40, 67, 86, 135
Gilbert, Major, E.H. St George, 63, 90, 221, 238, 241
Goodliffe, Major Guy Vernon, 141-142, 152-153, 190-191, 240
Graham, Captain H.J.C. 'Harry', 101, 153, 162, 175, 178, 181, 187-188, 190, 192, 217-218, 242
Grant-Thorold, Lieutenant-Colonel R.S., 72, 138, 244
Gregorie, Brigadier-General H.G., 120, 243

Haig, General/Field Marshal Sir Douglas, 143, 146, 154–55, 163, 169, 173, 181, 192, 197, 216, 259–60
Haig-Brown, Lieutenant-Colonel A.R., 78, 221, 243
Haking, Lieutenant-General Sir Richard, 85, 86, 90, 93
Herbert, Sir Ivor, 27
Hobkirk, Brigadier-General C.J., 187, 189
Homfray, Lieutenant-Colonel H.R. 33, 39, 44, 57, 60, 63-64, 72
Hone, Captain P.F., 83, 141, 157, 190, 222, 243
Hore, Lieutenant-Colonel C.B., 138-140, 219, 244
Horne, Major-General H.S., 92-93, 181, 225

Johnson, Lieutenant-Colonel R.I.B., 200-201, 244
Jones, Lieutenant-Colonel B.J., 71, 138, 150, 244
Jones, 2/Lt H., 165
Jones, 2/Lt V.T., 165, 168

Kennedy, Lieutenant-Colonel William, 150-151, 161, 179, 244
Kitchener, Field Marshal Lord, 24–25

Lloyd Evans, Lieutenant-Colonel Owen, 35, 71
Lloyd George, David, 23-24, 35, 64, 214
Lyne, Captain, C.V., 90, 93

Mackinnon, General W.H., 27-29, 32-34, 39
May, Lieutenant R.W., 190-191, 244
Metcalfe, Lieutenant-Colonel H.C., 178-80, 186, 219, 246, 252
Montgomery, Captain J.S., 141, 217
Montgomery, Muirhead, Captain A.J., 141, 190-191, 208, 247
Montgomery, Captain William, 110–12, 113–14, 139, 217

Nugent, Major-General Oliver, 107–8, 259

O'Connor, Major E.R., 198, 200-201, 207, 211, 247

Peyton, Major-General Sir William Elliot, 131, 201, 204, 211-212, 218, 247

Philipps, Major-General Ivor, 27-28, 37-38, 68, 77, 224-225
Plowman, Max, 122–23, 258, 261
Plunkett, Lieutenant-Colonel James, 95, 158–61, 163, 165, 168, 192, 195, 197–98, 200–201, 203, 205–10, 217, 219
Plymouth, Lord R.G.W., 24, 28, 68
Ponsonby, Major-General Sir John, 152–53, 171, 173, 175, 178, 180, 187–88, 197, 216–17, 219, 242, 246, 248
Pope, Lieutenant-Colonel E.A., 36–37, 72, 77–78, 90, 96, 138, 212, 221
Prentice, Major, R.E.S., 73-73, 248
Prichard, Brigadier-General C.S., 90, 134
Pritchard, Captain C., 88-89
Pugh, Captain S.W., 57, 63-64, 248

Ruggles-Brise, Major-General Harold, 41, 48, 79, 98, 139–40, 152–53, 202, 211–12

Saunders Lewis, Second Lieutenant John, 55, 63–64, 66, 145
Soames, Major A.G., 74, 83, 92, 135, 138, 141, 219, 249
Spender, Wilfred, 104-105, 108, 114-116, 188, 201, 217

Starrett, Private David, 54, 106, 109, 111, 131-132, 170, 185-186, 194, 217-218
Stewart-Moore, Lieutenant J.L., xiv, 113, 116, 218
Style, Brigadier-General R.C., 40, 57, 72-73, 134

Tabor, Major S., 194
Thorneycroft, Major-General Alexander, 105, 201
Thomas, Brigadier-General Sir Owen, 34-35, 62, 259

Watts, Major-General H.E., 224-225
Watts-Morgan, Captain David, 30, 246
Warden, Lieutenant-Colonel H.L., 172, 177, 179-180, 250
West, Major, W.G., 180, 184
Wetherall, 2/Lt Eric, 211
Whitworth, Captain, Eric, 66, 73, 91, 95, 135, 137–38, 144
Wilkie, Lieutenant-Colonel C.J., 28, 31–33, 90, 138, 221
Williams, 2/Lt Morris Meredith, 55, 78, 90, 95, 135, 138, 141, 221, 251
Withycombe, Brigadier-General W.M., 108–9, 114–15

Places

Aldershot, 16, 40, 47–48, 57-58, 60, 66-67, 93, 114, 149, 238, 240, 246

Bac St Maur, 184–86
Belfast, 108, 110, 112, 114, 124, 127, 254–55, 258–59
Birkenhead, 25–27, 214
Bourlon, 155–59, 164, 170, 172, 187, 189–90, 216, 222–23, 225, 231, 252, 258
Bourlon Wood, 51, 130, 152, 154–60, 163–65, 169, 171, 176, 178, 221–23, 225, 231–32, 244–45
Bully Grenay, 81-82

Cambrai, 151, 154–56, 159–60, 162, 164–65, 173, 228–29, 247, 256–58, 260
Canada, 104–106, 128, 239, 242, 248-249
Cardiff, 24, 27–29, 31, 33-34, 43, 56, 60, 62, 68, 130, 162, 222, 238, 240, 243
Contalmaison, 223–25
Croisilles, 164, 173, 175–76, 260

Deganwy, 34-35, 40, 61
Doullens, 80, 105, 131, 133

Ervillers, 80, 174, 176–78, 186

Fifteen Ravine, 143-144, 147, 215
Fontaine-Notre-Dame, 156, 159–60

Gallipoli, 54, 91, 239, 243–44, 247, 255, 257
Gonnelieu, 144, 228
Graincourt, 158, 161–62, 228, 233

Ireland, 43, 50–53, 107, 110, 116–17, 119–20, 123, 126, 129, 255, 260

La Vacquerie, 146–49, 215, 238
Lillers, 78, 80
Llandudno, 35, 47, 52, 56, 61, 63, 64
Loos, 82–84, 93, 132
Lucheux, 153–57
Lys, 80, 125, 170, 181-183, 185, 187, 190, 202, 206-208, 215, 220

Mametz Wood, 23, 223–25, 257, 259, 261

Newport, 36–37, 40, 63–64
Nieppe, 80, 182, 206–7

Porthcawl, 28, 30–33, 40, 42, 56–57, 61–63, 130, 221
Prees Heath, 40, 56, 62, 64–66
Roubaix, 80, 209–10

Scheldt, 209-210
Somme, 23, 80, 90–91, 93, 110, 112–13, 122–23, 131–32, 143, 224, 242, 256–60

St Leger, 174, 176–78
Strazeele, 186-187, 217

Thiepval Wood, 110–11
Tunnel Trench, 164–65

Valley Trench, 168
Villers-Plouich, 141, 144, 146-147, 149, 215

Wales, 23–24, 27–28, 34, 53–55, 130–31, 214, 221, 223, 248–49, 255, 259, 261–62

Formations/Units

Western Command, 27–31, 37–38, 43–44, 46, 239
First Army, 81, 85, 90, 92, 181
Second Army, 202, 204, 210
Third Army, 85, 151, 153, 155, 163–64, 173, 215
Fourth Army, 85, 90, 94, 132–33, 146, 148, 204, 223, 225
Fifth Army, 132, 165, 173, 210–11

Welsh Army Corps (WAC), 23–25, 27–36, 38–41, 54, 60–61, 64, 66, 68, 70, 258–59, 261
II Corps, 170–71, 204
III Corps, 143, 150–51, 154–56
IV Corps, 155–56, 181
V Corps, 155-56, 170-71, 173
VIII Corps, 171, 187, 241
XI Corps, 79, 85, 93
XV Corps, 90, 93, 133-34, 142, 144, 146-48, 150, 181-82, 187, 198, 204, 206, 210-11, 224-25

Guards Division, 156, 160
Portuguese Divisions, 170, 181-183, 189, 190
33rd Division, 134, 152, 171
34th Division, 170, 176, 182
35th (Bantam) Division, 79, 93-95, 103, 150, 215
36th (Ulster) Division, 77, 98, 105–6, 108, 110–11, 113, 115, 121, 188, 217
38th (Welsh) Division, 23, 39–40, 62, 68, 77, 79,
40th (Bantam) Division, 23, 40–41, 47, 49, 67, 70, 79, 82, 85–86, 88–90, 92–97, 101, 103, 131–33, 139–41, 143–44, 146, 148, 150-52, 154–57, 159-63, 169-70, 173, 175, 177-81, 183, 187-88, 192, 197-98, 201-04, 206-07, 210, 212-17, 222
41st Division, 79, 90, 93, 216
43rd Division, 28, 37-39, 62
62nd (West Riding) Division, 156-57, 160-61

Welsh Bantam Brigade, 23–69, 164, 214, 219
4 Guards Brigade, 176-77
118 Brigade, 48-49,
119 Brigade, 23, 25, 29, 36, 40-44, 46-47, 49, 51-56, 58-60, 62-63, 70-71, 73-79, 83, 85-86, 90-91, 93, 95, 97-100, 105, 117, 131, 133, 141, 143-46, 148-50, 152, 154, 157, 159-60, 162, 164, 169-70, 172-73, 176-79, 183, 186-87, 190, 192, 193, 195, 197-99, 200, 202-04, 206-07, 209-10, 212-17, 219, 222
120 Brigade, 47-48, 79, 90, 133, 140, 144, 146, 154-55, 160, 171-72, 175, 178-79, 183, 185-88, 192, 204, 206, 213
121 Brigade, 47-48, 79, 90, 133, 148, 153, 157-60, 171-72, 175, 179, 181, 184-85, 187, 190, 201, 205-06, 213, 217,

13th East Lancashire Regiment, 192–93, 195-98, 200, 203–04, 206–11
13th East Surrey Regiment, 48, 172-73, 176-79, 183-85, 187, 200, 222
8th Entrenching Battalion, 171
9th Entrenching Battalion, 171, 242
10/11th Highland Light Infantry(HLI), 171-72
14th Highland Light Infantry, 47-48, 179
21st Middlesex Regiment, 49, 150, 172-173, 176-178, 182-185, 187, 191, 220
12th North Staffordshire Regiment, 192-93, 195, 197-98, 200, 203-04, 207, 208-11, 219
13th Royal Inniskilling Fusiliers (RIF), 192-93, 195-98, 200, 203-04, 207-08, 210
9th Royal Irish Rifles (RIRifles), 58, 79, 104, 106-10, 111-14, 128, 131, 188, 216-17
19th Royal Welsh Fusiliers (RWF), 34-35, 38, 40, 43-46, 49-50, 52, 56, 58, 61-64, 71-72, 75-77, 79, 83, 93, 95, 98-100, 138, 144-46, 148-50, 152-53, 159, 161, 163, 165, 168, 171, 218, 222
12th South Wales Borderers (SWB), 23, 36-39, 40-46, 49-50, 52-56, 58, 61-64, 66, 68, 72-73, 75-77, 79, 81-83, 87-89, 90-91, 93, 95-101, 133-35, 138, 143-46, 148-50, 152-53, 158-59, 161-63, 165, 168-69, 171, 212
Thorneycroft's Mounted Infantry, 105, 119, 131, 201
225 Tunnelling Company, 82
12th Welsh Regiment, 36, 39, 49-50
17th Welsh Regiment, 28-29, 38-39, 49-50, 55, 79, 100, 138, 140-141, 143-144, 146-149, 151-153, 160-161, 163, 165,165, 168, 170-171, 221-222
18th Welsh Regiment, 32, 38-39, 49-50, 100, 152, 170, 182-185, 187, 221-222